ENCYCLOPAEDIA OF PETROLEUM SCIENCE AND ENGINEERING

ENCYCLOPAEDIA OF PETROLEUM SCIENCE AND ENGINEERING

(Volume 16)

Applied Remote Sensing and Hydrogen : The Worlds Future Energy Mix

S.L. Sah

KALPAZ

Encyclopaedia of Petroleum Science and Engineering

Rs. 900

ISBN: 81-7835-102-1 (Set)
ISBN: 81-7835-757-7 (Vol. 16)

Published in 2009 in India by
Kalpaz Publications
C-30, Satyawati Nagar,
Delhi-110052
E-mail: kalpaz@hotmail.com
Phone : 9212729499

Lasser Type Setting by: Quick Media, Delhi
Printed at : Young Art Press, Delhi - 92

Dedicated to the Geophysicists, Geologists, Engineers, Scientists, Universities, Organisations, Teachers, Students, and other working in different disciplines of petroleum science and engineering

"There has been far too much emphasis on rights and far too little on obligations. If obligations were undertaken, rights would naturally follow from them."

Pt. Jawahar Lal Nehru

"The woods are lovely, dark and deep
But I have promises to keep
And miles to go before I sleep
And miles to go before I sleep....."

Robert Frost

CONTENTS

PREFACE

"It is not an if—we are going to have to change. Oil is simply going to be gone."

—Dennis Weaver, American actor, 2008

The world's energy requirements are growing rapidly. The World Economic Outlook 2007 predicts that world energy needs would grow by 55 percent from 11.4 BTOE to 17.7 BTOE during 2005 to 2030. China and India alone are expected to account for 45 percent of this increase. Oil crisis is changing business practices and lifestyles. High oil prices affect everybody, from the poor man to the captain of industry. Every one should do what they can to ease the burden. It is good news that the jump in oil prices has induced firms to be more energy and cost efficient. Now people must follow suit. The fact is that there are no quick fixes to reverse the rising cost of living caused by high oil prices. People, therefore, will need to adapt to changing market conditions. Belt-tightening is a correct and necessary response, for businesses as well as for individuals. The dramatic rise in the price of crude has already led to a drop in demand from the United States and Europe. J. Paul Getty said, "Oil is like a wild animal, whoever captures it has it". It does not matter how much oil we have left, who has it, or how long it will last. Sheik Zaki Yamani said, "The Stone Age did not end for lack of stone, and the Oil Age will end long before the world runs out of oil".

Relying solely on oil for fuel is no longer a sustainable option. Alternative sources of energy need to be made available commercially. We simply have to step up research in solar, wind and biofuel energy from sources like the jatropha plant, biomass and waste, and perhaps sugarcane or maize crops. The world's top industrialized nations and leading oil consumers pledged to fight skyrocketing energy prices by increasing-efficiency and accelerating investment in new technologies, while urging producers to expand production. The G-8 countries : the United States, Russia, Japan, Germany, France, Italy, Canada and Britain laid out ways of cutting their dependence on oil in a statement. They pledged to launch 20 demonstration projects by 2010 on so-called "carbon capture and storage," which would allow power plants to catch emissions and inject them into underground storage spaces. The International Energy Agency, in a report estimated the world would have to construct 32 new nuclear power plants each year from now (June, 2008) until 2050 as part of effort to cut global greenhouse gas emissions by 50 percent. "I think we are on the verge of a new nuclear age and that will be a positive thing for the world," said John Hulton, British Secretary of state for business enterprise and regulatory refornr, 2008.

Part-one of this encylopaedia gives about the applied remote sensing. The growing activities of multispectral remote sensing of the earth from space with the use of satellites and space shuttles point to need to ponstantly monitor our terrestrial environment. Interest in remote sensing has grown so rapidly in recent years that the literature on this subject has becomes staggering. Applications using remotely sensed data from Aerospace platforms are increasingly diverse especially because scientists from different disciplines have found these data useful. The interdisciplinary nature of remote sensing has made it a valuable integrating tool in the study of the environment. In view of these, this part has been written stressing the practical applications of remote sensing to mankind in different parts of the terestial environment. The applications have been selected carefully from among those that have proven to be significant. These applications have been classified by subjects and by the portion of the electromagnetic spectrum within which the data are required. Information about the object concerned is conveyed to the observer through electromagnetic energy which is the information carrier and thus provides the communication link. Remote sensing data as basically wavelength-intensity information which needs to be decoded before the message can be fully understood. Electromagnetic radiation is a form of energy transfer in the free space, which exhibits both wave and particle properties. In order to detect the electromagnetic energy which exists in a wide range of wavelengths and frequencies, different varieties of remote sensing instruments on required.

Part-two of this encyclopaedia gives about the hydrogen : the world's future energy mix. We must understand the future hydrogen economy. Clean air and unlimited fuel supply could make hydrogen the alternative fuel of choice for the future. It is an attractive conception where our energy needs are met by clean-burning hydrogen, produced by renewable sources like wind power and solar energy. This vision is not just around the corner by any means, but transition is gathering steam, and hydrogen certainly has a part to play in the world's energy mix within the foreseeable future. Hydrogen's main attraction is that it can be produced from water or from any hydrocarbon fuel, or even from energy sources of the future that we cannot envision yet. Hydrogen fuel cells are already being tested in vehicles and used commercially in micropower plants, which generate electricity where it is needed instead of transmitting it over long distances. The oil/energy industry pioneers in promoting hydrogen are BP and Shell, both based in Europe, and America's Chevron Texaco. They have joined with several of the world's major automakers in demonstrating hydrogen fuel cell vehicles and fueling stations. ONGC Energy Centre Trust, India, dedicated to holistic research in non-conventional energy sources in the premises of Rajiv Gandhi Urja Bhavan coming up in New Delhi, has taken up 3 projects : (1) thermal-chemical reactor for hydrogen, (2) geo-bio reactors, and (3) fuel cell. Nearly one million vehicles will be running on Indian roads by 2020 using hydrogen which also be used to produce approximately

1000 MW of electricity according to the roadmap prepared by a steering group set up by the government to promote the gas as future fuel. After finalizing a hydrogen energy roadmap, the government is now preparing a strategy to harness solar energy as part of efforts to promote renewable energy sources in the country. The ministry of non-conventional energy sources is making a Solar Photovoltaic Technology Roadmap for the country upto 2022, in line with the 11th, 12th and 13th Five Year Plans.

The aim of this encyclopaedia is to make interconnections among the different disciplines of petroleum science and engineering like applied remote sensing and hydrogen : the world's future energy mix.

At the end of this encyclopaedia seven appendixes have been included. These appendixes will give more information to readers about interesting topics besides the petroleum science and engineering.

This encyclopaedia will help to promote understanding and communication among users. It is suitable for geophysicists, geologists, scientists, universities, organizations, teachers, students and other working in different disciplines of petroleum science and engineering.

The author will be grateful for comments and criticism which might help to improve the later edition of this encyclopaedia. Contact number is 91-135-2435487.

Some of the material of this encyclopaedia has been taken from the books and the papers published in different journals. I am thankful to all of them who have contributed to the development of this encyclopaedia.

Rishikesh (India), 2008

S.L. Sah

1

APPLIED REMOTE SENSING

Introduction

Applied remote sensing should be aimed at benefiting mankind through the use of an interdisciplinary approach. Remote sensing as a space-age technology provides a convenient tool to scientists for a better monitoring of the earth—the human habitat. Remote sensing refers to the group of techniques of collecting information about an object and its surrounding from a distance without physically contacting them. Normally, this gives rise to some form of imagery which is further processed and interpreted to produce useful data for application in agriculture, archaeology, forestry, geography, geology, planning and other fields. The prime objective of remote sensing is to extract environmental and natural resources data related to our earth. Information about the object concerned is conveyed to the observer through electromagnetic energy, which is the information carrier and thus provides the communication link. Remote sensing data as basically wavelength-intensity information which needs to be decoded before the message can be fully understood. This decoding process is analogous to the interpretation of the remotely sensed imagery which impinges heavily on our knowledge of the properties of electromagnetic radiation.

Detailed Encyclopaedia

This encyclopaedia is arranged in alphabetical order. The detailed encyclopaedia is given below :

Atmospheric Environment

The atmosphere or the gaseous realm which surrounds our earth exercises a great impact on the activities of mankind. In the lowest 80 km. of the atmosphere, there is a homogenized mixture of gases composed predominantly of nitrogen (78.08 percent by volume), oxygen (20.95 percent), argon (0.93 percent) and carbon dioxide (0.033 percent). The remaining gases, in decreasing order of percentage by volume, are neon, helium, krypton, xenon, hydrogen, methane and nitrous oxide, which add up to less than 0.003 percent of the total volume. In the lower atmosphere water vapour is always present from 1 percent to 4 percent. Ozone gas is present at the surface of the earth and it is 0.00007 percent by volume. Carbon dioxide is able to absorb heat, thus it permits the lower atmosphere to be warmed by the incoming solar radiation and the emitted longwave radiation from the earth's surface. Carbon dioxide is also an effective emitter of radiation which helps to cool the upper atmosphere. The atmosphere is held to the earth by gravitational pull. Thus, the air thins out and the pressure decreases as we go up the atmosphere. The atmosphere is vertically subdivided into four layers : (1) troposphere (0-12.5 km), (2) stratosphere (12.5-50 km), (3) mesosphere (50-80 km), and (4) thermosphere or ionosphere (beyond 80 km.). See Fig. 1. The human population lives in the tropopause, the lowest layer of the atmosphere, where virtually all the clouds and weather occur. We collect data by remote sensing to understand better the dynamic circulatory processes of the atmospheric system. The data required are basically three types : (1) temperature, (2) pressure, and (3) humidity.

The collection of meteorological data has been traditionally ground based with the use of barometers, thermometers, anemometers, rain-gauges and sunshine recorders distributed in a dense network of stations over a country. To collect pressure, temperature and humidity data

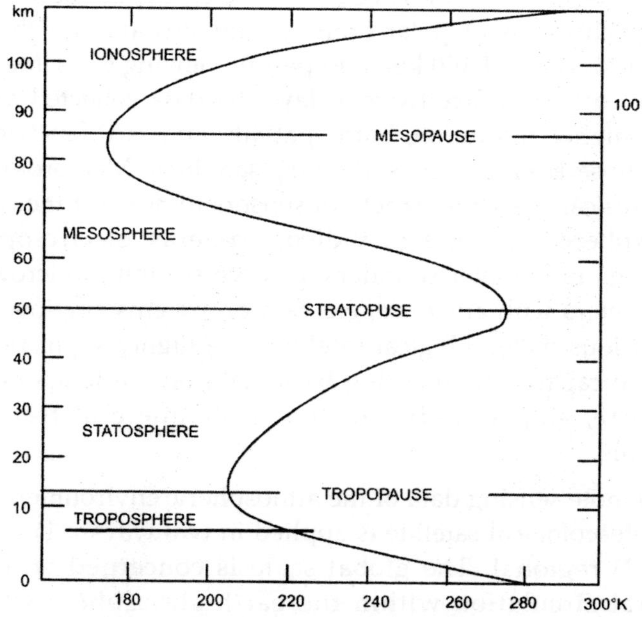

Fig. 1. Characteristics of the thermal structure of the atmosphere upto the lower part of the ionosphere (After LO, 1986).

in the upper atmosphere, a radiosonde is used. This consists of a small barometer, a thermometer and a hygrometer built into a cage which is carried by a balloon upto a height of about 30 km. A tiny radio, powered by batteries is also contained in the cage to telemeter the data back to earth. From the track of the balloon, wind speeds and directions can be computed. Radars have also been used to measure the intensity of rain and snow. Doppler radars have been used to detect tornadoes and other forms of storms. Now great variety of meteorological satellites are used which provide ideal platforms for remote sensing of meteorological phenomena in both the lower and upper atmosphere of the earth. The geo-stationary satellites at an altitude of 35,800 km. give global views of the earth over the same sub-satellite point every day and permit continuous collection of data. However, they cannot see the poles because of the earth's curvature. The sun-synchronous or polar orbiting satellites are launched to an altitude about 1,100 km. and permit viewing the same spot on the earth's surface twice a day. The data collected are of much higher resolution, both spatially and radio-metrically, than those from the geostationary satellites. Meteorological satellites carry a wide variety of sensors to monitor the earth-atmosphere system, e.g., Vidicon cameras, electro-optical scanners, radiometer sounders, passive scanning microwave radiometers with antennee, etc. Sensor systems employed by the various meteorological satellites are highly sophisticated and are capable of collecting basic data on the temperature, pressure, and humidity of the atmosphere at frequent intervals.

Remote sensing data of the atmospheric environment sent by meteorological satellite is applied in two ways : (1) global, and (2) regional. The global scale is concerned with the general circulation within the earth-atmosphere system whereas the regional scale focuses on phenomena that occur within a small area of the earth, of about 10 to 100 km. across, such as, studies of tornadoes, thunderstorms or urban heat islands. Availability of the satellite data in image and non-image forms obtained at frequent time intervals permits three approaches to processing the data for various applications : (1) the visual or computer-assisted interpretation of the spatial patterns of the original two-dimensional imagery, (2) the mathematical analysis of the one-dimensional non-image radiation measurements to derive useful meteorological parameters, and (3) the detection of trends or patterns of changes of weather phenomena by comparing one-dimensional or two-dimensional meteorological data acquired at different times. These approaches in combination with scale factor lead to remote sensing applications in (1) applied macroclimatology with special emphasis on the radiation budget of the earth-atmosphere system; atmospheric moisture and circulation patterns and (2) mesoscale and synoptic scale analysis of weather phenomena for forecasting purposes. Heat and moisture are continuously being exchanged between the earth and the atmosphere. See Fig. 2. In the long run, the

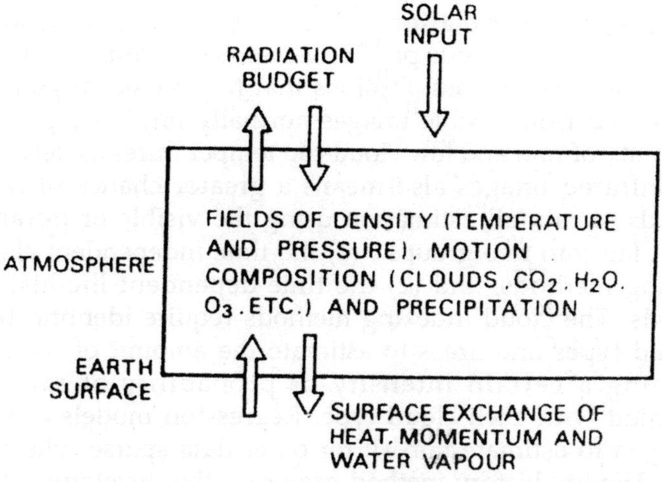

Fig. 2. Basic components of the radiation budget of the earth-atmosphere system (After LO, 1986).

earth-atmosphere system must return to space as much energy as it receives from the sun, the major energy source. The mean value of input from the sun is 1.95 cal/cm^2 min or 1.38 kW/m^2. Its name is solar constant. The solar constant measures the rate at which solar radiation is received at the top of the atmosphere on a unit surface normal to the incident radiation. The radiation budget describes the energy exchange between the earth and space upto about 50 km. altitude. The Earth Radiation Budget (ERB) experiment was equipped with a 22-channel radiometer. The ERB experiment has also been able to map the geographical distribution of the outgoing radiation fluxes from the earth's surface in both the coarser and the finer resolutions. The availability of geostationary satellite data permits the radiation budget of the earth-atmosphere system to be determined with greater accuracy.

Atmospheric Measurements

A number of significant characteristics of the remote sensing data has been applied to study our atmosphere. Much of the remote sensing data comes from space platforms. The scope of remote sensing applications to the atmospheric environment is wide and their outcome has great practical importance. Important atmospheric measurements are given below :—

1. Rainfall Estimation : Visible and thermal infrared satellite images of clouds provide a means to estimate rainfall. This is based on the assumptions that high cloud brightness as observed from visible images normally implies a greater probability of rain and low cloud-top temperatures as detected from infrared images also means a greater chance of rain. Methods of rainfall estimation using the visible or infrared images fall into two groups : (1) the time-independent cloud indexing methods, and (2) the time-dependent life-history methods. The cloud indexing methods require identification of cloud types and areas to estimate the amount of rainfall, assuming a certain intensity or probability of rainfall associated with each cloud type. Regression models can be employed to estimate rainfall for other data sparse cells. See Fig. 3. The life-history method examines the development of convective clouds from a time-sequence of geo-stationary satellite images over individual grid cells. The interval between consecutive pictures must be short. The passive microwave method is used for rainfall estimation. The passive microwave sensor detects thermal emission the intensity of which is linearly related to the blackbody temperature corresponding to the brightness temperature. The brightness temperature is also affected by the direction of polarization of the electromagnetic wave. Three constituents of the atmosphere are : water vapour, oxygen and liquid water droplets. By selecting the appropriate frequencies, the microwave sensor can either look through or look at the atmosphere. The frequency intervals best suited for measurement of rain are less than 20 GHz and close to 30 GHz (Barrett and Martin, 1981). Microwave radiometry from satellites has been used to remotely measure rainfall from Nimbus 55 (using ESMR-5 at 19.35 GHz frequency). The ESMR-6 at 37 GHz frequency is more sensitive to liquid water droplets and, when massing in both polarization components, is capable of giving a more accurate rainfall estimation over land. The brightness temperature at 37 GHz becomes insensitive to changes in rainfall rate once rainfall rates exceed 8 mm/hour.

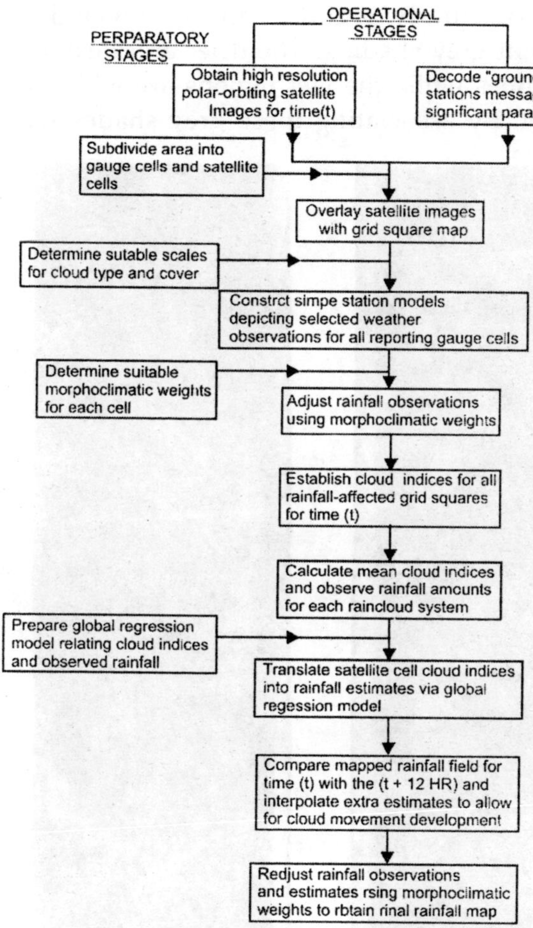

Fig. 3. Flow diagram of the cloud indexing method in rainfall estimation (After LO, 1986).

2. Water Vapour Analysis : The moisture content of the atmosphere is another important parameter which can be measured directly from satellite images. The Nimbus-4 satellite carried the Temperature-Humidity Infrared Radiometer (THIR), which monitored radiation in the 6.5-7.2 μm water vapour absorption region with a 23 km. spatial resolution.

The radiation so monitored principally came from emission in the 500-250 mb region of the upper troposphere. By examining the photo-facsimile imagery in the 6.7 μm channel, moisture-rich or cloudy regions can be detected by the different levels of grey shading. The drier areas exhibit dark grey to black tones while the wet regions are white or light gray. See Fig. 4. By associating these grey shades with the

Fig. 4. Nimbus 4 THIR photofacsimile imagery in the (*a*) 6.7 μm, and (*b*) 11.5 μm spectral regions at local midnight over the western USA on orbit 2565, 16 October, 1970 (After LO, 1986).

radiosonde soundings, an experienced analyst can obtain a good idea of the vertical stratification of the moisture content. From the same imagery, it would be possible to estimate the mixing ratio, i.e., the mass of water vapour compared to the mass of dry air within which the water vapour contained, in the atmosphere. The geo-synchronous METEOSAT monitors the earth with a water vapour channel (5.7-7.1 μm) at a more frequently (half-hourly) interval in a higher spatial resolution (5 km.) then the polar-orbiting Nimbus-4, thus giving a global view of the moisture pattern of the middle troposphere (300-600 mb).

3. Wind Field Analysis : Satellite data have also been employed in determining wind speed and wind direction. The water vapour imagery could be used to infer the directions of horizontal wind flows. Wind flows at different levels can be inferred from cloud motion as revealed by the animated photography of the spin-scan clouds cameras onboards some geo-synchronous satellites such as the Applications Technology Satellites (ATS). This method can give about the same accuracy as wind speeds derived from radiosondes. The cross-correlation technique computes the cross-correction coefficients between two sequential digital data sets measured by computer. This has been applied to single-layer clouds and multiple-layer clouds in low, middle and high levels. Another approach in automatic cloud tracking was to make use of pattern recognition technique.

4. Prediction of Severe Storms : Thunderstorms often form within straight or arc-shaped cloud lines. The severe weather elements tended to have cold minimum cloud top temperatures and large rates of growth. By measuring the areal expansions of the cold areas through time, one can detect and monitor the growth rates of the storm. Storms penetrating the tropopause were found to have a higher probability of producing damaging hail. A strong relationship was observed to exist between the onset of large hail and cloud-top temperatures getting colder than the environmental tropopause temperature, accompanied by a rapid vertical growth of cloud. Another approach to predict storm intensity is to make use of microwave data in the 19.35 GHz region from ESMR-5 to measure the distribution and intensity of rainfall within tropical cyclones which are positively related to storm intensity.

5. Weather Analysis and Forecast : The availability of polar-orbiting and geosynchronous satellites as platforms for remote sensing of the atmosphere has provided valuable data to improve the accuracy of short-term weather forecasting, particularly for data-sparse areas of the world, such as the tropics. The construction of synoptic weather charts is greatly facilitated with the availability of visible and infrared imagery. Most of the data are also available in digital form which facilitates computer processing. This makes possible near real-image display of the cloud pattern over a place. Much useful information can be extracted from the interpretation of the satellite images obtained in the visible and thermal infrared channels of the remote sensors. The weather images show mostly clouds. These remote sensors give a good idea of the spatial distribution and vertical extension of the clouds. The configuration and structure of these cloudy areas suggested that the distinction of the four types of cloud configurations, e.g., cloud bands, vortex configurations, cellular cloudiness and uniform cloud areas, would be useful to weather analysis and forecast. The availability of passive microwave data and an active spaceborne radar system will certainly improve our ability to monitor rainfall, temperature, humidity and winds in the lower atmosphere.

Atmospheric Temperature Structure

Temperature measurements can be made by using the emission spectrum of carbon dioxide centred at a wavelength of 15 μm in the infrared. Carbon dioxide is present in the atmosphere, uniformly mixed to within 1 or 2 percent. Its emission spectrum when viewed from above will be dependent only on the vertical distribution of the atmospheric temperature. These temperature measurements are particularly affected by the presence of clouds. The remote temperature sounding of the atmosphere from a satellite was made from TIROS, SIRS (Satellite Infrared Spectrometer), and IRIS (Infrared Interferometer Spectrometer). Microwave spectrometers and Scanning Microwave Spectrometer

(SCAMS) have also been used to measure atmospheric temperature from satellite platforms. Passive microwave sensors have the advantage of being able to measure the temperature profile under cloud-covered conditions. Mostly they are used to measure temperature, water vapour and liquid water. The five spectral channels of the SCAMS were selected in the water vapour band (22.235 GHz), the atmospheric wind at 31.650 GHz, the oxygen band at 52.85 GHz, 53.85 GHz and 55.45 GHz (Staelin et.al., 1977).The primary surface temperatures determining the microwave emission are surface temperature and surface emissivity or dielectric properties of the surface. The product of these two parameters gives the brightness temperature of the surface. The last channels of SCAMS were selected at the oxygen absorption band which measured the average temperature of layers about 10 km. thick centred near altitudes of 2, 6 and 13 respectively. Because radiation sources occur at different heights in the atmosphere, gradients of transmission with respect to the logarithms of pressure known as weighting functions can be computed for each carbon dioxide channel of the instrument. In other words, the weighting functions describe the region of atmosphere from which the radiation detected in the different spectral channels originates. See Fig. 5. For best results both infrared and microwave observations should be employed together.

The radiation and temperature measurements from the satellite platforms can be extended to study earth surface radiation characteristics in the rural and urban environments. An important area of investigation is desertification caused possibly by increased surface albedoes which produce subsequent rainfall deficits. The increased albedo results in a net radiative loss which gives rise to general subsidence and drying over the area, thereby inhibiting or reducing the convection necessary for rain. The increased surface albedoes may be natural or man-made as a result of improper land management. The top of the atmosphere is referred to as planetary albedo. Another interesting applications of radiation

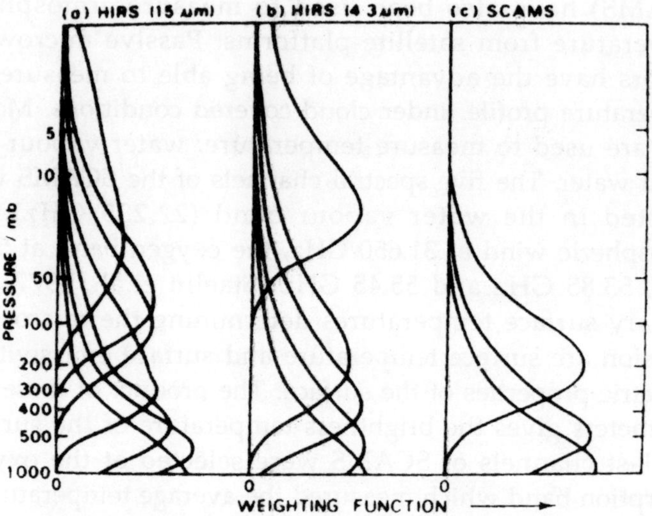

Fig. 5. Weighting functions for instruments sounding the temperature of the lower atmosphere on the Nimbus 6 satellite for (*a*) 15 μm channels, (*b*) 4.3 μm channels, and (*c*) channels of SCAMS (After Houghton, 1979).

budget and temperature measurements from satellite remote sensing is the urban heat island study, which illustrates the usefulness of polar-orbiting thermal infrared satellite data in microclimatological investigations. The application was based on a four-layer surface model to infer the surface energy fluxes, moisture availability and thermal inertia from HCMM radiance data. After the solution the daytime and night-time surface layer models, the satellite radiance data were input into these models to produce a series of maps for surface temperature, sensible heat flux, moisture availability and thermal inertia. See 6. The heating up of the urban area caused differential heating which resulted in small-scale circulations. The urban heat island was therefore attributable to the presence of surfaces that could not retain moisture which was due to the result of inadvertent human modifications of the land cover.

Satellite images record cloud patterns from which one can deduce the three-dimensional structure of wind and pressure

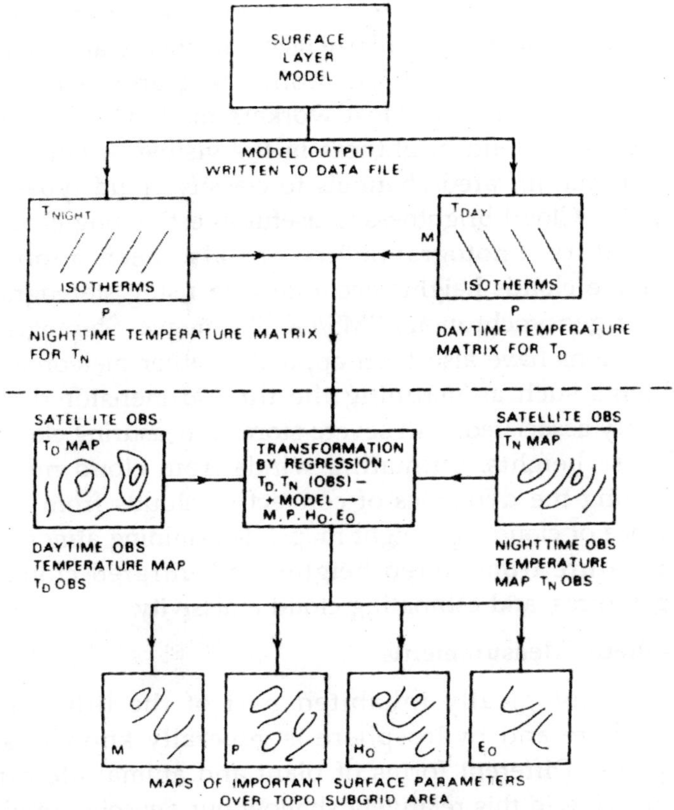

Fig. 6. Flow diagram for inferring surface parameters from satellite observations (After LO, 1986).

fields. This makes use of four factors : (1) condition of stability in the atmosphere, (2) vertical or horizontal motion in the troposphere, (3) contrasting temperature or humidity characteristics, and (4) the modifications in air masses and air streams caused by the underlying topography. Satellite images are used to identify the different types of clouds. Three major types of clouds are : (1) cirrus or curly clouds, (2) stratus or layered clouds, and (3) cumulus or curly clouds. With the use of satellite images, the viewing is vertically, from above. Meteorological satellite images have been used for the preparation of cloud charts or nephanalyses which show the distribution of cloudiness over an area. Better cloud information will be particularly useful in energy and moisture budget modeling, rainfall monitoring and sea surface temperature mapping. Most workers made use of spectral features, i.e., cloud brightness in the visible, water vapour and thermal infrared channels to classify cloud types with computer. Cloud brightness is useful in estimating cloud-top temperature. Photogrammetry has also been applied to determine clouds heights accurately by using stereographic pairs of geosynchronous SMS/GOES images. Stereographic observations have also been applied to other meteorological problems such as mapping the three-dimensional cloud geometry associated with severe storms, measuring cloud top and base heights, estimating winds from cloud motions, examining the dynamics of convective clouds from a time sequence of cloud top height maps, determining atmospheric temperature from stereo heights and infrared cloud top temperatures, and estimating cloud emissivity.

Biospheric Measurements

The biologically inhabited part of the lithosphere, atmosphere and hydrosphere is generally known as the biosphere. Different forms of plant and animal life can be found living in this relatively shallow but densely populated zone of the interface between the atmosphere and lithosphere or hydrosphere. Here, the focus is on the plant life and its related phenomena which have a direct impact on the well-being of the human population. Plants comprise the greatest bulk of the total world biomass, i.e., volume of living material, both above and below the lithosphere and in the hydrosphere. In the study of vegetation, crops and soils, there is invariably the need to carry out surveys with a view to discover their spatial distribution, structure and type. This information is indispensible for the purpose of management in agriculture and forestry, for informed decision-making in planning, for feasibility studies in land development projects and many engineering works. The spatial distribution emphasizes the locational variations in the characteristics of soils and plants. The pattern refers to the lay-out and arrangement of the soils units and plants in a particular location. The identification of the specific types of soils and plants permits individual homogeneous units to be defined and their extent delimited. All these information requirements can be effectively met with the use of conventional and modern remote sensing techniques coupled with minimal ground survey.

Biospheric Measurements (By Aerial Photography)

The role of aerial photography remains dominant in providing information on the distribution, structure and type of vegetation, crops and soils. The distinctiveness of tonal and textural variations of the photographic images and the superior spatial resolution are among the factors which have contributed significantly to the success of aerial photography applied to the study of the biosphere. In vegetation studies it permits accurate metric data relating to heights and volumes to be obtained photogrammetrically. The employment of colour infrared film also aids greatly in extracting qualitative data of the vegetation. In countries with an abundant forest cover, an inventory of the forest to determine the volume of the timber resources is necessary for economic and management purposes. The method of identification of tree species was developed by the use of morphological characteristics of trees, such as crown shape, branching habit and foliage characteristics for identification clues. The most useful morphological characteristics from the vertical aerial photographic point of view are crown shapes, texture and branching habits. Crown shapes can be generally described as oval, down, cylindrical, conical, rounded, wide-spreading and flat-topped. See Fig. 7. Branching characteristics of trees can be described according to the length and thickness of branches; variation in branch size, the branch direction, whether ascending, horizontal or drooping; the branch form, weather straight, crooked or twisted; the arrangement of

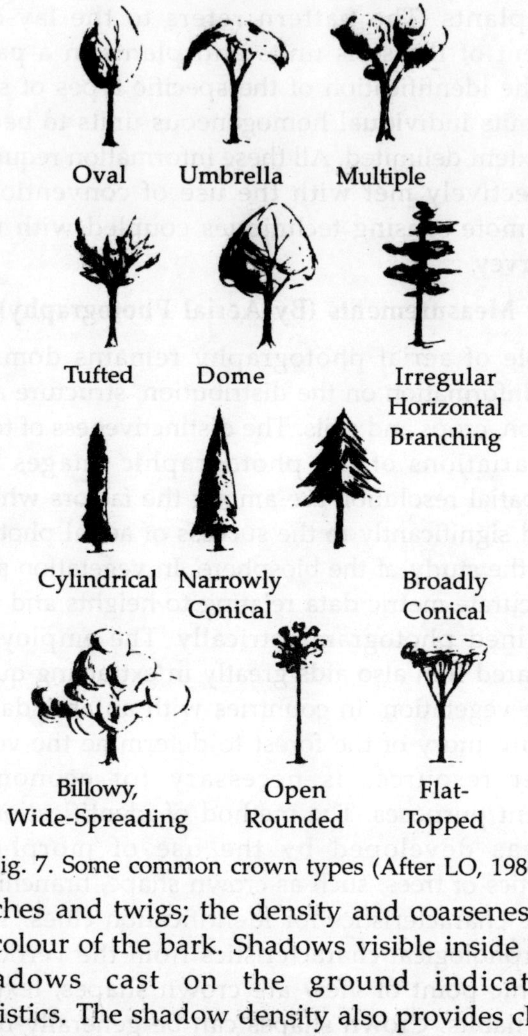

Fig. 7. Some common crown types (After LO, 1986).

branches and twigs; the density and coarseness of twigs and the colour of the bark. Shadows visible inside the crown and shadows cast on the ground indicate crown characteristics. The shadow density also provides clues to the degree of the crown and foliage; the darker the shadow the more compact. Tree type identification depends on tone and texture but not crown shape. One major limitation of the application of aerial photography to forest inventory or woodlands survey is that it cannot adequately take into account the well developed structure in terms of layering, i.e., the layers of canopy, understorey, shrub, herb and ground.

Fig. 8. Diagrammatic representation of vegetation stratification (After LO, 1986).

See Fig. 8. The aerial photographs focus attention to the uppermost layer, i.e., the tree canopy. But correlations exist between the canopy and the other layers of the forest. Another approach in the use of aerial photography in vegetation study is to detect damage caused by diseases or pests to the vegetation. Morphological damage involves a change in the shape or outline of the vegetation. Physiological damage involves a changes in function as expressed by a deviation from a normal pattern, such as decrease in photosynthates, deterioration of chloroplasts, interruption of translocates, including water, etc. A first visual symptom of physical damage is yellowig of the foliage. Any morphological changes are best described on the basis of form, texture and boundary pattern. The changes in spectral reflectance caused by physiological damage will affect normal colour or colour infrared film. The damage vegetation may be the result of an environmental stress, such as air pollution (sulphur dioxide) or a biotic stress, such as insects. See Table 1.

Table 1. Selected stress agents and key for noticable strain symptoms (After LO, 1986)

Stress	*Key Strain Symptoms*
Abiotic – Environmental	
Water deficit (drought)	Small fliage, wilting
Water excess (flood)	Topography-related, discoloured to dead foliage
Air pollution (e.g. SO_2)	Affects many species, interveinal necrosis and chlorosis, decrease from source
Wind (storm)	Broken stems
Fire (ground)	Burn scar, blackened ground
Acid rain	Top dieback, lower fliage appear healthy
Biotic – Insects	
Bark beetles (Douglas fir)	Red-brown and faded foliage
Defoliators (spruce budworm)	Bare branches, seasonal red-brown foliage
Terminal feeders (white pine weevil)	Dead leader
Sucking insects (woolly aphid)	Yellowed foliage, thin crown
Leaf miners (birch leaf miner)	Discoloured foliage
Biotic – Diseases	
Stem rusts (blister rust)	Dead top or leader
Root rots (Fomes, Poria)	Thin foliage, dead trees in pockets
Leaf wilts (Dutch elm)	Entire or part of crown with no dead or discoloured foliage.

Aerial photography of varying scales in black-and-white panchromatic, colour and colour infrared films has been extensively employed to identify farm crops in different climatic environments. Tone, texture and association were three major clues which helped in the identification of the farm crops. In order to standardize images, a densitometer was used to measure quantitatively the tone values of all objects, which were then adjusted relatively to the tone of a reference object. The texture of the photographic image of individual crops varied with the external characteristics of the crops and the way in which they were planted, cultivated and harvested. Textural characteristics were also, to a certain extend, associated with variations of soil moisture. One could therefore describe textures of fields as "lined", "plaid-like", "corduroy", "striped", "swath" or "mottled". The use of association of objects such as straw stack, hay stack, herds of cows, etc., has helped photo-interpreters to identify a field of oats, a field of hay and a rotation pasture respectively. The identification of farm crops was also attempted using colour and colour infrared photography. An increasing number of photographic variables is being employed for the crop identification purpose. Variations in the infrared reflection from the crops are the result of chlorophyll breakdown in the mesophyll tissue before visible symptoms of stress or infection appear. The density levels of colour infrared photographs ca be related to the infection level of diseases of crops in fields. The higher the level of infection, the lower will be the infrared reflectance from the crop. The colour infrared photography proved to be an effective tool to detect pre-visual crop stress caused by the defects of the irrigation system. The nature and pattern of the colour variations of the crop indicate the probable source of the stress. There are three layers of soil : (1) the topsoil, (2) the subsoil, and (3) the parent material. The topsoil is the most extensively weathered horizon and contains the most organic matter. The aerial photographs are used to locate changes in the land surface patterns that may relate to different soil properties (White 1977). There is a close relationship between the kinds of soil and the nature of the parent material, relief, climate, vegetation and age of the landform. A sandy soil reflects more radiant energy than a clay soil. Soils with high organic matter give low reflectance. The reflectance is lower for a soil with rough surface. Tonal patterns were good indicators of different soil, but the correlations of photo-tone with organic matter content, moisture content, calcium carbonate content and siltiness of the soils were poor especially over large areas. The photographic tones were related to the lithological pattern and soil surface characteristics. The colour infrared displays a greater contrast between bare soil (blue) and vegetation (red). A higher degree of wetness is reflected by a darker blue colour.

Biospheric Measurement (By Multispectral Remote Sensing Techniques)

Multi-spectral sensing makes use of different spectral bands of the electromagnetic spectrum to differentiate between objects or to determine the physical condition of objects based on the amount of reflectance in each band. Computer processing is normally required because of the large number of multispectral data. Now, applications of multispectral remote sensing have focused on the estimation of the amount and distribution of vegetation. A knowledge of the vegetation amount permits vegetation yield to be estimated. When applied to crop growth, crop yield can be predicted (Curran, 1980). The amount of green vegetation can be measured by the green Leaf Area Index (LAI), green biomass or percent cover. The LAI is the area of green leaves per unit area of ground. The biomass is the mass of the green vegetation per unit area, usually measured by harvesting and weighing vegetation. Percent cover of green vegetation can be measured by photographing upwards into the vegetation canopy from the forest floor. The percentage cover was calculated with a dot grid. Estimation of green leaf area index (LAI) is based on reflectance from a vegetation canopy. The intensity of the reflectance is dependent on the wavelength used and the three components of the vegetation canopy, e.g., leaves, substrate, and shadow. Leaves reflect weakly in the blue and red wavelengths but strongly in the near infrared wavelengths. See Fig. 9. The reflectance of vegetation substrates varies

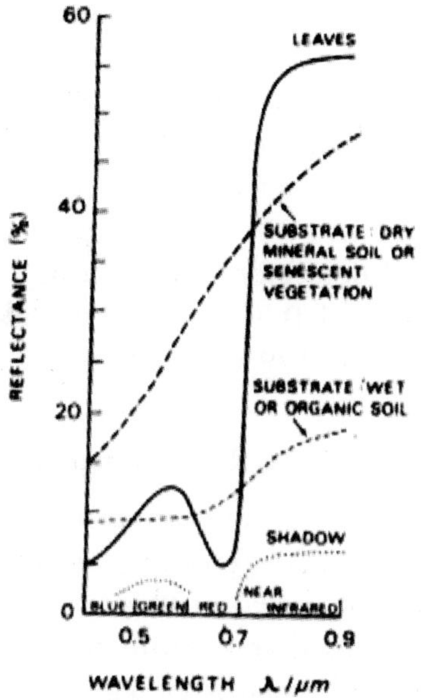

Fig. 9. Reflectance properties of three components of a vegetation canopy, leaves, shadow and mineal or organic subtrate (After Curran, 1983).

according to the nature of the substrate, i.e., senescent vegetation, light-toned mineral soil, or dark-toned organic soil. The shadow component in a vegetation-canopy is very dark in the visible wavelengths with radiation strongly absorbed by leaves, but appears fairly dark in the near infrared wavelength with radiation slightly absorbed by leaves. The angle of the sun controls the area and the darkness of the shadow. The look-angle of the sensor determines the amount of substrate (soil) visible to the sensor. As the look-angle moves from the vertical, less soil and more vegetation will be visible. A homemade, hand-held biomass meter was constructed which was capable of measuring the canopy reflectance at 0.58 μm (red) and 0.80 μm (near-infrared). The ratio of the red and near-infrared reflectances was then related to the dry biomass data collected at 25 sample plots of blue grama grass, each plot being $^1/_4$ m^2 in area. A linear relationship was established between the two, showing a correlation of 0.98 for all 25 plots measured. This was found adequate for biomass estimation of shortgrass to midgrass canopies. The results of one flight line of 12-band multispectral imagery over the Pawnee National Grassland, Colorado, USA indicated that with the use of a simple ratio of the two spectral bands most closely representing the red and near-infrared bands used in the hand-held biomass meter, which happened to be 0.66 - 0.72 μm and 0.80 - 1.00 μm respectively, a correlation coefficient R of 0.79 was obtained for 26 ground-truth biomass samples.

Biospheric Measurements (By Radar Imagery)

The use of imaging radar, an active microwave remote sensing system, to study vegetation, crops and soils is somewhat limited because much of these can be done better with the conventional black-and-white aerial photography. However, in tropical and equatorial regions which tend to be cloud-covered most of the time, imaging radar is the only sensor which has the capability of penetrating thick layers of clouds to obtain timely land cover information. According to Morain (1976), radar images can reveal three main kinds of vegetational information : (1) geographic pattern, (2) gross structure and physiognomy, and (3) type identification. The image tone and texture are two major parameters employed to identify and delineate vegetation types. They are affected by surface roughness and dielectric properties of the terrain features as well as the incidence angle, polarization and frequency of the radar system. Tone is a function of the wavelength of the system being used and the viewing angle. See Fig. 10. Leaf size, leaf area, leaf/twig ratio, percentage of ground cover and moisture condition can affect the radar image tones. Texture is affected by height variability of vegetation. Forests display coarser textures than grass or shrubs. The finer is the resolution, the more prominent is the texture. Polarization affects tone and texture of vegetation. A bright return on HV imagery indicates the heterogeneous

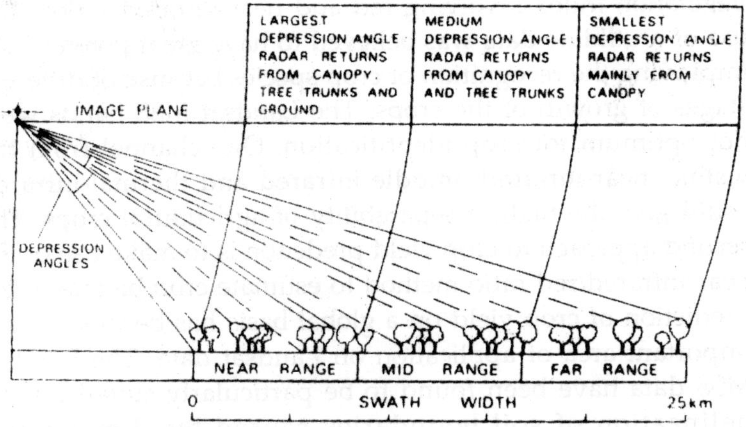

Fig. 10. SLAR signature differences in a uniform vegeation unit on level terrain (After LO, 1986).

nature of the imaged material. For homogenous materials there should be little difference between HH and HV reflectances. SLAR can at best be a reconnaissance vegetation survey tool. The accuracy of crop discrimination with radar can be further improved with multidate data. The multidate data alone were more informative than the spectral and polarization data. Frequencies above 8 GHz were best for crop discrimination. The HH polarization has been found to be more sensitive to row direction than HV.

Biospheric Measurements (By Satellite Data)

The Landsat MSS data which are available in four spectral bands can be visually interpreted with the aid of a colour additive viewer to manually delineate forest from non-forest land, or to separate between water, conifers, muskegs and herdwood stands. However, it would be difficult to visually differentiate tree species from the small-scale coarse-resolution colour composite. The importance of terrain in affecting the reflectance of the species was also observed. The Landsat data also open up opportunities to forecasting and estimating crop production. One approach is to identify agricultural crop types and estimate the area covered by the crops. Another approach is to estimate the vegetation amount using a

Vegetation Index involving red and near-infrared ratios. The use of mutlidate data was believed to have great potential for improving the recognition of crop species because of different stages of growth of the crops. The Landsat MSS bands were not optimum for crop identification. One channel from the visible, near-infrared, middle-infrared and thermal-infrared could give the highest separability of agricultural crops. The second approach to crop yield predciton is to make use of the near-infrared/red ratio method to estimate crop biomass. The prediction of crop yield on a global basis has become a very important area of application on Landsat data. The Landsat MSS data have been found to be particularly suited for the delineation of soil boundaries caused by climatic and vegetative differences which otherwise are not observable on conventional aerial photographs with restricted areal coverage. Soil boundaries can also be revealed by differences in parent materials and relief, which are all detectable visually from Landsat images (band 5 and/or band 7). A typical approach is to use image enhancement and classification techniques to produce a spectral map of cover types which are then correlated with soil characteristics. Such an approach is more successful in the arid or semi-arid environment where the vegetation cover is sparse. The enhanced imagery was found to be particularly helpful in locating soil unit boundaries in the field. There was a good match between the spectral pattern and the mapped soil boundary lines. The spectral patterns in the enhanced image appeared to be more similar to the field data than those produced simply by spectral signature classification.

Biospheric Measurements (By Thermal Infrared Imagery)

Thermal infrared sensors in the windows at 3-5 μm or 8-14 μm at aircraft altitude are specifically applied to measure the surface temperature of the vegetation, crops and soils either in the form of high-resolution imagery or in digital format, amenable to computer processing. From a knowledge of surface temperature, inference can be made of the soil moisture. A knowledge of temperature and moisture will permit vegetation or crop vigour to be determined. Soil moisture information is important to the agriculturalist. A soil consists of varying portions of water and air in the voids according to the moisture content. A soil with a high proportion of air will exhibit large day and night contrasts of surface temperature, while a soil containing a low proportion of air will show relatively small temperature variations. By acquiring thermal infrared data of an area in the same 24 hours (pre-dawn and early afternoon), the thermal inertia of the area can be found and employed as an indicator of subsurface moisture content. The thermal infrared sensor can be used to measure the temperature of a crop canopy from which the water tension within the plant itself can be inferred. The difference between crop canopy temperatures and ambient air temperatures is measured at the time of maximum solar heating. The daily sun of this temperature difference is then a value for the "Stress Degree Day (SDD)". Canopy temperatures acquired about an hour and a half past solar noon were well correlated with pre-dawn plant water tension, a irameter directly related to plant growth and development. The only other climatic parameter of importance was light. The potential yield of a grain crop was proportional to the summation of daylight minutes over the beginning and end of the heading period during which daily average air temperature was greater than the base temperature.

Catrographic Presentation

Remote sensing has been applied to collect qualitative and quantitative data of our terrestrial environment which comprises the atmosphere, the lithosphere and the hydrosphere. The data are more usually spatial in nature and are presented in the form of maps. These maps are thematic maps because they tend to display the spatial variations of a single phenomenon or the relationship between phenomena. The thematic map is more usually small scaled and its accuracy is assessed by the correctness of the spatial pattern displaced. Thematic mapping is possible only when a base map is available. This base map displays topographic features, such as roads, settlements, rivers, coastlines, water bodies and elevations in the form of contours, in their correct positions. A large-scale map of this type is called a topographic map. There are certain requirements to be met by the topographic map in terms of the accuracy of the positions of the points (planimetric or horizontal accuracy) and the accuracy of the elevations (height or vertical accuracy). These accuracy requirements are normally quite stringent.

Conventional aerial photography provides the major source of data for topographic mapping using the theory of photogrammetry. Photogrammetry is the science and art of obtaining reliable measurements from photographs, but it is always closely related to photo-interpretation because one needs to now what one is measuring. In order to meet the stringent standards of heights and planimetric accuracies, a metric camera is used to acquire the photography. The camera has been calibrated to determine the position of its principal point, the position of the projection centre and the principal distance. This is necessary to ensure that the photographs can reconstructed as exactly as possible the stereomodel produced at the time of photography. The aerial camera makes use of a 23×23 cm format stable base film for photogrammatric missions. Normally, vertical aerial photography is preferred for topographic mapping. The aerial photography produces stereomodels when viewed under a stereoscope, which form the basis for measurement of heights and positions in topographic mapping. The movement of the floating mark is transferred to the plotting pencil of a pantograph arm so that contours and planimetric details can be directly plotted from the stereomodel. An analogue photogrammetric plotting machine is equipped with orientation elements and shifts for each photographic carriage, thus permitting a correct reconstruction of the stereomodel for measurement by the floating dot. Good ground controls are absolutely essential if accurate topographic maps are to be produced from aerial photography.

Orthophotography is a process which transforms the central projection of an aerial photograph into the orthographic projection required of a map. The orthophotograph produced is essentially a photographic reproduction of the aerial photograph in which the distortions of images due to tilts and relief have all been removed. This is achieved by a method called differential rectification. The terrain is broken down into a number of flat areas at different heights above the datum, each of which is then rectified. This can be carried out mechanically by an analogue photogrammetric instrument. Orthophotography has thus speeded up topographic mapping from aerial photographs. With the advances in electronics and computer technology, a high degree of automation in photogrammetry becomes possible. The three for approaches are : (1) image correlating, (2) the fully analytical approach, and (3) the hybrid system. The image correlation technique makes "use of cathode ray tubes, photomultipliers and an electrical analogue computer. The fully analytical approach is to make use of a digital computer to solve mathematically for the unknowns in the collinearity equations which relate the model coordinates an image coordinates together in matrix form. In view of the high cost of the analytical plotters, a common approach is the hybrid system or computer-assisted analogue plotting system.

Cartographic Presentation (Infrared Imagery And SLAB)

The imagery is produced continuously as the aircraft progress along its flight path. Thus, each point on the film strip is exposed at a different time and consequently the correspondence between image position and ground position is directly affected by the flight trajectory. The image is also obtained indirectly through the photographic copying of the display on a cathode ray tube using a moving film. In the case of the thermal infrared imagery, the scanning in effect produces a cylindrical surface for the image, thus giving rise to a scale compression along the scan direction, which increases away from the nadir line while in the flight direction the image scale remains unchanged, thus producing a quasi-panoramic distortion. Konecny (1972) strongly recommended the use of auxiliary data to help improve the metric accuracy of the thermal infrared imagery. On the whole, thermal infrared imagery is not too suitable for topographic mapping purposes if the stringent standards in planimetry and elevation of the resultant maps are to be met (LO, 1986). But its use in thematic mapping is justified.

Side-looking radar (SLAB) imagery is an active microwave sensing system which possesses the greatest potential for topographic mapping and as a source of valuable cartographic data. Its capability of penetrating clouds is the greatest asset and explains its use in topographic mapping in such countries as Panama, Brazil, Venezuela, Colombia and Peru. However, its use in topographic mapping suffers from poor spatial resolution and a complicated geometry which is best handled with an analytical approach. Since SLAB is also a line scanning system which measures, "echo" time, there are two commonents in the spatial resolution of the resultant image : azimuth resolution in the flight direction and the range resolution in the across-track. The former depends on the widths of the antenna beam while the latter depends on the length of the emitted pulse. The scale distribution suggests compression that increases towards the nadir line. In making use of the SLAR imagery for topographic mapping, it is necessary to correct for a member of errors caused by the geometry of the range projection, changes in exterior orientation and incorrect inner orientation. A common approach to produce maps quickly from SLAR imagery is by "mosaicking". The mosaicking method is restricted by the presence of great relief. It is possible to carry out topographic mapping using stereo radar images, in particular, synthetic aperture radar because of its much better spatial resolution. They can be used to interpolate coordinates between known points. Reasonably accurate maps can be obtained provided look angles are not less than 40° off-nadir, with intersection angles of about 15°.

Cartographic Presentation (Space Platforms)

For topographic mapping applications, use of space platforms would mean fewer photographs to handle and few grounds points needed for control. A commonly used space platform is an earth satellite which revolves around the earth in a circular orbit from an altitude of at least 180 km. There are three ways by which imagery can be acquired from the satellite : (1) by film cameras, (2) by vidicon cameras with radio transmission of the stored image to ground stations, and (3) by optical-mechanical scanning with a radio transmission. If topographic mapping is to be carried out, metric aerial cameras should be employed. Essentially, vertical photographs with 60 percent forward overlap are obtained. Several days are required to cover a given area. Because the satellite travels very fast in space, image movement compensation is necessary, which involves moving the film in its focal plane during exposure to prevent blurring of the image. The use of vidicon cameras with radio transmission produces an electronic image. The image produced by the vidicon cameras should still possess the properties of conventional photography. The big advantage of the vidicon camera is its light weight and its eraseable surface. The vidicon camera can produce numerous photographs per day over a considerable period, e.g., a year or two. Optical-mechanical scanners with radio transmission of data to ground stations are used to acquire imagery. The scanning is carried out with a rotating mirror whose axis is parallel to the flight direction of the spacecraft. The radiation received is projected onto an array of detectors, each one of which senses the intensity of the radiation in different parts of the electromagnetic spectrum. The scanning speed is high and the image is built up sequentially element by element from successive signals as the space-craft moves forward. The intensity of radiation at each element can be converted to a numerical value which is then recorded on magnetic tape. This record is transmitted to a ground station where it is rerecorded and used to control a cathode ray tube to produce the final image on film, e.g., Multi-spectral Scanner (MSS) of Landsat, Return Beam Vidicon (RBV) camera. Two possible approaches to improve the usefulness of satellite imagery in topographic mapping are : (1) to use a metric camera and physical recovery of the film, and (2) to use a vertical line-array camera system designed for stereoscopic coverage.

Geographic Information Systems

With the advent of high-resolution multi-spectral remote sensing from space platforms, the volume of data concerning our terrestrial environment becomes too large to be effectively utilized. This explains the need to carry out geographic data processing with the aid of a computer. In a geographic information system, the data should be referenced in a manner which will allow retrieval, analysis and display on spatial criteria (Tomlinson, 1972). A geographic information system should at least consist of a data processing subsystem, a data analysis subsystem and a information use subsystem. See Fig. 11. The data processing subsystem includes data

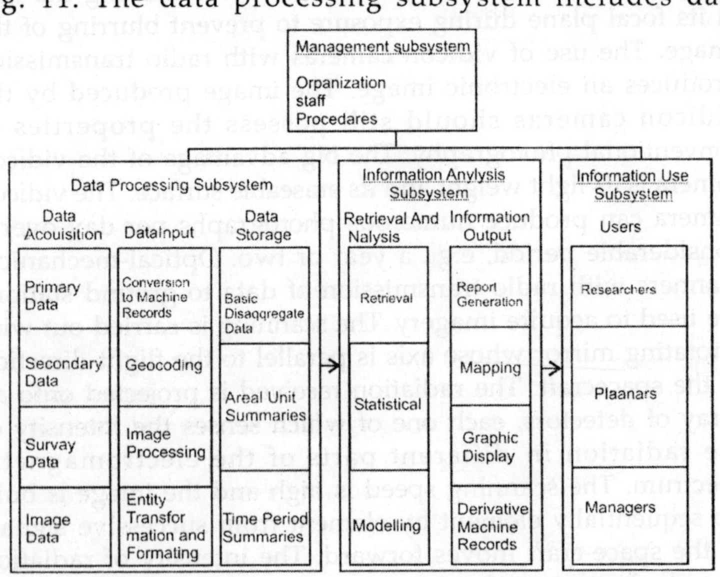

Fig. 11. Information system elements (After Tomlinson, 1972).

acquisition, input and storage. The data analysis subsystem includes retrieval, analysis and output of information in various forms. The information use subsystem permits relevant information to be applied to the problem. In the design of a geographic information system, specialized graphic input and output components often play a dominant role in shaping the architecture of the remainder of the system. There are three broad categories of data for input to the system : (1) alpha-numeric, (2) pictorial or graphic, and (3) remotely sensed data in digital form. Alphanumeric data are available in computer-readable form. The input of pictorial or graphic data, such as maps and photographs, requires the use of a digitizer which converts the features into strings of coordinate values. An optical scanner or a scanning densitometer is used to convert the graphic material to computer-readable form automatically. This records spatial data in narrow strips across the data surface, thus producing the raster format. The raster format includes grids or cells or matrix data-structure. The order of the data element is determined by their geographical positions. Remotely sensed data generated by multispectral scanners or high-resolution vidicon cameras from space platforms, are in raster format. However, these spectral data have to be restored, enhanced, filtered or geometrically transformed by the techniques of image processing before they can be incorporated into the geographic information system. One important problem is to effect an interface between raster information and geographic information system coordinates, i.e., vector format (LO,1986). A common approach is to develop a set of transformation equations (Meyer, 1984). When multispectral image data sets are used, there is the need to register them together. A common practice is to reconstitute the image data sets in such a way that they are geometrically connected and registered to a common map base of the geographic information system. This registration is accomplished by resampling techniques which involve defining new pixel positions on the map base and filling them with data determined by nearest neighbour or interpolation algorithms. The output devices from the geographic information system are incremental plotters, vector display cathode ray tubes and raster displays and matrix plotters which all show correspondence with the input device. Line printers are effective low-cost output device commonly employed.

In a geographic information system, algorithms are required to transform the raw data into meaningful information in the form of cartographic products. These data are conventionally divided into point types, line-types and region-types based on their geometry. Altogether there are six types of binary relations to consider : point-to-point, point-to-line, point-to-region, line-to-line, line-to-region, and region-to-region. Algorithms have to be written to deal with them. There are two major approaches to internal data organization in a geographic information system : the cellular organization and linked organization, which correspond roughly to discrete and continuous data respectively. Cellular organization makes use of a matrix of cells of uniform size, and the data are stored on each cell. The organization corresponds directly to the raster format for input and the matrix format for output. Linked organization makes use of coordinate values. Thus, point entities are described directly by their coordinates, line entities by a chain of coordinates, regions with nominal data by their boundaries and regions with numerical data by contour curves. This data organization corresponds directly to the format of data entered through a digitizer and output by an incremental plotter; it is highly storage space. Linked organization makes use of coordinate values, maps and contour maps. Its disadvantages are the complexity of software development in updating and editing data. External data organization involves examination of the implementation, operation and characteristics of the data. This relates to the performance of the computer system required to carry out all of the operations designed. There are two forms of auxiliary data organization: the data bank and the data base. A data bank is "separation" oriented with the information segregated either on the basis of the type of entity or on its geographical unit or both. Data are generally maintained on disk or tape files. A data base, on the other hand, is interaction oriented. It adds inter-entity relations to the information. The data exhibit a part-whole relationship which is said to be hierarchically organized. Thus, subdivision of a region and tributaries of a river are examples of this approach. On the whole, non-geometrical information may be organized into a data base while the geometric information may be organized as a data bank. Four geographic information systems are given below :-

1. ***The ODYSSEY System*** : This system was designed by the Laboratory of Computer Graphics and Spatial Analysis at Harvard University, USA (Teicholz, 1980).
2. ***Geographic Information Retrieval and Analysis System (GIRAS) :*** This geographic information system developed by the USA Geological Survey is oriented specifically to land use and land cover maps as the data source (LO, 1986).
3. ***Image Based Information System (IBIS) :*** IBIS is an image-based geographic information system designed to employ digital image processing technology to : (1) interface remotely sensed data with other spatially referenced information, and (2) perform interactive data base storage, retrieval and analysis operations (Bryant and Zobrist, 1976).
4. ***A Photogrammetric Urban Information System*** : Lo, 1981 has developed an urban information system based on input from aerial photography. Flow diagram of the photogrammetric urban information system is given in Fig. 12.

Human Population

The impact of population growth on global resources, the global environment and global development remains a major

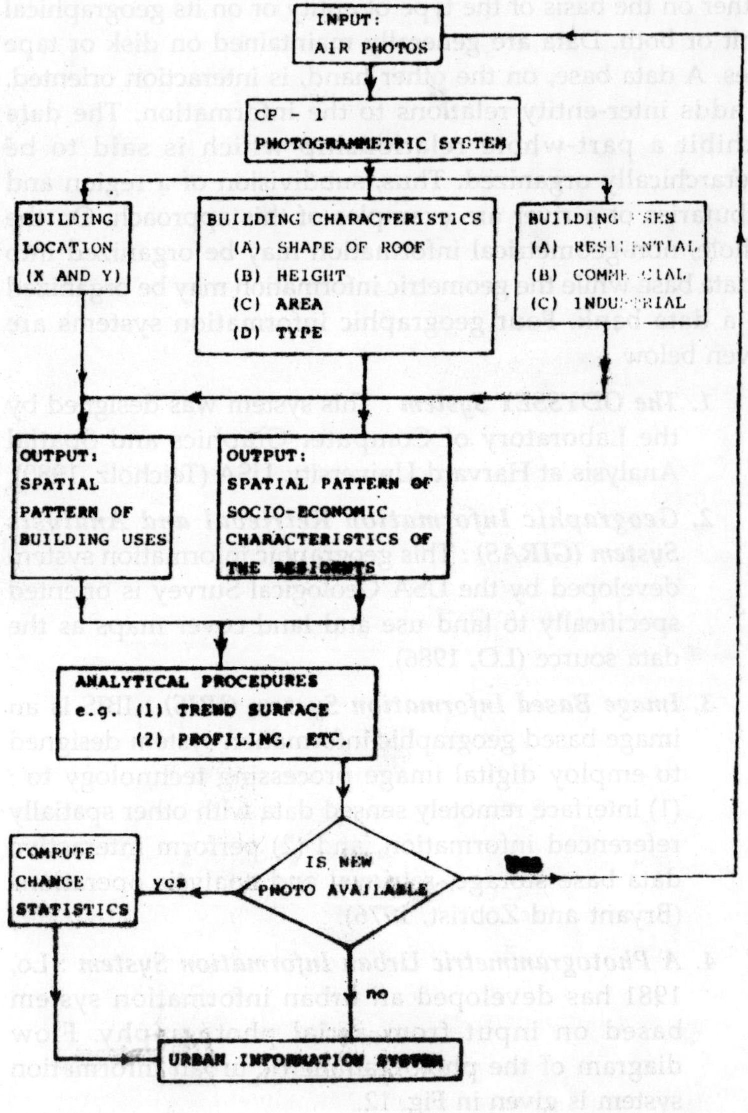

Fig. 12. Flow diagram of the photogrammetric urban information system (After LO, 1986).

challenge to be faced by mankind. Remote sensing data provide a synoptic view of the terrestrial environment, an obvious application is to map the spatial distribution of population and to examine the impact the human presence has brought to the living environment. An outgrowth from this application is to devise methods to estimate population number in an area which is essential information required to estimate the spatial distribution of population when planning the economic development of a region or a country. The extraction of information in these two areas of application involves two fundamental approaches of remote sensing : (1) the visual approach of image interpretation, and (2) the formulation of appropriate mathematical models to yield the data desired. A significant contribution of photographic data is the comprehensive view they give to a site which makes the strategic assessment of a region of interest possible. The ultimate aim of archaeology is to reconstruct the overall picture of a human community, its economy and setting. The use of large-scale vertical and oblique aerial photographs provides enough details to locate and map the remains of the ancilliary features and then interpret how the people of the past made use of natural resources found in their region. The discovery of archaeological sites from aerial photographs is based on evidence produced by tone or colour changes. The most important evidence is provided by vegetation markings caused by differential growth of vegetation responding to hidden differences in the soil beneath. The occurrence of these vegetation markings is affected by season, weather and moisture conditions. Another important source of evidence are soil markings which occur when earth works have been nearly leveled and become visible or when the soil is bare after ploughing or has only the thinnest covering of vegetation. The colour and tone contrast depend on the sub-soil. The contrast shows best after a long period of rain and wind in the area. Other considerations include the effect of sunlight and shadows which can emphasize subtle differences in relief. The time of photography and direction of orientation in the case of oblique photography all help in the detection of complicated archaeological sites. The application of remote sensing to archaeology has been confined to the use of large-scale vertical or oblique aerial photography because of the need of emphasize vegetation and soil markings, i.e., the basic clues for archaeological site discovery. Now non-photographic remote sensors have begun to be employed for application in archaeology. The radar imagery was found to be capable of detecting the archaeological features such as ancient cities, raised roads, edges of extensive paved zones and canals, which all exhibited radar signatures. The poor spatial resolution of the radar data restricts the accuracy of the estimate that one can make of the areal extent of the swamps and the intricate canal system which in turn affects the estimation of the population density in the area. But the usefulness of radar imagery in resolving archaeological problems in climatically difficult environment is confirmed.

Human Population Distribution and Mathematical Modelling

The present population distribution pattern can be inferred from the settlement pattern in macro-scale revealed by imagery acquired from space platforms. Tobler (1969) observed that the built-up area of a settlement should be proportional to the population according to the following equation

$$r = aP^b \qquad \text{...(1)}$$

where r is the radius of a circle of the same area of the settlement, P is the population, a is a coefficient and b is an exponent. The coefficient a provides a useful indication of settlement packing which reflects the characteristics of the individual society in spatial organization. Equation (1) can be employed to compute the population of a settlement with the input of the built-up area measured directly from imagery or maps. Another useful source of remote sensing data for the study of the settlement is the Shuttle Imaging Radar - A (SIR-A) data obtained with a synthetic aperture imagery radar (in L-band frequency) from the Space Shuttle Columbia in November 1981. The radar image has a ground resolution of about 40m and a scale of 1:500,000. As radar scattering is affected by the degree of surface roughness, vegetation and man-made structures, particularly settlements are most distinctive, because the walls of buildings from corner reflectors with the surface or because of the abundance of metallic structure or both. From Figure 13 which shows a

Fig. 13. Shuttle Imaging Radar-A data of Dezhou area, China taken on November 12, 1981 (Courtesy of Jet Propulsion Laboratory and National Aeronatics and Space Administration).

part of the North China Plain to the north of Chinan, the hamlets, villages, towns and cities as well as the road network are clearly delineated. The thermal infrared data provide insights into another aspect of spatial population distribution, i.e., the heat energy pattern of the population. A comparison of a DMSP (defence meteorological satellite programme) night time image of eastern USA with a population map of the same area produced by the US Bureau of Census (1973) clearly reveals the close correlation between the two. See Fig. 14 and 15. These IUA (Illuminated Urban area) density patterns of individual cities can be plotted by a computer as three dimensional perspective drawings. See Fig. 16. It represents a way whereby urban energy consumption pattern can be quantitatively measured from remotely sensed imagery. Apart from the problem of accuracy, population changes so quickly that many of the census data becomes out-of-date as soon as

Fig. 14. DMSP thermal infrared image of Eastern USA (After LO, 1986).

they are published. Therefore there is a need to regularly update the census data so that accurate population statistics are available for use in planning the economic development of a country. Population estimation from remote sensing data is no way replaces censuses conducted at regular ten-year intervals by countries. The value of the method is its low and efficiency in providing accurate and up-to-date estimates of population for the planners at any point in time. There are four types of approaches in the use of remote sensing data for population estimation. They are given below :-

1. Estimation Based on Measured Land Areas : The allometric growth module in the form of $A = aP^b$ can easily be applied in reverse to compute an estimate of the population

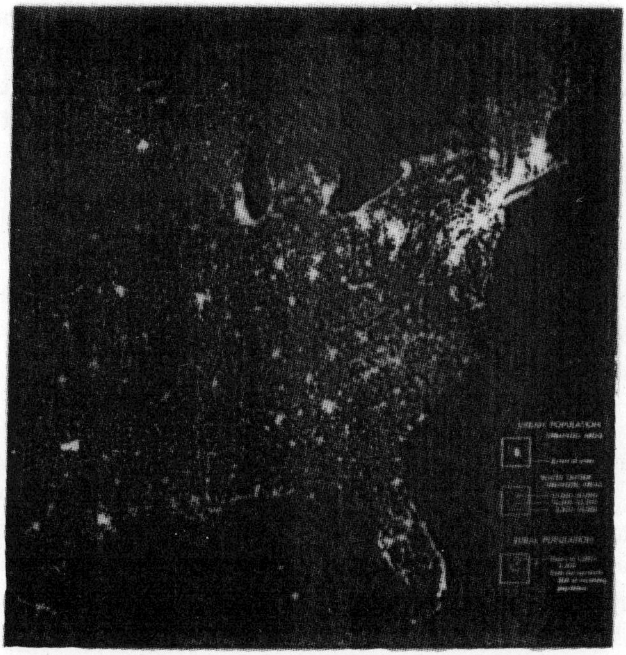

Fig. 15. Night-time population distribution map of easteem USA in 1970 (After LO, 1986).

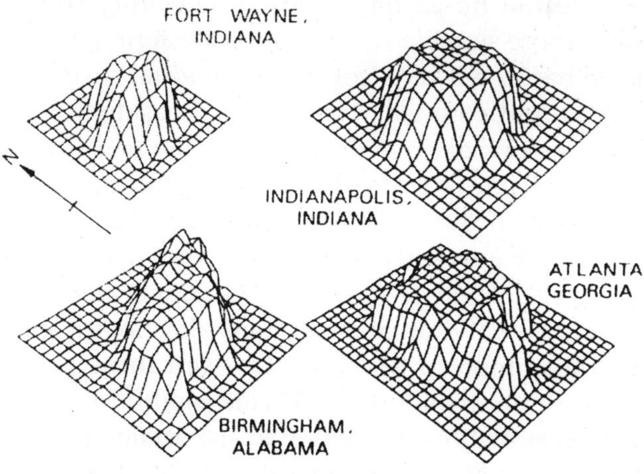

Fig. 16. Three-dimensional perspectives of the energy consumption patterns represented by the IUA domes of four cities in estern USA (After Welch, 1980).

P provided the built-up area of a settlement A is known. The accuracy of the estimated population figure obviously depends on the validity of the mathematical model employed. In applying the allometric growth model to estimate the population modified the equation to

$$P = aA^b \quad ...(2)$$

or

$$\log P = \log a + b\log A \quad ...(3)$$

where P is the estimated population and A is the built-up area of the settlement. In addition, a linear regression in the form of

$$P = a + bA \quad ...(4)$$

was introduced to explain the more rapid growth of larger cities. This approach is only suited to estimate the overall population of a settlement and appears to be more suited for use with small-scale aerial photography or even imagery acquired from space platforms such as Landsat. This approach is most interesting in the sense that one can formulate and test new mathematical models with a view to arrive at a more reliable estimation of population from remote sensing data.

2. ***Estimation Based on Counts of Dwelling Units :*** This approach is more suitable when large scale aerial photography is available because it requires that individual dwelling types be identified and counted. The factor of resident density or number of persons per dwelling unit is obtained from census statistics if available or from sample surveys on ground. Apart from the practical difficulty of identifying and counting the dwelling units correctly, one should also note that the assumption of one single household occupying one dwelling unit may not be valid in cities of many developing countries. It is not uncommon to have two or even three households sharing the same dwelling units. This method usually gives rise to underestimation of population, especially if it is applied to the urban area (Clayton and Estes, 1980). Even in a rural area a village house may contain more than one household. To avoid this difficulty the household concept was abandoned

and the number of persons actually living in the village house was determined in the field. Another application to estimate the rural population employed an ingenious method of sampling to combine with the counting of dwelling units from the aerial photographs at a scale of 1:20,000. This method is most interesting and demonstrates clearly the usefulness of statistical sampling in aiding population estimation from aerial photographs for a developing rural environment. The approach of counting dwelling units would face more problems in an urban environment where high-rise residential buildings abound. It is also possible to replace the dwelling unit count with a dwelling unit length measurement. It appears that length measurement is only practicable in the case of a homogenous terraced or back-to-back residential housing area. There is also the added difficulty of scale distortion caused by relief displacement and tilts of aircraft. It is therefore more common to rely on dwelling unit counts.

3. Estimation Based on Measured Land Use Areas : It involves interpreting and measuring the land-use of an area with special attention given to the residential use which is further subdivided into distinctive classes according to the cultural characteristics of the study area. The population density associated with each residential land use category is obtained by sample survey in the field or from existing census data. The population P of the area can be determined by the following equation :

$$P = \sum_{i=1}^{n} AiDi \qquad ...(5)$$

where A_1, A_2, ... A_n are the areas devoted to residential land use categories 1 to n, and D_1, D_2,........, D_n are the corresponding population densities associated with residential land use categories 1 to n. This approach is much more efficient than the house count approach. In an area where dwelling units are extremely mixed up, this approach of population estimation is particularly valuable. In developing countries where illegal squatter structures usually occur in the rural-urban fringes of the cities, an estimation of the squatter population can be most efficiently obtained from aerial photographs with this method. A knowledge of the squatter population figure and their spatial distribution is indispensable for the development of public housing in these countries. The estimated squatter population was found to be accurate within ±2 per cent. This approach of population estimation has been improved upon by Thompson (1975) who advocated the use of a base population count obtained from the census.

4. Estimation Based on Spectral Radiance Characteristics by Individual Pixels : With the increasing availability of multi-spectral data from satellites such as Landsat, population estimate can be carried out with a higher degree of automation. An area with low population density was assumed to have more natural components, i.e., vegetation cover or base soil, than another area of high population density where artificial structures are dominant. By using a grid size of 500 × 500 m area, the relationship between population and spectral radiance characteristic was expressed as follows :

$$P = Ax_1 + Bx_2 + Cx_3 + Dx_4 + E \qquad ...(6)$$

Where P is the population in a 500 × 500m area, and x_1, x_2, x_3, x_4 are the spectral reflectance values of the four bands of the Landsat MSS data. The major weakness of this method is the presence of the non-residential structures which have no direct relationship with population density, e.g., schools, railway stations, churches, etc. But this method does permit population density maps or population distribution maps of a region to be displayed by the computer with ease and is useful for geographic information system development.

Human Population Socio-Economic Characteristics

Another type of demographic data which are useful to planners are socio-economic characteristics of the population. These can only be inferred through indirect evidence of housing types and environmental characteristics from aerial photography. Human groups occupy physical space and facilities as a result of their interaction and adjustment to the environment. Thus, the directly observable physical data from the aerial photographs have meaningful sociological correlations. In this way, a method of correlation photo-interpretation or "inventory-by-surrogate" can be developed. The sociological characteristics of residential sub-areas from other statistical sources were studied to see whether they were related to the photodata. It was confirmed that significant differences between zones in the city existed in educational status, average monthly rentals and adult crime rates. Another observation was the consistency in correlation between the prevelance of single-family houses and socio-economic status of the urban sub-areas in terms of occupational status, education, income, rental values and ethnic composition. Finally, these social and physical data were combined by means of the Guttman Scaling. Technique to form a single continuum defining the exact position or rank of each sub-area in relation to every other sub-area in the sample. A scale of "residential desirability" of USAs cities was constructed, based on the four photo-data categories. Another scale, the "socio-economic status scale", could also be constructed using the five social data items of : (1) median annual income, (2) prevalence of within-dwelling crowing, (3) prevalence of home ownership, (4) prevalence of social disorganization, and (5) educational achievement. These two scales were found to be strongly correlated. Thus, physical data extracted from aerial photographs can be employed to predict the social structure of the city. Urban poverty was closely associated with residential areas located adjacent to the Central Business District (CBD), industry and major urban arteries. These were also found to be strongly correlated with low income, unemployment, low education achievement, family crowding, crime, low health status and lack of community facilities. Metivier and McCoy (1971) discovered that house density was the most significant criterion for the identification of sub-standard housing on the photographs, which served also as an index of socio-economic conditions. House density which was expressed as the number of houses per hact. for each block was strongly and negatively correlated with median family income, with average house value, with average rent and with high percentage of non-white population. In the case of a city in a developing country, where a great influx of population from a rural area has severely strained the housing situation, the urban poverty region lies not only in the old slum area of the city centre with deteriorating structure but also in the flimsy squatter structures on the periphery of the city. Aerial photography can be usefully employed to detect these poverty-stricken regions. The availability of sequential aerial photographs could reveal clearly the pattern of growth or decline of these squatter areas and provide a basis to evaluate the government's land use policy (LO, 1979). The environmental variables, notably those relating to vegetation and housing conditions, can be more conspicuously revealed by colour infrared photography.

As for the study of present population, there is a greater variety of remotely sensed aerospace imagery being used. Along with the conventional aerial photography, thermal infrared line scanner as well as synthetic aperture radar have been employed. The space platforms have provided data which are suitable for use in testing macro-scale models or population distribution on the earth. A great deal of attention has been given to population estimation from remotely sensed imagery acquired from both aircraft and spacecraft. Socio-economic characteristics of the human population can be inferred indirectly from aerial photographs through correlating them with the directly observable physical structures. This approach depends heavily on field work and is characterized by a high degree of generalization. Much investigation is needed before this approach is operationally useful.

Image Interpretation

Remote sensing is applied to collect information needed for a better understanding of four various components of our environment : (1) the biosphere or the life-bearing layer, (2) the atmosphere or the gaseous layer, (3) the hydrosphere or the water layer, and (4) the lithosphere or the solid earth crust. Remote sensing plays primarily the role of a surveying, inventorying and mapping tool for environmental features. Image interpretation is an important part of remote sensing. There are two methods of image interpretation which are given below :-

1. Manual Approach : Remote sensing data are basically records of reflected and emitted electromagnetic energy patterns presented as picture-like images which are highly varied in nature. In order to extract meaningful information out of these data, one has to exercise one's judgement to sieve the significant features out of the insignificance. This is the first stage of image interpretation known as detection. Detection is aided by the spatial, spectral, radiometric and temporal characteristics of the data. Spatial resolution refers to the ability of the recording system in distinguishing closely spaced objects. Larger objects tend to attract more attention than smaller ones. See Figs. 17, 18 and 19 (Low, 1986). In

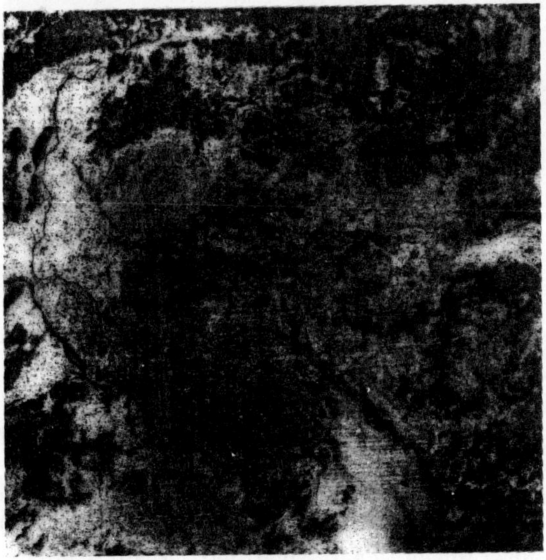

Fig. 17. Landsat image : Pearl River delta area of China acquired on 25 December, 1973 (band 5) (After LO, 1986).

Fig. 18. Landsat image : Pearl River delta area of China acquired on 25 December, 1973 (band 7) (After LO, 1986).

Fig. 19. Landset image : Pearl River delta area of China acquired on 19 October, 1979 (band 5) (After LO, 1986).

figure 17 the field patterns are not two clearly revealed along the coast or inland, but in figure 18 the reflected infrared band gives the strong contrast between land and water which helps to pick out the larger fields on the coast and the numerous reservoirs on the hills. On the other hand, the vegetation is more clearly shown as dark-toned patches in band 5. The sediments carried by the river into the sea are more distinctly recorded on the band 5 pictures than on the band 7 picture which shows water as black. This indicates the importance of spectral resolution. Spectral resolution is the recording of the same scene in different spectral intervals. The finer the spectral interval the better is the spectral resolution which provides the rationale for multispectral or multiband remote sensing. By superimposing all four spectral bands of the Landsat image together a false colour composite is formed, which provides better information of the area. It is clear that the spatial and spectral resolution are interrelated. Radiometric resolution is to provide better contrast so that a greater number of discriminable grey steps between the black and white limits is achievable. Finally, temporal resolution refers to the use of imagery acquired at given time-intervals of the year to detect changes that have occurred. Figure 19 is a band 5 Landsat photograph of the same Pearl River delta area taken on 19 October 1979. Because harvesting has not yet taken place, the field patterns are more apparent. A comparison of Fig. 19 and Fig. 17 reveals changes in land use and coastal sedimentation patterns in the area. Another notable feature is the much lighter tone of the river water for the October scene than that for the December scene, where the river water is dark-toned. The difference is due to the higher water volume in the wet October month, which causes a greater degree of turbulence in the rivers.

The detection stage naturally leads on to the recognition and identification stage in which the image interpreter has to exercise general, local, as well as specific levels of reference to allocate objects into known categories. In recognition and identification, the non-geometric image characteristics of tone or colour, texture, pattern, shape, shadow, size and situation normally gives clues. Tone is a record of energy reflectance or remittance which has different meanings according to the spectral sensitivity of the detector or film employed. Thus, light tone water in a thermal infrared image suggests it presence of warm water, whereas in black-and-white photography, it is the result of light reflecting to the camera lens. Similarly, the colour of an image depends on whether true colour or colour infrared film is used. Texture, is related the frequency of tone change, which gives one an impression of the degree of roughness or smoothness of the imaged features. Pattern, is the spatial arrangement of objects in the image. Shape, gives the general form or outline of an object. Helped by shadows, the shape factor is very useful in object identification and recognition. Long shadows tend to emphasize linear features. The size or dimensions of an object is an essential clue to the identification of objects of similar shape and can be used as a standard for comparison. Finally, the situation or location of objects in relation to the others is always helpful where other characteristics fail to give clues. The final stage of the interpretation is classification, producing spatial data which can be displayed as maps or for incorporation into a geographic information system by the computer.

2. ***Computer-assisted Approach :*** This approach involves a number of steps. First of all, the analogue image data have to be converted into digital form. This is done by means of a digitizing TV scanner or a microdensitometer. The second step is data processing, which is a group of procedures to "clean-up" the raw input data, such as correcting geometric and radiometric distortions. This is then followed by feature extraction. Possible features are spatial, spectral and temporal. For supervised classification, sample areas are selected from the image data for more detailed examination. Training sets of data are then compiled. These training sets are sub-samples from the image whose identification is completely known. These will be treated as stereotypes of particular classes of data

with which unknown areas can be compared. Another approach is unsupervised classification in which no training samples are used. The partitioning of the feature space is carried out by the method of cluster analysis which can identify natural groupings of patterns. The nature of each grouping is determined afterwards by field checks. Supervised classification is still too slow to handle a massive influx of satellite multispectral data. For optimal analysis, hybrid procedures incorporating the advantage of both supervised and unsupervised classification have been evolved.

Land Use and Land Cover Mapping

Since land use and land cover data are most essential to planners who have to make decisions concerning land resource management, they are strongly economic in nature. These data are usually presented in map form accompanied by area statistics for each category of land use and land cover. The use of remotely sensed imagery is particularly appropriate for the production of these maps. Land is a raw material of a site, which is defined in terms of a number of natural characteristics, namely, climate, geology, soil, topography, hydrology and biology (Aldrich, 1981). Land use is man's activities on and in relation to the land, which are usually not directly visible from the imagery. Land use has been studied from many diverse view-points so that no one single definition is really appropriate in all different contexts. Land cover describes the vegetational and artificial constructions covering the land surface. These are all directly visible from the remotely sensed imagery. Three general classes of data are included in land cover : (1) physical structures built by human beings, (2) biotic phenomena such as natural vegetation, agricultural crops and animal life, and *(3)* any types of development. Thus, based on the observation of land cover as a proxy, one hopes to infer human activities and land use. Therefore, land used and land cover mapping require some arbitrary decisions to be made and the resultant maps inevitably contain some degree of generalized information according to their scales and the purposes of applications. A good classification scheme should be easy to use with no ambiguity in defining each land use and land cover category. The level of accuracy of the resultant maps is closely related to the classification scheme which should take into account the final map scale. The use of ground survey methods allows the adoption of a smaller land parcel as the mapping unit and the production of more detailed maps on a large scale. Now-a-days, most land use and land cover surveys make use of aircraft or satellite imagery. The use of the smallest recognizable parcel of land for interpretation should give as much detail as possible so that the uses can be grouped into the categories most appropriate to the needs for the researchers and planners. The functional approach is activity-oriented, e.g., agricultural, grazing, forestry, urban activities, etc. The morphological approach emphasizes land cover, e.g., arable land, grassland, woodland, moorland, built-up area, etc. United States Geological Survey's land and land cover classification is given in Table 2. The scheme emphasized a rather coarse level of mapping - Level I and II. The whole system is "resource-oriented" rather than "people oriented". Land cover is used as the principal surrogate for interpreting activity. The USGS land use and land cover classification system has been used in other countries of the developed and developing world with slight modifications (Allan, 1980).

Table 2. Land use and land cover classification system for use with remote sensor data (After LO, 1986).

Level I	*Level II*
1. Urban or Built-up Land	11 Residential
	12 Commercial and Services
	13 Industrial
	14 Transportation, Communications, and Utilities
	15 Industrial and Commerical Complexes
	16 Mixed Urban or Built-up Land

Continued to......

Level I	*Level II*
	17 Other Urban or Built-up Land
2. Agricultural Land	21 Cropland and Pasture
	22 Orchards, Groves, Vineyards Nurseries, and Ornamental Horticultural Areas
	23 Confined Feeding Operations
	24 Other Agricultural Land
3. Rangeland	31 Herbaceous Rangeland
	32 Shrub and Brushy Rangeland
	33 Mixed Rangeland
4. Forest land	41 Deciducus Forest Land
	42 Evergreen Forest Land
	43 Mixed Forest Land
5. Water	51 Streams and Canals
	52 Lakes
	53 Reservoirs
	54 Bays and Estuaries
6. Wetland	61 Forested Wetland
	62 Nonforested Wetland
7. Barren Land	71 Dry Salt Flats
	72 Beaches
	73 Sandy Areas other than Beaches
	74 Bare Exposed Rock
	75 Strip Mines, Quarries and Gravel Pits
	76 Transitional Areas
	77 Mixed Barren Land
8. Tundra	81 Shrub and Brush Tundra
	82 Herbaceous Tundra
	83 Bare Ground Tundra
	84 Wet Tundra
	85 Mixed Tundra
9. Perennial Snow or Ice	91 Perennial Snowfields

Land Use and Land Cover Mapping (By Aerial Photography)

The aerial photographs have to be assembled together in the form of a mosaic to define the area of interest. The minimum area to be interpreted should also be defined. It should be the a smallest area that one can interpret with certainty. This requires the application of the following image characteristics : size, shape, shadow, texture, tone, pattern, site and association. The area of each category of land use and land cover is measured by using a dot grid, a planimeter or a digitizer. Finally, a report has to be written to provide the regional setting, to explain the method of data acquisition, to assess the accuracy of the maps and to summarize the land use patterns of the study area. This method is applicable to rural land use mapping in a hilly country. Due to the complexity of human activities and the high density of buildings, mapping the land use of an urban area is always difficult, both from the ground or from aerial photography. The photography required should normally be of large scale, say not smaller than 1:50,000. For detailed urban land use studies, especially those concerned with industrial activity, the optimum photo scale was 1:2,500. This approach has mostly been applied to urban land use mapping in developing countries where aerial photography is the more easily available form of remote sensing data. Land use change detection using aerial photography has been applied to both rural and urban areas and found to be an efficient method of discovering the development trends of a region. Change detection involves the use of sequential aerial photography over a specific region from which the land use map for each data was mapped and compared. A land use change map between two time periods is usually produced. A modern approach to land use change detection in a more complex and rapidly changing environment involves the use of the computer. The study area Lagos, Nigeria encompassed urban built-up areas, urban vacant land and non-urban land. See

Fig. 20. The computer approach permitted a high degree of

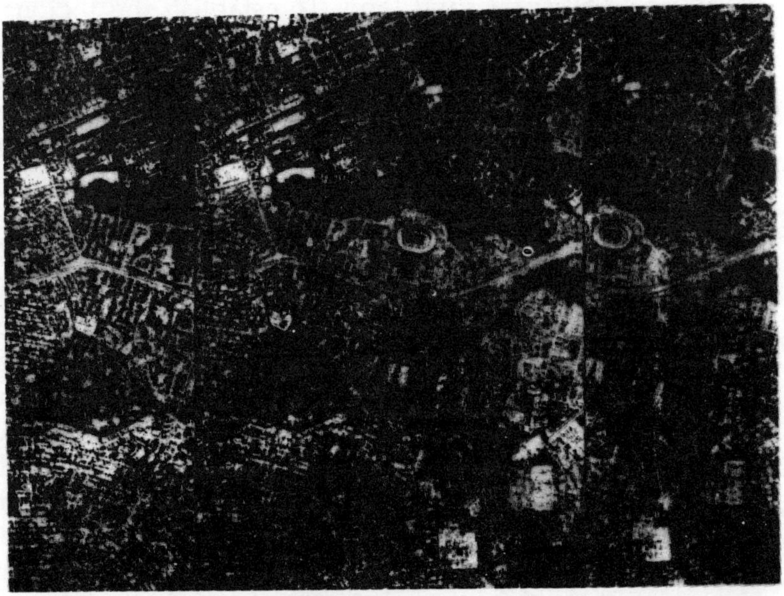

Fig. 20. Stereotriplet of part of central mainland Lagos, 1974 (After LO, 1986).

flexibility and the generation of a large volume of land use data. The land use change revealed the rapid increase of the residential land use and a strong lateral expansion of the urban area of Lagos (Nigeria).

Land Use and Land Cover Mapping (By Radar Imagery)

The use of radar imagery to map land and land cover has attracted a great deal of attention because the radar imagery is an all-weather system which complements the aerial photography well. Also, the radar image appears visually similar to the aerial photograph and familiar image characteristics such as tone, texture, pattern, shape and association can be applied to the interpretation of the radar imagery. In addition, the areal coverage of the radar imagery obtained by Side-Looking Airborne Radar (SLAR) in much wider than that of aerial phlography, thus facilitates the detection of the overall land use pattern. It is used for mapping small-scale rural land. To establish the regions, physical and cultural features of the environment had to be interpreted from the radar imagery. Henderson (1975) was able to detect five major components of a land use region: (1) surface configuration, (2) natural vegetation, (3) field patterns and size, (4) settlement pattern, and (5) transportation and communications network. The combination and intermixing of the relevant environmental characteristics had to appear homogenous and distinct if compared to the adjacent areas. The radar imagery was in the form of a continuous film strip which facilitated the description of the areas and detection of changes. In delineating these regions, collateral materials have to be used. Environmental modulation reduced the level of land use detail visible in the Northeast compared to that of the Midwest and West, USA as a result of the much more fragmented and complex landscape elements of the Northeast. See Fig. 21. For

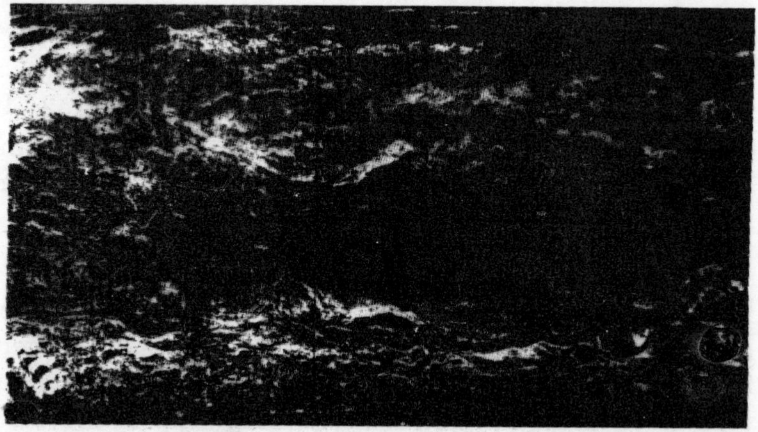

Fig. 21. K-band imagery of Connecticut River Valley, USA (Aftr LO, 1986).

the radar imagery, forest vegetation was an important environmental factor contributing to the variation in the amount of land use information. In the North-west, forest stands were found virtually everywhere, thus connecting drainage, relief, transportation and settlement features. In such a situation, large-scale radar imagery is required. The application of radar imagery to urban land use mapping is possible with the improved spatial resolution (10 × 10 m) and the availability of multiple wavelength and multiple polarization systems. Applications using small-scale real aperture K-band SLAR imagery at 1:250,000 scale indicated the possibility of identifying gross pattern of industrial, residential and open space uses in the city, but their boundaries could not be mapped in great detail. For the latter purpose, a large-scale radar imagery has to be used to improve the accuracy of the interpretation of urban land use. In radar imagery, shadows are no signal areas. To compensate for the loss of information, multiple looks of the same scene at different angles should be carried out. As the radar is also sensitive i surface roughness, the availability of multiple wavelength data allows the fiscrimination of variations in the surface roughness within the urban area. i good quality synthetic aperture radar image, detailed land use mapping ! the urban area was possible using a manual approach. The accuracy of turban land use mapping using radar imagery is still inferior to that achievable with aerial photography, because of the lack of correspondence between the fform and the function. The advantage of the radar sensors seems to lie in giving additional information to that of the aerial photography by virtue of its exploitation of the microwave portion of the electromagnetic spectrum. Several new approaches have been presented to the use of radar imagery for land use classification of urban areas, having taken into account of the importance of the depression angle of the sensor's radiation and orientation of the imaged feature. A new approach was to use a "squint" mode of acquiring the synthetic aperture radar data as a means of eliminate the strong cardinal effect caused by the orientation of streets in the urban area. Another approach was the acquisition of height information as a measure of surface roughness of the urban area using synthetic aperture radar. Building height information permits a better understanding of the morphology of the urban environment (LO, 1971).

Land Use and Land Covering Mapping (By Satellite Imagery)

The procedures of manual and digital analyses of satellite data for land use mapping have been well established. Manual approach of analysis involved visual examining of the satellite image data which have been preprocessed to remove geometric distortions and radiometric errors. The original data are usually enlarged optically to permit the maximum detection of variations in tone, texture, pattern, shapes and other related image characteristics. Where multi-spectral data are available, as in the case of Landsat, false colour composites are normally employed for visual interpretation, although individual spectral band images of the scene will also be examined. Where a colour additive viewer is available, much more manipulation of the image data is possible through different combinations of spectral bands and colour filters. The concept of different levels of land use or land cover details interpretable according to the different scales of the imagery, and hence, the spatial resolution quality is normally adopted. The use of Landsat imagery for land use mapping has been particularly popular in the developing countries for rapid extraction of the needed data or to update old ones. Usually, multistage approach was adopted. This means the inter-correlation of all available data, ground truth data, aerial photography and satellite data. Landsat imagery provides an overall picture of the country which forms the basis for more details data collection using a combination of field work and aerial photography. Landsat MSS data could produce generalized land use maps with percentagesof accuracy ranging from 80 to 90. Skylab was a manned space station which orbited the earth from an altitude of 435 km at an orbital inclination of 50 degree. It included three major imaging systems : (1) the Multispectral Photographic Camera S-190A, (2) the S-190B Earth Terrain Camera, and (3) the Multispectral Scanner S-192, The photographic data acquired by S-190A and S-190B are of high spatial resolution. Higher building densities tended to reduce contrasts between urban landuse or cover classes particularly in the developing countries of Asia. Therefore, spatial resolution requirements for urban studies should vary with region. As an active system, the radar is weather independent and is more-or-less time-independent. Seasat carried a Synthetic-Aperture Radar (SAR). The SAR has a ground resolution cell of 25 × 25 m, and the imagery has a swath width of 100 km. See Fig. 22. Although Seasat was intended for monitoring the

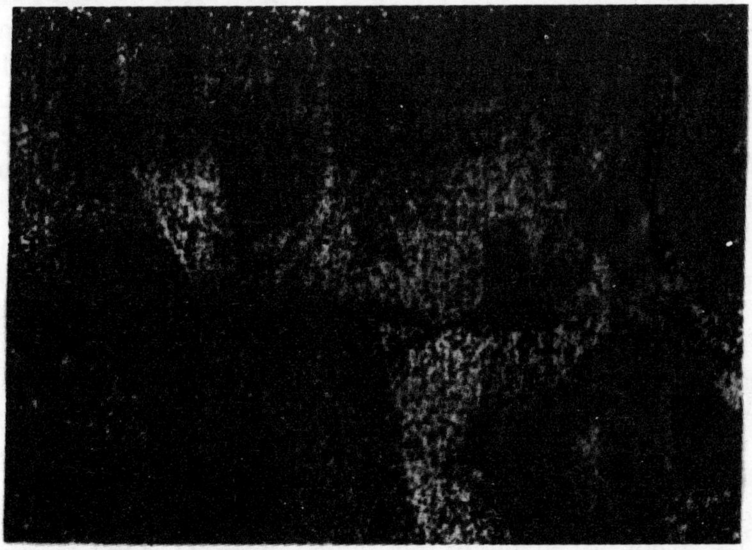

Fig. 22. Seasat-A SAR image of the East Anglia study area in the UK (After LO, 1986).

world's ocean surface, the SAR system also imaged land surfaces. With suitable field checking and supporting information from maps and aerial photographs, some land use categories could be mapped with reasonable reliability by SAR system. Its use for urban studies was also investigated. Digitally processed SAR imagery could be useful to urban studies at medium-to-large scale enlargements with a manual approach.

For land use and land cover mapping, there is a need to continuously update the data base to meet rapid changes in the environment caused by urbanization and industrialization. Only with the aid of computer techniques can we expect to carry out and use mapping with improved accuracy, that can be consistently repeated at regular time intervals. The digital approach is perhaps more appropriately used for land cover rather than land use mapping because it basically involves manipulation of the spectral data in number form to recognize or delineate patterns which have internal homogeneity. The major problem of digital analysis lies in the choice of the correct method of classification for the problem in hand. However, the accuracy of the classification depends on the nature of the data : the pixel size in relation to the degree of homogeneity of the land cover type. A line printer map of the classification is produced by the computer. The land use classes on the line printer map can be transferred to the base map by direct tracing or by means of a Bausch and Lomb Zoom Transfer-scope. See Fig. 23. Another data preprocessing technique used is filtering. This is aimed at smoothing the data by means of a digital filter. The digital approach of land use and land cover mapping using Landsat data can surely produce reasonably accurate results. Only by reducing the pixel size and by improving the pointing accuracy of the satellite can we expect a significant breakthrough in landuse and/or land cover mapping accuracy. One major advantage of the digital approach is the ease in updating the land use map of an area by comparing two Landsat scenes taken on two different dates, pixel by pixel. With the use of non-photographic and satellite remote sensing data for land use and land cover mapping, a major concern is the accuracy of the maps produced. There are two commonly employed methods to check the accuracy of the land use maps : (1) non-site specific accuracy, and (2) site-specific accuracy. Apart from the statistical methods developed to assess the accuracy of the land use and land cover maps produced from remotely sensed data, there were attempts to examine some specific causes of the errors. Best results were not always obtained with the smallest grid cell and less complex interpretation techniques often produced more accurate data. The type of environment studied seemed to have an impact on the accuracy.

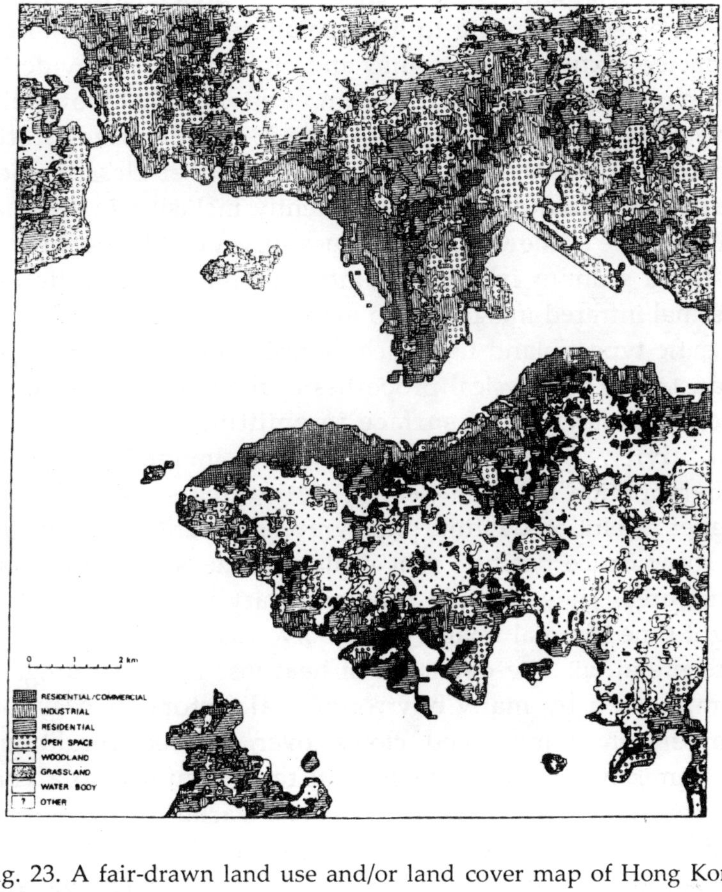

Fig. 23. A fair-drawn land use and/or land cover map of Hong Kong (After LO, 1986).

Land Use and Land Cover Mapping (By Thermal Infrared Imagery)

The spatial resolution of the thermal line scan system is rather coarse and that its emphasis has been to record thermal emission from the land cover. The tonal variations of the thermal infrared imagery are closely related to the emissivities of the materials that make up the land cover. It would not be possible to classify subtle land uses based on emissivities alone. The interpretation of thermal infrared imagery required and understanding of the intensity of infrared energy emitted by an object according to its absolute temperature, thermal capacity, texture, background and emissivity. It provided a wide variety of information unavailable from the photographic system alone. The USGS (United States Geological Survey) land use and land cover classification system was founded to be sufficiently inclusive to serve as an adequate framework for land-use surveys, utilizing thermal infrared scanner imagery. A more common application of thermal infrared imagery is to map or detect heat loss from a specific type of land use, such as residential, commercial or industrial. The physical properties of the material determine the efficiency of the surface in emitting energy, i.e., its emissivity. The daytime thermal imagery permits differentiation between clear or ice-covered snow while the higher resolution daytime photograph facilitates identification of snow or ice patches, roof vents, chimneys and other roof structures. They provide supplementary information to the night-time thermal imagery to resolve cases of doubts in the interpretation. The detection of heat loss from buildings is complicated by many environmental factors such as sky temperature, wind speed, cloud cover, and roof conditions. The emissivities of the roofs tend to be confined to a very narrow range so that the observed variation in rooftop emissivities has only a minimal effect on the temperatures depicted in the thermal image. Ground surveys and interviewing of the residents are normally required if accurate mapping of heat losses is to be achieved.

Lithospheric Environment

The lithosphere is the solid realm called the earth where the human population lives. It is the source of chemical elements and compounds vital to life. These substances are released during interactions between the earth's surface and the atmosphere, in the presence of heat and water which are essential components of the hydrological cycle. As a result, physical disintegration and chemical decomposition of the solid rock occur, leading to the formation of soils on the surface of the earth. In addition, the lithosphere also supplies the mineral resources, i.e., hydrocarbons, metals, and non-metals, that are most essential to man's economic well-being. The earth itself is made up of four concentric zones : (1) the solid inner iron-nickel core, radius 1255 km, (2) the liquid outer iron-nickel core, radius 2221 km, (3) a mantle of ultramafic rock, radius 2895 km, and (4) the crust thickness from 16 to 40 km. The crust is the most important form the human population point of view because all relief features are found there. The term lithology refers to the crust and the uppermost mantle which combine to from the earth's rigid shell. The crust is much less dense than the mantle and is largely composed of oxygen (46.6 percent by weight), silicon (27.7 percent by weight), aluminium (8.1 percent by weight) and iron (5.0 percent by weight). The other elements include calcium, sodium, potassium and magnesium which are essential for soil fertility and plant growth. The crust is much thicker under the continents than beneath the ocean basins. The upper layer of the continental crust is granitic (sial) and the lower layer is basaltic (sima). It is separated from the mantle by a surface called the Mohorovicic discontinuity. The application of remote sensing to the lithospheric environment has focused on the crust with a view to extract geologic, geomorphologic and hydrologic information. The major objectives of the remote sensing are to detect, identify and map earth features on the surface and subsurfaces and to infer the processes at work through the synoptic vantage point afforded by the imagery acquired from aerospace platforms, e.g., elusive lithological and structural information as well as for the more directly observable landform, land cover and water availability characteristics. Rmote sensing is suited for use in studying the dynamic aspect of the terrain features, particularly the genetic origin of landforms in geomorphologic applications, e.g., study of coastal changes or river channel changes or glacier retreats. The qualitative approach provides identification and description of the terrain features, e.g., tone, pattern, texture, and form or relief. The quantitative approach involves metric measurement of the terrain characteristics, e.g., linear, area, volume height and direction data. Then dip-slope measurements are especially important to geologists, geomorphologists and hydrologists. The measurement of image tone or density with the aid of a microdensitometer. There is a strong correlation between image density data and the corresponding terrain features.

Lithospheric Environment Measurements (By Active and Passive Microwave Imagery)

The Side-Looking Airborne Radar (SLAR) imaging system is the most important active remote sensing system which is capable of acquiring imagrey over areas constrained by adverse weather conditions. The SLAR image may be compared to a low sun angle aerial photograph. This is an advantage which permits subtle terrain features and lineaments to be enhanced. Even the same feature imaged at different locations will give distinctly different shadow lengths. The radar imagery is particularly suited to land-form analysis from which geological and hydrological inferences can be made. The commonly used radar wavelengths for geological applications are 0.8 cm (K band), 3 cm (X band) and 25 cm (L band). It is possible therefore to experiment with multi-channel radar imaging in addition to the use of dual polarization (HH and HV) and different look-directions. Both the real aperture and synthetic aperture radars have been employed. Radar shadows are the result of the interaction between the depression angle β of the radar beam and the slope of the terrain α facing away from the beam. The interaction between the depression angle of the radar beam and terrain slope permits a qualitative approach to classify land forms into mountains, high hills, low hills and plains based on radar shadow lengths. For mountainous areas, radar shadowing occurs for over half of the range; for hills, radar shadowing occurs for less than half of the range. In particular, for the low hills, the tonal change from front to back is gradual; for high hills, the tonal change is abrupt. For plains, a uniform tonal signature is observed at the macro-scale but a salt and pepper appearance is obvious at the micro-scale. The different vegetation covers may cause darker or lighter tones. In all cases, no radar shadows should be found. The shadow patterns of the radar imagery help to emphasize relief and structure. With suitable tonal contrasts and a proper orientation of the flight line, lineaments on the earth's surface are easily detected. The detection of these lineaments can be lead to the discovery of geological structures, which are indicators of the occurrence of mineral resources. It was found that the radar data added 27 percent more lineaments (faults, fractures, contacts, etc.) to those mapped from Landsat images. These lineaments were then analyzed to find the area of concentration and the directional trends. From such an analysis, one could locate areas where numerous fault intersections occurred, leading to the discovery of an anticline which could be oil-bearing.

McCoy (1969) found that the radar imagery at a scale of 1:200,000 could produce drainage information comparable to that derived from a 1:62,500 topographic map. The radar shadows in steep mountainous areas tend to enhance the first-order streams on the one hand but observe large areas on the other. In areas of low relief, no shadows occur and small streams can only be detected by vegetation changes which causes variations in film density. In areas of rough topography, multiple looks of the terrain by the imaging radar can produce much more information of first-order streams. See Figs. 24 and 25. Low relief and forest cover tend to suppress details of drainage. The orientation of the drainage channels in relation to the radar beam obviously affects their detectability, with considerable loss of detail in drainage systems oriented orthogonally to the flight line. The character of the drainage system would have a direct effect on the

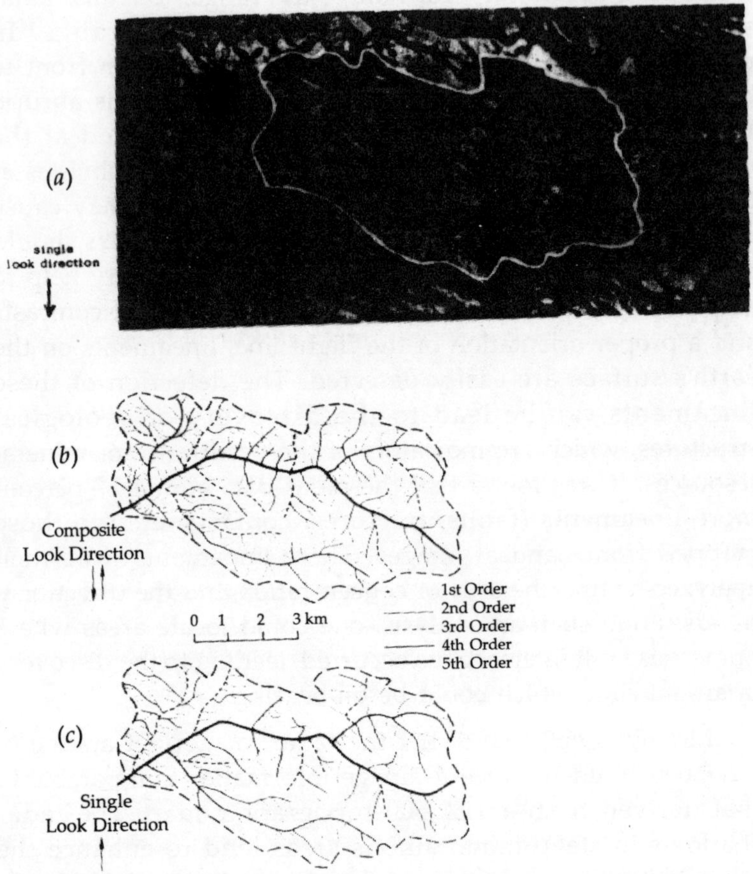

Fig. 24. (*a*) K-band radar image of Trinchera Creek, Colorada. (*b*) Interpeted drainage orders using compositę look-dirction. Fig. 25. (*c*) Interpreted drainage orders using single-look direction. (After McCoy, 1969).

amount of network detail imaged The radar performance in detecting drainage channels was relative poor especially in detecting first-order and second-order streams. The best performance was achieved with the X-band like-polarized (HH) imagery which provided 64 percent of the actual drainage network. The same type of radar imagery was also most effective in recording channel detail and in identifying rapids and depositional features such as point-bars. Lakes were readily identifiable on all X-band like polarized (HH) radar imagery. Muskeg and equatic vegetation were also easily differentiated because of their unique signatures. The SLAR imagery is important as a reconnaissance tool in hydrological studies. Based on the concept that the presence of a given vegetation group is related to an ecological system where biological conditions are in balance with the physical environment. Amazon vegetation types are given in Fig. 26. Geological mapping requires studying the radar return from the various vegetation types, i.e., the degree of surface roughness affecting the image texture and tone. The application of the technique was illustrated with three examples of interpretation in the floodplain, sedimentary terrain, and igneous and metamorphic terrain, all with dense forest covers. In the flood plain, the radar return from the alluvial deposits such as sand beaches and levees which are usually associated with grassland vegetation was controlled by ground surface roughness and moisture content. For the forested areas in the swamp and plateau, the radar return was scattered by tree canopies, hence a function of vegetation surface roughness. In the sedimentary terrain the changes of landforms were revealed by textural changes in the radar image, which corresponded to lithological contacts. The diabase sills were easily mapped because of the relatively uniform fine texture and grey tone on the radar images, indicating some etlaphic control of a unique vegetation assemblage of true canopy to topographic relief. Faults could also be delineated even under the thick tropical rainforest. In the igneous and metamorphic terrain, the different rock types were detected on radar images by characteristic landforms, drainage and structural patterns as well as the distribution of vegetation. The igneous and metamorphic rock complex was covered largely by thick tropical rain forests. The hilly topography and V-shaped valleys were the result of deep erosion partly controlled by fracture patterns. The coarse

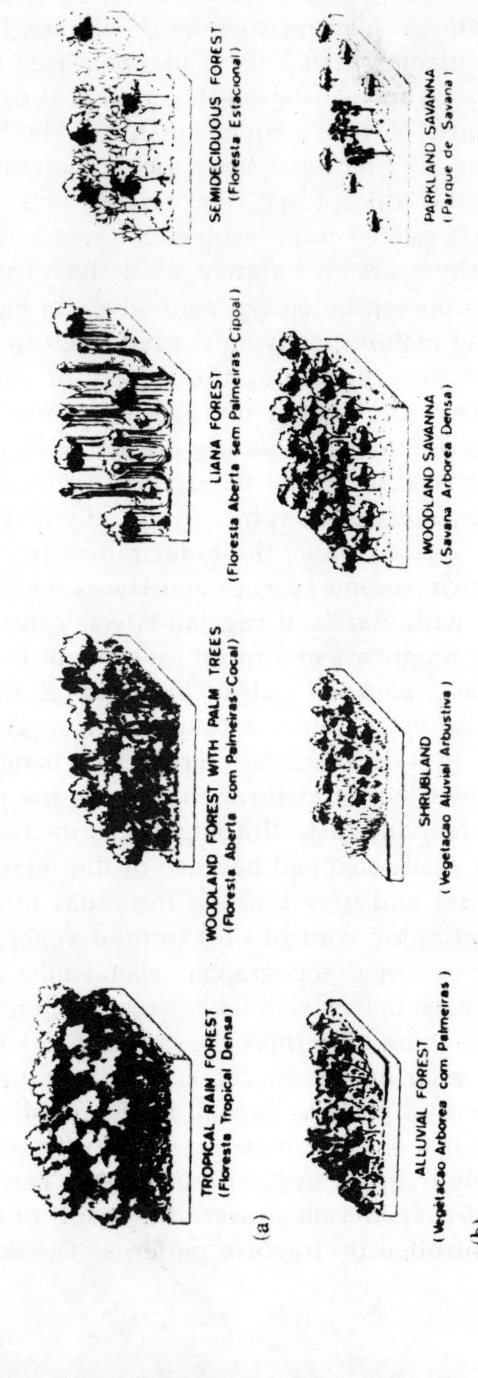

Fig. 26. Amazon vegation types (After LO, 1986).

textural areas of the radar image were found to be associated with granites and grandiosities after field. checks. It demonstrated the usefulness of SLAB as a reconnaissance geological tool.

Surface deposits in desert regions is mapped by SLAB system. See Fig. 27. According to the brightness of the radar return, physiological setting as well as drainage pattern and texture, six radar-rock units of the surface deposits in the Bristol Lake/Granite Mountain area were discriminated. See Fig. 28. Notice the very great contrast in tone between the very bright "cobble-boulder fan deposits and the very dark playa deposits, a result of the difference in the size of these deposits and their moisture-relation capability. An area of application in hydrology where both active and passive microwave remote sensing can contribute in snowfield or snow cover mapping. The extent of snow cover, the stored amount of water and the state of the snow metamorphism, in particular the data of the snow-melt and the intensity of runoff, area of prime importance of hydrology and water management in large regions. The active microwave in the form of radar using ka-band frequencies can be used to map accurately the area! extent of the snowfields and glaciers. In addition, the freshly fallen, dry snow can be differentiated from the old snow based on the difference in their brightness of radar return. For quantitative estimation of the runoff from the snow, the passive microwave remote sensor has to be used. The intensity of microwave radiation received is a function of the temperature, density crystal size and free water content of the snow layer and is commonly referred to as the brightness temperature Tβ. One can relate snow conditions with the equivalent amount of water stored in each type of snow cover. Only the uppermost surface layer actually contributes to the observed radiation. At longer wavelengths, the effect of water equivalent on the brightness temperature is much less pronounced. Thus, by using the difference of brightness temperatures at 36 GHz and 18 GHz one can estimate the water equivalent. The combination of a passive microwave radiometer with a synthetic aperture radar is ideal

Fig. 27. X-band radar mosaic of the Birstol Lake-Granite Mountain area, California (After LO, 1986).

in mapping both the areal extent and the brightness temperature of the snow cover.

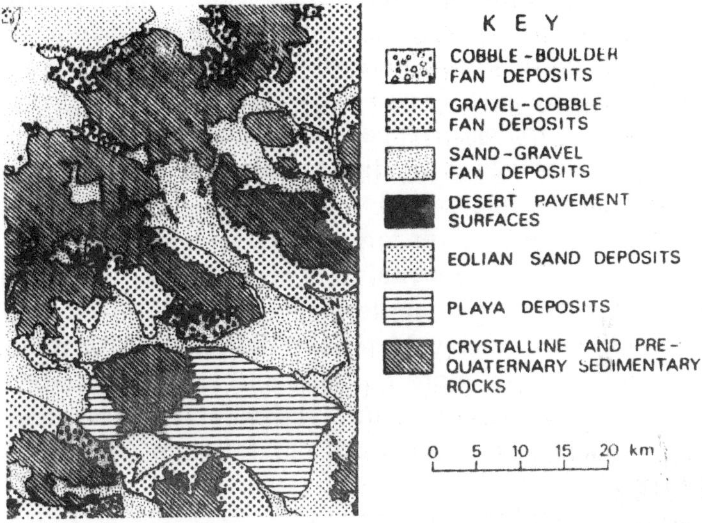

Fig. 28. Interpretation of surface deposits from the radar mosaic in previous figure (After LO, 1986).

Lithospheric Environment Measurements (By Aerial Photography)

Conventional vertical aerial photography is used in the study of the lithospheric environment through its excellent spatial resolution and the stereoscopic capability which facilitates the extraction of detailed qualitative and quantitative information of the surface features, e.g., landforms, drainage patterns, soils, land use and land cover. In geology, the use of aerial photography is to unravel the lithological and structural characteristics of an area. In lithological interpretation, or the recognition of rock types from aerial photographs one should combine geomorphological and structural analysis together in a regional setting so that one should start by recognizing the climatic and erosional environments. A generalized photogeological legend or key was developed based on photographic envidence alone to suggest the type of the rock. Mekel (1978) emphasized the importance of photographic characteristics of sedimentary, igneous and metamorphic rock types as an aid to interpretation. It was observed that areas of sedimentary rock might yield more information on lithology and structure than those formed by igneous and metamorphic rocks. Differential erosion due to the occurrence of alternating resistant and less resistant beds as well as banding indicated by vegetation cover have helped the interpretation. Intrusive igneous rocks tend to be homogeneous over large areas, frequently exhibiting joints or fractures. Extrusive igneous rocks are usually associated with special landforms such as volcanoes and are more readily identifiable. Metamorphic rocks may be revealed by characteristically more rounded and subdued landforms, the occurrence of folding in a sedimentary area plus the presence of cleavage, schistosity or foliation, banding and fracturing.

In structural interpretation, the purpose is to detect the attitude of beds, folds, faults and joints, from which the structural relationships of the rocks in the area can be deduced. Because of the close correlation between structure and relief, a good knowledge of geomorphology is required. Drainage, relief, lineaments and vegetation, tone or colour and texture can all throw light on the bed-rock distribution and structural relations of the area. The detection of photo-lineament in terms of its type, orientation and length is an important step to the understanding of the geological structure of an area. The stereoscopic capability of aerial photography facilitates the study of relief in the qualitative approach. In studying the attitudes of the beds, the strike and dip of the bedding planes can also be determined from aerial itographs. Drainage pattern plays an especially important role in structural interpretation. The form and density of the drainage network provide clues to the underlying geology and hydrology. The drainage pattern can be structurally controlled and the drainage density depends on the infiltration-runoff ratio controlled by the resistance and permeability of the surface material. See Fig. 29. The highest density occurred in shales, medium density in phyllites,

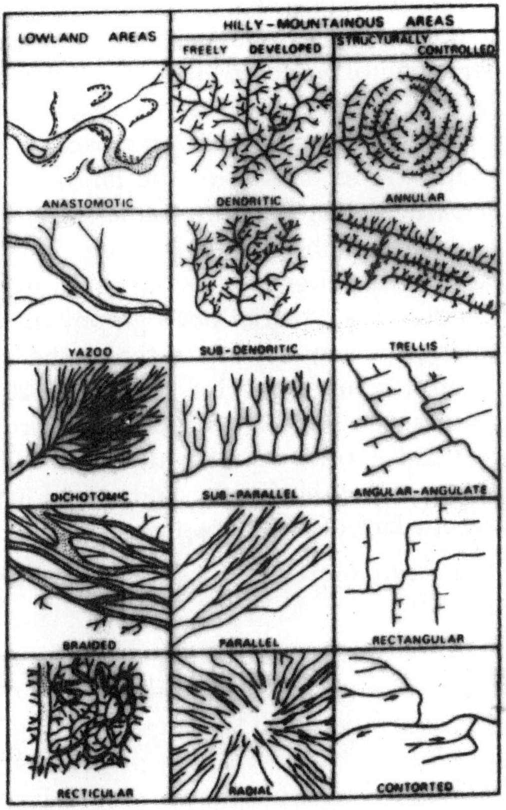

Fig. 29. Major types of drainage patterns.

granites, sandstones and siltstones, and the lowest density in limestones and gravels. It was observed that bifurcation ratios range normally between 3.0 and 5.0 for watersheds in which geological conditions do not distort the drainage pattern. Any abnormal bifurcation ratios will indicate the occurrence of dominant geological control. Also, abnormal bifurcation ratios may be related to flood discharges so that basins with a high bifurcation ratio would yield a low but extended peak flow whereas basins with low bifurcation ratio would produce sharp peaks. An understanding of the watershed geometry is important in hydrology. Hence, one sees the close relationships among geological structures, landforms and hydrological characteristics. These relationships are useful in predicting the potential environments for mineral resources. In geomorphology, the interpretation of aerial photographs is more direct and descriptive because landforms are highly visible. In the genetic approach, the processes responsible for the formation of the landforms are to be inferred. Of particular importance is the study of the large-scale processes such as the temporal change in land forms or sediment movement patterns in estuaries. In hydrology, the main application areas of aerial photography lie in recording and monitoring the amount of water in the surface and subsurface environments. The visible portion of the electromagnetic spectrum (0.4 – 0.7 μm) is particularly suited to delineate flood plains, detect water turbidity or colour, monitor changes in depth of water bodies and identify snow and ice on the surface of the lithosphere.

Lithospheric Environment Measurements (By Satellite Remote Sensing)

The introduction of satellite remote sensing has revolutionized the study of our lithospheric environment. The general availability of the land resources satellite remote sensing data such as Landsat to the public has resulted in an increasing number of applications taking advantage of the regional perspective afforded by these data and the wide capabilities of the multi-spectral sensors. Much emphasis has been placed on the development of the softwares for general-purpose and specific applications, e.g., geologic remote sensing, applied geomorphology, and satellite hydrology. The synoptic view of the earth from space provides the best vantage point to study the relationships between landforms and major structural features. The first use is in the mapping regional structures and lithology. Based on an interpretation of Landsat images the existence of major thrust faults on the north and south sides of Tien Shan in China was noted. This was particularly clear on the south side where folded sedimentary formations were visible. Likewise other strike-slip faults were recognized from Landsat images in Altyn Tagh and Kunleen mountains. From this, the relative motions of the Indian subcontinent and Eurasia could be deducted and it was concluded that crustal deformation extended over a large area with as much as 1,000 km of lateral movement along subparallel strike-slip faults, similar to the San Andreas fault system. Spaceborne radar imaging systems have complemented the Landsat multispectral sensors, e.g., Seasat SAR, and Shuttle Imaging Radar-A (SIR-A). See Figs. 30 and

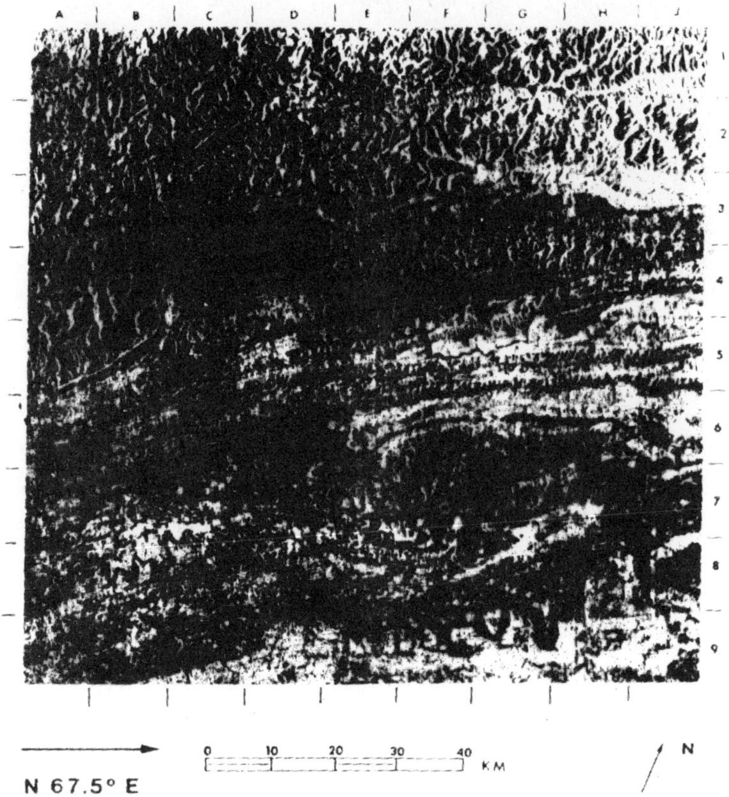

Fig. 30. Mosaic of optically correlated Seasat SAR imagery of the Cumberland Plateau area between Tennessee and Kentucky, USA (After Ford, 1980).

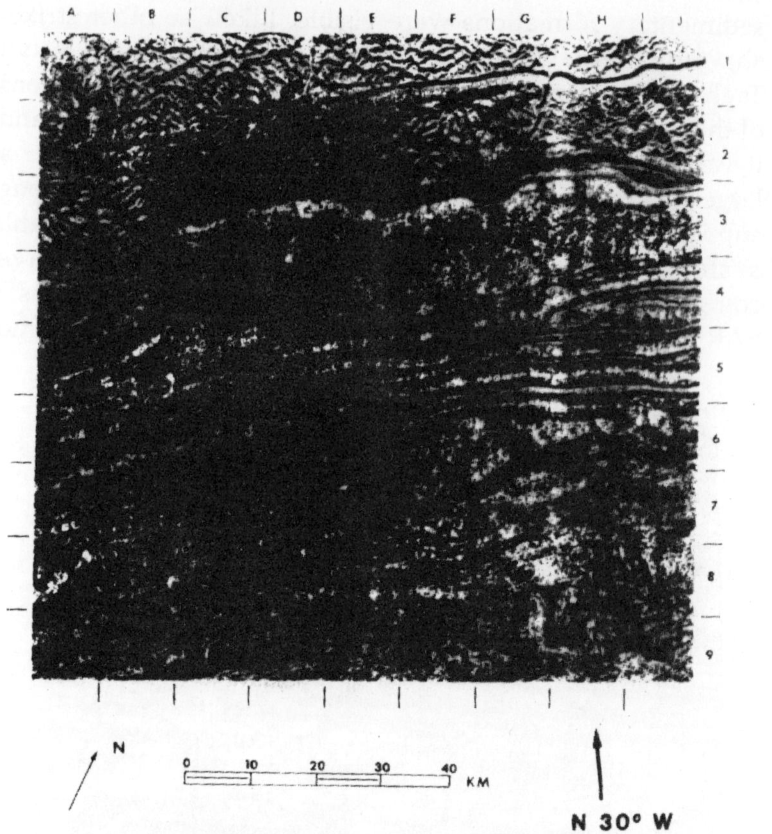

Fig. 31. Lansat MSS (band 6) of the area covered by Seasat SAR in previous figure (After Ford, 1980).

31. The number of minor geomorphic lineaments mapped from the SAP images was greater than that mapped from the corresponding Landsat MSS image by a factor of about 2. Landsat MSS images did not show any significant geometric distortion. It was found that the SIR-A radar imagery could locate most lineaments that were less than 15 km. in length, which the Seasat SAR failed to locate. The different types of satellite imagery have also been used for the extraction of lithologic information. When the vegetation cover exceed 10 percent of the surface area, recognition of rock

types by reflectance alone is not possible. As far igneous rocks, they can be recognized by their irregular shape and image texture. Generally, granite exhibits a darker tone than the surrounding rocks but texture provides the more useful clue. Metamorphic rocks are even more difficult to recognize if they do not show foliation planes or planes of schistosity. For the extraction of lithologic information, ratio enhancements by compter have been found to be most fruitful. In a colour ratio composite, the hydrothermally altered areas appear as green to dark green and brown to red brown. It is possible to make use of geobotanical information in combination with the colour ratio composite images to locate mineral resources. Geobotanical associations are found to be closely related to regional lithologic variations whereas barren areas and certain shrubs and herbs are specifically related to the concentrations of metals. The ultramic rocks could only support lesser amounts of vegetation then the surrounding rocks and exhibited a rounded topography, an accurate map of ultramafic rocks could be obtained with the Landsat imagery.

There are numerous applications of satellite imagery for landform analysis, e.g., desert and volcanic landforms on the global scale. This involved identification, description and measurement of characteristic forms and structures of the sand bodies, with a view to determine the distribution pattern of various dune types and their classification as well as to infer the processes responsible for each dune type. The study of the desert sand seas was continued with colour handheld photography by the crew members of Skylab-4 in 1973 from an altitude of 435 km. This high-resolution photography permitted detailed identification of the components of each sand dune pattern and gave a better understanding of the depositional environments of aeolian sand bodies by means of sand-distribution mapping.

The relationship between the sand distribution and the surface wind regimes could be established to provide insights into the processes of sand dune formation. Satellite imagery has been employed for volcanic activity monitoring and landform study. One of the most useful applications of Landsat imagery is to detect landform changes before and after a volcanic eruption. The handheld colour photography which was obtained by Skylab-4 crew members provided details on volcanic ring infrastructures and caldera landforms through the display of subtle differences in coastal landforms, topographic texture, relief, drainage pattern and albedo. In this way, relationships between geomorphology and structure could be shown. SIR-A data have also been applied to study volcanic landforms (Masursky, 1982). The coarse surface texture of the lava flows tended to give bright radar returns, thus distinctly outlining each lava flow or eruptive centre. Clear water transmits radiant energy in the blue-green band and absorbs energy in the near infrared band. Turbid water with heavy concentrations of sediment also reflects some of the radiation in visible wavelengths but absorbs nearly all the near infrared energy. Thus, on the band S (0.6-0.7 μm) image of Landsat MSS image, the sediments in the rivers and along the coastal can be easily distinguished. Another useful characteristic of water is that it has the highest specific heat of any substance. It is possible to detect water or moisture by sensing the emitted thermal energy as cool areas during warm days or as warm areas on cool nights. Snow was the first "earth resource" observed from space by US satellite TIROS-1 in April, 1960. Another approach to map snow is to use the passive microwave sensors, i.e., the Electrically Scanning Microwave Radiometer (ESMR) carried onboard Nimbus 5 and Nimbus 6. The microwave radiometer detect the brightness temperature of snow. As the liquid water in the snow increases, the brightness temperature increases.

Lithospheric Environment Measurements (By Thermal Infrared Scanner)

Thermal infrared scanner data normally trap the reflected and emitted radiant energy in the two transmission windows of 3-5 μm and 8-14 μm. There are two major approaches in applying these scanner data to the geological, geomorphological and hydrological studies of the lithosphere: (1) the direct visual correlation of the thermal image data with the ground features, and (2) the quantitative analysis of repetitively acquired images using a theoretical thermal model. Thermal infrared images can display surface temperature variations of the ground and are most effective in picking out high temperature targets such as active volcanic craters, hot springs, hot gases and forest fires. The temperature contrast of these targets to the background is high and their temperatures are relatively constant with respect to time. According to Wien's displacement law, the wavelength of peak radiant emittance shifts to the shorter wavelengths with increasing blackbody temperature. Thus, the most suitable wavelengths to use to detect these high temperature targets lie in the 1.0 - 6.0 μm region. The major problem is to ensure that solar heating is eliminated so as not to confuse it with the geothermal heat sources to be detected. The best time for the thermal infrared survey should be the evening or night-time when the interference from solar heating is absent. The use of thermal infrared imagery to detect ground-water discharge has also been found to be most effective. The best time to acquire the thermal infrared images for this type of I detection was during the predawn hours and the best season was winter when the river temperature was about the same as the land temperature about 4°C and ground-water discharges were relatively warm about 10°C to 15°C. The temperature anomaly between the land and ground-water gives rise to a tonal contrast in the pre-dawn thermal infrared imagery which helps to emphasize structural lineaments. The thermal infrared imagery is used to detect near-surface conductive heat transfer which shows only low-level temperature anomalies. Thermal intertia refers to the resistance of a material to a change of temperature. The maximum thermal contrast occurs just prior to sunrise and about 1.5 hours after mid-day. The thermal intertia of a dry material is found to be linearly correlated with its density. Minerals and rocks high in silica, e.g., quarz, granite, rhyolite, have high thermal intertia while those low in silica and high in iron, e.g., olivine, gabbro, basalt, have low thermal intertias. The addition or moisture to dry soils will significantly increase their thermal inertia as a result of the changes in specific heat and conductivity. Thus, by mapping the thermal intertias one can discriminate rock types in areas where vegetation cover is thin. This makes the technique useful for geological mapping in arid and semi-arid regions. The thermal intertia of the ground surface is estimated from two primary variables : (1) the diurnal temperature range (ΔT) and the albedo (A). Multispectral thermal infrared sensing is used for the detection of silicate rocks and minerals (SiO_4). They display spectral emittance minima in the 8-12 μm wavelength region. This phenomena is believed to be caused by interatomic vibrations. This occurrence of the major molecular absorption bands is the thermal infrared can be made use of in the discrimination of the silicate rocks from the non-silicate rocks, which exhibit quite different emittance minima.

Major Imaging Sensor Systems

In order to detect the electromagnetic energy which exists in a wide range of wavelengths and frequencies, different varieties of remote sensing instruments are required. Here remote sensing instruments capable of producing images of the environment in a form suitable for visual interpretation are given below :-

1. Photographic Cameras : The most commonly employed sensor is the conventional photographic camera designed to detect energy in the visible 0.4-0.7 μm) and near infrared (0.7-0.9 μm) portions of the electromagnetic Npectrum. This has been made possible with the use of suitable black-and-white or colour films sensitized to these spectral regions. In order to enhance the contrast between the object and background of interest in the result-ant photograph a yellow filter is normally employed at the time of photography to eliminate the Rayleigh scatter in the atmosphere. Lens system of photographic cameras should be aberrations free. In aerial cameras designed for topographic mapping purposes, the lens distortion is cut down to ±6 μm. See Fig. 32. Most of the

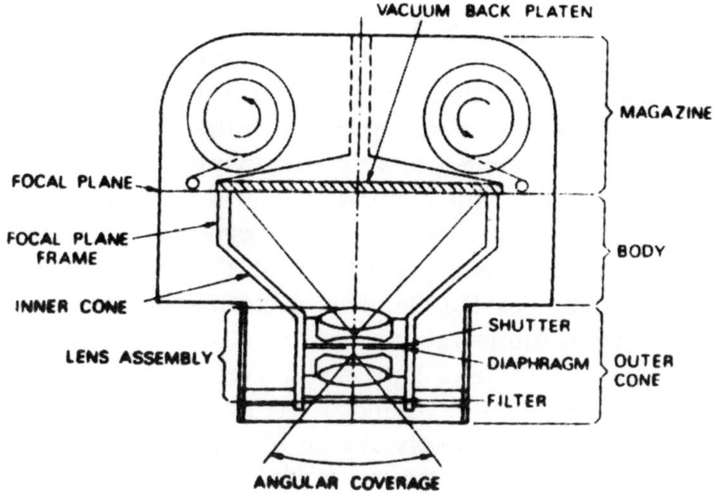

Fig. 32. Components ot an aerial camera (After Moffitt and Mikhail, 1980).

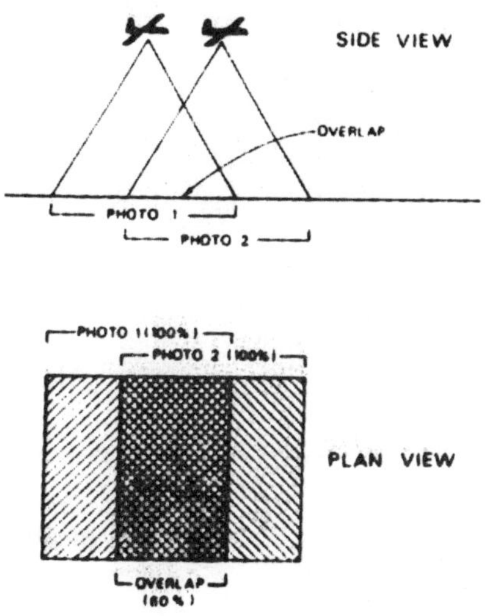

Fig. 33. Flight configuration in stereoscopic aerial photography.

photography is obtained from aircraft with such a metrically accurate camera for photogrammetric purposes. This usually involves vertical aerial photography of the terrain with 60 percent forward overlap between successive frames of photographs along a flight strip and 15 to 20 percent lateral lap between two adjacent flight strips. See Fig. 33. This flight configuration permits aerial photographs to be viewed stereoscopically to give an impression of the third dimension, thus facilitating the interpretation and mapping of the terrain features by the analogue approach. Geometrically, the vertical aerial photograph gives a central perspective projection with the lens idealized as a point fixed at a distance from the negative plane. See Fig. 34. The electromagnetic energy is reflected from the terrain to pass through the lens and is regarded as a bundle of light rays traveling in straight-line paths. Thus, by similar triangles, the normal scale S of the vertical aerial photograph can be found by the following equation :-

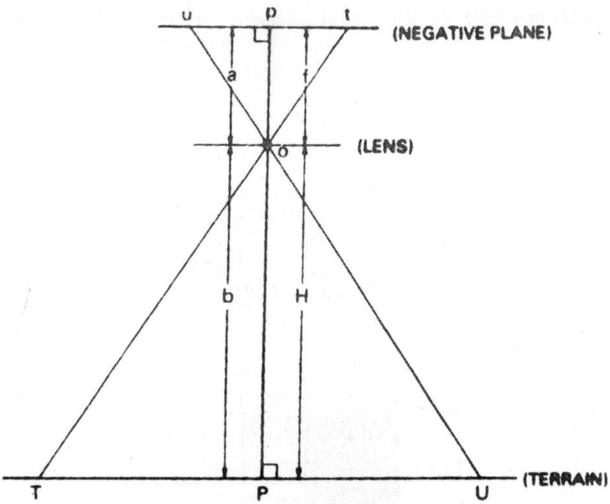

Fig. 34. The central perspective projection of a vertical photograph over the terrain.

$$S = f/H \qquad \text{...(1)}$$

When *f* is the focal length of the camera and H the flying height from the ground, However, if the relief of the terrain is taken into account, the scale of the photograph at point A will be given as :-

$$S = f/(H - h_A) \quad \text{...(2)}$$

Where h_A is the height of the point A from the datum. The average scale of the photograph S_{AV} should take into account the average terrain height so the equation (2) becomes as :-

$$S_{AV} = f/(H - h_{AV}) \quad \text{...(3)}$$

In aerial photography the whole area covered by the photograph is acquired instantaneously. Photographic film consists of a base and a thin layer of chemical emulsion on top. The emulsion is made up of silver halide crystals or grains of different sizes ranging from 0.1 to 1 μm^3 embedded in a solidified gelatine. The halide ions are commonly bromine or iodine. The standard film type of aerial photography is the panchromatic black-and-white film which has a spectral sensitivity ranging from 0.35 to 0.70 μm. Another type of film is the infrared black-and-white film which has a spectral sensitivity in 0.34-0.52 μm and 0.60-0.90 μm. Leaf mesophyll of vegetation is highly reflective and water bodies are highly absorptive of infrared radiation. These factors, coupled with its ability to penetrate haze make infrared black-and-white film ideal for rural landuse and land cover mapping. Now-a-days, increasingly more remote sensing applications make use of colour films because the human eyes can distinguish a greater number of colour shades than grey tones. A true colour film consists of three layers of emulsion each sensitized to one of the three primary colours, blue, green and red. Colour infrared film reacts most strongly with vegetation which is exhibited in varying shades of red, according to the amount of reflectance from the leaves. This kind of film has been most extensively used in environmental remote sensing applications. Multiband photography is possible with the use of an array of synchronized cameras, such as the four-

Hasselblad-camera array, The multiband photographs are in smaller format such as 60 mm or 90 mm, than the usual 230 mm format of the mapping aerial camera.

2. ***Electro-optical Detectors :*** Electro optical detectors are transducers which "transform electromagnetic radiation into electrons or electrical signals from a scene viewed. The detector elements behave like the grains of the photographic film and produce an analogue electrical record of each point of the scene scanned according to the nature of the incoming electromagnetic radiation. There are two basic classes of detectors : (1) quantum, and (2) thermal, depending on the physical processes by which the electromagnetic radiation input is converted to electrical output. Quantum detectors can be further subdivided into two groups: (1) photo-emissive detectors, and (2) solid-state detectors. In photo-emissive detectors, the photo-electrons are emitted into a vacuum or gas upon absòrption of photons from incident radiation. They can only be employed for sensing in the ultraviolet and visible spectrum, e.g., photo tubes and photo-multipliers. The solid-state detectors comprise both photoconductive and photovoltaic devices which use similar materials but operate differently. Photoconductive detectors are typically made from silicon and germanium doped with various materials. The usual measure of performance of a detection system is the signal-to-noise ratio (S/N). The performance of the detectors for remote sensing applications should also be evaluated with respect to their spectral responsivity and the speed, linearity and dynamic range of response. The resolving power of the system is detérmined by the packing density of the detector elements. In order to illustrate the working of electro-optical detectors as imaging sensors, two examples are given below :-

(a) Vidicon Television Camera : The vidicon camera is a form of image tube. Its principal application is sensing in the visible and near infrared portion of the electromagnetic spectrum, i.e., upto 0.85 μm. It makes use of an optical system (camera lens) to focus an optical image onto a photosensitive surface of an electron gun which then converts the image into electronic form, either as charge pattern on a storage device or in a non-storing mode, traveling electrons. The vidicon television camera is based on the photoconductive process. See Fig. 35. A photoconductive target is coated on a

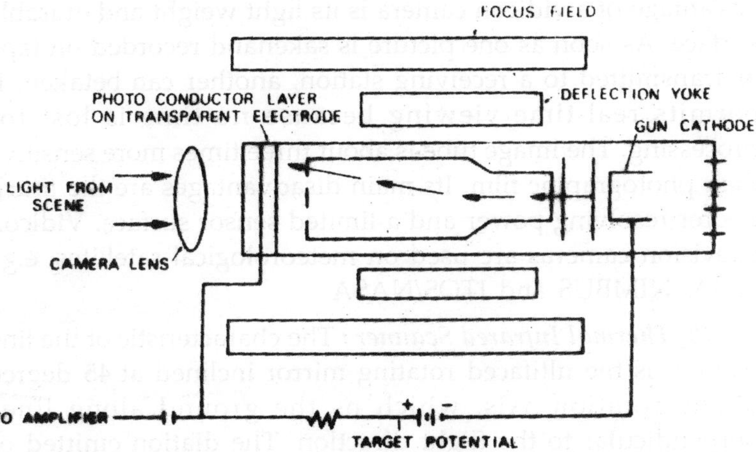

Fig. 35. Diagrammatic representation of a vidicon camera (After Tomlinson, 1972).

transparent electrode which has a positive charge. Before exposure, the target is first scanned by an electron beam in the dark, which deposits a uniform layer of negatively charged electrons on its rear surface. As the mechanical or electronic shutter is opened for a short while, an image is focused on the photo-conductive target. Light incident on the target increases its conductivity locally and electrons escape to the electrode which also acts as a conductor. The cathode of the electron gun produces an electron beam which is attracted to the positively charged electrode. In the dark areas, the electron beam passes through in proportion to the brightness of the illumination. This creates a current at the electrode. By scanning the image, line by line with the aid of the deflection coils, the image is displaced in a cathode ray tube (CRT) and can be photographically recorded. After the completion of scanning, the photoconductive target is removed of residual electrons and is ready for another new picture. For remote sensing from space a low velocity scanning is normally used with the additional advantage that the video signals can be transmitted to the earth with small frequency bandwidth and low power requirements. The great advantage of a vidicon camera is its light weight and erasable surface. As soon as one picture is sakenand recorded on tape or transmitted to a receiving station, another can betaken. It permits real-time viewing because no time is lost for processing. The image tube is about three times more sensitive than photographic film. Its main disadvantages are the much poorer resolving power and a limited sensor surface. Vidicon television cameras are used on meteorological satellites, e.g., ESSA, NIMBUS and ITOS/NASA.

(b) Thermal Infrared Scanner : The characteristic of the line scanner is the ultifaced rotating mirror inclined at 45 degree to the rotation axis, which ns the ground along lines perpendicular to the flight direction. The diation emitted or reflected from the ground is projected by the rotating mirror onto the detector which senses the intensity of the radiation in a specific part of the electromagnetic spectrum and converts it to electrical signals. These signals are used to modulate the intensity of a single-line cathode ray tube (CRT) to expose an image line on the photographic film which is made to advance at a rate proportional to flight velocity of the sensor platform. Thus, as the sensor platform moves forward, successive new scan lines of the ground surface are swept. Together the continuous scan lines give a real-time image of the ground surface sensed. See Fig. 36. It is also possible to record the scanner data on magnetic tape which is later employed to reconstruct the image. In the case of the thermal infrared scanner, the detectors commonly used belong to the photoconductive type. For sensing in the 1-5.5 μm infrared window, indium antimonide (InSb) or indium arsenide (InAs) detectors are used, whilst for the 2-14 μm window, mercury-doped germanium (GeHg) or mercury-cadmium-

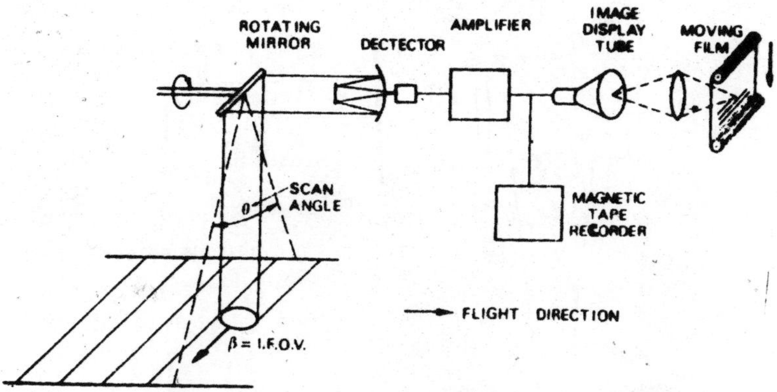

Fig. 36. Operation of a line scanning system.

telluride (HgCdTe) detectors are employed. The spatial resolution of thermal imagery is determined by the instantaneous field of view (IFOV), the platform height the scan angle 0 of the scanner. For civilian applications, the IFOV ranges between 1.5 to 2.5 milliradians, and the best ground resolution is obtained at the point directly beneath the sensors, i.e., the nadir. In order to improve the spatial resolution, a smaller IFOV needs to be used, but this would mean an increase in scanning speed which is at 6000 scans per minute. The thermal resolution or the ability of the system to detect small radiometric temperature differences is dependent on the sensitivity of the detector element employed, which is dependent on the detector area and of quency bandwidth of operation.

3. ***Multispectral Scanners :*** The optical-mechanical or "whiskbroom" scanner can operate in any wavelength region so that by using detectors sensitized diation in several spectral channels, multispectral data can be collected ultaneously. Advances in detector fabrication technology makes possible Iconstruction of multi-element detector arrays. By placing a detector array in the image plane of the spectrometer, each detector sees the same slit image in its proper spectral region. See Fig. 37. It is possible to manufacture multispectral

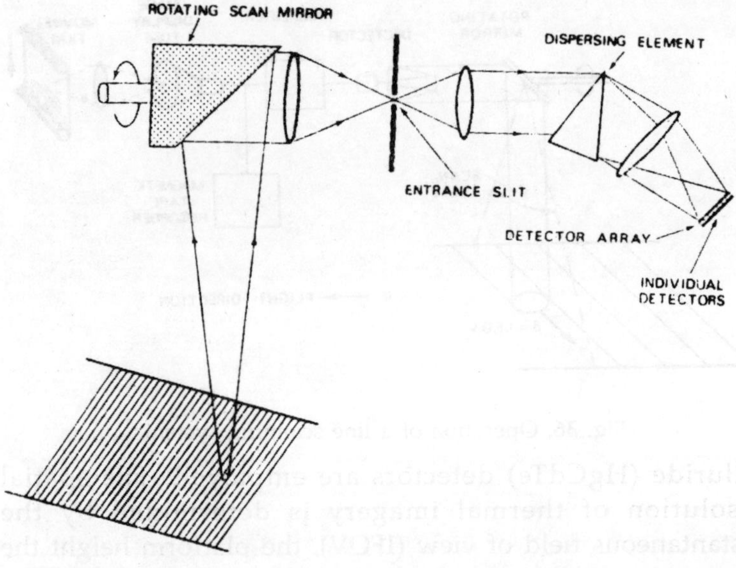

Fig. 37. Scheme of multispectral dispersive scanner (After Lowe, 1980).

scanners to sense in 24 separate spectral channels, but such a large amount of spectral data requires the use of high speed digital computer to help in the analysis. For practical application a smaller number of spectral bands is used, e.g., multispectral scanner system (MSS) employed in the Landsats. It provides images of the earth simultaneously in four spectral bands : (1) 0.5-0.6 μm, (2) 0.6-0.7 μm, (3) 0.7-0.8 μm, and (4) 0.8-1.1 μm. Altogether 24 detectors are used, 6 in each band. It is also possible to make use of solid-state detectors operating in the pushbroom mode. In pushbroom scanning, only the forward motion of a sensor platform is used to sweep a linear array of detectors oriented perpendicularly to the flight direction across a scene being imaged. One array is used for each spectral channel. There are no moving parts in this system. This will eliminate complex geometric distortion and it has better signal-to-noise ratio. But this system needs many more detectors for the array.

Microwave Imagers

These imagers make use of antennae to collect radiation information in the microwave wavelengths, i.e. 100 cm - 0.1 cm or 0.3 - 300 GHz in frequencies from the ground. They are generally classified into passive and active types.

1. Passive Microwave Imagers : Passive microwave sensing collects thermal emission from the earth's surface in the microwave spectrum. The commonly employed spectral bands are separated into microwave regions, each of which is given a letter designation, e.g., from P to W. See Table 3.

Table 3. Microwave and radar wavebands (After Ulaby et al., 1981).

Designations	*Frequency (GHz)*	*Wavelength (cm)*
P	0.225–0.390	133-77
L	0.390–1.550	77–19
S	1.550–4.20	19–7.1
C	4.20–5.75	7.1–5.2
X	5.75–10.90	5.2–2.8
K	10.90–36.0	2.8–0.83
Ku	10.90–22.0	2.8–1.36
Ka	22.0–36.0	1.36–0.83
V	46.0–100.0	0.65–0.54
W	56.0–100.0	0.30–0.54

The district advantage of microwave sensors is their capability to penetrate clouds, although water vapour and oxygen can still hamper them, pecially if microwaves at higher frequencies are used. Passive microwave sensors detected emitted, reflected and transmitted radiation within the 1 mm to 300 mm wavelengths. The strength of the passive microwave radiation largely depends on the temperature and dielectric properties of the material rather than on the surface roughness. The dielectric property of a material is characterized by its dielectric constant. The large dielectric constant for water at 20°C is about 80 which makes passive microwave remote sensing useful in monitoring water resources. Microwaves with lower frequencies are more sensitive to moisture content changes. The radiation emitted in the microwave region from surfaces is polarized. If the electrical vector is parallel to the earth surface, it is called horizontal (H) polarization. Microwave remote sensing is employed to detect the H component of the emitted radiation only. The passive microwave imager is a mechanical scanning device which consists of a parabolic reflector. At the center of the reflector is a small antenna which collects the radiant energy and feeds it into the receiver amplifier. Scanning is achieved by mechanically rotating the antenna to produce a conical scan at a constant angle of tilt with respect to the direction of motion of the sensor platform. See Fig. 38. Nimbus-5 meteorological satellite uses electrically scanning microwave radiometer (ESMR). The spatial resolution of the resultant imagery is dependent on the antenna size so that the ground resolution is determined by the antenna bandwidth, sensor platform height and scan angle. The beamwidth b is expressed as :-

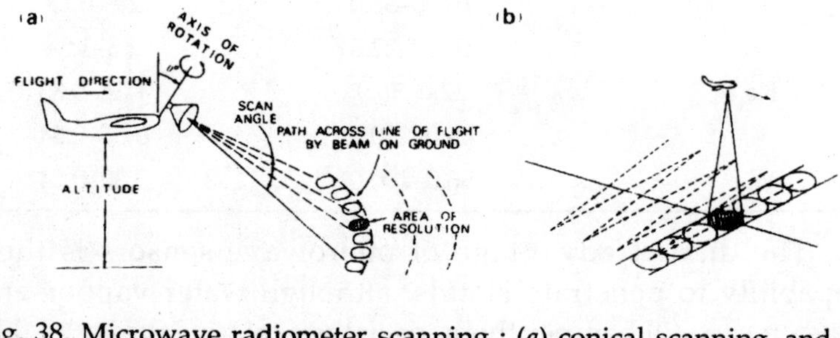

Fig. 38. Microwave radiometer scanning : (*a*) conical scanning, and (*b*) cross-track scanning in the plane normal to the direction of flight (After Ulaby et al., 1981).

$$b = \lambda/d \qquad ...(1)$$

where λ is the wavelength and d is the antenna diameter. High spatial resolution requires a fast scan rate which is detrimental to temperature resolution. Passive microwave imager shows correct scale in the flight direction but incorrect in the scan direction, in addition to the errors oduced by variations in sensor platform height and attitude.

2. ***Active Microwave Imagers :*** Active microwave remote sensing involves the sending out of a pulse of microwave energy to a target from the sensor and then measuring the return or reflected signal. This method of sensing is known as radar. Radar was designed for measuring distances and determining locations of objects. This system operates in single wavelength within the 35-9.1 GHz frequencies in the microwave spectrum, which fall mainly in the X and K bands. A major advantage of radar is its all-weather, day and night operational capability. The strength of the return signal in radar is determined by the surface roughness and the dielectric properties of the terrain rather than the temperature of the material. A commonly used radar imaging system is the Side-Looking Airborne Radar (SLAR) which produces imagery of the terrain on one or both sides of the aircraft flight line. An antenna is mounted on the belly of the aircraft parallel to its longitudinal axis and hence to the flight direction over the terrain. From the antenna, a short pulse of energy of a specific wavelength is transmitted in a fan which lies approximately in a plane perpendicular to the flight line. See Fig. 39. When

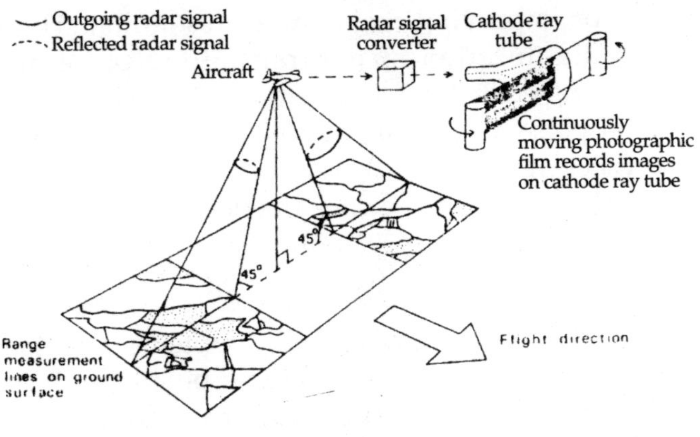

Fig. 39. Operation characteristics of Side-Looking Airborne Radar (SLAR) (After Cooke and Harris, 1970).

the pulse strikes a target, a signal is returned and detected by the receiver on the aircraft which converts it to a video signal to modulate the intensity of the electron-beam of a cathode ray tube to give a line trace of the terrain. This is transferred by a lens to a photographic film which is moved forward at a velocity proportional to the velocity of the aircraft. As the aircraft moves forward in its flight, scanning of the terrain in the flight direction or azimuth is accomplished and a series of lines is recorded onto the film, which builds up a two dimensional image of the terrain. In recording the line trace of the terrain, either a slant range or ground range presentation is possible. The appearance of the terrain on the radar image depends on the incidence angle of the radar beam rather than the absolute range of the aircraft. Therefore, in der to avoid ambiguity in imaging, the terrain directly beneath the aircraft is not imaged. SLAR images also exhibit shadows because of the oblique dar beam illumination to targets. The shadow length of terrain features will crease directly with relative relief and incidence angle and inversely with depression angle. The spatial resolution of the SLAR system is determined by the antenna beam width in the along-track or azimuth direction and the pulse length in the across-track or range direction. A small beam-width is desirable for improving the azimuth resolution. The pulse length or the duration of the transmitted pulse and the depression angle combine to determine the range resolution, The typical pulse lengths are between 0.05 and 0.1 μs. There are two types of radars : (1) real aperture, and (2) synthetic aperture. The synthetic aperture side-look radar is preferred for use in spacecraft.

Natural Hazards (Earthquakes)

Earthquakes, landslides, volcanic eruptions, and flood are natural hazards that kill thousand of people and destroy billions of dollars of property each year. Various forms of remote sensing have been used for these activities. Earthquakes are caused by the abrupt release of strain that has built up in the earth's crust. Most zones of maximum earthquake intensity and frequency occur at the boundaries between the moving plates that form the crust of the earth. Earthquakes are common along the San Andreas fault that forms part of the boundary between the North America and Pacific plates. Major earthquakes also occur within the interior of crustal plates such as those in the southeast United States, China, and Russia. Remote sensing is very useful for seismic risk analysis, which estimates the geographic distribution, frequency, and intensity of seismic activity without attempting to pinpoint specific earthquakes. This analysis is essential for locating and designing dams, power plants,.and other projects in seismically active areas. One method of seismic risk analysis is based on the study of instrumentally orded earthquakes and historic records of earthquakes. The second method of seismic risk analysis is base don the recognition of active faults, , which are defined as breaks along which movement has occurred in Late Quaternary, or Holocene time (past 11,000 years). Remote sensing analyses and field studies of active faults provide a geological record that extends our instrumental and historic records. Surface faulting during large shallow earthquakes is more universal than has been recognized. Analysis of this geomorphic evidence and radiometric age dating of earlier events are two techniques that have not been fully utilized. The following general relationships between faulting and earthquakes in California were noted by Allen (1975):-

1. Virtually all large earthquakes (magnitude greater than 6.0 on the Richter scale) have resulted from ruptures along faults that had been recognized by field geologists prior to the events.
2. All of these faults have a history of earlier displacements in Quaternary and possible Holocene times.
3. All the earthquakes have been relatively shallow, not exceeding about 20 km in depth. Most earthquakes

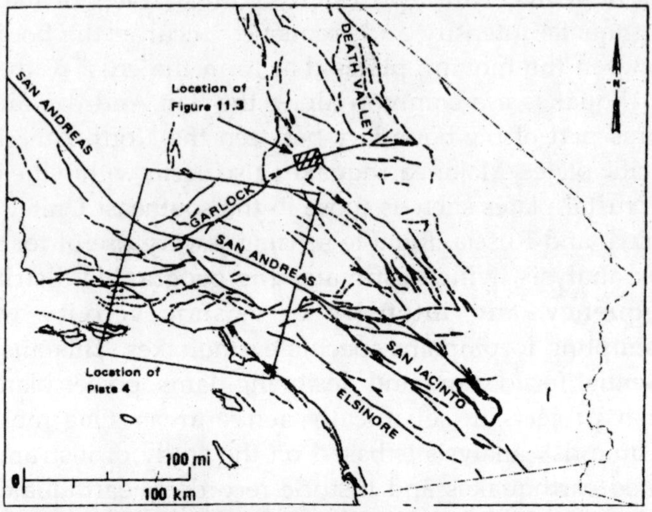

A. FAULTS WITH QUATERNARY DISPLACEMENTS. AREAS SHOWN BY PLATE 4 AND FIGURE 11.3 ARE OUTLINED.

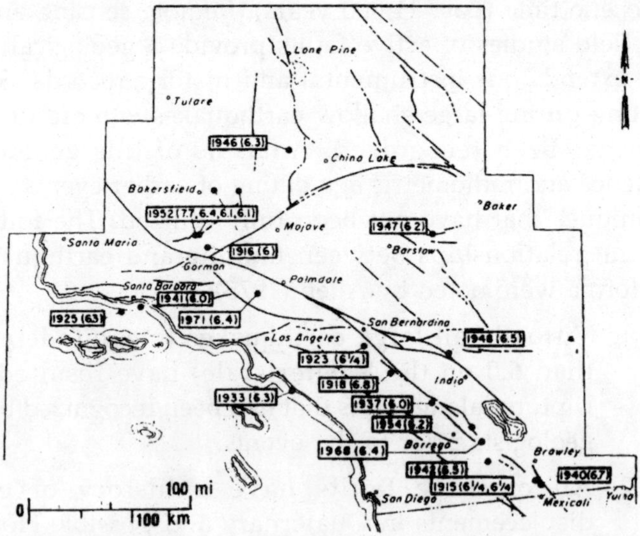

B. EARTHQUAKES OF MAGNITUDE 6.0 AND GREATER, 1912–1974.

Fig. 40. Relationship of Quaternary faulting to earthquakes in southern California (After Allen, 1975).

large than magnitude 6.0 have been accompanied by surface faulting, as have many of the smaller events.

4. The larger earthquakes have generally occurred on the longer faults.
5. Generally only a small segment of the entire length of a fault zone has broken during any single earthquake.

Comparing the Landsat MSS image of the Los Angles region with the map of faults having Quaternary displacements shows that most of these faults are evident on the Landsat image. Additional faults are recognizable in TM images because of their higher spatial resolution. See Fig. 40. The map of major earthquakes in southern California between 1912 and 1974 show that, with few exceptions, these have occurred in the areas of Quaternary faulting, Typical topographic features associated with active strike-slip faults are shown on the Skylab image of Fig. 41. The left-lateral,

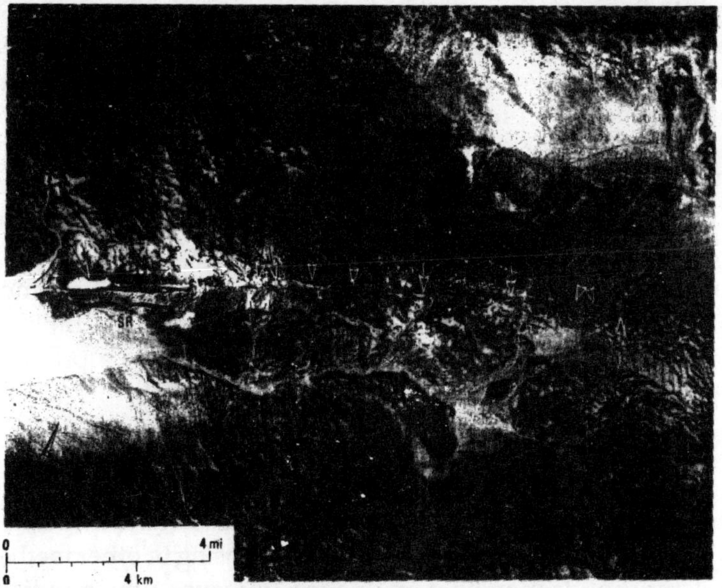

Fig. 41. Skylab earth-terrain-camera photograph of the Garlock fault, California (After Merifield and Lamar, 1975).

strike-slip placement of the Garlock fault is indicated by the offset drainage channels in this figure. A fault zone is comprised of active and inactive faults; the entire belt of faults may be hundreds of kilometres in length and several kilometres in width. A fault trace is the surface expression of an individual active fault. Landsat MSS images are excellent for recognizing the continuity and regional relationships of faults. The higher spatial resolution of Landsat RBV and TM images records many of the topographic features indicative of active faulting. Stereo viewing of aircraft and LFC photographs provides detailed information on geomorphic features formed by faulting. Thermal IR images of arid and semiarid areas may record the presence of active faults with little or no surface expression, such as the San Andreas and Superstition Hills faults. The highlights and shadowing effects on low-sun-angle aerial photographs can emphasize topographic scarps associated with active faults, such as in the Carson Range, Neveda. Radar images also emphasize subtle features along active fault zones, as shown in the SIR-A image of the Sorong fault in Irian Jaya, Indonesia. Mosaics of Landsat images are used to analyze regional relationships of earthquake epicenters to faults and lineaments. Known faults are well expressed on the Landsat MSS mosaic of the Cook Inlet region in Alaska together with numerous lineaments that had not previously been mapped. See Figs. 42 and 43. In the central interior of Alaska, epicentres of the largest earthquakes occur at the intersections of lineaments or faults that are recognizable on Landsat images. Combining physical data and remote sensing information is a promising approach to quake risk analysis.

Natural Hazards (Landslides)

Landslides occur on the land and on the seafloor in areas underlain by unstable materials. Individuals landslide events are difficult or impossible to diet by remote sensing or other methods. Existing solids may be d on images, however, which indicates that an area is slide-prone and should be avoided or used with great care. Stereo pairs of aerial photographs have long been

Fig. 42. landsat mosaic of south-central Alaska compiled from Landset MSS band-5 images acquired in early November 1972 (Courtesy U.S. Department of Agriculture Soil Conservation Service).

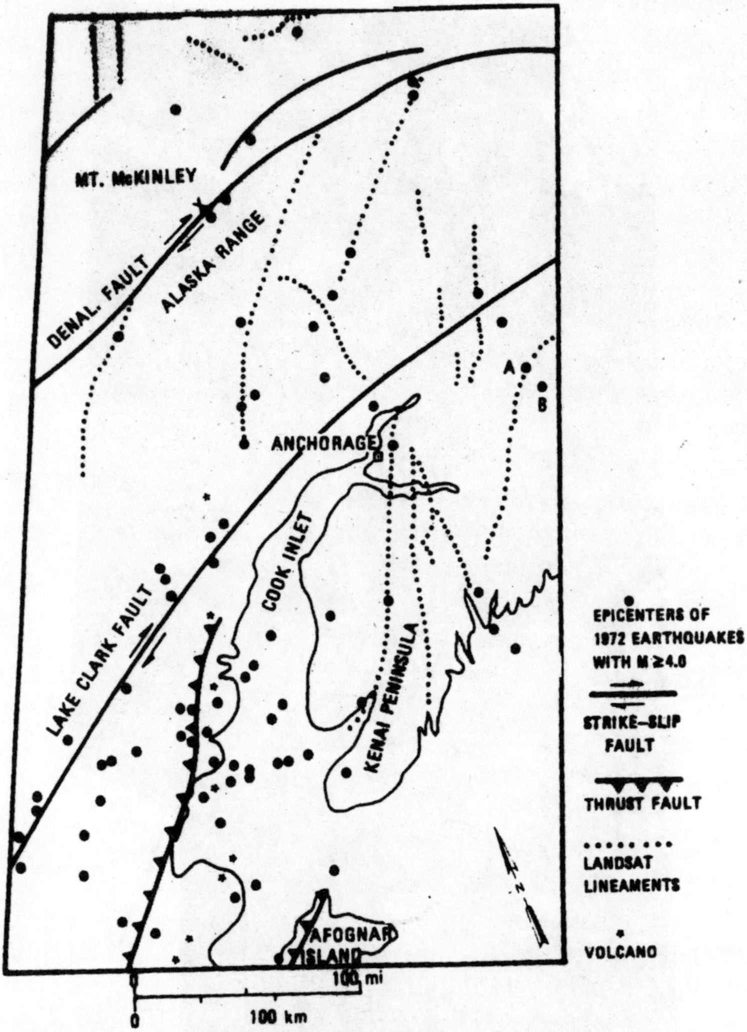

Fig. 43. Interpretation map of Landsat mosaic of south-central Alaska with epicenters plotted for earthquakes in 1972 (After Gedney and Van Womer, 1974).

used to recognize solids and slide-prone terrain. High soil moisture lubricates unstable material and is a major factor in landslides. Thermal IR images have been used to recognize dam ground associated with landslides in California. Evaporative cooling on the damp ground produces a cool signature on aircraft thermal IR images. Satellites, radar, and side-scanning sonar have expanded our capability to recognize unstable terrain where slides occur. The prehistoric Blackhawk landslide originated on the north flank of Blackhawk Ridge in the San Bernardino Mountains and moved northward for 9 km. into the Mojave Desert. Figure 44 shows two remote sensing images and a map of the Blackhawk slide. Erosion had created an over-steepened slope in the highly fractured bedrock, which collapsed along an arculate front. The debris trapped a cushion of air during its descent that lubricated the mass, enabling it to flow several kilometres. In the Skylab photograph the headward scarp of the original debris fall is shadowed, but the characteristic crescent form is apparent. The distal lobe of the slide has a characteristic hummocky appearance. The toe and lateral margins of the slide form a pressure ridge 15 to 30m high that stands slightly above the surface of the slide. A northwest-flowing ephemeral stream has deposited younger alluvium over the central portion of the slide. In the Skylab photograph, the slide debris is darker than the stream and desert alluvium. The radar image has poorer resolution than the Skylab photograph but portrays major features of the slide. The coarse debris and hummocky surface are rough and produce a bright signature relative to the darker signature of the finer-grained alluvium. The pressure ridges have narrow, bright signatures.

The Mississippi Delta consists of unconsolidated, water saturated, fine-grained sediment. The gentle depositional slopes around the margin of the delta are unstable and may collapse to form submarine landslides and related features. Because the delta is an oil-producing region, it is important to map slide-prone areas before installing production platforms and seafloor pipelines. The turbid water prevents remote sensing by visible means. Bright signatures in sonar images record shadow zones or smooth surfaces. Dark

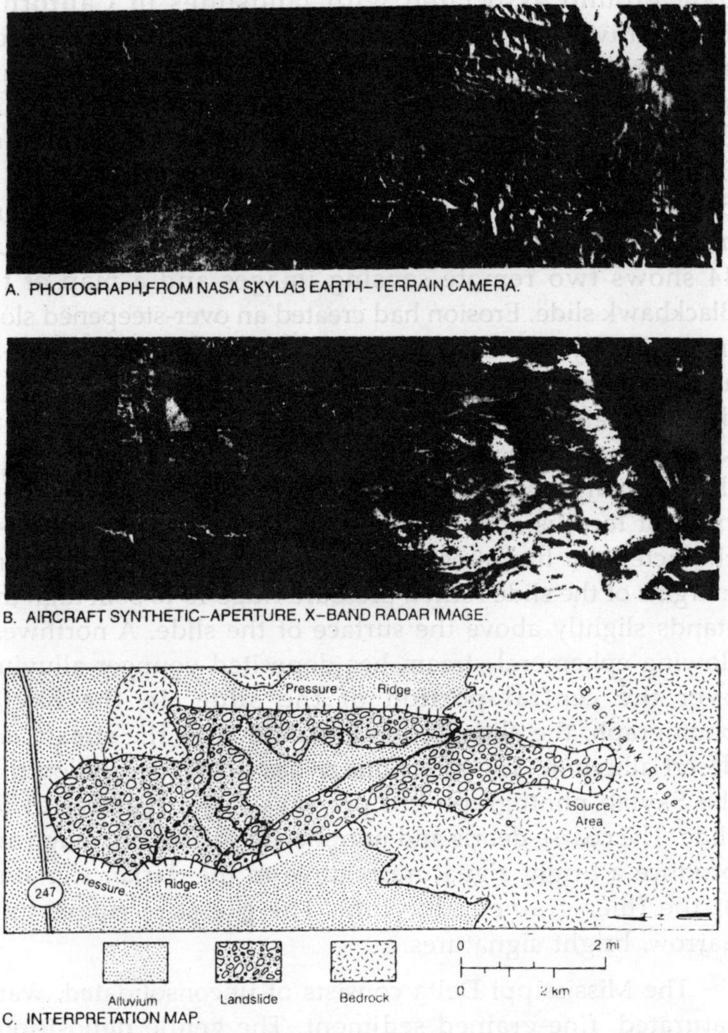

Fig. 44. Blackhawk landslide, San Bernardino Mountains, California (After Sabins, Jr., 1987).

MOSAIC OF SIDE-SCANNING SONAR IMAGES. FROM PRIOR, COLEMAN, AND GARRISON (1979, FIGURE 2). COURTESY D. B. PRIOR, COASTAL STUDIES INSTITUTE, LOUISIANA STATE UNIVERSITY.

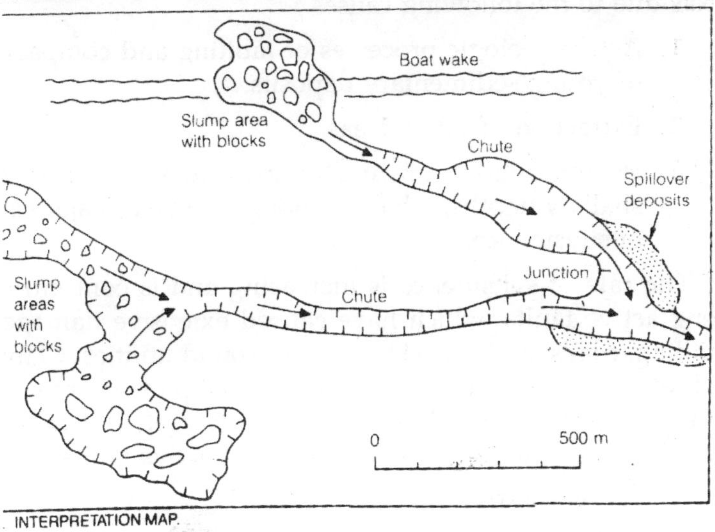

INTERPRETATION MAP.

Fig. 45. Submarine landslides, Mississippi Delta, Gulf of Mexico (After Sabins, Jr., 1987).

signatures recorded strong returns from scarps facing the sonar pulse and from rough surface. See Fig. 45. As shown in the interpretation map, the slides originates at lobate slump areas where the sediment collapses to form irregular blocks. The slump material moves downslope through narrow, steep-sided channels (chutes) that merge at junctions. At the junctions, the slump material may leave the chute and form spillover deposits. Extensive systems of slumps and chutes have been mapped in the delta with sonar.

Natural Hazards (Land Subsidence)

Land subsidence is downward movement in which lateral movement predominates. Subsidence results from removal of underlying support and can have serious effects on man-made structures. Surface subsidence upto several metres in depth can be caused by extraction of subsurface fluids. When subsidence occurs in populated and industrialized coastal areas, the resulting flooding can be a major problem. In the past upto 2.5 m of land subsidence has occurred in Houston, Texas due to the following causes :-

1. Active geologic processes of faulting and compaction of young sedimentary deposits.
2. Extraction of oil and gas.
3. Widespread pumping of groundwater from the shallow depths, which is thought to be a major cause of subsidence.

The rate of subsidence is increasing and is concentrated along active faults, which have caused extensive damage to building, roads, and especially underground utilities. Clanton and Verbeck (1981) acquired oblique aerial photographs with normal colour and IR colour films and interpreted them using the following criteria to identify traces of active faults :-

1. Faults scraps
2. Sag ponds along fault traces
3. Differences in drainage pattern on opposite sides of faults
4. Linear tonal anomalies caused by higher soil moisture on the down-thrown sides of faults

5. Vegetation anomalies.

These criteria have been sued to prepare map showing the locations of active faults. In areas of limestone terrain, groundwater can dissolve the bedrock to produce underground caverns that may collapse and cause surface subsidence. Areas of incipient sink-holes have anomalously high surface moisture. A few aircraft thermal IR images show cool areas that may be indicators of future sinkholes.

Natural Hazards (Subsurface Coal Fires)

Coal mining produce large volumes of waste rock, which includes combustible material such as contaminated coal, carbonaceous shale, and pyrite. Large refuse dumps containing millions of tones of this material are present at coal-mining areas throughout the world. Surface fires or spontaneous combustion may ignite the dumps, and the resulting fire may spread to abandoned coalmines. Such fires in refuse dumps and mines are common, and some have been burning for over 50 years. Subsurface fires .istitute three major hazards given below :-

1. The large volumes of carbon monoxide and sulfur dioxide gases released at the surface are potentially dangerous.
2. Fires in abandoned mines may cause surface-subsidence problems.
3. The fires may interfere with mining operations.

Coal fires are controlled by shutting off the air supply. This is accomplished either by coating the dumps with clay or by injecting water and slurries through holes drilled into the combustion zone. For such measures to be effective, the underground fire must be accurately located. Thermal IR images have proven useful for this purpose. Processing the magnetic-tape record enhances the areas of maximum surface radiant temperature so that coal fires are readily distinguishable from water. The enhanced image emphasizes the active burning fronts, and it is apparent that the narrow, elongate dump is the site of the most intense burning. IR images are valuable for planning fire-control programmes and for evaluating the effectiveness of control measures. Correlating IR images of coal-mine fires with temperature measurements in boreholes, we get the following conclusions :-

1. Fires at shallow depth (less than 10m) are readily detectable.
2. Fires at intermediate depths (less than 10m to 30m) are detectable where heat is carried to the surface by convection in open cracks or where the fire has been burning long enough (several years or more) for heat to reach the surface by conduction.
3. Deep fires (greater than 30m) are detectable only where heat reaches the surface by convection in open cracks.

Remote sensing methods are useful for recognizing areas subject to natural hazards, e.g., earthquakes, volcanic eruptions, landslides, and floods. Images are also useful for assessing the damaged caused by these hazardous events and for planning relief and rehabilitation efforts. Prediction of specific events is a desirable, but much more difficult, objective.

Natural Hazards (Volcanoes)

On the basis of their activity, volcanoes may be classified as : (1) active, erupted at least once in historic time, (2) dormant, no historic eruptions, but probably capable of erupting, and (3) extinct, incapable of further eruptions. Hazards to people and property from active volcanoes include (1) lava flows, (2) hot avalanches, mudflows, and floods; and (3) volcanic ash and gases. Eruptions can be costly and dangerous. Warning signs of increasing volcanic activity and means of detection are given below :

1. Earthquakes caused by magma intrusion are detected by seismometers.
2. Changes in shape of a volcano caused by magma intrusion are recorded by tiltmeters and by repeated, precise surveys, including aerial photographs.

3. Steam-driven ejection of old rock and ash is monitored by visual observations, radar observations, photography, and studies of ejecta (material erupted by the volcano).

4. Increased emission of heat and gas may be detected from visible fumes, increased stream flow, avalanches from melted snow, and change in chemistry of the meltwater. Ground temperature may be measured directly with probes or remotely by IR scanners and radiometrs.

Mount St. Helens, in the southwest part of the state of Washington, several times in the 1800s and has long been recognized as an active volcano. The major explosive eruption of May 18, 1980 was thoroughly monitored and studied (Sabins, 1987). Numerous remote sensing such as the pair of aerial photographs were acquired before and main eruption. Figure 46(A) is a Seasat radar image acquired 2 years before the blast. The high elevation of the volcano and the steep depression angle of Seasat cause the severe displacement of the peak toward the radar look direction. The post-blast X-band aircraft image (Fig. 46B) was acquired at a low depression angle, which enhances topographic features such as the crater walls, lava doma, and mudflows on the south flank. Thermal IR images were acquired before and after the eruption. Numerous aircraft thermal IR images were acquired and analyzed in the months following the eruption. See Fig. 47. The repetitive coverage, regional scale, and low cost of thermal IR images from satellites make this an attractive method for monitoring volcanoes. Landsat TM band 6 acquires thermal IR images with a ground resolution cell of 120m, which should prove useful for monitoring volcanic activity, especially on nighttime image, when the interfering effects of solar heating are absent. The plume from the 1973 eruption of the Russian volcano Tiatia on Kunashir Island shows clearly on Landsat MSS images. The ability to monitor size and distribution of volcanic plumes may prove useful in

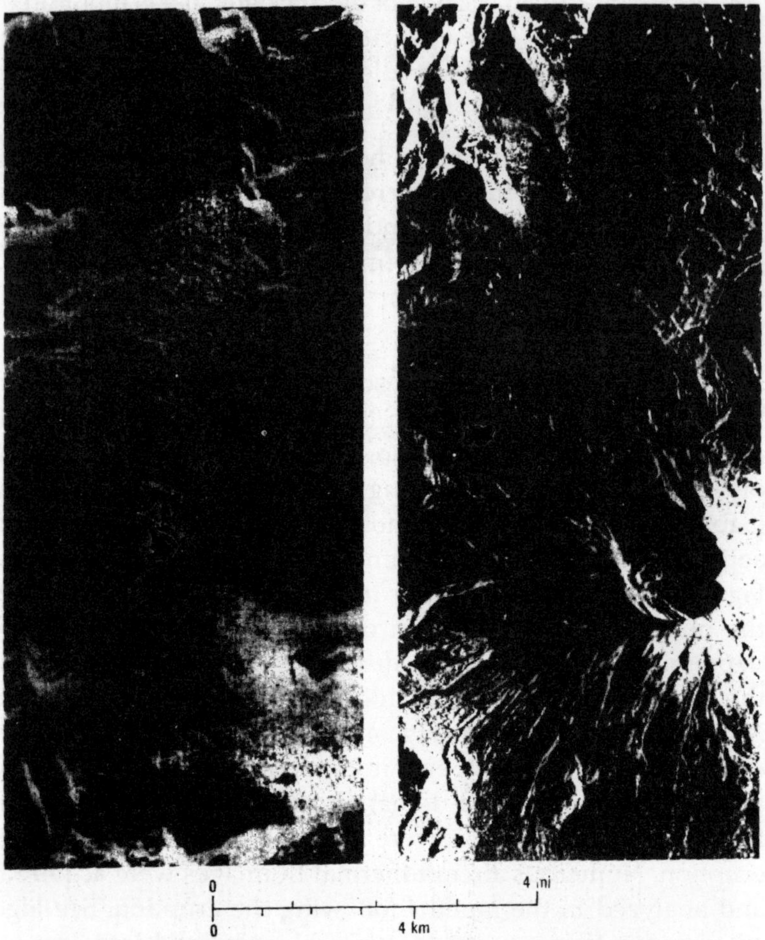

A. SEASAT L-BAND IMAGE ACQUIRED AUGUST 13, 1978. LOOK DIRECTION TOWARD NORTHEAST.

B. AIRCRAFT X-BAND IMAGE ACQUIRED JULY 7, 1980 LOOK DIRECTION TOWARD WEST

Fig. 46. Radar images of Mount St. Helens acquired before and after the May 18, 1980, eruption (After Sabins, Jr., 1987).

planning the rehabilitation of areas covered by ash, Landsat images are used to delineate flooded areas. Landsat images have also been used for flood-damage assessment. Flooded area are typically cloud covered and are rarely recorded on Landsat images. However, radar, with its cloud-penetration capability,

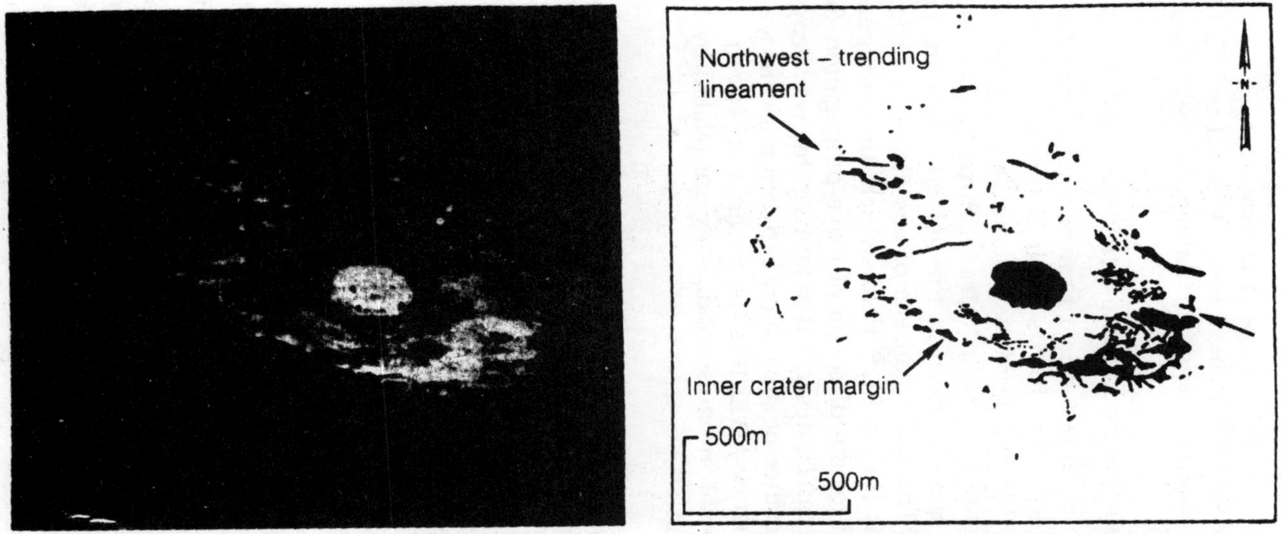

A. THERMAL IMAGE (8 TO 14 μm). BRIGHT SIGNATURES ARE HOT AREAS.

B. INTERPRETATION MAP. BLACK SPOTS INDICATE HOTTEST TEMPERATURES.

Fig. 47. Nighttime thermal IR image of Mount St. Helens acquired August 20, 1980 (After Friedman et al., 1981).

is well suited to monitor floods. It is desirable to have an operational radar satellite system, such as Seasat or SIR, that can provide all-weather images for damage assessment and reclamation work.

Principle Electromagnetic Remote Sensing

Electromagnetic radiation is a form of energy transfer in the free space, which exhibits both wave and particle properties (Hunt, 1980). According to its wave properties, the electromagnetic energy is seen to travel through space in a plane harmonic wave pattern at the velocity of light, i.e., about 3×10^8 m/s. The wave consists of one electric (vertical) and one magnetic (horizontal) field, which are orthogonal to each other and to the direction of wave propagation. See Fig. 48. The wave can be described in terms of the wavelength λ which is the distance of separation between adjacent wave peaks or its frequency f which is the number of wave peaks passing a fixed point in one second. They are related by the following equation :

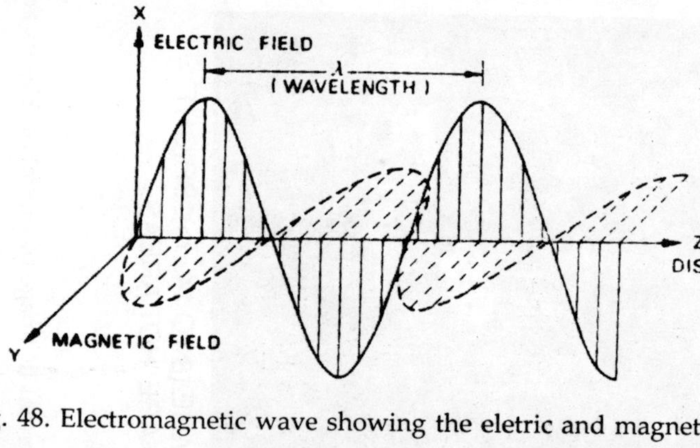

Fig. 48. Electromagnetic wave showing the eletric and magnetic fields.

$$\lambda f = c \qquad ...(1)$$

where c is the velocity of light. These wave properties as exhibited by electromagnetic radiation represent interaction between energy and matter on a macroscopic scale. Electromagnetic energy is also observed to be transferred in discrete units called quanta or photons. This gives rise to the particle properties of electromagnetic radiation. The energy of radiation E is related to the frequency f via a constant value known as Planck's constant h which is 6.6256×10^{-27} erg sec. It is given by the following equation :-

$$E = hf \qquad ...(2)$$

By substitution into equation (1) we can relate the particle and wave perties of electromagnetic radiation as :-

$$E = hc/\lambda \qquad ...(3)$$

Thus, the energy of the photon varies directly with the frequency and ely with the wavelengths of the radiation. These properties represent actions between energy and matter on an atomic and molecular scale. It is observed that all bodies with a temperature of above absolute zero (°K or –273°C) will emit electromagnetic radiations over a broad range of wavelengths. As the absolute temperature T of a body changes, the wavelength of the maximum radiation λ_{max}, or the dominant wavelength, also shifts or is displaced according to the following equation :

$$\lambda_{max} = \alpha/T \qquad ...(4)$$

where α is a constant equal to 2898 μmK. This is known as Wien's displacement law. Fig. 49 shows the shift of the

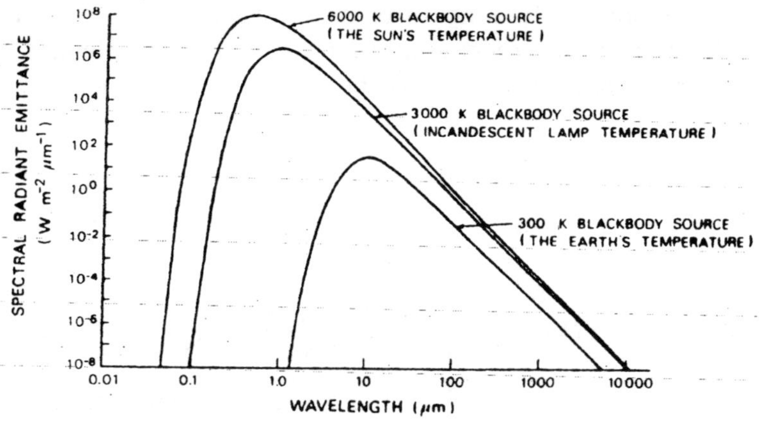

Fig. 49. Spectral radiant emittance curves for 6000K, 3000K and 300K blackbody sources (After Slater, 1980).

dominant wavelengths to the shorter region as the blackbody temperatures increases from 300K to 6000K. The black body is a hypothetical body which absorbs all the radiation incident upon it and emits the maximum amount of radiation at all wavelengths. It would reflect no light, hence it is black colour. The total amount of radiation emitted by a black body, i.e., the radiant emittance W, is proportion to the fourth power of the absolute temperature T in Kelvin of the body such that

$$W = \sigma T^4 \qquad ...(5)$$

Where W is the energy radiant per second per unit area of the surface of the body, and σ is the Stefan-Boltzmann constant equal to 5.669×10^{-12} w/cm^2K^4. As the temperature increases, the radiant energy emitted by an object increases very rapidly. This is known as the Stefan-Boltzmann law. But for a real body, the equation (5) becomes as :-

$$W = \Sigma\sigma T^4 \qquad ...(6)$$

Where Σ is the emissivity of the body which lies between 0 and 1. The Wien's displacement law and the Stefan-Boltzmann law are combined together into a more general law defined from quantum theory known as Planck's law which expresses the amount of energy $E(\lambda)d\lambda$, present in the radiation from a perfect emitter and having a wavelength in the range from λ to $\lambda + d\lambda$ by the following equation :-

$$E(\lambda) = \frac{C_1}{\lambda^5[\exp(C_2/\lambda T) - 1]} \qquad ...(7)$$

Where, C_1 and C_2 are constants. Equation (7) can be written as :

$$E(\lambda) = \frac{3.74151 \times 10^8}{\lambda^2[\exp(1.43879 \times 10^4)/\lambda T - 1]} \qquad ...(8)$$

where E(λ) is in $Wm^{-2}\mu m^{-1}$ and λ is μm. Therefore, the computed E(λ) is the radiant energy given in watts, within a spectral interval of 1 μm, emitted from a blackbody having an area of $1m^2$ into a hemisphere (Slater, 1980). The form of this curve is shown in figure 49. The area under the curve is evaluated as:-

$$\int_0^\infty E(\lambda)d\lambda = \sigma T^4 \qquad ...(9)$$

By arranging the electromagnetic radiation according to wavelength, frequency or energy, a continuum of energy called electromagnetic spectrum can be defined. In remote sensing, the more useful regions of the electromagnetic spectrum are the visible (0.4 – 0.7 μm), the reflected infrared (0.7 – 3 μm), the thermal infrared (3-5 μm and 8-14 μm) and the radar (0.3 – 300 cm) regions.

For terrestrial remote sensing, the most important natural source of electromagnetic radiation is the sun which has a surface temperature of about 6000K and radiates energy covering wavelength regions in Ultraviolet, visible and infrared. The dominant wavelength occurs at 0.5 μm (green light) which is visible to human eyes. This represents the reflected solar energy which permits us to see earth features. The surface temperature of the earth is about 300 K and its dominant wavelength occurs at 9.7 μm, which falls in the thermal infrared region of the electromagnetic spectrum. This represents the emitted energy from the earth and is more easily detected at night because of its much lower magnitude in comparison with the reflected solar energy. In remote sensing, the wavelength of 2.5 μm is used as the upper limit for reflected solar energy whilst the wavelength of 6 μm is the lower limit for self-emitted thermal energy. Electromagnetic energy, as it carries information from the earth to a remote sensor in the air or space, is seriously attenuated by its passage through the atmosphere. The atmosphere contains gas molecules and aerosol particles such as water droplets, dust and smoke, which give rise to scattering and absorption of the electromagnetic energy. In order to obtain good quality imagery, proper filter systems have to be employed on the remote sensors to eliminate or minimize scattering effects. See Fig. 50. In the atmosphere, electromagnetic radiation is

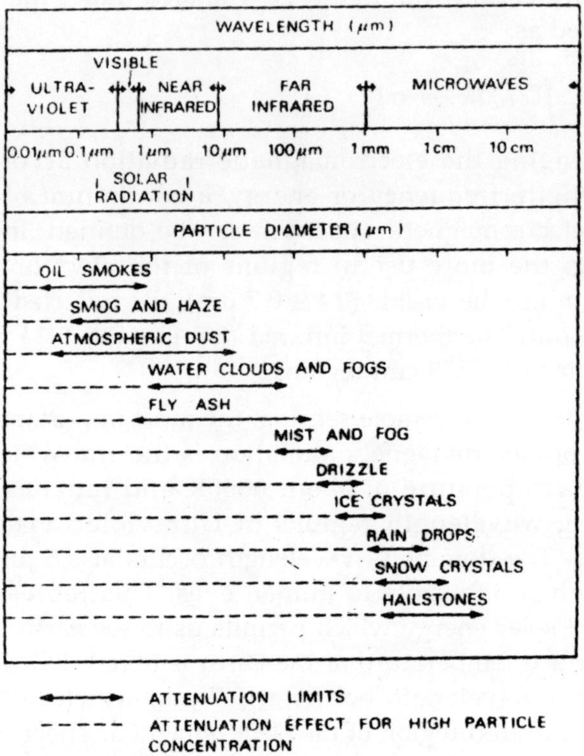

Fig. 50. Attemation to radiation of different wavelengths by common atmospheric constituents other particles (After Tomlinson, 1972).

effectively absorbed by gas molecules, e.g., water vapour, carbon dioxide, oxygen and Ozone (O_3). There are certain "spectral windows" in the atmosphere through which the electromagnetic energy of certain wavelengths can be fully transmitted, e.g., 3 to 5 μm and 8 to 14 μm through which emitted thermal energy from the earth can be transmitted. Similarly, the window in the 1mm to 1m wavelength region permits radar and microwave energy to be transmitted. Attenuation coefficient is the factor by which the radiation through a medium is reduced in traveling a distance of one wavelength in the medium. See Fig. 51. When the electromagnetic energy eventually reaches the earth, it is

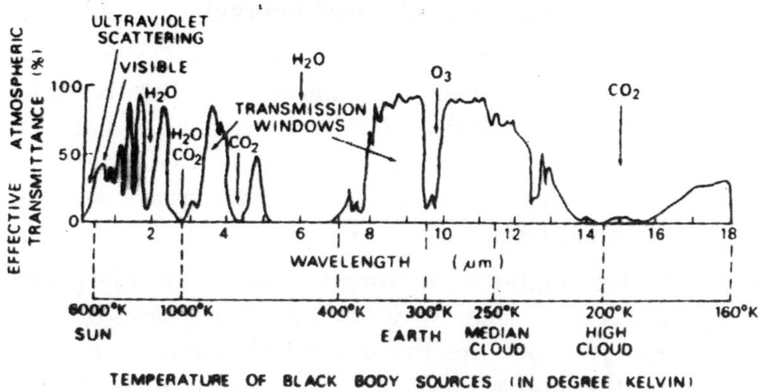

Fig. 51. Radiation transmission through the atmosphere by radiant energy of different wavelengths (After Tomlinson, 1972).

further modified through interacting with features on the earth's surface. Some of the energy is reflected and the rest enters the features as a refracted wave front which may either be absorbed, or transmitted through the features, depending on the nature of the materials making up these features and the wavelengths of the energy. The diffuse reflections of terrestrial objects give rise to colour information, and are most useful as a source of spectral data in remote sensing. The energy absorbed by the earth will eventually be released again in the form of heat as emitted energy. Added to the geothermal energy emitted from the interior of the they form another important source of electromagnetic radiation for sensing. Total energy detected can be given by the following equation :

Total energy detected = source energy – absorbed energy – transmitted energy – reflected energy + emitted energy ...(10)

Equation (10) provides the basis for passive remote sensing, i.e., employing radiation naturally reflected or emitted from the terrain. Active remote sensing utilizes electromagnetic radiation provided by the sensor itself.

Resource Exploration (Geothermal Energy)

Geothermal energy is obtained from subsurface reservoirs of steam or hot water that are shallow enough to be drilled and exploited economically. Most of the steam and hot water is used to generate electricity, but some is used directly for heating, as in Iceland. The following conditions are necessary for a geothermal reservoir :

1. A large, high-temperature heat source must be present at relatively shallow depth. Intrusive masses of young igneous rock are the usual heat source, and most geothermal areas are associated with surface or subsurface igneous rocks of Cenozoic age.
2. Porous and permeable reservoir rocks filled with steam or hot water must occur near the heat source. A variety of rocks can serve as geothermal reservoirs. In the Imperial Valley, California, poorly consolidated sandstones of late Tertiary age are the reservoir rocks. At the Geysers in northern California, the reservoir occurs in highly fractured sedimentary and volcanic rocks.
3. A natural recharge system must replenish the reservoir with water as steam or hot water is produced.
4. An impermeable zone above the reservoir is necessary to prevent the escape of steam and hot water. Convective flow to the surface would dissipate the heat on an unconfined reservoir. Heat losses due to thermal conduction through the rocks are relatively minor because of the low thermal conductivity of rocks.

Some geothermal reservoirs have no visible or thermal expression at the surface and are not detectable by remote sensing methods. Many geothermal reservoirs, however, have surface thermal expressions ranging in intensity from a minor increase in ground temperature to the presence of hot springs and geysers. Hot springs and geysers commonly occur along faults and fractures that allow hot water to escape from the reservoir. Thermal springs and zones of hydrothermal alteration associated with a geothermal area in Mexico have been interpreted from thermal IR images. At the Geysers area, hot springs and fumaroles were also detected on thermal IR images and there was some local evidence of higher ground temperatures. However, there was littie evidence of a regional surface temperature anomaly on the images of the Geysers area. Iceland is the site of frequent volcanic eruptions, including six since 1946, and associated geothermal activity. Space heating and hot water for the capital city of Reykjavik have long been supplied from geothermal sources. The 17 high-temperature geothermal areas are concentrated along the zones of active rifting and volcanism. Vatnajokru is an ice cap approximately 100 km in diameter that overlies two known high-temperature geothermal areas. The aerial photograph and thermal image show the Kverkfjoll geothermal area, which is located on the northern edge of the Vatnajokull ice cap. See Fig. 52. As shown on the interpretation map of Fig. 53, the geothermal area is located between the Kverkjokull outlet glacier on the east and a re-entrant of bedrock on the west. The thermal IR image is not rectilinearized, which accounts for the geometric »iipression at the east and west margins. The ice and bedrock have ely cool signatures (dark tones). The geothermal features, the melt water, and the bedrock ridges that confine the outlet glacier have warm signatures. The north-trending geothermal feature is at least 2 km. long and includes two separate hot areas at the north-east end. Near the south margin of the image, warm signature mark concentric crevasses and an ice cauldron subsidence feature that are caused by subsurface melting of the glacier. The warm stream emerging from the snout of the outlet glacier is melt-water that has flowed along the base of the glacier from a subglacial geothermal source. The topographic expressions of some geothermal features are detectable on the aerial photograph, but are less pronounced than on the IR image.

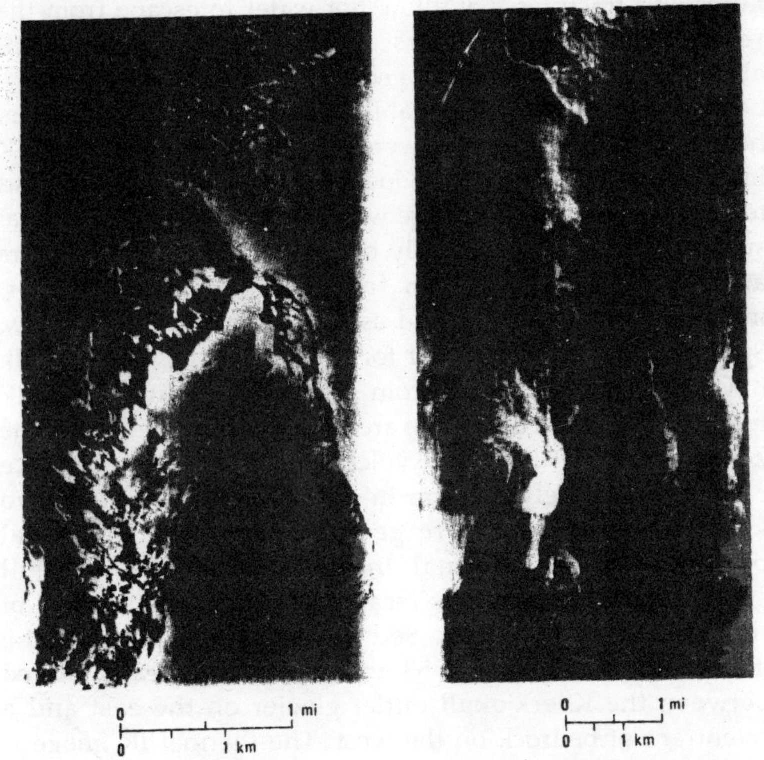

A. AERIAL PHOTOGRAPH ACQUIRED AUGUST 24, 1960, BY THE U.S. AIR FORCE.

B. NIGHTTIME THERMAL IR (1.0 TO 5.5 μm) IMAGE (NOT RECTILINEARIZED). ACQUIRED AUGUST 22,1966, BY THE U.S. AIR FORCE, CAMBRIDGE RESEARCH LABORATORIES.

Fig. 52. Kverkfjoll geothermal area and Kverkjokull outlet glacier, Ialand (After Friedman et. al., 1969).

Geothermal vents and hot springs have been detected on thermal IR images in such diverse localities as Japan, Italy, Ethiopia, and the United States. Remote sensing is especially useful in remote areas where the surface expression of geothermal activity has not been located by conventional means. Thermal IR images are ideal for detecting fumaroles, steaming ground, and hot springs associated with very active geothermal areas such as Iceland and Yellow-stone National

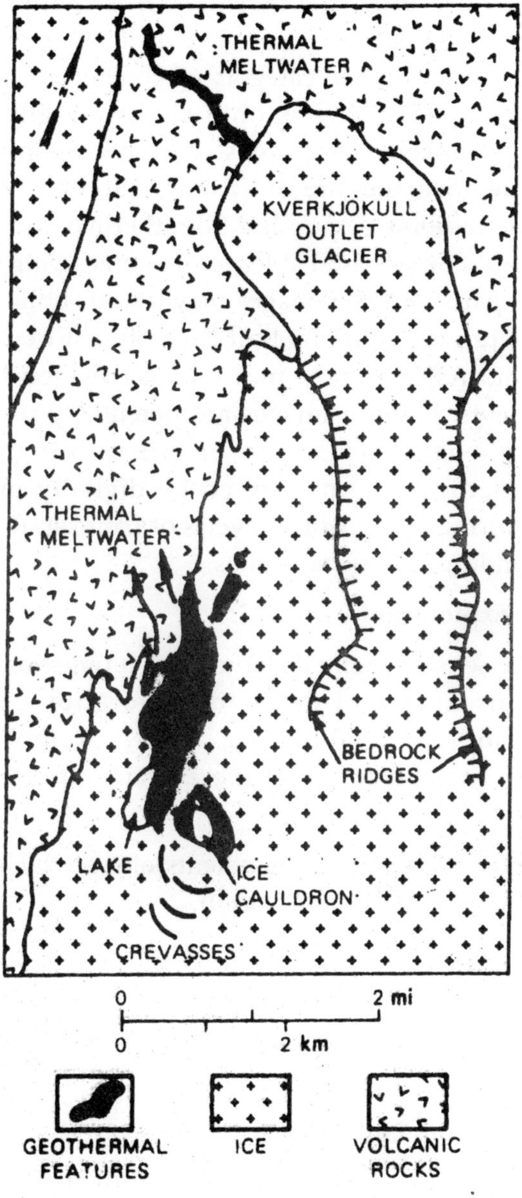

Fig. 53. Interpretation map of the thermal IR image of the Kverkfjoll geothermal area (After Friedman et al., 1969).

Park. There are blind geothermal areas that lack surface thermal or alteration expression. Between the active areas and the blind areas is a broad category of geothermal areas where the surface temperature is only slightly higher than the surrounding areas. These areas with low-intensity surface temperature anomalies are difficult to detect on IR images or on airborne radiometer profiles. Both thermal and reflectance images should be acquired at least three times ping the diurnal cycle. Comparison of the images may reveal subtle anomalies. An 8-to-14 μm image in the Raft River area if Idaho revealed a weak thermal anomaly that was confirmed by ground measurements. Landsat images are potentially useful during mining of coal. The status of trip mining and land reclamation may be monitored by digitally processing i acquired during the repetitive cycles of Landsat. Roof falls are hazards underground coal mines.

Resource Exploration (Mineral)

Remote sensing methods have great promise as techniques for both aissance and detailed exploration of nonrenewable resources (Sabins Jr., 1987). Remote sensing has proven valuable for mineral exploration in following four ways :-

1. Mapping regional lineaments along which groups of mining districts may occur.
2. Mapping local fracture patterns that may control individual ore deposits.
3. Detecting hydrothermal altered rocks associated with ore deposits.
4. Providing basic geological data.

In many mineral provinces, mining districts occur along linear trends that range from tens to hundreds of kilometres in length. These trends are referred to as mineralized belts or zones, and many deposits have been found by exploring along the projections of such trends. The availability of Landsat images has enabled geologists to evaluate the relationship between mineral deposits and linear structural features. Other lineaments are formed by linear ridges, aligned ridges, and tonal boundaries. Within a mineral province, areas with numerous fracture intersections are good prospecting targets because fractures are conduits for one-forming solutions. Local fracture patterns are fnappable on enlarged Landsat images, especially those acquired at low sun angles and those that have been digitally filtered to enhance fractures. Many ore bodies are deposited by hot aqueous fluids, called hydrothermal solutions, that invade the host rock, or country rock. During formation of the ore minerals, these solutions also interact chemically with the country rock to alter the mineral composition for considerable distances beyond the site of ore deposition. The hydrothermally altered country rocks contain distinctive assemblages of secondary, or alteration, mineral that replace the original rock constituents. Alteration minerals commonly occur in distinct sequences, or zones of hydrothermal alteration, relative to the ore body. These zones are by changes in temperature, pressure, and chemistry of the hydrothermal solution at progressively great distances from the ore body. At the time of ore deposition, the zones of altered country rock may not extend to the surface of the ground. Later uplift and erosion expose successively deeper alteration zones and eventually the ore body itself. Not all alteration is associated with ore bodies, and not all ore bodies are marked by alteration zones, but these zones are valuable indicators of possible deposits. Fieldwork, laboratory analysis of rock samples, and interpretation of aerial photographs have long been used to explore for hydrothermal alteration zones. In regions where bedrock is exposed, multispectral remote sensing is useful for recognizing altered rocks because their reflectance spectra differ from those of the country rock. Fig. 54 shows the reflectance spectra of hydrothermally altered rocks and minerals.

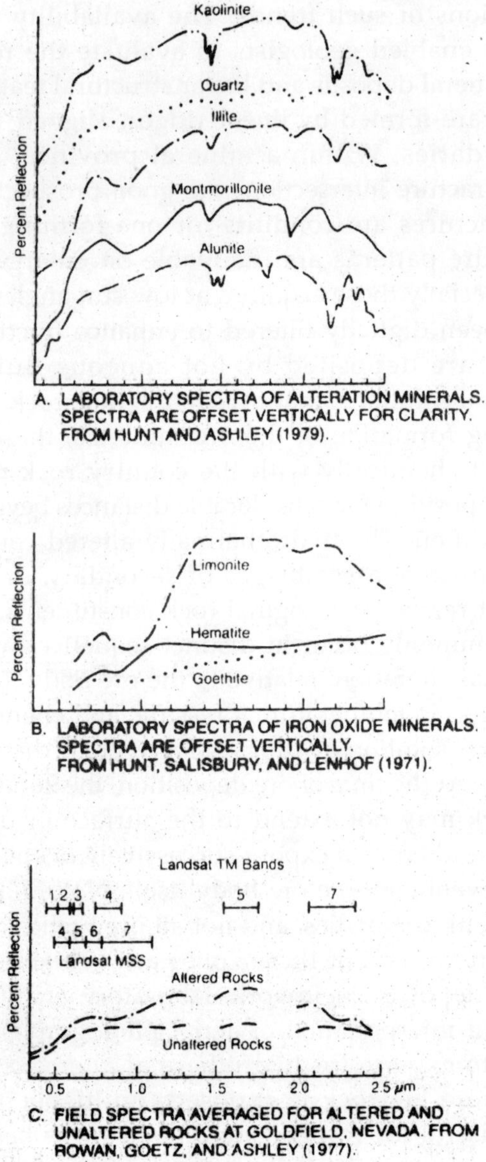

Fig. 54. Reflectance spectra of hydrothermally altered rocks and minerals (After Sobins, Jr., 1987).

Resource Exploration (Oil and Natural Gas)

The search for oil in unemployed onshore areas, such as portions of Africa and China, normally follows a pattern. It begins with regional reconnaissance and is succeeded by progressively more detailed and expensive steps that culminate in drilling a wildcat well. Wildcat wells are exploratory tests in previously undrilled areas, whereas development wells are drilled to produce oil and gas from a previously discovered field. A typical exploration programme proceeds as follows:-

1. *Regional Remote Sensing Reconnaissance :* Small-scale Landsat mosaics covering hundreds of thousands of square kilometres are especially useful in this phase. The objective is to locate sedimentary basins, which are areas underlain by thick sequences of sedimentary rocks. These basins are essential for the formation of oil and gas fields.

2. *Reconnaissance Geographical Surveys :* Aerial magnetic surveys are made to produce maps that record the intensity of the earth's magnetic field. Sedimentary basins have lower magnetic intensities than do areas underlain by non-sedimentary rocks such as granite and volcanic rocks. The aerial magnetic maps thus can confirm the presence of sedimentary basins. Surface gravity surveys are made that record the intensity of the earth's gravity field. Sedimentary rocks have a lower specific gravity than non-sedimentary rocks. Hence sedimentary basins are shown by lower values on the gravity maps. Gravity and magnetic maps may also show regional structure features.

3. *Detailed Remote Sensing Interpretation :* Individual digitally processed Landsat images are studied to identify and map geological structures, such as anticlines and faults, that may form oil traps. Promising structures may be mapped in detaile using

stereo pairs of aerial photographs. Radar images are used in regions of poor weather where it is difficult to acquire good photographs and Landsat images. At this stage, geologists go into the field to check the interpretation and collect samples of the exposed rocks.

4. ***Seismic Surveys :*** Explosives or mechanical devices are used to transmit waves of sonic energy into the subsurface, where they are reflected by geological structures. The reflected waves are recorded at the surface and processed to produce seismic maps and cross sections that show details of subsurface geologic structure.
5. ***Drilling :*** Wildcat wells are drilled to test the subsurface targets. The success rate in 1983 of wildcat wells drilled in the United States was only 17.5 percent.

The essentially all-weather capability and the ability to enhance geological structure in forested terrain have made side-looking airborne radar for oil exploration, especially in tropical regions. One can readily iret lithologic terrains and geological structures from these images. Landsat and radar images may be analyzed for surface evidence of geologic structures such as folds and faults that may form petroleum traps at depth. Some oil fields are marked at the surface by direct indications of the underlying hydrocarbons. Surface seeps of oil and gas that have leaked from subsurface traps are a well-known example. The original Drake well in Pennsylvania was located on the basis of oil seeps. In the early 1900s, oil fields were located in California on the basis of oil seeps. The recognition of oil and gas seeps is called direct detection. Escaping oil and gas may interact with surface rocks, soil and vegetation to produce anomalous conditions that may be clues to the underlying hydrocarbon deposit.

Classic examples of rock alteration occur at the Cement and Velma oil fields in southern Oklahoma. Sandstone outcrops in the area are typically red, but over the fields they are tan and gray. Gypsum ($CaSO_4.nH_2O$) is locally replaced by calcite ($CaCO_3$) over the fields. The colour change from red to gray has long been attributed to escaping hydrocarbons that have chemically reduced the red iron oxide in the sandstone to a noff-red iron compound. Donovan (1974) recognized another surface alteration effect, i.e., the secondary calcite and dolomite ($Ca_{1/2}Mg_{1/2}CO_3$) in the surface rocks have unusual carbon isotopic lues. These values indicate that hydrocarbons leaking from the reservoir were oxidized and the carbon incorporated into the secondary carbonate [minerals of the surface rocks. Similar carbon isotopic values occur over the Davenport oil field in central Oklahoma.

Each of the three following examples illustrates a particular aspect of remote sensing for oil exploration :-

1. Kenya: Chevron Overseas Petroleum acquired an exploration license in eastern Kenya and completed a photogeologic and field study in 1972. Landsat MSS images of the area became available in 1973 and were complied into the mosaic that was interpreted by Miller (1975). See Fig. 55. The drainage patterns on the interpretation map provide valuable geographic reference in this region of generalized base maps. See Fig. 56. Much geologic information is present on the Landsat images despite the relatively featureless nature of the terrain. Lineaments are a major feature in Kenya. The Lagh Bogal lineament that trends northwest is particularly significant because it marks the northeast boundary of a sedimentary basin that was confirmed by later geophysical surveys. See Fig. 57. Young volcanic flows from the black pattern in the west-central part (Fig. A). In the southeast part, large arcuate tonal bands may represent depositional patterns in elastic beds. A dark lobe extends southeast from the northwest part of the image and marks the outcrop of crystalline basement rocks with discernible

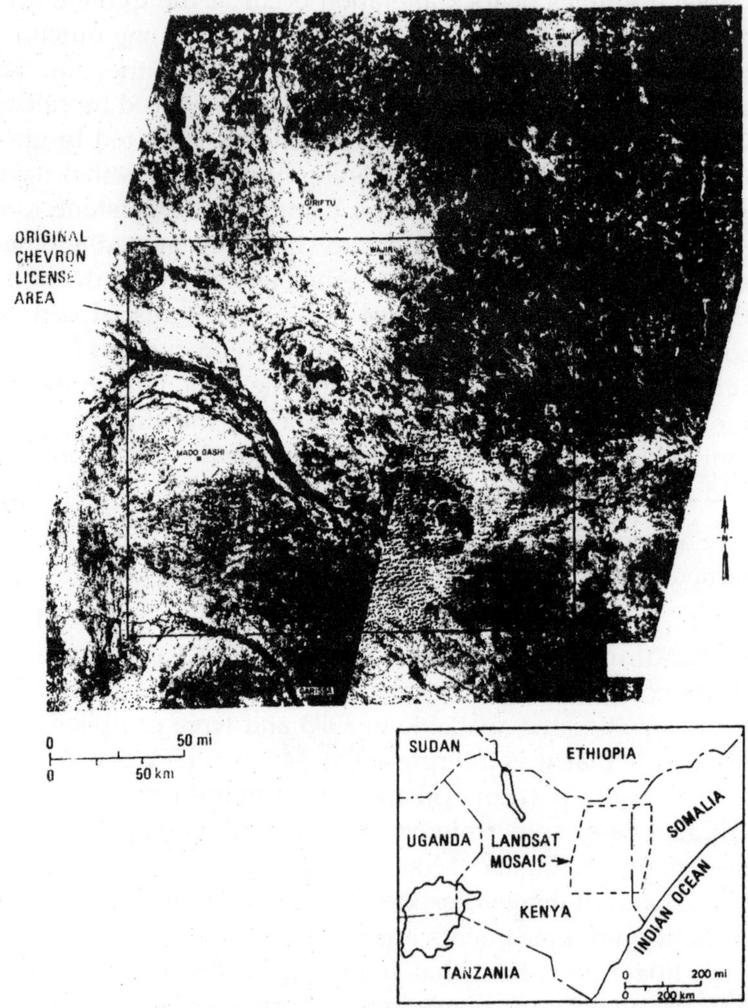

Fig. 55. Mosaic of eastern Kenya compiled from Landset MSS band-7 images (After Miller, 1975).

foliation trends. The image in Fig. B covers the southwest part, where dark basement rocks, with north-trending foliation patterns, crop out in the south-west part of the image. East of the basement outcrops, and probably in fault contact, are sands and clays of Pliocene age that form a triangular light-

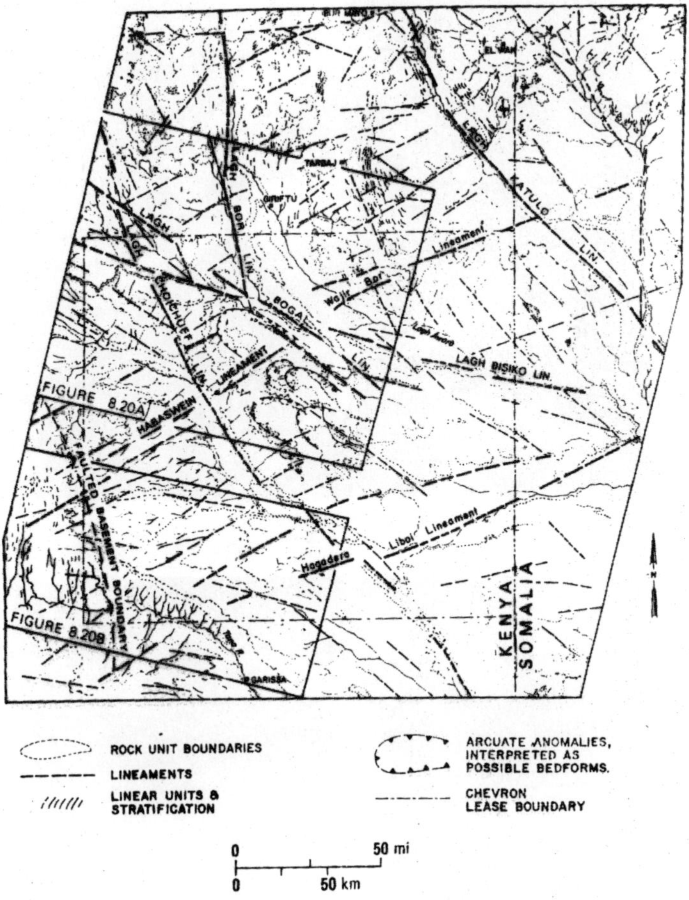

Fig. 56. Interpretation of Landsat mosaic of eastern Kenya (After Miller, 1975).

coloured outcrop through which flows the Tana River with its associated vegetation. North of the river, the Pliocene strata are capped by a dark layer of duricrust. In the southeast part, a thin wedge of strata with a gray tone occurs between the duricrust and the underlying light-toned strata. The eastward expansion of this wedge represent basinward thickening of

A. NORTHWEST PART OF THE CHEVRON LICENSE AREA.

B. SOUTHWEST PART OF THE CHEVRON LICENSE AREA.

0 40 mi
0 40 km

Fig. 57. Landset MSS band-5 images that cover parts of the Chevron exploitation license area in Kenya (After Millar, 1975).

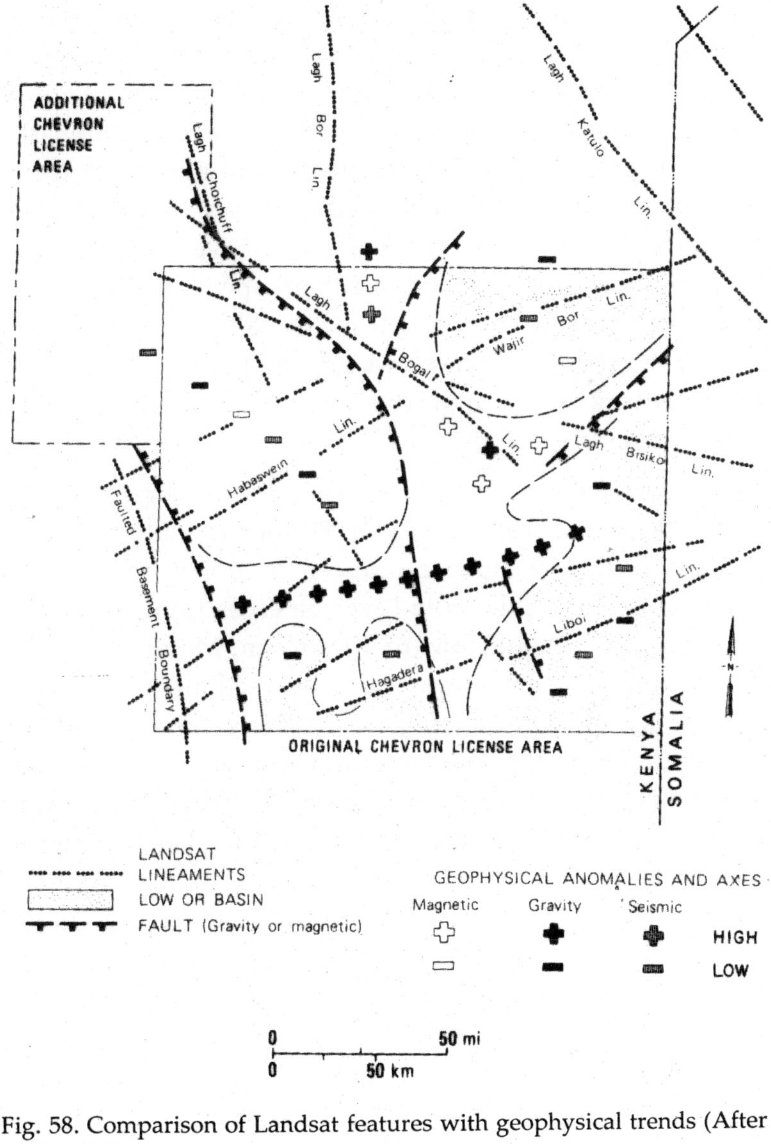

Fig. 58. Comparison of Landsat features with geophysical trends (After Miller, 1975).

the sedimentary section that was first observed on the Landsat image. Fig. 58 shows the results of gravity, magnetic, and seismic surveys. The Lagh Bogal lineament coincides in part with a subsurface fault, independently interpreted from the geophysical surveys, that forms the northeast boundary of the basin. Geophysical data indicate that the west border of the basin is not a single major fault zone but a combination of faulting and tilting. The northeast and northwest trends of the image lineaments in the northeast part are parallel with the gravity and magnetic positive trends. Several wildcat wells were drilled to test geophysical prospects but were dry because subsurface conditions were not conducive to hydrocarbon generation. However, the geophysical surveys and drilling confirmed the accuracy of the geologic interpretations of Landsat images.

2. ***The Sudan:*** Chevron compiled a mosaic of Landsat MSS images at a scale of 1:1,000,000 for the southern part of the Sudan. Fig. 59 shows a reduced-scale version of part of the mosaic. The White Nile River emerges from the swamp and flows northward toward Khartoum. Miller recognized the presence of a previously unknown sedimentary basin in the vicinity of the present day Sudd swamp. He also analysed the drainage patterns and noted that while there were numerous local bends and meanders, the major streams were relatively straight at the regional scale of the Landsat mosaic. These stream lineaments were interpreted as the expression of faults that formed the boundaries of the major basin and smaller sub-basins. Chevron then made aerial magnetic surveys that confirmed the existence of the sedimentary basin. A gravity survey added details to the evolving regional picture. The seismic surveys defined a number of potential oil traps, and wildcat drilling began in 1977. The first five wells were dry, but in 1979 the first oil was discovered in Sudan at Abu Gabra. Subsequently drilling discovered the Heglig, Unity, and Melut fields. See Fig. 60. Landsat

Fig. 59. Mosaic of Landsat MSS band-5 images of southern Sudan showing the outline of the original Chevron exploration concession area (After Sabins, Jr., 1987).

data were also employed in the operational phase of the project. Southern Sudan has a dry season and a wet season with drastically different terrain conditions. These terrain classification maps were valuable to the seismic crews for planning operations.

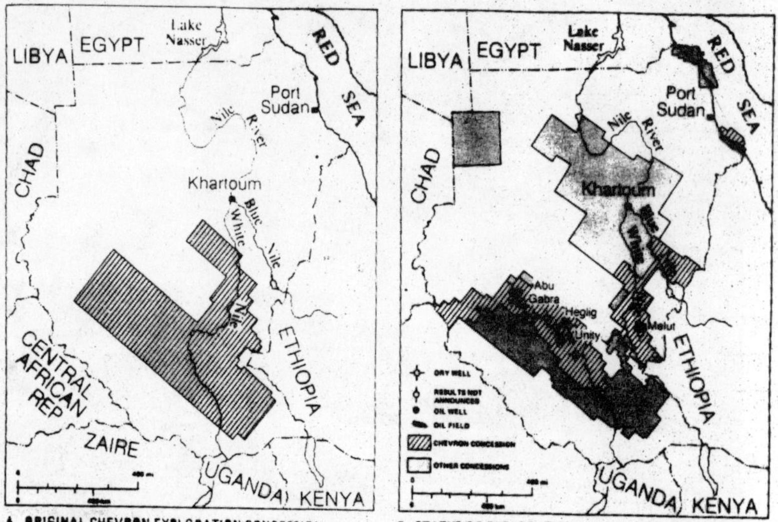

A. ORIGINAL CHEVRON EXPLORATION CONCESSION GRANTED IN 1974.

B. STATUS OF EXPLORATION AND CONCESSIONS IN 1982.

Fig. 60. Maps showing status of oil exploration in the Sudan (After Sabins, Jr., 1987).

3. ***Northwest Colorado :*** Northwest colarado is a mature exploration area where the surface structures have been drilled and one can directly evaluate the relationship of Landsat features to oil and gas fields. See Fig. 61. The major geologic features and the local structures associated with oil and gas fields are shown in the map of Fig. 62. The White River and Vinta Mountain uplifts and the Piceance Creek and Sand Wash basins are well expressed. The Piceance Creek basin contains major oil shale reserves of the Green River Formation (Eocene age) that crops out around the basin margins. The Grand Hogback monocline separating the Whiter River uplift from the Piceance

Fig. 61. Landsat MSS band-5 winter image of northwest Colorado (After Sabins, Jr., 1987).

Creek basin is especially prominent on the image. The Rangely anticline, in the southwest part of the map, is a major Chevron oil field that is outlined by strike ridges of resistant Cretaceous sandstones surrounding the eroded Mancos Shale outcrops in the core. The asymmetry of the anticline is indicated on the image by the gentle dip slopes on the north flank and the steeper slopes on the south. The Blue Mountain anticline to the north is equally well expressed, but is non-productive. Moffat, lies, and Thornburgh are small oil fields trapped at anticlinal closures that are outlined by resistant sandstone ridges on the image. The Danforth Hills and Wilson Creek oil fields are also anticlinal structures but are marked on the image by a change to very fine texture. The Piceance Creek gas field is formed by an anticline that is clearly indicated by the radial drainage pattern and by the streams that "wrap around" the structure.

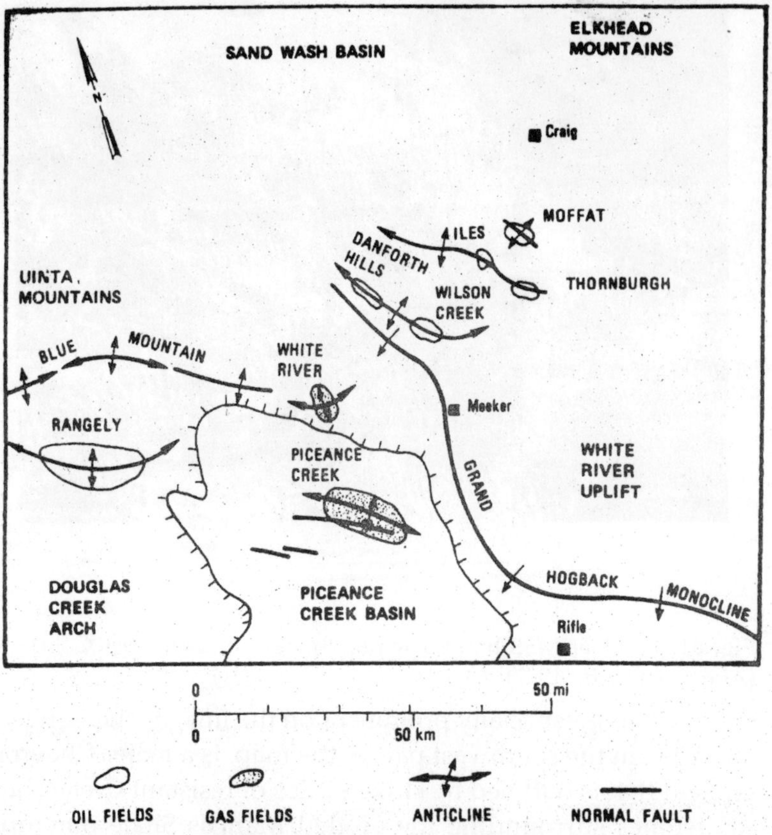

Fig. 62. Location map of northwest Colorado showing oil and gas fields and associated structural feaures (After Sabins, Jr., 1987).

Resource Exploration (Uranium)

The solutions that deposited the uranium also altered the host rocks and caused local colour anomalies on the outcrops. Aerial photographs have used extensively in exploring for these areas of altered rock. Digital processing of Landsat CCTs has the potential to recognize subtle alteration effects that may be obvious to the eye or on aerial photographs. Most uranium deposits in the United State occur in non-marine fluvial sandstone and conglomerate beds of the Colarado Plateau, Rocky Mountain basins, and southern Texas. See Fig. 63 for Uranium deposit model. Granite, granitic detritus,

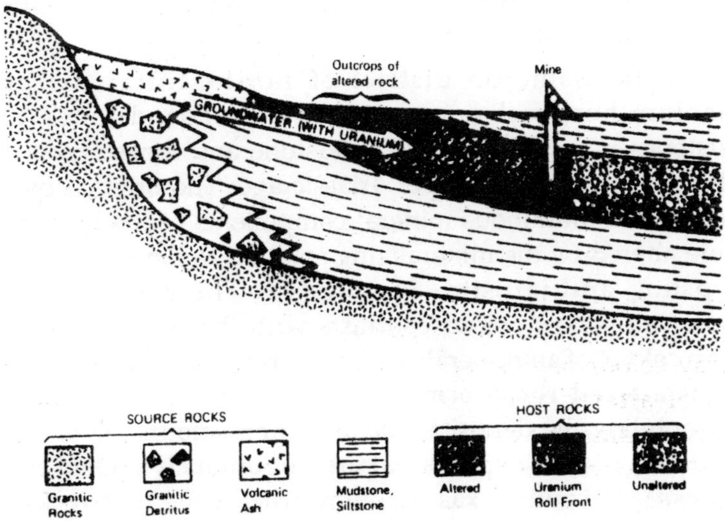

Fig. 63. Model for the formation of sedimentary uranium deposits (After Sabins, Jr., 1987).

and silicic volcanic ash and flows contain disseminated uranium in concentrations upto 10 parts per million. Some of this uranium is leached from the source rocks by oxygen-rich groundwater that then migrates into porous sandstone and conglomerate beds carrying the uranium in solution. Within these sedimentary rocks, the migrating water encounters reducing conditions caused by the presence of organic material, natural gas, or hydrogen sulphide and pyrite. The change from oxidizing to reducing conditions causes the uranium to precipitate as oxide minerals, primarily uranimite, that coat sand grains and fill pore spaces in the host rock. The ore deposits typically contain from 0.1 to 0.5 percent U_3O_8 and occur as tabular layers or as arcuate bodies called roll fronts. Later uplift and erosion may expose the ore to secondary oxidation. Outcrops of altered host rock are clues to possible ore deposits below the surface. The unaltered host rocks are typically drab in colour and contain organic carbon and pyrite. Oxidation by the migrating solutions destroys the carbon and converts the dark pyrite to iron oxide minerals that impart characteristic yellow, red, and brown colours to the altered rocks.

In the Cameron district of north-central Arizona, uranium host rocks are conglomerates, sandstones, and siltstones inter-bedded with mudstone and limestone of the Chinle Formation of Upper Triassic age. The original pyrite, calcite, and aluminous mineral components of the host rocks were altered by the mineralizing solution to limonite, alunite, gypsum, and jarosite. See Fig. 64. The resulting light brownish yellow colour contrasts with the typical purple to gray colour of unmineralized parts of the Chinle Formation. as of altered rock form elongate halos upto 400m long surrounding the deposits. The alteration colours are valuable guides to the ore deposits but are not uniquely related to ore deposits. In south Texas uranium district, the host rocks are channels filled with sandstone or conglomerate in the Catahoula Tuff. One important exploration method is to map the occurrence oi outcrops of the channels filled with potential host rocks. Geologic mapping in this area of low relief is hampered by lack of outcrops, non-distinctive rock types, a partial cover of younger gravel, and restricted land access. The U.S. Geological Survey conducted airborne scanner surveys to map the sandstone channel deposits. The nighttime thermal IR image showed that the sandstone channels had distinct bright signatures that contrast with the dark signatures of the clay-rich tuff units. These nighttime thermal IR signatures were consistent with the densities and thermal characteristics. At Lisbon Valey, Utah, uranium occurs in the Chinle Formation (Triassic age), which is poorly exposed at the surface. The present day white outcrops of Wingate Sandstone record the subsurface geochemical conditions that precipitated uranium in the Chinle Formation. This ability

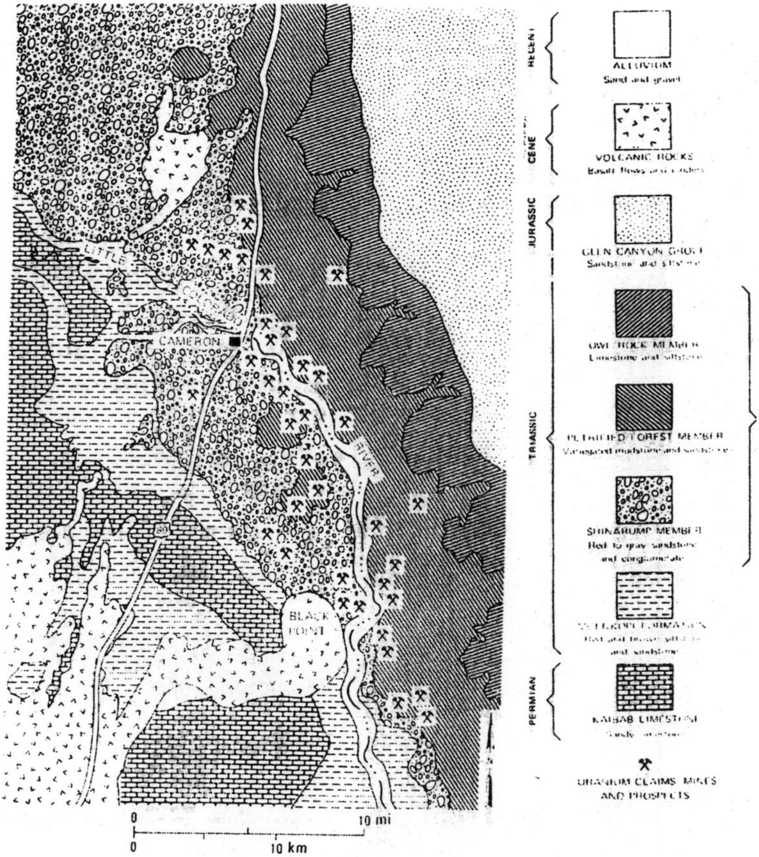

Fig. 64. Geologic map of the Cameron uranium district, north-central Arizone (After Chenoweth and Megbly, 1971).

to recognize anomalous colour patterns may be useful in uranium exploration. Landsat MSS was a new tool for mineral exploration; Landsat TM was a major improvement with its higher spatial resolution and additional spectral bands. Within the atmospheric window from 2.0 to 2.5 μm, kaolinite, montmorillonite, illite, and alunite have distinctive absorption features in their reflectance spectra as shown in Fig. 65. All four minerals have an absorption minimum near 2.2 μm, but the exact location of the minimum is different for each mineral. The air-borne imaging spectrometer (AIS) has the capability of recording detailed spectral features and thereby the potential for identifying specific alteration minerals.

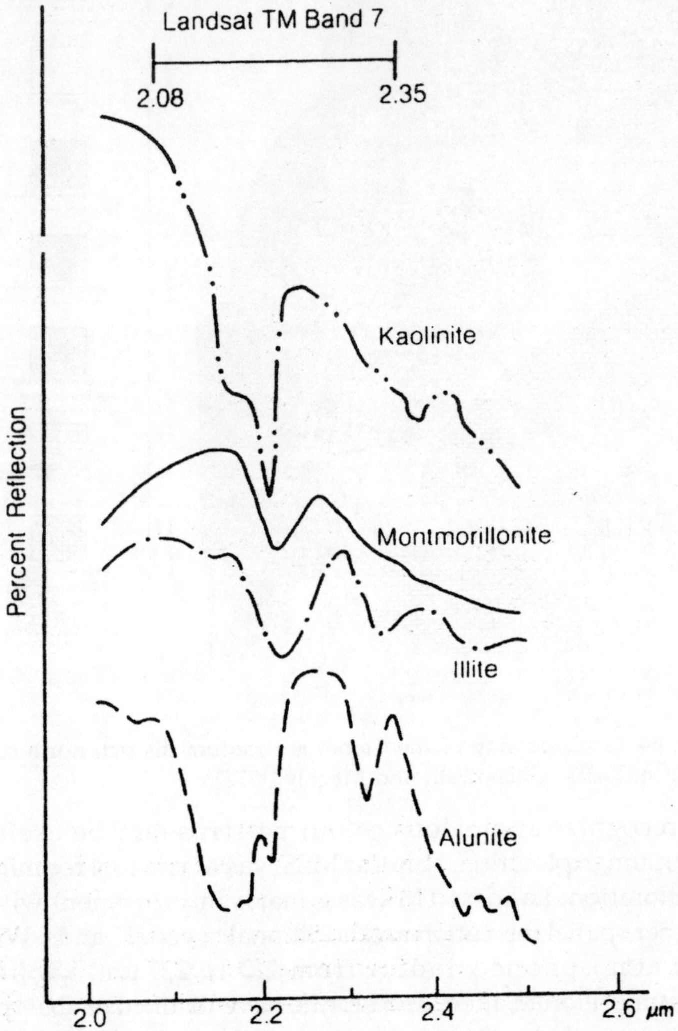

Fig. 65. Laboratory spectra of alteration minerals in the 2.0 to 2.5 µm atmospheric window (After Sabins, Jr., 1987).

In most of the temperate and humid climate zones of the world, deposits are commonly concealed beneath a cover of soil and on. The composition of residual soil reflects the composition of the underlying bedrock from which the soil was derived by weathering processes. Geochemical exploration techniques involve collecting water and soil samples and analyzing their metal content. Areas with high metal concentrations are then tested by core drilling. Vegetation growing in mineralized soil may have higher metal content in its tissue than vegetation in normal, or background, soil. This concentration of metals in vegetation is the basis for biogeochemical and geobotanical prospecting methods. These techniques are not applicable in areas where the soil has been transported, e.g., alluvial and glacial soils. Bio-geochemical exploration cosists of collecting vegetation samples that are analysed chemically for high metal concentrations that may indicate a concealed ore deposit. Geobotanical exploration searches for unusual vegetation conditions that may be caused by high metal concentration in the soil. The major geobotanical criteria for recognizing concealed ore deposited are : (1) lack of vegetation, (2) indicator plants, and (3) physiological changes, e.g., abnormal size, shape, and spectral reflectance characteristics of leaves, flowers, fruit, or entire plants. Chlorosis or yellowing of leaves results from an upset of the iron metabolism of plants that may be caused by an excess concentration of copper, zinc, manganese, or other elements. Field spectrometers measured reflectance of trees growing in normal soil and in mineralized soil overlying the deposit. See Fig. 66. Red spruce and balsam fir growing in the mineralized soil had higher metal concentrations than trees of the same species in unmineralized soil. In the reflected IR spectral region, the mineralized balsam firs have a higher reflectance than the normal trees, whereas mineralized red spruce have a lower reflectance than the normal trees. In the green spectral pn, the mineralized trees of both species have a higher reflectance. Geophysical Environmental Research operates a nonimaging airborne system acquires detailed

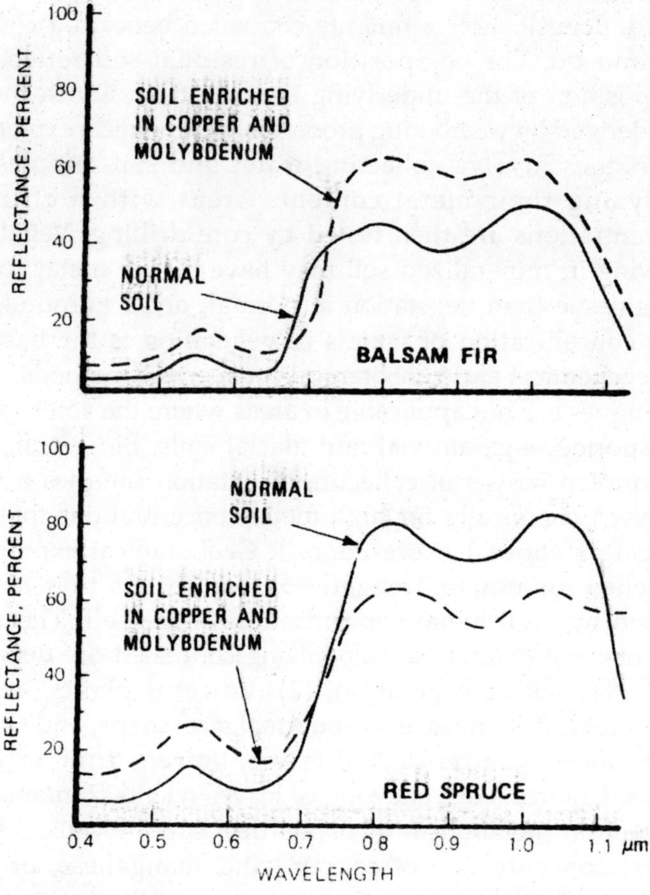

Fig. 66. Reflectance spectra of balsam fir and red spruce, growing in normal soil and in soil enriched in copper and molybdenum (After Yost and Wenderoth, 1971).

reflectance spectra. In the green band (0.5 to 0.6 μm) ance is higher for trees in the mineralized area. Beginning at a wavelength of about 0.7 μm, vegetation spectra have a steep upward slope to the high reflectance values in the IR region. See Fig. 67. This steep slope is shifted slightly toward shorter wavelength for the conifers growing in the mineralized area. This shift, called the blue shift, has been noted in vegetation over several mineralized areas and has exploration potential.

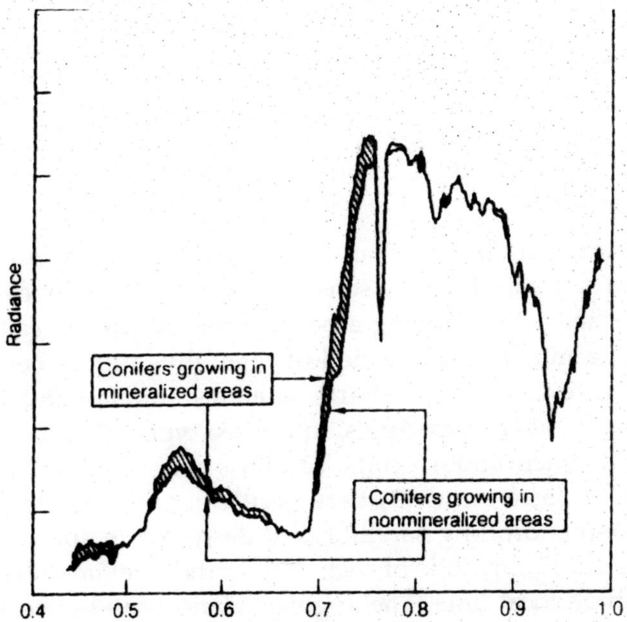

Fig. 67. Airborne reflectance spectra of conifers in the Cotter Basin, Lewis and Clark Country, Montana (After Collins et. al., 1983).

Space Platforms and Imaging Systems

The use of spacecraft orbiting regularly around the earth from a height of several hundreds of kilometres makes regular surveillance of the earth with suitable remote sensing devices, e.g., rockets, artificial satellites, manned or unmanned space vehicles. Details of these devices are given below :-

1. Rockets : These play an important part in space exploration. Earlier rockets were used as platforms for photographic systems. The coverage of these rockets photographs was very restricted because the rocket had to be fired vertically upwards and it had to land not far from its launching site. Also, the rocket went up and down so fast that the camera had at the most, only 8 minutes to take photographs about the earth. In 1972 the Skylark Resources Rocket (Hoare, 1972) was developed. Technical design improvements made automatic stabilization of the payload possible and, a programmed horizontal rotation by the electronic control unit, so that a larger area could be covered by the photographic system during the rocket 'rajectory. After re-entry into the earth's atmosphere a parachute recovery system permitted speedy recovery of the payload. In recent years the interest in resources rockets has dropped considerably.

2. ***Earth Satellites :*** The earth satellite provides an ideal platform space for I remote sensors. The earth satellite revolves around the earth following a pecific orbit. A satellite can stay aloft for a much longer period of time, thus nitting constant surveillance of the earth. Earth satellites are classified, ding to their orbital characteristics, into three types: (1) those with near sun-synchronous orbits, (2) those with equatorial geo-synchronous its, and (3) those with general orbits. Sun-synchronous orbiting satellites are designed in such a way that the ascending node of each orbit of the satellite will occur at the same local time. The angular relationship between the sun and the satellite's orbital plane is kept constant. In order to see as large an area of the earth as possible, the orbital inclination of the satellite is near to 90 degree or near-polar so that the coverage of the earth visible from the satellite is extended nearby between the two poles. Such a satellite is about 1000 km above the earth's surface, e.g. Landsat satellite series, and Heat Capacity Mapping Mission (HCMM) satellite. Geo-synchronous orbiting satellites remain overhead a specific point on the earth's surface. They are also known as geo-stationtary. The orbital period of these satellites is equal to the earth's rotation. This orbital height is 35,800 km. Such a geosynchronous orbit occurs over the equator, e.g., Applications Technology Satellites (ATS) for meteorological applications, and for communication applications. General satellites have neither a sun-synchronous nor a geosynchronous orbit.

3. ***Landsat Resources Satellites :*** The first three Landsats which share common orbital and image system characteristics

can be regarded as the first generation resources satellites in the series. Landsat 4 which was successfully launched on 16 July 1982 initiates a new generation of high-resolution resources satellites. The orbits of the Landsat series are all sun-synchronous. For the first three Landsats, the orbit inclination angle is about 99.1 degree, the orbital period is about 103.3 minutes, and the altitude of the satellite varies between 880 km. and 940 km. It takes 18 days for the satellite to return to the same spot on earth again. The coverage pattern des 14 per cent cross-track imagery overlap at the equator, which increases as the latitude increases so that at latitude 80 degree the image is as much as 85 percent. This gives rise to stereoscopic viewing tialforthe Landsat images. The imaging systems onboard Landsat 1,2 and 3 are return beam vidicon (RBV) cameras and the multi-spectral scanners (MMSS). See Table 4. It is capable of producing high-resolution pictures consisting of 4125 scan lines and 4500 picture elements per scan line, which is equivalent to a ground resolution of about 80m. The three cameras could image the 185 × 185 km area every 25 seconds. See Fig. 68. The MSS on the first three Landsat satellites is capable of imaging the earth's surface in four spectral bands simultaneously through a single optical system. There are 6 detectors for each band so that altogether 24 detectors are used for the MSS. Six lines of data are scanned at one time for a distance of 185 km long on the ground. During each scan, the electromagnetic radiation coming from the earth's surface and its atmosphere is reflected by the mirror into reflecting telescope optics and focused on fibre optic bundles of the detector array located in the focal plane of the telescope. The size and arrangement pattern of these fibre optic bundles determine the instantaneous field of view (IFOV) of the detector. Each detector produces a voltage according to the amount of radiation received. The voltage, which is an analogue signal, is converted to digital value by a multiplexer. The IFOV is 79×79 m, which is separated at an internal of 56 m on the ground between each sample. The radiation measurements have to be assigned to the 56×79m dimension in order to maintain the spatial relationship. This nominal dimension of 56×79m area is called a Landsat picture element or pixel. A geometrically corrected Landsat MSS scene of 185×185 km in area, normally consists of about 2340 lines and about 3240 pixels per line. A new generation of sensor :em is carried on-board Landsat 4, aiming at improving the spatial on, spectral separation, geometric fidelity and radiometric accuracy of the data.

Table 4. The spectrald wavelength intervals detected by the remote sensing systems on Landsatss 1 and 2 (After Taranik, 1978).

Data Channel	*System*	*Type of Radiation*	*Wavelength (μm)*	*NASA Code*
1	RBV	Visible, yellow-green	0.475–0.575	Band 1
2	RBV	Visible, green-red	0.580–0.680	Band 2
3	RBV	Visible, red-invisible IR	0.690–0.830	Band 3
1	MSS	Visible green	0.5–0.6	Band 4
2	MSS	Visible red	0.6–0.7	Band 5
3	MSS	Invisible reflected IR	0.7–0.8	Band 6
4	MSS	Invisible reflected IR	0.8–1.1	Band 7
(5)	MSS	(Invisible thermal IR)	(10.2–12.6)	(Band 8)*

*Landsat 3 MSS, channel not on Landsats 1 and –2.

4. *Seasat :* It is the first satellite designed to observe the earth's oceans with wave sensors. The satellite was launched into space on 28 June 1978 by NASA and Jet Propulsion Laboratory in a near-circular orbit with an indination angle of 108 degree at an altitude of 800 km. It circled the earth 14 times a day, covering 95 percent of the oceans on earth every 36 hours. There were 5 sensors onboard : (1) a radar altimeter (ALT), (2) a Seasat-A scatterometer system (SASS), (3) a synthetic aperture radar (SAR), (4) a visible and infrared radiometer (VIRR), and (5) a scanning multichannel microwave radiometer (SMMR). Seasat-1, however, failed in orbit on 10 October 1978 as a result of a massive short circuit in its

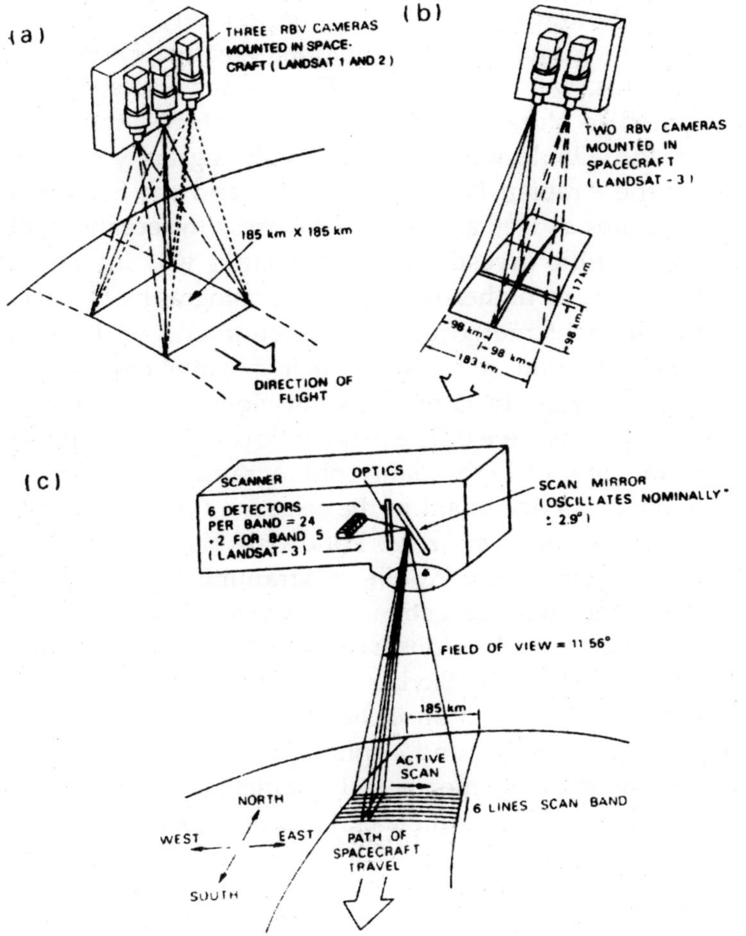

Fig. 68. Remote sensing systems on Landsats 1, 2 and 3 : (*a*) Therecamera RBV system on Landsats 1 and 2, (*b*) Two-camera RBV system on Landsat 3, and (*c*) Multispectral Scannar System (MSS) (After Taranik, 1978).

electrical system. But some useful data were already acquired during the 98 days of its useful life.

5. *Manned spacecraft* : With manned spacecraft, more direct control is possible in obtaining imagery of the earth from space. The orbiting altitude was about 161 km. at perigee and about 260 km. at apogee. For Gemini IV and V two specific photographic experiments, namely (*a*) Synoptic Terrain Photography and (*b*) Synoptic Weather Photography Experiments, were carried out. The former was specifically concerned to show major geologic structures, their form, colour and albedo with priority for photography over East Africa, the Arabian Peninsula, Mexico and the South-West United States as well as their coastal areas for oceanographic and geographic investigations. The latter was intended to provide a set of higher-resolution I photographs to cover a broad range of meteorological phenomena with special emphasis on cloud systems and their dynamic changes at 90 minute intervals. In later flight missions, more advanced cameras systems were d, The panoramic camera made possible the production of high quality photography of a large area of the lunar surface to aid in the selection ^potential landing sites and exploration areas. Following the completion of (Mercury, Gemini and Apollo programmes, a much larger spacecraft-the ab space station was launched on 14 May, 1973 which made possible lobservation of the earth for more extended periods. The Skylab followed a orbit at a nominal altitude of 435 km and an inclination angle of 50 degree. In mission numbers 2,3, and 4, photography of the earth was obtained by the crew members. In particular for Skylab-2, the Earth Resources Experimental Package (EREP) was carried onboard. This included three novel imaging systems: (1) the Multispectral Photographic Camera S-190A which was an array of six matched 70mm format cameras, (2) the Multispectral Scanner S-192 which operated in the visible and reflected Wrared bands, and (3) the High Resolution Camera S-190B. Both the S-190A and S-190B cameras which were equipped with image motion compensation were designed to provide photographs for topographic mapping applications. The successful orbital test flight of the space shuttle April 1981 ushered in a new-era of terrestrial remote sensing. The space shuttle is a much more flexible spacecraft than the Skylab space station and Provide an ideal platform for collecting remote sensing data and for testing advanced sensor systems because of its ability to carry the instruments into space and return them to the ground for recalibrating and refurbishing. In the second test flight of the Space Shuttle Columbia on 12th November 1981, the Office of Space and Terrestrial Applications-1 (OSTA-1) payload was carried into orbit. The OSTA-1 payload consisted of five experiments to the earth and its atmosphere, of which the Shuttle Imaging Radar A (SIR-A) experiment is most interesting. SIR-A was a side-looking, synthetic which looked at the earth's surface with horizontally polarized microwave radiation transmitted at L-band frequency (1.278 GHz) at an incidence angle of 50 degree. The ground resolution was about 40 m. About; 10 million km^2 of radar image of the earth were obtained by the space shuttle, Preliminary investigations of the radar images have revealed the of the data in studying structural and geomorphic features such as faults, folds, outcrops, and sand dunes in the tropical and arid regions on earth (Elachi et.al., 1982).

The Hydrosphere

The hydrosphere is a liquid water realm characterized by free flows in response to unequal stresses. The characteristics of fluid are the same as gases, exhibiting a layered arrangement according to density in order to maintain an equilibrium at rest. At a result, one expects a close interaction between the atmosphere and the hydrosphere at their interface. In nature water can also occur as a solid (ice) when the temperature is below its freezing point. The ocean is the dominant member of the hydrosphere and occupies 70 percent of the earth's surface. The ocean affects our climate and is in turn affected by the atmosphere, acting both as a heat reservoir for storing, distributing and releasing solar energy, and as the major source of atmospheric moisture. It collects the detritus of man and nature and is also an important source of petroleum. Its currents are used to dispense sewage and wastes. It is also an important source of food.

Developments in space remote sensing techniques have provided a better understanding of hydrosphere. It is customary to study four major characteristics of the ocean, namely, physical, biological, geological and chemical. The physical characteristics examine the properties of sea water such as temperature and density, oceanic circulation such as surface currents, deep water circulation, waves and tides and water mass descriptions. Biological characteristics examine the living organisms in the ocean, the fish and plants. Geological characteristics study the properties of different types of sediments deposited in the bottom of the oceans, seas and their coastal areas. Chemical characteristics deal with the composition of the sea water, such as its salinity, acidity, basicity and degree of pollution. The same remote sensor being employed to extract physical, biological, geological, and chemical characteristics of the marine environment.

The Hydrosphere (Biological Characteristics)

Sea-water colour refers to the spectrum of upwelling radiance just beneath the sea surface. The light coming directly from the sun is partly reflected at the sea surface and the remaining is transmitted into the sea. The transmitted energy is absorbed or scattered by the water molecules and other substances in it. Part of the light (3 to 5 percent) is scattered backward into the atmosphere again. Phytoplankton are the most important constituents. Phytoplankton are mostly microscopic and unicellular organisms restricted to the photic zone of the sea where the highest productivity is found. Photosynthesis by the phytoplankton takes place here. The phytoplankton contain chlorophyll a, the dominant photosynthetic pigment which strongly absorbs the energy in the blue and red regions of the visible spectrum. The sea water also contains sediments brought down by rivers and dissolved organic matter. Sea water can be divided into two classes. Case-1 water contains phytoplankton and their by-product which laigely determine the optical properties of the water body. Cash-11 water contains resuspended sediments, dissolved organic matter and terrigenous particles from rivers and glaciers. Different types of water have shown sufficient change in optical properties closely related to the amount of dissolved or suspended material to be distinguished by passive remote sensing. A small portion of the incident energy is caused by fluorescence torn dissolved and particular organic substances. By fluorescence, one is iring the wavelengths of light active in photosynthesis. Different types Ifhytoplankton seem to exhibit different intensities of fluorescence n. One specific remote sensor designed for the study of living marine through the detection of the variation in the concentration of phytolankton pigments is the Coastal Zone Colour Scanner (CZCS). The instrument is an imaging multispectral scanner operating in six spectral bands with an instantaneous field of view of 825 μ rad (0.047°) for a nadir field of view of about 800m from a spacecraft altitude of 955 km in a sun-synchronous orbit. The first five bands belong to the visible spectrum with which phytoplankton pigments detection, estimation and mapping can be carried out. The distribution of chlorophyll α can be carried out with multispectral scanness carried aboard aircraft. Chlorophyll α is regarded as an important environmental parameter indicative of the water quality, nutrient contents and pollution effects in coastal zones, not simply as an indicator of water productivity. The fluorescence of the green algae can be measured directly with laser induced fluorometer flying at low altitudes by aircraft.

The marine environment is full of other living organisms such as fish, seaweed, and algae which contribute significantly to the food chain. A large number of fish types found near the surface of the sea are detectable and aerial photography has been used quite successfully this purpose. For optimum results aerial photography should only be taken in clear, cloudless skies at solar angles between 20° and 50° from the horizontal to enhance contrast and to avoid glare. The indirect method makes use of sea temperature, wind direction, water salinity and water colour all collectable from remote sensors to locate fish. All these parameters are measurable with some degree of confidence from satellite platforms using appropriate sensors. Algae which are aquatic plants living in the bottom of the sea are easily detected by remote sensors. The blue-green algae occurred in dense masses at the sea surface during warm late summer periods. They served as indicators for wind-generated surface currents or internal waves. These algae depended on phosphate for their mass growth and can be indicative of a possible entrophication of the Baltic. They are capable of nitrogen fixation from the air and their occurrence is connected with the nitrogen budget of the Baltic.

The Hydrosphere (Chemical Characteristics)

Salinity and sea-surface temperature are two major factors controlling isolation of water in the sea. Salinity measures the total amount of salts in sea water. It is measured in parts per thousand and is usually between 33 parts per thousand and 38 parts per thousand (O/00) with the norm of 35 parts per thousand. Salinity also has a great impact on fie growth and distribution of phytoplankton as well as the abundance and fiigration of shrimp and fish population. In the estuarine environment where fresh and sea water mix, the change in salinity and sea water temperature is particularly significant. The microwave emission of sea water is dependent on temperature and salinity. The apparent temperature of sea water is dependent on salinity. The dielectric constant of sea water therefore seems to depend on salinity. It is known that microwave emission from sea water is more dependent on salinity at lower microwave frequencies and more dependent on temperature at higher frequencies. By selecting the L-band (1.43 GHz) frequency, a passive microwave radiometer can be used to measure remotely the salinity of sea water. Satellite platforms can be used to make salinity measurements. A second approach is to make use of landsat MSS digital data.

Water quality refers to the chemical, physical and biological characteristics of water in the hydrosphere. The chemical characteristics include the organic and inorganic substances such as heavy metals, pesticides, detergents and petroleum. All types of remote sensors have been employed to measure the chemical pollutants such as oil slicks and sewage sludge plumes in the hydrosphere. One important parameter indicative of the pollution strength of wastes in water is the biochemical oxygen demand. Highly polluted water has a large biochemical oxygen demand or a high content of dissolved oxygen. Most of the oil spills were associated with vessels. It was found that ultraviolet, thermal infrared and microwave sensors were potentially suited to oil detection. The presence of an oil film tends to reduce the surface roughness of the ocean giving more specular reflection so that the object-to-background contrast ratios are enhanced. Passive microwave sensors appear to have the potential to identify oil type and thickness at sea. Radar is the most suitable tool to map oil slicks because of its large area! coverage on a single image. The synthetic-aperture system detected surface concentrations of oil from all directions significantly better than the real-aperture system. A multispectral approach in remote sensing is more appropriate if early detection and monitoring of oil in the marine environment are to be achieved. See Fig. 69.

The Hydrosphere (Geological Characteristics)

Turbidity refers to the churning up of sediments by water to form a dense, heavy flow especially in the sea. As the water becomes more turbid, the transmittance of light through the water becomes more difficult and the reflectance becomes stronger, rendering the suspended sediments highly visible. The colour of turbid water is also distinctly different from that of clear water. Both low-altitude aerial photography and space satellite imagery have been used to measure turbidity and to map the pattern of sediment concentration. Remote sensing of the coastal zones can provide data on sediment volume, characteristics and depositional areas. By using a microdensitometer to measure image brightness, turbidity could be quantitatively determined. Photography was taken

Fig. 69. Seasat SAR image of the Santa Barbara Channel, Southern California where numerous natural seeps of oil, tar and gas exist in the coastal zone (After LO, 1986).

in mid-afternoon in order to eliminate sun glint. Landsat images provide a synoptic view of the coastal region and are ideal for mapping turbidity or suspended sediment distribution pattern. For mapping suspended sediment concentrations, it was found that the pattern appeared most distinctly in band 5 (0.6-0.7 μm). If one wishes to distinguish between different sediment types, the reliance on a single spectral band is not enough because different wavelengths penetrate different depths and help to separate different sediment types. Colour density slicing helped to delineate more clearly the suspended sediment patterns and to distinguish turbidity levels.

Bathymetry refers to the measurement of water depth. It depends on the degree of penetration of water achievable by the radiant energy of a certain wavelength. With remote sensing it is possible to determine the depth of water upto 30m. Both conventional aircraft and satellites provide platform to sense the water surface and the ocean bad. Large-scale aerial photography has to be obtained of the water area and the water depth is determined according to tonal variations, especially in the coastal areas. Water penetration and reflectance from the sea bad depend on the sun's azimuth and elevation angle in relation to the water surface and the sea bed, the nature of the sea bed, the direction of wave propagation and the sea state. Landsat MSS data, band 4 (0.5-0.6 μm) which covers the green or orange range of the visible spectrum, is generally preferred for the detection of water depth. Both the conventional aerial photography and Landsat MSS data are passive remote sensing. A more accurate remote sensing system for depth determination has to be an active one. The laser system is best employed in deep water areas. The synthetic aperture radar produces imagery for use in indirectly inferring water depths. Lodge (1983) identified three classes of features observable on Seasat SAR images of the sea that can be correlated with changes in depth.

The Hydrosphere (Physical Characteristics)

Water has great capacity for, and conductance of, heat. The temperature of sea water is a vital parameter in understanding the role of the ocean as a heat reservoir. Changes in temperature cause variation in the properties of the sea water and the life it supports. The temperature of the ea water can be measured with a standard mercury thermometer from a water sample collected at the rear of the ship. There are a large number of space satellites equipped with thermal infrared (8-15 μm) sensors designed for sea surface temperature measurement. The spectral radiance emitted by the sea is therefore partially absorbed by the atmosphere before reaching the satellite sensors. If the pressure, temperature and relative humidity profile is unknown, the accuracy of the corrected sea surface temperatures (SSTs) can still be obtained by the multispectral method. This involves making radiance measurements in two infrared wavelengths, one between 7 μm and 9 μm and the other between 10 μm and 12 μm. A straight forward application of thermal infrared imagery to map SST patterns without involving atmospheric correction problems was demonstrated by Zhing and Klemas (I982) who combined the remote sensing data with the synchronous or quasi-synchronous measurements in situ by vessels in the study area. See Fig. 70. The Scanning Multichannel Microwave Radiometer (SMMR) which was carried abroad the Seasat and Nimbus-7 satellites was designed specifically for the determination of global sea surface temperatures and wind speeds from space under different atmospheric conditions.

The detection of sea ice in the polar regions has great significance in climatic research and navigation activity. See ice occupies vast areas of the world's oceans, about 10 percent in the Northern Hemisphere and 13 percent in the Southern Hemisphere. The sea ice floats and is subject to large seasonal and annual variations in extent and composition. It insulates the ocean from the much colder air overlying it, thereby reducing the heat flux from the ocean. Its high albedo insulates the ocean from solar heating and hence the sea ice cover acts as a heat sink to cool the air and to reduce the turbulence in the atmosphere. The movement of the ice towards the open ocean helps to cool down the ocean water in the high latitudes. Winds and currents play a major role in the motion of the ice as well as the melting and forming of the ice. The ice concentration changes all the time, thus causing change in the heat flux. From the navigation point of view, the dynamic nature of the ice floes represents a major

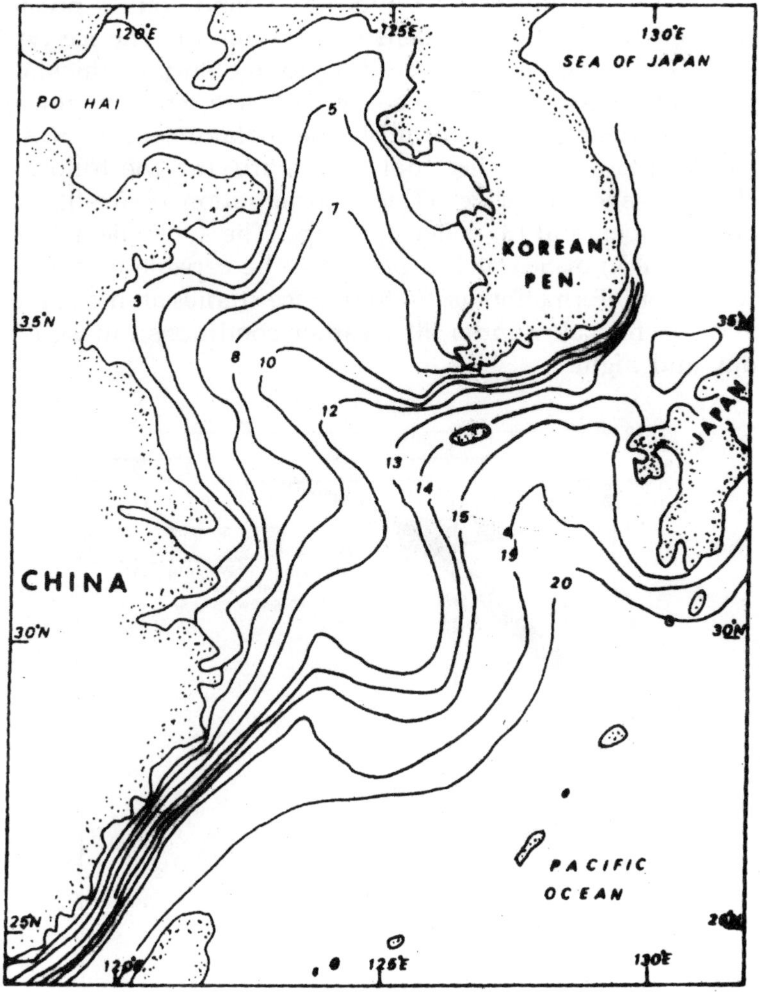

Fig. 70. Winter sea surface temperature (SST) pattern in the Yellow Sea and East China Sea (After LO, 1986).

hazard and an understanding of their movement patterns is essential. Microwave remote 'ensing is a suitable approach to sea ice detection. Since the relative dielectric constant of sea ice is normally very much lower than that of sea water, an ice-covered ocean has a higher emissivity than an ice-free ocean.

Sea ice and open water can be easily distinguished. Differentiating different ice types and conditions is possible with passive microwave sensors. See Fig. 71. The ice types are generally classified according to age and, or thickness. Another approach to detect sea ice is to sue active microwave remote sensing in the form of side-looking radars (SLAR). SLAR was a promising tool for identifying the following characteristics or sea ice : (1) ice concentration, (2) ice-floe size and number, and (3) water openings. The synthetic aperture radar (SAR) of Seasat has proved to be capable of giving a wealth of information useful for sea ice studies at micro, meso and macro-scales under all weather conditions during both day and night.

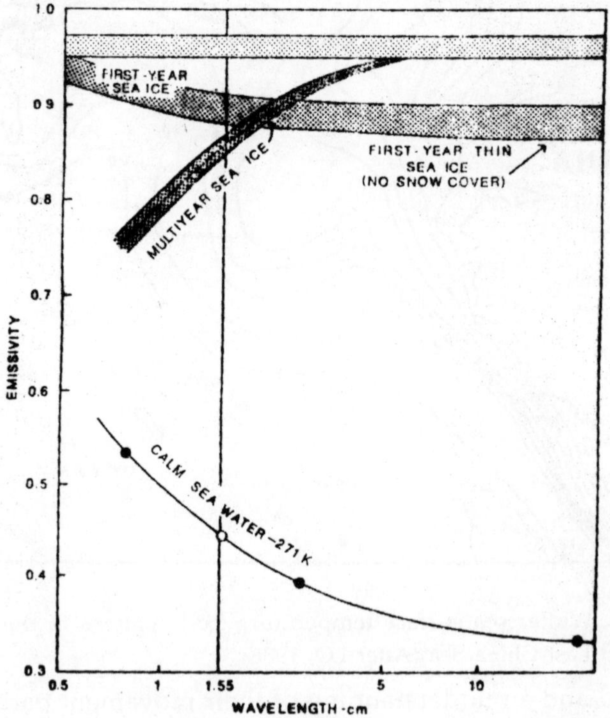

Fig. 71. Spectra of the three radiometrically distinct ice types and of open water (After LO, 1986).

The circulation of waters in the oceans involves both horizontal movements of water across the surface and vertical-horizontal movements within the body of ocean water itself. These movements depend on the difference in the density of water which is in turn influenced by its temperature and salinity. The horizontal movements of water at the surface also depend on the wind flows which are controlled by atmospheric pressure distributions. These surface movements are in the form of currents and drifts which can be easily detected by a variety of remote sensing techniques. The deep ocean circulation is not directly evident from the sea surface. One approach to detect current is to interpret patterns of water turbidity from aerial photographs. From the aerial photographs, the source of the suspended fine-grained sediments which caused the turbidity pattern could be located. The use of a space platform permits a better vantage point to carry out oceanographic interpretations from photography. The high-resolution Landsat imagery is better suited to detect surface water circulation. The water was classified according to the levels of turbidity observed. Thermal infrared and radar imagery can be used to detect surface currents. The thermal infrared imagery can detect water masses of contrasting temperatures, e.g., Gulf Stream off the eastern North Atlantic. The synthetic aperture radar onboard Seasat has also been able to pick-out the boundaries of the Gulf Stream clearly. The difference in water temperature on the two sides of the current gives rise to a change in wind stress, with smaller wind stress occurring on the colder side. See Fig. 72. This produces a difference in backscattering. The Seasat SAR which has a wide swath (100 km) is suitable to monitor the evolution of large-scale current systems in the ocean.

Sea state refers to the degree of surface roughness in the sea. This is closely related to wind stress at the interface between the hydrosphere and the atmosphere expressed in the form of waves. It is usual to distinguish between two types of waves the capillary and gravity waves. The capillary waves are small

Fig. 72. The Gulf Stream off Cape Hatteras as imaged by Seasat SAR on 31 August, 1978 (After LO, 1986).

rippies with less than 1.73 cm in wavelength. Their shape is controlled by surface tension of the water and approximates a sinusoidal form but with slightiy V-shaped troughs. Gravity waves have much longer wavelengths and are controlled by gravitational forces. The strength of the waves is determined by wind velocity, the fetch or the distances of water surface over which the wind blows and the duration of the wind blowing. Aerial Photography can be used to determine wind directions and gravity wave heights in the sea. More accurate determination of wave heights using photography requires the application of photogrammetry. Satellite remote sensors have been developed for the observation of ocean waves. These are the precision radar altimeter and the synthetic aperture radar. The radar altimeter measures the distance of the satellite above the earth and the mean roughness of the earth's surface. The sea surface is sampled at a specific rate. The synthetic aperture rader (SAR) is the second wave sensor which produces an image of the sea surface. Seasat SAR imagery is most suited for use to study on a synoptic scale the generation and propagation of long ocean waves in the open ocean. The distribution of the short gravity waves recorded by the Seasat SAR shows correlation with a number of significant larger scale phenomena, such as local wind structure, long gravity waves, current shear boundaries and occasionally the local bathymetry. Trains of internal waves can also be detected by Seasat SAP as alternating bands of rough and smooth sea surface. These waves have longer wavelengths (800m-1000m) and are dispersive in nature. The change in sea-state has also been studied with Landsat MSS images. A rough see will always appear lighter than a calm sea in Landsat MSS band 7 imagery.

References

1. Aldrich, F.T., 1981; Land use data and their acquisition : In lounsbury, J.L., Sommers, L.M. and Fernald, EA. (eds) Land Use : A Spatial Approach, Kendall-Hunt Publishing Company, Dubuque, Iowa, USA, pp. 79-95.

2. Allan, J.A., 1980; Remote sensing in land and land use studies; Geography, Vol. 65, pp. 35-43.
3. Allen, C.R., 1975; Geological criteria for evaluating seismicity; Geological Society of America Bulletin, Vol. 86, pp. 1041-1057.
4. Barrett, E.G. and Martin, D.W.,1981; The use of satellite data in rainfall monitoring; Academic Press London.
5. Bryant, N.A. and Zobrist, A.L., 1976; IBIS: a geographic information system based on digital image processing and image raster data type; Symposium Proceedings on Machine Procesing of Remotely Sensed Data, 29 June-1 July; Laboratory for Applications of Remote Sensing : Purde University, West Lafayette, Indiana USA.
6. Clamton, U.S. and Verbeek, 1981; Photographic portrait of active faults in the Houston metropolitan area, Texas in Etter, E.M. ed., Houston area environmental geology-surface faulting, ground subsidence, and hazard liability Houston Geological Society, Houston, Texas, pp. 70-113.
7. Clayton, C. and Estes, J.E., 1980; Image analysis as a check on census enumeration accuracy; Photogrammetric Engineering and Remote Sensing, Vol. 46, pp. 757-674.
8. Curran, P. 1980; Multispectul remote sensing of vegetation amount; Progress in Physical Geography, Vol. 4, pp. 315-341.
9. Denovan, T.J. 1974; Petroleum microseepage at Cement field, Oklahoma-evidence and mechanism; Bulletin of the American Association of Petroleum Geologists, Vol. 58, pp. 429-426.
10. Elachi, C. et.al., 1982; Shuttle imaging radar experiment; Science, Vol. 218, pp. 996-1003.
11. Henderson, F.M., 1975; Radar for small-scale land-use mapping; Photogrammetric Engineering and Remote Sensing, Vol. 41, pp. 307-309.
12. Hoare, D.N., 1972; The Skylark earth resource rocket; paper presented to the 22nd International Geographical Congress, Montreal, Canada.
13. Hunt, G.R., 1980; Electromagnetic radiation : the communication link in remote sensing; In Siegal, B.S. and

Gillespie, A.R. (eds.). Remote sensing in Geology; John Wiley, New York, pp. 5-045.

14. Konecny, G., 1972; Geometric aspects of remote sensors; Invited paper for Commission IV, Twelfth Congress of the International Society of Photogrammetry, Ottawa, Canada.
15. Lo, C.P., 1971; A typological classification of buildings in the city centre of Glasgow from aerial photographs; Photogrammetria, Vol. 27, pp. 135-157.
16. Lo, C.P., 1976; Geographical Application of Aerial Photography; Crane Russak, New York.
17. Lo, C.P., 1979; Surveys of squatter settlements with sequential aerial photography - a case study in Hong Kong; Photogrammetria, Vol. 35, pp. 45-63.
18. Lo, C.P., 1981; A photogrammetric urban information system using the CP1 plotter; Photogrammetric Record, Vol. 1 0, pp. 311-329.
19. Lo, C.P., 1986; Applied remote sensing; Longman Scientific & Technical, Longman Group UK Limited, Longman House, Burnt Mill, Harlow, Essex CM20 2JE, England, pp. 393.
20. Lodge, D.W.S., 1983; Surface expressions of bathymetry on SEASAT synthetic aperture radar images, International Journal of Remote Sensing, Vol. 4, pp. 639-653.
21. Masursky, H., 1982; Volcanic field east of Raton, New Mexico, in Cimino, J.B. and Elachi, C (eds) Shuttle Imagery Radar-A (SIR-A) Experiment; Jet Propulsion Laboratory, Pasadena, pp. 4.19-4.12.
22. McCoy, R.M. 1969; Drainage network analysis with K-band radar magery; Geographical Review, Vol. 59, pp. 493-512.
23. Mekel, J.F.M. 1978; The use of aerial photographs and other images in geological mapping; International Institute for Aerial Survey and Earth Sciences, Enschede, the Netherlands.
24. Metivier, E.D. and McCoy, R.M. 1971; Mapping urban poverty housing from aerial photographs; Proceedings

of the Seventh International Symposium on Remote Sensing of Environment; University of Michigan, pp. 1563-1569.

25. Meyer, W.L., 1984; Integration of remotely sensed data into geographic information; In Richason, Jr. B.F. (ed.) Proceedings PECORA VII Symposium, Remote Sensing : An Input to Geographic Information Systems in the 1980s, American Society of Photogrammetry, Falls Church, Virginia, pp. 3-14.
26. Miller, J.B.,1975; Landsat images as applied to petroleum exploration in Kenya; NASA Earth Resources Survey Symposium, NASA TM X-58168, Vol. 1-8, pp. 605-624.
27. Morain, S.A., 1976; Use of radar for vegetation analysis: In Lewis, A.J, (ed.) Geoscience Applications of Imaging Radar Systems, Remote Sensing of the Electromagnetic Spectrum, Vol. 3, pp. 61-78.
28. Sabins, JR., Floyd F.,1987; Remote Sensing, Principles and iterpretation; second edition, W.H. Freeman And Company, New York, pp. 449.
29. Slater, P.N., 1980; Remote Sensing : Optics and Optical Systems; Addison Wesley : Reading, Mass; London.
30. Staelin, D.H. et.al., 1977; Microwave spectroscopic imagery of the earth, Science, Vol. 197, pp. 991-2003.
31. Teicholz, E., 1980; Geographic information system : the ODYSSEY project; Journal of the Surveying and Mapping Division, American Society of Civil Engineers, Vol. 106, pp. 119-113.
32. Thompson, D., 1975; Small area population estimation using land use data derived from high altitude aircraft photography; Proceedings of the American Society of Photogrammetry, Fall Convention, pp. 673-696.
33. Tobler, W., 1969; Satellite confirmation of settlement size coefficients; Area, Vol. 1, pp. 30-34.
34. Tomlinson, R.F. (ed.), 1972; Geographical Data Handling; IGU Commission on Geographical Data Sensing and Processing, Ottawa, Canada.
35. White, L.P. 1977; Aerial photography and remote sensing for soil survey; Clarendon Press, London.

36. Zheng, Q.A. and Klemas, V. 1982; Determination of winter temperature patterns, fronts, and surface currents in the Yellow Sea and East China from satellite imagery; Remote Sensing of Environment,Vol. 12, pp. 201-218.

REFERENCE FOR FIGURES

1. Alien, C.R., 1975; Geological criteria for evaluating seismicity; Geological Society of American Bulletin, Vol. 86, pp. 1041-1057.
2. Chenoweth, W.L. and Magleby, D.N., 1971; Mine location map, Cameron Uranium area, Coconino Country, Arizona; U.S. Atomic Energy Commission Preliminary Map 20.
3. Collins, W., Chang, S.H., Raines G., Canney F. and Ashley, R.P., 1983; Airborne biogeophysical mapping of hidden mineral deposits; Economics Geology, Vol. 78, pp. 737-749.
4. Cooke, R.U. and Harris, D.R.; 1970; Remote sensing of the terrestrial environment - principles and progress; Transactions of the Institute of British Geographers, No. 50, pp. 1-13.
5. Curran, P.J., 1983; Multispectral remote sensing for the estimation of green leaf area index; Philosophical Transactions of Royal Society of London, Series A, Vol. 309, pp. 257-270.
6. Ford, J.P., 1980; Seasat orbital radar imagery for geologic mapping : Tennessee-Kentucky-Virginia; The American Association of Petroleum Geologists Bulletin, Vol. 64, pp. 2064-2094.
7. Friedman, J.D., Williams R.S., Palmason G. and Miller C.D., 1969; Infrared surveys in Iceland; U.S. Geological Survey Professional paper 650-C, pp. C89-C105.
8. Friedman, J.D., Frank D., Kieffer H.H. and Sawatzky, 1981; Thermal infrared surveys of the May 18 crater, subsequent lava domes, and associated deposits in Lipman, P.W. and Mullineaux (eds.), The 1980 eruption of Mount St. Helens, Washington; U.S. Geological Survey Professional Paper 1250, pp. 279-293.

9. Gedney, L. and Wormar, J. Van, 1974; Earthquakes and tactonic envolution in Alaska; Third ERTS-1 Symposium, NASA SP-351, Vol.1, pp. 745-756.
10. Houghton, J.T., 1979; The future role of observations from meteorological satellites; Quarterly Journal of the Royal Meteorological Society, Vol. 105, pp. 1-23.
11. Lo, C.P., 1986; Applied remote sensing; Longman Scientific & Technical, Longman Group UK Limited, Longman House, Burnt Mill, Harlow, Essex CM20 2JE, England.
12. Lowe, D.S., 1980; Acquisition of remotely sensed data, in Siegal B.S. and Gillespie, A.R. (eds.), Remote Sensing in Geology, John Wiley, New York, pp. 59.
13. Lowell, J.D. and Guilbert, J.M. 1970; Lateral and vertical alteration-mineralization zoning in porphyry ore deposits; Economic Geology, Vol. 65, pp. 373-408.
14. McCoy, R.M., 1969; Drainage network analysis with K-band radar imagery; Geographical Review, Vol. 59, pp. 493-512.
15. Merifield, P.M. and Lamar, D.L.; 1975; Active and inactive faults in Southern California viewed from Skylab; NASA Earth Resources Survey Symposium, NASA TM X-58168, Vol. 1, pp. 779-797.
16. Miller, J.B., 1975; Landsat images as applied to petroleum exploration in Kenya; NASA TM X-58168, Vol. 1-B, pp. 605-624.
17. Moffitt, F.H. and Mikhail, E.M., 1980; Photogrammetry; Harper and Row, New York, pp. 76.
18. Sabins, Jr., Floyd F., 1987; Remote Sensing, principles and interpretation, 2nd edition, W.H. Freman and Company, New York, pp. 449.
19. Slater, P.N., 1980; Remote sensing : optical systems; Addison-Wesley, Reading, Mass.
20. Taramik, J.V., 1978; Characteristics of the Landsat Multispectral Data System, Open File Report 78-187, US Geological Survey.
21. Tomlinson, R.F., 1972; Geographical data handling, vol.1, International Geographical Union Commission on

Geographical Data Sensing and Processing for the UNESCO/IGU Second Symposium on Geographical Information Systems; Ottawa, Canada.

22. Ulaby, F.T., Moore, R.K. and Fung, A.K., 1981; Microwave Remote Sensing, Active and Passive, Vol.1, Fundamentals and Radiometry; Addison-Wesley, Reading, Massachusitts, London, pp. 423.

23. Welch, R., 1980; Monitoring urban population and energy utilization patterns from satellite data; Remote Sensing of Environment, Vol. 9, pp. 109.

24. Yost, E. and Wenderoth, S., 1971; The reflectance spectra of mineralized trees; Proceedings of Seventh International Symposium on Remote Sensing of Environment, University of Michigan, Vol. 1, pp. 269-284, Ann. Arbor, Mich.

Annexure–1

BASIC GEOLOGY FOR REMOTE SENSING

On images of land areas, the terrain is a direct expression of the geology of the area. Many interpreters are concerned with nongeologic subjects (such as land use, environment, or forestry), but an understanding of the geology will contribute to the overall understanding of the image.

Rock Types

Rocks belong to three major categories: sedimentary, igneous, and metamorphic. These are described in the following sections.

Sedimentary Rocks

Material that has been transported and deposited by water or wind forms sedimentary rocks characterized by layers, called *beds* or *strata,* formed during deposition. The surfaces separating strata are called *bedding planes.* Outcrops of sedimentary strata typically have a banded appearance on images. *Sedimentary rocks* are divided into the broad categories of clastic and chemical rocks.

Clastic Rocks Erosion of older rocks produces fragments and particles that are transported and deposited to form *clastic rocks.* After deposition, the fragments are compressed and cemented to form rocks. The consolidated rocks are classified on the basis of particle size before consolidation, as follows:

Consolidated rocks	*Unconsolidated particles*
Conglomerate	Boulders and gravel
Sandstone	Sand
Siltstone	Mud
Shale	Clay

Clastic rocks differ in their resistance to erosion: sandstone and conglomerate typically form ridges, but shale and siltstone form valleys.

Chemical Rocks Minerals dissolved in water may be removed from solution to form *chemical rocks,* either by chemical precipitation or by uptake into organisms whose shells and skeletons form sediments after death. Algae and shellfish remove calcium carbonate from sea-water as the mineral caicite. which accumulates to form the rock called *limestone.* Half of the calcium atoms in in calcite may be replaced by magnesium to form the rock called *dolomite.* Evaporation of seawater produces deposits of gypsum, anhydrite, and salt. Because of its low density, salt may migrate upward into the overlying strata to form cylindrical plugs called *salt domes.*

Open spaces between the grains of sedimentary rocks are called *pores* and contain fresh or salt water or, less commonly, oil and gas.

Igneous Rocks

Igneous rocks are rocks that have cooled from molten material. They arc assigned to the classes of intrusive and extrusive rocks.

Intrusive Rocks

Molten rock, called *magma,* that invades country rock (areas of older rock) cools to form *intrusive rocks.* Based on the relationship to the country rock, intrusive rocks are classed as batholiths, dikes, and sills (Figure A.I). *Batholiths* are large, irregularly masses of intrusive rock that cut across the of the country rock. Erosion of the overlying rocks exposes outcrops of the batholith rock. Tops are commonly.cut by intersecting fractures, called *joints,* that give a distinctive appearance to locks on images. Typical batholithic rocks crop the Peninsular Ranges of southern California and the Adirondack Mountains of New York.

As shown in Figure A.I, country rocks are commonly r stratified. Tabular bodies of igneous rock that led parallel with the layers are *sills,* such as the Palisades sill that crops out along the west bank of the Hudson River. New York.

Tabular bodies of intrusive rock that cut across the country rock are called *dikes.* Erosion of the overlying country rock may expose dikes in the form of ridges, such as the Chinese Wall at Yellowstone National Park. Some dikes are less resistant to erosion than the surrounding country rock and weather to form depressions. On images, dikes are recognized by their linear shape and cross-cutting relationships to the country rock.

As the intruded magma slowly cools, silicate minerals form relatively coarse crystals that are visible to the unaided eye. There are two major types of intrusive rocks, classed according to silica content :

1. *Granite,* which has a high silica content and is typically light gray to pink.

2. *Gabbro,* which has a relatively low silica content and high content of iron- and magnesium-bearing minerals. Gabbro is dark and has a higher density than granite.

Extrusive Rocks

Magma may reach the surface as a liquid called *lava,* which cools to form lava flows. The lava may also be explosively ejected into the air as cinders and ash that can accumulate as volcanoes, *or cinder cones* (Figure A.I). Because lava cools rapidly at the surface, the resulting *extrusive rocks* are very fine-grained. Three major categories of extrusive rocks are

1. Rhyolite: the extrusive equivalent of granites. Rhyolite has a high silica content and is typically pink.

2. Andesite: a rock having intermediate silica cont Andesite volcanoes form the "ring of fire" around the Pac Ocean and make up the Andes of South America and t

Cascade Range of northwestern United States. Mount St. Helens is an andesite volcano.

*3. **Basalt:*** the extrusive equivalent of gabbro. Basalt has a low silica content and a high content of iron- and magnesium-bearing minerals. Basalt is dark and has a relatively high density. Flows of basalt with rough surfaces are called *aa;* those with smooth, ropey surfaces are called *pahoehoe.* Both flow types occur in the Pisgah Crater area together with a volcanic cone of basalt cinders.

Metamorphic Rocks

Heat and pressure may transform igneous and sedimentary rocks into *metamorphic rocks.* As shown in Figure A.1, the heat and pressure associated with intrusive rocks may convert original country rock into the following kinds metamorphic rock:

Original rock	*Metamorphic equivalent*
Sandstone	Quartzite
Shale and siltstone	Schist
Limestone	Marble

Intensive regional compression and deep burial can also produce metamorphic rocks.

Structural Geology

Stresses within the earth's crust may deform the rocks to produce geologic structures that may be mapped on various types of images. Most sedimentary rocks were deposited as horizontal strata, but later uplift and tilting caused the strata to become inclined.

Strike and Dip

Geologists use the terms *strike* and *dip* to describe the orientation and degree of inclination. The line formed by the intersection between an inclined surface and a horizontal plane is the *strike* of the inclined surface (Figure A.2). The orientation of the strike is described by its geographic azimuth, in this case N45°E. *Dip* is measured in the vertical plane oriented normal to the strike and measures the inclination below horizontal of the inclined surface in degrees. In Figure A.2. the Jip is 30° toward the southeast. The strike-and-dip symbol is used to record the *attitudes* of structures on geologic maps. Exposed bedding planes of dipping strata are called *dip slopes*. Erosion of dipping strata produces ledges called *antidip scarps* (Figure A.2) that face the opposite direction from dip slopes.

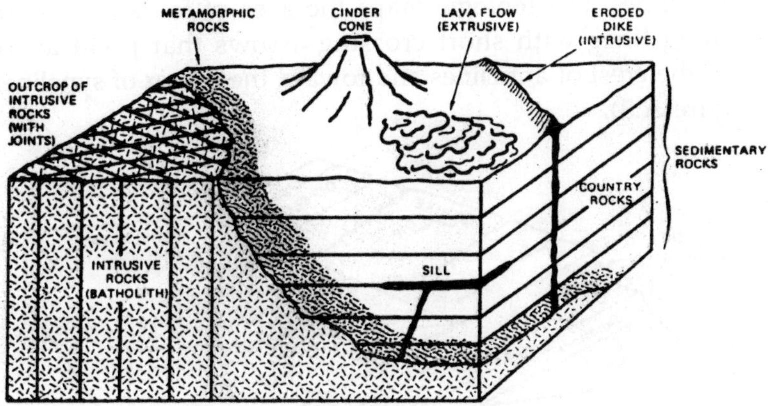

Fig. A.1. Intrusive and extrusive rocks.

The ability to recognize strike and dip is fundamental for interpreting geologic structure from remote sensing images. Except for highly deformed areas, beds generally dip less than 45°, and the following criteria apply. Dip slopes are relatively broad and are traversed by relatively long streams that flow in the direction of dip. Antidip scarps are narrow and have a few short drainage channels that flow opposite to the dip direction. The orientation of shadows and highlights is an important key for interpreting images acquired with inclined illumination, such as low-sun-angle aerial photographs and radar images. If the scene in Figure A.2 were photographed in the morning with sun shining from the southeast, the dip slope would form a bright expanse and the shadowed antidip scarp would form a narrow dark band; in the afternoon the highlights and shadows would be reversed.

Folds

Compressive stresses form folds called anticlines and synclines. As shown in Figure A.3. in *anticlines* the beds dip away from the axis; in *synclines* the beds dip toward the axis. Note orientation of the strike-.and-dip symbols and the attitude of the dip slopes. Also, note the arcuate outcrop patterns that mark the *plunge* of a fold. Hrosion exposes older beds in the center of anticlines and younger beds in the center of synclines. *On* geologic maps the axes of folds are slumn by long lines with short crossing arrows that point away from the crest of anticlines and toward the center of synclines (Figure A.3).

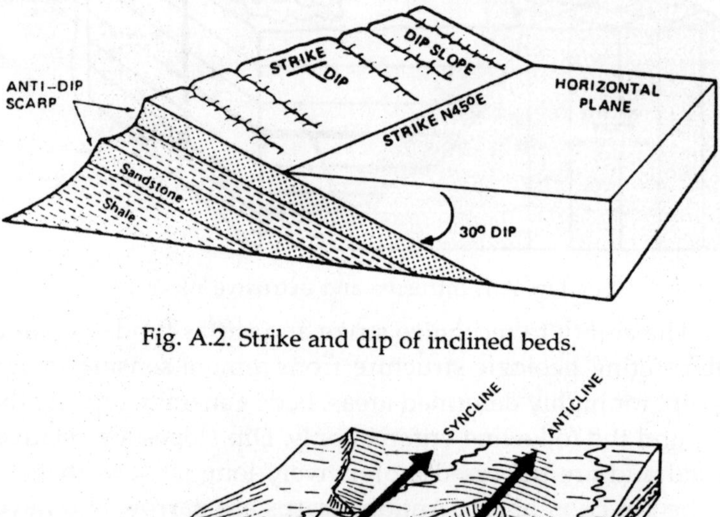

Fig. A.2. Strike and dip of inclined beds.

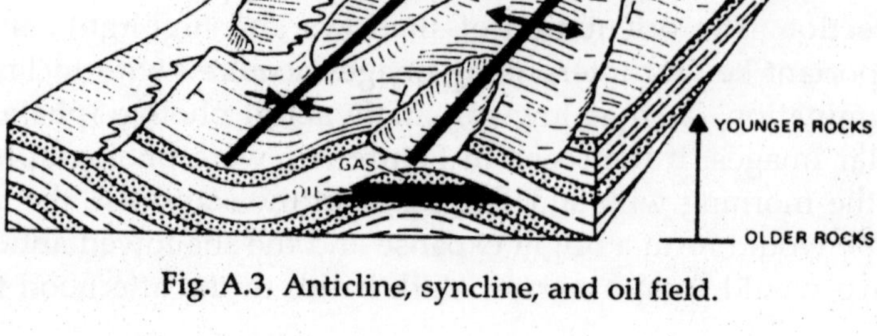

Fig. A.3. Anticline, syncline, and oil field.

Organic matter contained in shales *(source rocks)* generates oil and gas, which migrate into the pore spaces of sandstones and limestones *(reservoir rocks).* Rocks in the subsurface are also saturated with water. Because hydrocarbons are less dense than water, oil and gas float on the water, becoming concentrated in the high points of structures, such as crests of anticlines. Such concentrations may form oil fields (Figure A.3).

Oil fields also occur along faults and in ancient reefs, sandbars, and river channels.

Joints and Faults

Joints, mentioned earlier in connection with batho-liths, are intersecting sets of fractures along which no movement has occurred (Figure A.1). Erosion along joints produces linear depressions that are readily interpreted on images. *Faults* are fractures along which appreciable movement has occurred. Strike-and-dip terminology is also used to describe the attitude of fault surfaces. Faults are assigned to the following categories according to the kind of relative movement.

Normal Faults

The relative movement of rocks on either side of a fault is indicated by arrows, as shown in Figure A.4. *Normal faults* dip less than 90° and the rocks on the upper side of the fault have moved downward relative to those on the lower side. Topographic escarpments caused by faults are called *fault scarps.* In the Basin and Range Province of the United States, normal faults separate the uplifted mountain ranges from the intervening down-dropped basins, as shown in the Landsat mosaic of Nevada in Chapter 4. The uplifted blocks are called *liorsts* and the down-dropped basins are called *graben.*

Thrust Faults

Thrust faults are horizontal or gently dippirrgfaults in which the rocks overlying the fault have moved up and over the rocks below the fault (Figure A.4). Thrust faults are common in the Central Range of Irian Jaya.

Strike-Slip Faults

Faults along which the rocks have moved lateally are *strike-slip faults* (Figure A.4). Because of their steep dip, strike-slip faults have linear surface traces, as seen by the traces of the San Andreas and Garlock faults in the Landsat image of the Los Angeles region. The offset of freatures on opposite sides of a strike-slip faults is used to determine the relative displacement. In Figure A.4 an observer standing on the stream and looking across the fault at the offset channel will note that the lateral displacement of the stream is toward the right, making this a right-lateral, strike-slip fault. In left-lateral faults the features are displaced to the left.

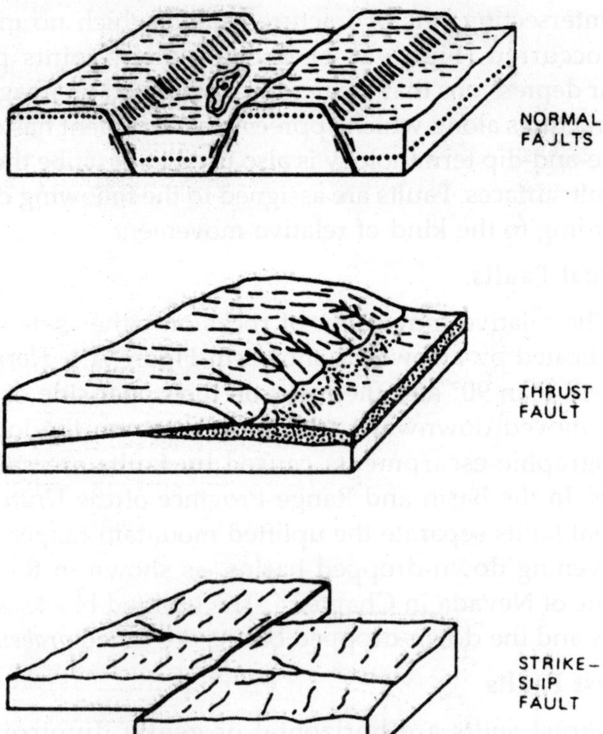

Fig. A.4. Types of faults.

Source: Sabins, 1987.

Annexure–2

GLOSSARY (APPLICABLE TO REMOTE SENSING)

The following glossary includes terms, abbreviations and acronyms commonly employed in remote sensing.

Absorption band : Wavelength interval within which electromagnetic radiation is absorbed by the atmosphere or by other substances.

Absorptivity : Capacity of a material to absorb incident radiant energy.

Active remote sensing : Remote sensing methods that provide their own source of electromagnetic radiation to illuminate the terrain. Radar is one example.

Additive primary colours : Blue, green, and red. Filters of these colors transmit the primary color of the filter and absorb the other two colors.

Adiabatic cooling : Refers to decrease in temperature with increasing altitude.

Advanced very high resolution radiometer (AVHRR) : Cross-tekmultispectral scanner on a NOAA polar-orbiting sat-acquires five spectral bands of data (0.55 to U fun) with a ground resolution cell of 1.1 by 1.1 km.

Air base : Ground distance between optical centers of succes-7 live overlapping aerial photographs.

Aerial magnetic survey : Survey that records variations in the earth's magnetic field.

Airborne imaging spectrometer (AIS) : Along-track multispec-tral scanner with spectral bandwidth of 0.01 μm.

Airborne visible and infrared imaging spectrometer (AVIRIS) : Experimental airborne along-track multispectral scanner under development at JPL to acquire 224 images in the spectral region from 0.4 to 2.4 μm.

AIS : Airborne imaging spectrometer.

Albedo (A) : Ratio of the amount of electromagnetic energy reflected by a surface to the amount of energy incident upon it.

Along-track scanner : Scanner with a linear array of detectors oriented normal to flight path. The IFOV of each detector sweeps a path parallel with the flight direction.

Alteration : Changes in color and mineralogy of rocks surrounding a mineral deposit that are caused by the solutions that formed the deposit. Suites of alteration minerals commonly occur in zones.

Amplitude : For waves, the vertical distance from crest to trough.

Analog display : A form of data display in which values are shown in graphic form, such as curves. Differs from digital displays, in which values are shown as arrays of numbers.

Angular beam width : In radar, the angle subtended in the horizontal plane by the radar beam.

Angular field of view : Angle subtended by lines from a remote sensing system to the outer margins of the strip of terrain that is viewed by the system.

Angular resolving power : Minimum separation between two resolvable targets, expressed as angular separation.

Anomaly : An area on an image that differs from the surrounding, normal area, For example, a concentration of vegetation within a desert scene constitutes an anomaly.

Antenna : Device that transmits and receives microwave and radio energy in radar systems.

Aperture : Opening in a remote sensing system that admits electromagnetic radiation to the film or detector.

Apollo : U.S. lunar exploration program of satellites with crews of three astronauts.

Apparent thermal inertia (ATI) : An approximation of thermal lated as one minus albedo divided by the dif-ndaytime and nighttime radiant temperatures.

ASA index : Index of the American Standards Association designating film speed, or sensitivity to light. Higher values indicate higher sensitivity. The ASA index has been re-placed ISO index.

ATI : Apparent thermal inertia.

Atmosphere : Layer of gases that surrounds some planets.

Atmospheric correction : Image-processing procedure that compensates for effects of selectively scattered light in multispectral images.

Atmospheric window: Wavelength interval within which the atomosphere readily transmits electromagnetic radiation.

Attitude: Angular orientation of a remote sensing system with respect to a geographic reference system.

AVIRIS: Airborne visible and infrared imaging spectrometer.

Azimuth: Geographic orientation of a line given as an angle measured in degrees clockwise from north.

Azimuth direction: In radar images, the direction in which the aircraft is heading. also called *flight direction.*

Azimuth resolution: In radar images, the spatial resolution in the azimuth direction.

Background: Area on an image or the terrain that surrounds an area of interest, or target.

Backscatter: In radar, the portion of the microwave energy scatered by the terrain surface directly back toward the antenna.

Backscatter coefficient: A quantitative measure of the intensity of energy returned to a radar antenna from the terrain.

Band: A wavelength interval in the electromagnetic spectrum. For example, in Landsat images the bands designate specific wavelength intervals at which images are acquired.

Base—height ratio: Air base divided by aircraft height. This ratio determines vertical exaggeration on stereo models.

Batch processing: Method of data processing in which data and programs are entered into a computer that carries out the entire processing operation with no further instructions.

Bathymetry: Configuration of the seafloor.

Beam: A focused pulse of energy.

Binary: Numerical system using the base 2.

Bit: Contraction of *binary digit,* which in digital computing represents an exponent of the base 2.

Blackbody: An ideal substance that absorbs all the radiant energy incident on it and emits radiant energy at the maximum possible rate per unit area at each wavelength for any given temperature. No actual substance is a true blackbody, although some substances, such as lampblack, approach its properties.

Brightness: Magnitude of the response produced in the eye by light.

Brute-force radar: See real-aperture radar.

Byte: A group of eight bits of digital data.

Calibration: Process of comparing an instrument's measurements with a standard.

Calorie: Amount of heat required to raise the temperature of 1 g of water by 1°C.

Camouflage detection photographs: Another term for *1R colour photograph.*

Cardinal point effect: In radar, very bright signatures caused by optimally oriented corner reflectors, such as buildings.

Cathode ray tube (CRT): A vacuum tube with a phosphorescent screen on which images are displayed by an electron beam.

CCD: Charge-coupled detector.

CCT: Computer-compatible tape.

Centerpoint: The optical center of a photograph.

Change-detection images: A difference image prepared by digitally comparing images acquired at different times. The gray tones or colors of each pixel record the amount of difference between the corresponding pixels of the original images.

Charge-coupled detector (CCD): A device in which electrons are stored at the surface of a semiconductor.

Chlorosis: Yellowing of plant leaves resulting from an imbalance in the iron metabolism caused by excess concentrations of copper, zinc, manganese, or other elements in the plant.

Circular scanner: Scanner in which a faceted mirror rotates about a vertical axis to sweep the detector IFOV in a series of circular scan lines on the terrain.

Classification: Process of assigning individual pixels of an image to categories, generally on the basis of spectral reflectance characteristics.

Coastal zone colour scanner (CZCS): A satellite-carried multi-spectral scanner designed to measure chlorophyll concentrations in the oceans.

Colour composite image: Colour image prepared by projecting individual black-and-white multispectral images, each through a different color filter. When the projected images are superposed, a color composite image results.

Colour ratio composite image: Colour composite image prepared by combining individual ratio images for a scene using a different color for each ratio image.

Complementary colours: Two primary colours of light (one additive and the other subtractive) that produce white light when added together. Red and cyan are complementary colours.

Computer-compatible tape (CCT): The magnetic tape on which the digital data for Landsat MSS and TM images are distributed.

Conduction: Transfer of electromagnetic energy through a solid material by molecular interaction.

Contact print: A reproduction from a photographic negative in direct contact with photosensitive paper.

Contrast enhancement Image-processing procedure that improves the contrast ratio of images. The original narrow range of digital values is expanded to utilize the full range of available digital values.

Contrast ratio: On an image, the ratio of reflectances between the brightest and darkest parts of the image.

Convection: Transfer of heat through the physical movement of heated matter.

Corner reflector: Cavity formed by two or three smooth planar surfaces intersecting at right angles. Electromagentic waves entering a corner reflector are reflected directly back toward the source.

COSMIC: Computer Software Management and Information Center, University of Georgia. This facility distributes computer programs developed by U.S. government-funded projects.

Cross-polarize: Describes a radar pulse in whichthe polarizataion direction of the return is normal to the polarization direction of the transmission. Cross-polarized image may be HV (horizontal transmit, vertical return) or VH (vertical transmit, horizontal return).

Cross-track scanner: Scanner in which a faceted mirror rotates about a horizontal axis to sweep the detector IFOV in a series of parallel scan lines oriented normal to the flight direction.

CRT: Cathode ray tube.

Cycle: One complete oscillation of a wave.

CZCS: Coastal zone colour scanner.

Data collection system (DCS): On Landsats 1 and 2, the system to acquired information from seismometers, flood gauges, and other measuring devices. These data were relayed to ground receiving stations.

Densitometer: Optical device for measuring the density of photographic transparencies.

Density, of images: Measure of the opacity, or darkness, of a negative or positive transparency.

Density, of materials ***(p):*** Ratio of mass to volume of a material, typically expressed as grams per cubic centimeter.

Density slicing: Process of converting the continuous gray tones of an image into a series of density intervals, or slices, each corresponding to a specific digital range. The density slices are then displayed either as uniform gray tones or as colors.

Depolarized: Refers to a change in polarization of a transmitted radar pulse as a result of various interactions with the terrain surface.

Depression angle ***(γ):*** In radar, the angle between the imaginary horizontal plane passing through the antenna and the line connecting the antenna and the target.

Detectability: Measure of the smallest object that can be discerned on an image.

Detector: Component of a remote sensing system that con-rotselectromagnetic radiation into a recorded signal.

Developing: Chemical processing of an exposed photographic to produce an image.

Dielectric constant: Electrical property of matter that influences radar returns. Also referred to as *complex dielectric constant*.

Difference image: Image prepared by subtracting the digital values of pixels in one image from those in a second image produce a third set of pixels. This third set is used to the difference image.

Diffuse reflector: Surface that reflects incident radiation nearly equally in all directions.

Digital display: A form of data display in which values are shown as arrays of numbers.

Digital image processing: Computer manipulation of the digital-number values of an image.

Digital number (DN): Value assigned to a pixel in a digital image.

Digitization: Process of converting an analog display into a digital display.

Digitizer: Device for scanning an image and converting it into numerical format.

Directional filter: Mathematical filter designed to enhance on an image those linear features oriented in a particular direction.

Distortion: On an image, changes in shape and position of objects with respect to their true shape and position.

Diurnal: Daily.

Doppler principle: Describes the change in observed frequency that electromagnetic or other waves undergo as a result of the movement of the source of waves relative to the observer.

Dwell time: Time required for a detector IFOV to sweep across a ground resolution cell.

Earth-terrain camera (ETC): A high-resolution camera carried on Skylab.

EDC EROS: Data Center.

Edge enhancement: Image-processing technique that emphasizes the appearance of edges and lines.

Ektachrome: A Kodak colour positive film.

Electromagnetic radiation: Energy propagated in the form of-an advancing interaction between electric and magnetic fields. All electromagnetic radiation moves at the speed of light.

Electromagnetic spectrum: Continuous sequence of electromagnetic energy arranged according to wavelength or frequency.

Emission: Process by which a body radiates electromagnetic energy. Emission is determined by kinetic temperature and emissivity.

Emissivity (E): Ratio of radiant flux from a body to that from a blackbody at the same kinetic temperature.

Emulsion: Suspension of photosensitive silver halide grains in gelatin that constitutes the image-forming layer on photographic film.

Energy flux: Radiant flux.

Enhancement: Process of altering the appearance of an image so that the interpreter can extract more information.

EOSAT: The commercial company that took over operations of the Landsat system in 1985.

EREP: Earth Resources Experiment Package, carried on Skylab and consisting of cameras and a multispectral scanner.

EROS: Earth Resource Observation System.

EROS Data Center (EDC): Facility of the U.S. Geological Survey at Sioux Falls, South Dakota, that archives, processes, and distributes images.

ERTS: Earth Resource Technology Satellite, now called Landsat.

ETC: Earth-terrain camera.

Evaporative cooling: Temperature drop caused by evaporation otaerfrom a moist surface.

False color photograph: Another term for *IR color photograph.*

Fir range: The portion of a radar image farthest from the aircraft or spacecraft flight path.

Film: Light-sensitive photographic emulsion and its base.

Film speed: Measure of the sensitivity of photographic film to light. larger nuumbers indicate higher sensitivity.

Filter, digital: Mathematical procedure for modifying values of numerical data.

Filter, optical: A material that, by absorption or reflection, selectively modifies the radiation transmitted through an optical system.

Flight path: Line on the ground directly beneath a remote sensing aircraft or spacecraft. also called *flight line.*

Fluorescence: Emission of light from a substance following exposure to radiation from an external source.

***F*- number:** Representation of the speed of a lens determined by the focal length divided by diameter of the lens. smaller numbers indicate faster lenses.

Focal length: In cameras, the distance from the optical center of the lens to the plane at which the image of a very distant object is brought into focus.

Format: Size of an image.

Forward overlap: The percent of duplication by successive photographs along a flight line.

Frequency (*v*): Nummber of wave oscillations per unit time or the number of wavelengths that pass a point per unit tiem.

***f*-stop:** Focal length of a lens divided by the diameter of the lens's adjustable diaphragm. smaller numbers indicate larger openings, which admit more light to the film.

CCP: Gipund-control point.

Gemini U.S.: program of two-man earth-oribiting spacecraft in 1% 5 and 1966.

Geometric correction: Image-processing procedure that corrects spatial distortions in an image.

Geostationary: Refers to satellites traveling at the angular velocity at which the earth rotates; as a result, they remain above the same point on earth at all times.

Geostationary Operational Environmental Satellite: A NOAA satellite that acquires visible and thermal IR images for me-leorologic purposes.

Geothermal: Refers to heat from sources within the earth.

Goddard Space flight center: The NASA facility at Greenbelt, Maryland, that is also a Landsat ground receiving station.

GMT: Greenwich mean time. This international 24-h system is used to designate the time at which Landsat images are acquired.

GOES: Geostationary Operational Environmental Satellite. Surface occurrence of iron oxide formed by the nattering of metallic sulfide ore minerals.

Granularity: Graininess of developed photographic film that isdelermined by the texture of the silver grains.

Gray scale: A sequence of gray tones ranging from black to white.

Ground-control point: A geographic feature of known location that is recognizable on images and can be used to determine geometric corrections.

Ground range: On radar images, the distance from the ground track to an object.

Ground-range image: Radar image in which the scale in the range direction is constant.

Ground receiving station: Facility that records data transmitted by a satellite, such as Landsat.

Ground resolution cell: Area on the terrain that is covered by the IFOV of a detector.

Ground swath: Width of the strip of terrain that is imaged by a scanner system.

GSFC: Goddard Space Flight Center.

Harmonic: Refers to waves in which the component frequencies are whole-number multiples of the fundamental frequency.

Heat capacity (*c*): Ratio of heat absorbed or released by a material to the corresponding temperature rise or fall. Expressed in calories per gram per degree centigrade. Also called *thermal capacity.*

Heat Capacity Mapping Mission (HCMM): NASA satellite orbited in 1978 to record daytime and nighttime visible and thermal IR images of large areas.

Highlights: Areas of bright tone on an image.

Hue: In the IHS system, represents the dominant wavelength of a color.

IFOV: Instantaneous field of view.

IHS: Intensity, hue, and saturation system of colors.

Image: Pictorial representation of a scene recorded by a remote sensing system. Although *image* is a general term, it is commonly restricted to representations acquired by non-photographic methods.

Image swath: See *ground swath.*

Incidence angle: In radar, the angle formed between an imaginary line normal to the surface and another connecting the antenna and the target.

Incident energy: Electromagnetic radiation impinging on a surface.

Index of refraction (*n*): Ratio of the wavelength or velocity of electromagnetic radiation in a vacuum to that in a substance.

Instantaneous field of view (IFOV): Solid angle through which a detector is sensitive to radiation. In a scanning system, the solid angle subtended by the detector when the scanning motion is stopped.

Intensity: In the IHS system, brightness ranging from black to white.

Interactive processing: Method of image processing in which the operator views preliminary results and can alter the instructions to the computer to achieve desired results.

Interpretation: The process in which a person extracts information from an image.

Interpretation key: Characteristic or combination of characteristics that enable an interpreter to identify an object on an image.

IR: Infrared region of the electromagnetic spectrum that includes wavelengths from 0.7 *um* to I mm.

IR colour photograph: Colour photograph in which the red-imaging layer is sensitive to photographic IR wavelengths, the green-imaging layer is sensitive to red light, and the blue-imaging layer is sensitive to green light. Also known as *camouflage detection photographs* and *false-color photographs.*

ISO index: Index of the International Standards Organization, designating film speed in photography. Higher values indicate higher sensitivity.

Isotherm: Contour line connecting points of equal temperature. Isotherm maps are used to portray surface-temperature patterns of water bodies.

Johnson Space Flight Center: A NASA facility in Houston, Texas.

JPL Jet Propulsion Laboratory, a NASA facility at Pasadena, California, operated under contract by the *California* Institute of Technology.

Ka band: Radar wavelength region from 0.8 to 1.1 cm.

Kernel: Two-dimensional array of digital numbers used in digital filtering.

Kinetic energy: The ability of a moving body to do work by virture of its motion. The molecular motion of matter is a form of kinetic energy.

Kinetic temperature: Internal temperature of an object determined by random molecular motion. Kinetic temperature is measured with a contact thermometer.

Kodachrome A Kodak colour positive film.

LACIE: Large Area Crop Inventory Experiment.

Landsat: A series of unmanned earth-oribiting NASA satellite that acquire multispectral images in various visible and IR bands.

Laplacian filter: A form of nondirectional digital filter.

Large-format camera (LFC): An experiment first carried on to Space Shuttle in October 1984.

Latent image: Invisible image produced by the photochemical fa of light on silver halide grains in the emulsion of film. le latent image is not visible until after photographic dtvelopment.

Layover: In radar images, the geometric displacement of the)fobjects toward the near range relative to their base.

L band: Radar wavelength region from 15 to 30 cm.

Lens: One or more pieces of glass or other transparent material itoped lo form an image by refraction of light.

LFC: Large-format camera.

Light: Electromagnetic radiation ranging from 0.4 to 0.7 *um* in wvelength that is detectable by the human eye.

Light meter: Device for measuring the intensity of visible radiation and determining the appropriate exposure of photographic film in a camera.

Lineament: Linear topographic or tonal feature on the terrain Notiimages, maps, and photographs that may represent I iffle of structural weakness.

Linear: Adjective that describes the straight line-like nature of features on the terrain or on images and photographs.

Line-pair: Pair of light and dark bars of equal widths. The number of such line-pairs aligned side by side that can be distinguished per unit distance expresses the resolving power of an imaging system.

Lineation: The one-dimensional alignment of internal components of a rock that cannot be depicted as an individual feature on a map.

Look direction: Direction in which pulses of microwave energy are transmitted by a radar system. The look direction is normal to the azimuth direction. Also called *range direction.*

Low-sun-angle photograph: Aerial photograph acquired in the morning, evening, or winter when the sun is at a low elevation above the horizon.

Luminance: Quantitative measure of the intensity of light from a source.

Mercury: U.S. program of one-man, earth-orbiting spacecraft in 1962 and 1963.

Microwave: Region of the electromagnetic spectrum in the wavelength range of 0.1 to 30 cm.

Minimum ground separation: Minimum distance on the ground between two targets at which they can be resolved on an image.

Minus-blue photographs: Black-and-white photographs acquired using a filter that removes blue wavelengths to produce higher spatial resolution.

Modular optoelectric multispectral scanner (MOMS): An along-track scanner carried on the Space Shuttle that recorded two bands of data.

Modulate: To vary the frequency, phase, or amplitude of electromagnetic waves.

Modulation transfer function (MTF): A method of describing spatial resolution.

MOMS: Modular optoelectric multispectral scanner.

Mosaic: Composite image or photograph made by piecing together individual images or photographs covering adjacent areas.

MSS: Multispectral scanner system of Landsat that acquires images at four wavelength bands in the visible and reflected IR regions.

Multiband camera: System that simultaneously acquires photographs of the same scene at different wavelengths.

Multispectral classification: Identification of terrain categories by digital processing of data acquired by multispectral scanners.

Multispectral scanner: Scanner system that simultaneously acquires images of the same scene at different wavelengths.

Nadir Point on the ground directly in line with the remote sensing system and the center of the earth.

NASA: National Aeronautical and Space Administration.

Near Range: Refers to the portion of a radar image closest to the aircraft or satellite flight path.

Negative photograph: Photograph on film or paper in which the relationship between bright and dark tones is the reverse of that of the features on the terrain.

NHAP: National High Altitude Photography program of the U.S. Geological Survey.

NOAA: National Oceanic and Atmospheric Administration.

Noise: Random or repetitive events that obscure or interfere with the desired information.

Nondirectional filter: Mathematical filter that treats all orientations of linear features equally.

Nonsystematic distortion: Geometric irregularities on images that are not constant and cannot be predicted from the characteristics of the imaging system.

Normal colour film: Film in which the colours are essentially true representations of the colours of the terrain.

NSSDC National Space Science Data Center.

Oblique photograph Photograph acquired with the camera intentionally directed at some angle between horizontal and vertical orientations.

OMS: Orbital maneuvering system.

Orbit: Path of a satellite around a body such as the earth, under the influence of gravity.

Overlap Extent to which adjacent images or photographs cover the same terrain, expressed as a percentage.

Panchromatic film: Black and white film that is sensitive to all visible wavelengths.

Parailax: Displacement of the position of a target in an image caused by a shift in the observation position.

Parallel-polarized: Describes a radar pulse in which the polarization of the return is the same as that of the transmission. Parallel-polarized images may be HH (horizontal transmit, horizontal return) or VV (vertical transmit, vertical return).

Pass: In digital filters, refers to the spatial frequency of data transmitted by the filter. High-pass filters transmit high-frequency data; low-pass filters transmit low-frequency data.

Passive remote sensing: Remote sensing of energy naturally reflected or radiated from the terrain.

Palh-and-row index: System for locating Landsat MSS and TM images.

Pattern: Regular repetition of tonal variations on an image or photograph.

Periodic line dropout: Defect on Landsat MSS or TM images in which no data are recorded for every sixth or sixteenth scan line, causing a black line on the image.

Periodic line striping: Defect on Landsat MSS or TM images in which every sixth or sixteenth scan line is brighter or darker than the others. Caused by the sensitivity of one detector being higher or lower than the others.

Photodetector: Device for measuring energy in the visible-light band.

Ptotogeology: Mapping and interpretation of geologic features lomaerial photographs.

Photograph: Representation of targets on film that results from the action of light on silver halide grains in the film's emulsion.

Photographic IR: Short-wavelength portion (0.7 to 0.9 μm) of the IR band that is detectable by IR color film or IR black and white film.

Photographic UV: Long-wavelength portion of the UV band (0.3 to 0.4 μm) that is transmitted through the atmosphere d is detectable by film.

Photomosaci: Mosaic composed of photographs.

Photon: Minimum discrete quantity of radiant energy.

Picture element: In a digitized image, the area on the ground represented by each digital number. Commonly contracted *pixel.*

Pitch: Rotation of an aircraft about the horizontal axis normal to its longitudinal axis that causes a nose-up or nose attitude.

Pixel: Contraction *of picture element.*

Polarization: The direction of orientation in which the electrical field vector of electromagnetic radiation vibrates.

Positive photograph: Photographic image in which the tones are directly proportional to the terrain brightness.

Previsual symptom: A vegetation anomaly that is recognizable on IR film before it is visible to the naked eye or on normal color photographs. It results when stressed vegetation loses its ability to reflect photographic IR energy and is recognizable on IR color film by a decrease in brightness of red hues.

Primary colours: A set of three colours that in various combinations will produce the full range of colours in the visible spectrum. There are two sets of primary colours, additive and subtractive.

Principal-component (PC): image Digitally processed image produced by a transformation that recognizes maximum variance in multispectral images.

Principal point: Optical center of an aerial photograph.

Printout: Display of computer data in alphanumeric format.

Pulse: Short burst of electromagnetic radiation transmitted by a radar antenna.

Pulse length: Duration of a burst of energy transmitted by a radar antenna, measured in microseconds.

Pushbroom scanner: An alternate term for an along-track scanner.

Radar: Acronym for *radio detection and ranging*. Radar is a active form of remote sensing that operates in the microwav and radio wavelength regions.

Radar shadow: Dark signature on a radar image representin no signal return. A shadow extends in the far-range directio from an object that intercepts the radar beam.

Radian: Angle subtended by an arc of a circle equal in lengtl to the radius of the circle 1 rad = 57.3°.

Radiant energy peak: λ_{max} Wavelength at which the maxi mum electromagnetic energy is radiated at a particulai temperature.

Radiant flux: Rate of flow of electromagnetic radiation measured in watts per square centimeter.

Radiant temperature: Concentration of the radiant flux from a material. Radiant temperature is the kinetic temperature multiplied by the emissivity to the one-fourth power.

Radiation: Propagation of energy in the form of electromagnetic waves.

Radiometer: Device for quantitatively measuring radiant energy, especially thermal radiation.

Random line dropout: In scanner images, the loss of data from individual scan lines in a nonsystematic fashion.

Range direction: See *look direction.*

Range resolution: In radar images, the spatial resolution in the range direction, which is determined by the pulse length of tk transmitted microwave energy.

Raster pattern: Pattern of horizontal lines swept by an electron beam across the face of a CRT that constitute the image display.

Ratio image: An image prepared by processing digital multi-spectral data as follows: for each pixel, the value for one tad is divided by that of another. The resulting digital values are displayed as an image.

Rayleigh criterion In radar, the relationship between surface roughness, depression angle, and wavelength that determines whether a surface will respond in a rough or smooth fashion to the radar pulse.

RBV: Return-beam vidicon.

Real-aperture radar: Radar system in which azimuth resolution is determined by the transmitted beam width, which is in turn determined by the physical length of the antenna and by the wavelength.

Real time: Refers to images or data made available for inspection simultaneously with their acquisition.

Recognizability: Ability to identify an object on an image.

Rectilinear: Refers to images with no geometric distortion in which the scales in the horizontal and vertical directions are identical.

Reflectance: Ratio of the radiant energy reflected by a body to the energy incident on it. Spectral reflectance is the reflectance measured within a specific wavelength interval.

Reflected energy peak: Wavelength (0.5 um) at which maximum amount of energy is reflected from the earth's surface.

Reflected IR: Electromagnetic energy of wavelengths from 0.7 *um* to about 3 *um* that consists primarily of reflected solar radiation.

Reflectivity: Ability of a surface to reflect incident energy.

Refraction: Bending of electromagnetic rays as they pass from one medium into another when each medium has a different index of refraction.

Registration: Process of superposing two or more images or photographs so that equivalent geographic points coincide.

Relief: Vertical irregularities of a surface.

Relief displacement: Geometric distortion on vertical aerial photographs. The tops of objects appear in the photograph lo be radially displaced from their bases outward from the photograph's centerpoint.

Remote sensing: Collection and interpretation of information atari an object without being in physical contact with the object.

Reseau marks: Pattern of small crosses added to photographs.

Rsotolion: Ability to separate closely spaced objects on an image or photograph. Resolution is commonly expressed as the most closely spaced line-pairs per unit distance that can tdistinguished. Also called spatial resolution.

Resolution target: Series of regularly spaced alternating light aid dark bars used to evaluate the resolution of images or photographs.

Resolving power: A measure of the ability of individual components, and of remote sensing systems, to separate closely spaced targets.

Reststrahlen band: In the thermal IR region, refers to absorption of energy as a function of silica content.

Return: In radar, a pulse of microwave energy reflected by the terrain and received at the radar antenna. The strength of a return is referred to as *return intensity.*

Return-beam vidicon (RBV): A system in which images are formed on the photosensitive surface of a vacuum tube; the image is scanned with an electron beam and transmitted or recorded. Landsat 3 used a pair of RBVs to acquire images.

Roll: Rotation of an aircraft that causes a wing-up or wing-down attitude.

Compensation system: Component of an airborne scanner system that measures and records the roll of the aircraft. This information is used to correct the imagery for distortion due to roll.

Rough criterion: In radar, the relationship between surface roughness, depression angle, and wavelength that determines whether a surface will scatter the incident radar pulse in a rough or intermediate fashion.

Roughness: In radar, the average vertical relief of small-scale irregularities of the terrain surface. Also called *surface roughness.*

Satellite: An object in orbit around a celestial body.

Saturation: In the IHS system, represents the purity of color. Saturation is also the condition where energy flux exceeds the sensitivity range of a detector.

Scale: Ratio of distance on an image to the equivalent distance on the ground. scan line Narrow strip on the ground that is swept by IFOV of a detector in a scanning system.

Scanner: An imaging system in which the IFOV of one or more detectors is swept across the terrain. scanner distortion Geometric distortion that is characteristic of cross-track scanner images.

Scan skew: Distortion of scanner images caused by forward motion of the aircraft or satellite during the time required to complete a scan.

Scattering: Multiple reflections of electromagnetic waves by particles or surfaces. scattering coefficient curves Display of scatterometer data in which relative backscatter is shown as a function of incidence angle.

Scatterometer: Nonimaging radar device that quantitatively records backscatter of terrain as a function of incidence angle.

Scene: Area on the ground that is covered by an image or photograph.

Seasat: NASA unmanned satellite that acquired L-band radar images in 1978.

Sensitivity: Degree to which a detector responds to electromagnetic energy incident on it.

Sensor: Device that receives electromagnetic radiation and converts it into a signal that can be recorded and displayed as either numerical data or an image.

Shuttle imaging radar (SIR): L-band radar system deployed on the Space Shuttle.

Sidelap: Extent of lateral overlap between images acquired on adjacent flight lines.

Side-looking airborne radar (SLAR): An airborne side scanning system for acquiring radar images.

Side-scanning sonar: Active system for acquiring images of tfcscafloor using pulsed sound waves.

Side scanning system: A system that acquires images of a strip of terrain parallel with the flight or orbit, path but offset to on side.

Signal: Information recorded by a remote sensing system.

Signature: Set of characteristics by which a material or an object may be identified on an image or photograph.

Silver halide: Silver salts that are especially sensitive to visible light and convert to metallic silver when developed.

Skylab: U.S.earth-orbiting workshop that housed three crews of Ike astronauts in 1973 and 1974.

Skylight: Component of light that is strongly scattered by the atmosphere and consists predominantly of shorter wavelengths.

Slant range: In radar, an imaginary line running between the antenna and the target.

Slant-range distance: Distance measured along the slant range.

Slant-range distortion: Geometric distortion of a slant-range image.

Slant-range image: In radar, an image in which objects are located at positions corresponding to their slant-range distances from the aircraft flight path. On slant-range images, the scale in the range direction is compressed in the near-range region.

SLAK: Side-looking airborne radar.

Smooth criterion: In radar, the relationship between surface roughness, depression angle, and wavelength that determines whether a surface will scatter the incident radar pulse in a smooth or intermediate fashion.

Software: Programs that control computer operations.

Sonar: Acronym for *sound navigation ranging*. Sonar is an active form of remote sensing that employs sonic energy to image the sealloor.

Space Shuttle: U.S. manned satellite program in the 1980s, officially called the Space Transportation System (STS). spectral reflectance Reflectance of electromagnetic energy at specified wavelength intervals.

Spectral sensitivity: Response, or sensitivity, of a film or detector to radiation in different spectral regions.

Spectral vegetation index: An index of relative amount and vigor of vegetation. The index is calculated from two spectral bands of (AVHRR) imagery.

Spectrometer: Device for measuring intensity of radiation absorbed or reflected by a material as a function of wavelength.

Spectrum: Continuous sequence of electromagnetic energy arranged according to wavelength or frequency. specular Refers to a surface that is smooth with respect to wavelength of incident energy.

SPOT: Systeme Probatoire d'Observation de la Terre. Unmanned French remote sensing satellite orbiting in the late 1980s.

Stefan-Boltzmann constant: 5.68×10^{-12} W . cm^{-2}. °K^{-4}.

Stefan-Boltzmann law: States that radiant flux of a blackbody it equal to (lie temperature to the fourth power times the Stefan-Boltzrnann constant.

Stereo base: Distance between a pair of correlative points on a stereo pair that are oriented for stereo viewing.

Stereo model: Three-dimensional visual impression produced by viewing a pair of overlapping images through a stereoscope.

Stereo pair: Two overlapping images or photographs that may be viewed stereoscopically.

Stereoscope: Binocular optical device for viewing overlapping images or diagrams. The left eye sees only the left image, and the right eye sees only the right image.

Subcene: A portion of an image thai is used for detailed analysis.

Subtractive primary colours: Yellow, magenta, and cyan. When used as filters for white light, these colors remove blue, green, and red light, respectively.

Sunlight: Bright reflectance of sunlight caused by ripples on water.

Sun-synchronous: Earth satellite orbit in which the orbit plane is nearly polar and the altitude is such that the satellite passes over all places on earth having the same latitude twice daily at the same local sun time.

Supervised classification: Digital-information extraction technique Jn which the operator provides training-site informaiion that the computer uses to assign pixels to categories.

Surface phenomenon: Interaction between electromagnetic radiation and the surface of a material.

Surface roughness: See *roughness.*

Synthetic-aperture radar (SAR): Radar system in which high azimuth resolution is achieved by storing and processing data on the Doppler shift of multiple return pulses in such a way as to give the effect of a much longer antenna.

Synthetic stereo images: Stereo images constructed through digital processing of a single image. Topographic data are used to calculate parallax.

System: Combination of components that constitute an imaging device.

Systematic distortion: Geometric irregularities on images that are caused by known and predictable characteristics.

Target: Object on the terrain of specific interest in a remote sensing investigation.

TDRS: Tracking and Data Relay Satellite.

Telemeter: To transmit data by radio or microwave links.

Ternan: Surface of the earth.

Texture: Frequency of change and arrangement of tones on an image.

Thematic mapper (TM): A cross-track scanner deployed on Landsat that records seven bands of data from the visible through the thermal IR regions thermal capacity *(c)* See *heat capacity.*

Thermal conductivity ***(K):*** Measure of the rate at which heat will pass through a material, expressed in calories per centimeter per second per degree Centigrade.

Thermal crossover: On a plot of radiant temperature versus time, the point at which temperature curves for two different materials intersect.

Thermal diffusivity ***(k):*** Governs the rate at which temperature changes within a substance, expressed in centimeters squared per second.

Thermal inertia ***(P):*** Measure of the response of a material to temporalure changes, expressed in calorics per square centimeter per square root of second.

Thermal IR: IR region from 3 to 14 um that is employed in remote sensing. This spectral region spans the radiant power peak of the earth.

Thermal IR image: Image acquired by a scanner that records radiation within the thermal IR bund.

Thermal IR multispectral scanner (TIMS): Airborne scanner that acquires multispectral images within the 8-to-14-um band of the thermal IR region.

Thermal model: Mathematical expression that relates thermal and other physical properties of a material to its temperature. Models may be used to predict temperature for given properties and conditions.

Tomography: Medical applications of thermal IR images. Images of the body, called *iherinograms,* have been used to detect tumors and monitor blood circulation.

TIMS: Thermal IR multispectral scanner.

TM: Thematic mapper.

Tone: Each distinguishable shade of gray from white to black on an image.

Topographic inversion: An optical illusion that may occur on images with extensive shadows. Ridges appear to be valleys, and valleys appear to be ridges. The illusion is corrected by orienting the image so that the shadows trend from the top margin of the image to the bottom.

Topographic reversal: A geomorphic phenomenon in which topographic lows coincide with structural highs and vice versa. Valleys are eroded on crests of anticlines to cause topographic lows, and synclines form ridges, or topographic highs.

Tracking and Data Relay Satellite (TDRS): Geostationary satellite used to communicate between ground receiving stations and satellites such as Landsat.

Trade-off: As a result of changing one factor, in a remote sensing system, there are compensative changes elsewhere in ksystem; such a compensating change is known as a tradeoff,

Training site: Area of terrain with known properties or char-itleristics that is used in supervised classification.

Transmissivity: Property of a material that determines the amount of energy that can pass through the material.

Transparency: Image on a transparent photographic materinl normally a positive image.

Transpiration: Expulsion of water vapor and oxygen by vegetation.

Travel time: In radar, the time interval between the generation of a pulse of microwave energy and its return from the terrain.

Unsuperviscd classification: Digital information extraction technique in which the computer assigns pixels to categories with no instructions from the operator.

UV: Ultraviolet region of the electromagnetic spectrum ranging in wavelengths from 0.01 to 0.4 μm.

Vegetation anomaly: Deviation from the normal distribution or properties of vegetation. Vegetation anomalies may be caused by faults, trace elements in soil, or other factors.

Vertical exaggeration: In a stereo model, the extent to which the vertical scale appears larger than the horizontal scale.

Visible radiation: Energy at wavelengths from 0.4 to 0.7 um that is detectable by the human eye.

Volume scattering: In radar, interaction between electromagnetic radiation and the interior of a material.

Watt (W): Unit of electrical power equal to rate of work done by one ampere under a potential of one volt.

Wavelength (λ): Distance between successive wave crests or other equivalent points in a harmonic wave.

Wien's displacement law: Describes the shift of the radiant power peak to shorter wavelengths as temperature increases.

X band: Radar wavelength region from 2.4 to 3.8 cm.

Yaw: Rotation rf an aircraft about its vertical axis so that the longitudinal axis deviates left or right from the flight line.

Source: Sabins, 1987.

2

HYDROGEN : THE WORLD'S FUTURE ENERGY MIX

Introduction

Hydrogen's main attraction as that it can be produced from water or from any hydrocarbon fuel, or even from energy sources of the future that we cannot envision yet. Like electricity, hydrogen carries energy that is produced from other sources and delivers it in the form of power and heat. Compared to electricity, however, hydrogen is easier to store-a vital distinction. It creates no harmful emission when used in an electro-chemical fuel cell to generate power. The only by-product is water. In the future, all of our energy needs could be met by hydrogen that is produced from renewable sources like wind power and solar energy. Hydrogen fuel cells are already being tested in vehicles and used commercially in micro-power plants, which generate electricity where it's needed instead of transmitting it over long distances. In a future hydrogen economy, fuel cells would power most of our vehicles, and micropower plants would proliferate, complementing our supply of electricity from the utility grid by providing extra power during periods of peak demand. Many barriers would need to be overcome to realise hydrogen's promise. Technology development would have to reduce the costs of manufacturing fuel cells, building a fueling infrastructure, capturing carbon dioxide emissions, and producing, storing, and transporting hydrogen.

Detailed Encyclopaedia

This encyclopaedia is written in the text format not in

alphabetical order for the benefit of readers. The detailed encyclopaedia is given below :

Concept and Vision

Hydrogen is not a source of energy like oil or natural gas-instead, production of hydrogen consumers energy. That is because hydrogen atoms are almost always bonded with other elements into compounds like water or hydrocarbon fuels, which require energy to break apart. Hydrogen certainly has a part to play in the world's energy mix within the foreseeable future. Hydrogen is usually considered an energy carrier-a way to transport and store energy that is produced from other sources. Like electricity, hydrogen does not exist freely in a usable form, but it can be made using natural gas or other primary energy sources. Compared to electricity, however, hydrogen is easier to store. Both hydrogen and electric power can be made from and fossil fuel or from any renewable resource, such as wind and solar energy. Hydrogen could complement electricity as an alternative energy delivery service. Hydrogen and electricity are closely related. This means that if hydrogen and electricity were both in widespread use, they could be substituted for each other fairly easily. Today natural gas is gaining on oil's market share and is perceived as its successor in many applications. In America and some developing countries, new power generating capacity has shifted toward natural gas, which in its liquid form is now shipped worldwide. Natural gas has less carbon and more hydrogen than oil, i.e., carbon to hydrogen ratio is roughly 1:4. Today over two-thirds of the fossil-fuel atoms we burn are hydrogen, not carbon. The next step eliminates both the burning and the carbon. By 2050, natural gas and hydrogen could replace oil and coal and eventually command 15 percent of the global energy market—"the same as King Coal in his hey-day". A decarbonized fossil fuel is, simply, hydrogen. To produce hydrogen from today's fuels, we would need to store the carbon somewhere safe, which is called sequestration. Hydrogen itself, once it has been produced from renewable energy or other sources, can be stored in a variety of ways. Traditionally, hydrogen gas has been compressed or liquefied for storage in tanks. It can also be used to produce other storable liquid fuels such *as* methanol and ammonia. Now technologies are being developed in which hydrogen can be attached to certain metals to form hydrides, and scientists are inventing ways to store hydrogen on microscopic carbon fibers.

Hydrogen is relatively safe compared to gasoline, propane, and other common fuels. Because hydrogen is so lightweight, it nould disperse upward if it leaked, instead of spreading into a dangerous pool that could be ignited. Also hydrogen cannot spill into the ground and contaminate the water supply as oil can, nor could it form a huge oil slick on the ocean. Space exploration was the first practical application for fuel cells, beginning in the 1960s. Today, fuel cells are recognized as a vanguard technology that could launch hydrogen into the world's energy mix. Hydrogen can also be used in engines and turbines to generate power. Chemical energy in the form of a fuel is fed into the cell, so it can generate electricity as long as it's getting fuel and oxygen. See Fig. 1. Hydrogen is

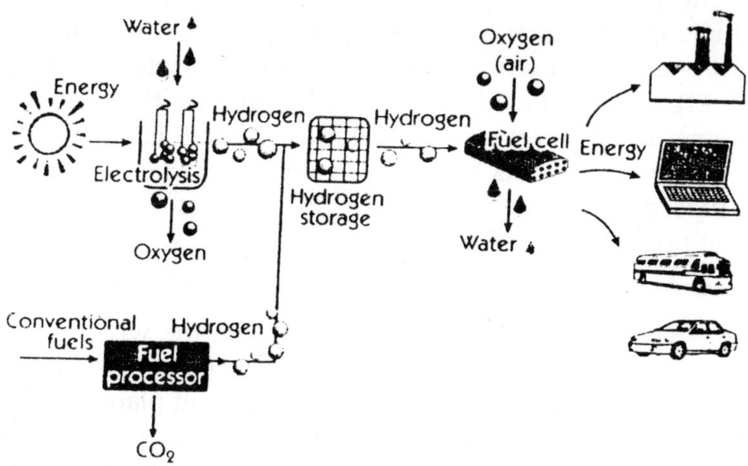

Fig. 1. Generation of hydrogen and its uses (Courtesy of SHELL).

the fuel cell's ideal fuel. Fuel cells work by combining hydrogen with oxygen from the air is an electrochemical process that is clean and flameless. Electric power and pure, distilled water, alongwith useful heat are produced. Today, fuel cells are emerging in the energy market place, not only in experimental vehicles but also in small power plants serving groups of homes and buildings and in large sizes powering factories and other industrial facilities. Today's fuel cells generata power much more efficiently than a car engine running on gasoline i.e., roughly $2^1/_2$ times more, according to nost estimates. Fuel cells capture 40 percent to 65 percent of hydrogen's energy and convert it to electricity. The U.S. electric power network converts only 33 percent to 35 percent of fuel energy into electricity on average and wastes most of the heat released during power generation. However, the service life of today's fuel cells is much too short, and fuel cell costs are 15 to 20 times too high for mass-market success. In a future fuel cells would be used in three ways: (1) transportation, (2) stationary fuel cell plants generating electricity from a fixed location, and (3) portable miniature fuel cells powering small appliances, e.g., laptop computers, cellular phones, and other hand-held devices. Fuel cell uses electrolytes which are liquids lor solids that channel charged particles inside the cell, e.g., phosphoric acid, molten carbonate, solid oxide, and polymer electrolyte membrane (PEM). One of the advantages of fuel cells is their modular design, i.e., connect several fuel cells together if more power is needed. Fuel cells have been anointed as the best bet for future micropower systems, e.g., engines and turbines modified to run on hydrogen or hydrogen/natural gas blends.

Drivers and Barriers

Several interrelated forces are driving the world's strial nations toward a hydrogen economy that could use fuel llls for much of its electricity, from multi-megawatt plants to home generators and car engines. Chief among these proved technologies are fuel cells, which could launch hydrogen the world's energy mix. The automotive industry is eering the development of practical, desirable hydrogen fuel cell-powered vehicles, joined by oil companies and equipment ufacturers. Environmental advocates find fault with some pathways toward a hydrogen future, most notably production of drogen from coal and nuclear power or even from natural gas. ling hydrogen from natural gas and other fossil fuels would ivolve some amount of air pollution, depending on the production ile. Many environmental activists would produce hydrogen only renewable sources like wind power and solar energy. Scientists are collecting data covering hundreds of years, and they are using computer models to estimate changes that have occurred over thousands of years before that. Some effects of global warming are already apparent, e.g. glaciers have begun melting, causing a measurable rise in sea levels. The United nations' Intergovernmental Panel on Climate Change (IPCC) estimated that if nothing is done to counteract global warming, planet's temperature could increase within the next century by a range of 1.4°C to 5.8°C. Moreover, the IPCC said unequivocally that human activities have contributed substantially to global warming over the past 50 years. Important organizations working on global warming are : (1) National Research Council, (2) Georgetown University, (3) United Nations, (4) National Academy of Science, and (5) European Environment Agency. Methane, the prime constituent of natural gas, is a potent greenhouse gas that has been indicated, alongwith CO_2, as a cause of global arming. Methane is released from leaky natural distribution systems, coal mines, rice paddies, livestock, fud municipal landfills. The United Nations had initiated the flyoto Protocol, a treaty that mandates reduction of greenhouse gas emissions. It uses 1990 as the starting point and calls for lecific percentage decreases below the level. Scientists Identified emissions of chlorofluorocarbons (CFCs) as a culprit in puncturing the earth's protective ozone layer.

Carbon dioxide emissions in the developing world (including China and India) are expected to surpass those in industrial countries before 2025. See Fig. 2. However, developing countries will still account for less than half of

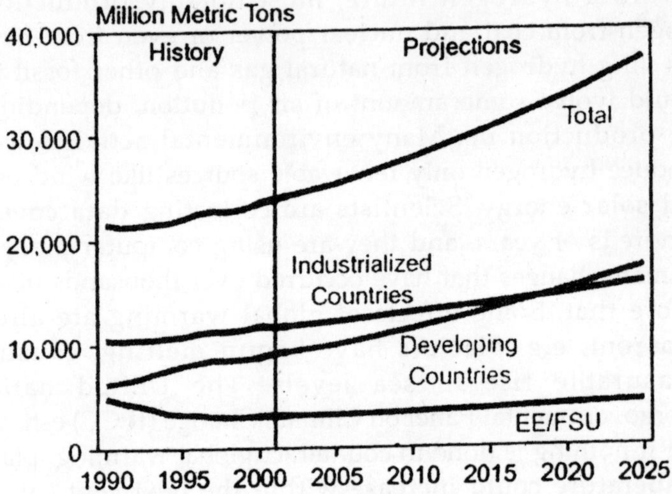

Fig. 2. Global carbon dioxide emissions by different regions (Courtesy of EIA).

global CO_2 emissions. Hydrogen-fueled micro-power could improve the lives of people dependent on primitive fuels, e.g., wood, charcoal, and cattle dung, Investment in cleaner, more efficient energy technologies in developing nations will be promoted by the U.S. Overseas Private Investment Corpn., under an agreement with the U.S. Department of Energy in 2004. The two agencies will support U.S. investment in environmentally sound economic growth in emerging uarkets. By any measure, hydrogen fuel cells are more efficient than traditional power generation plants based on combustion of fossil fuels and much more efficient than the lowly car engine. Hydrogen fuel cells can be applied in our transportation sectors for automotive power and in stationary plants for power generation on just about any scale, from homes to utilities. In the United States in 2002-03,, transportation accounted for about 33 percent of CO_2 emissions. See Fig. 3. In the electric power industry, the use

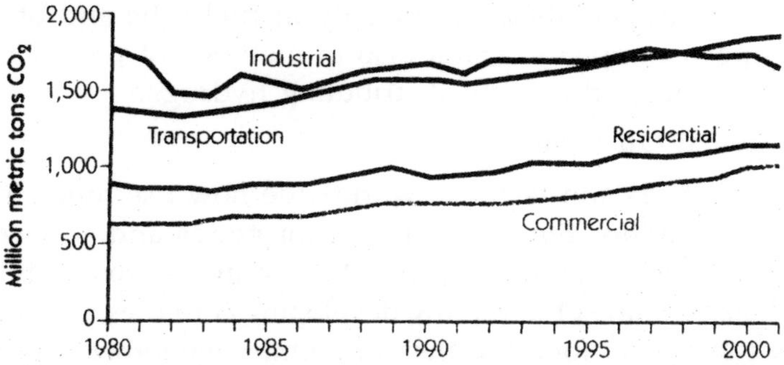

Fig. 3. U.S.A. carbon dioxide emissions (Courtesy of EIA).

of fossil fuels accounted for about 39 percent of total energy—related CO_2 emissions in 2002-03, and its share is projected to increase to 41 percent in 2025, said the U.S. Energy Information Administration (EIA). See Fig. 4. Hydrogen fuel cell vehicles and micropower could help control emissions from the transportation sector and from electric power operations. Running on hydrogen and oxygen, the fuel cell

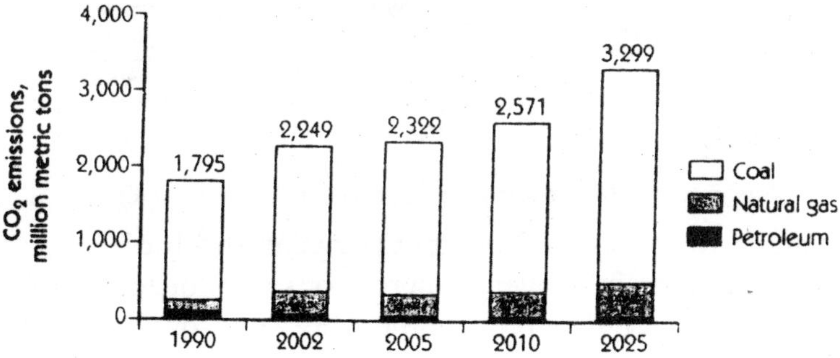

Fig. 4. U.S.A. electric power sector carbon dioxide emissions (Courtesy of EIA).

generates electricity for the motor, and the vehicle emits only water vapour. Hydrogen fuel cells in vehicles range in efficiency upto 60 percent. Fuel cells in stationary power generation rations operate at efficiencies upto 65 percent, and using cogenerated heat, a fuel cell system can approach efficiencies of 85 cent. Examples of technological innovation on the hydrogen abound, not only in fuel cells and other micropower appliances, but also in methods of producing, storing, transporting, and distributing hydrogen.

The global Oil Picture

Businesses and factories worldwide now use much less energy iproduce the same amount of goods and services. Nevertheless, global oil consumption continues to climb by the sheer volume of in rapidly developing countries and their increasing iaand for oil as their economies modernize. Today global oil demand is growing rapidly, not only in the United States, but in developing nations in Asia, South America and Africa. See Fig. 5. Through 2025, China's oil consumption is

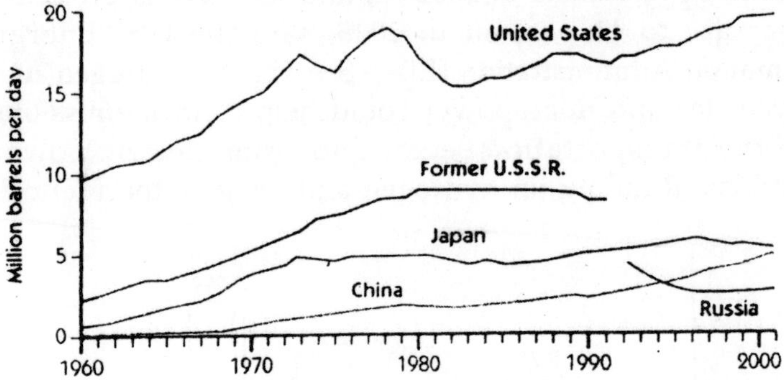

Fig. 5. Global oil consumer countries (Courtesy of EIA).

projected to grow at 4.8 percent per year and India's by 4.7 percent per year. In of overall energy consumption, developing Asia accounts for 40 percent of the increase through 2025. See Fig. 6. According to three forecasts of world oil production, the peak will occur no later than 2016. See Fig. 7. This view foresees annual production declines of about 2.5 percent over the 20 years following the peak. The U.S. EIA and many oil companies are more optimistic about the world's oil output. Using U.S. Geological Survey data, EIA projects healthy growth in production of conventional oil through 2020 and a peak around 2037-2047. See Fig. 8. The Middle East commands more than 40 percent of the world's oil, most of it around

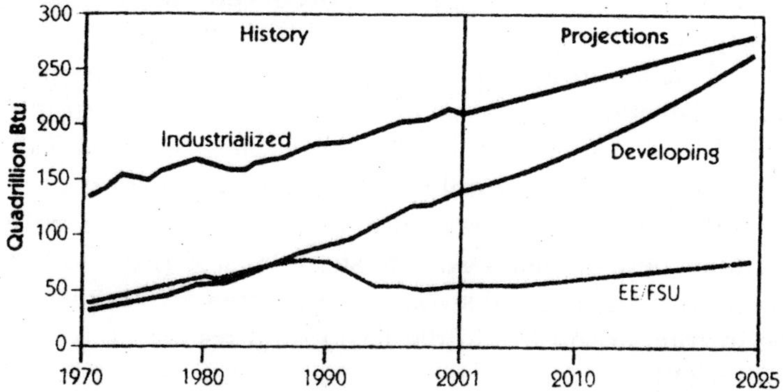

Fig. 6. Energy use in developing nations (Courtesy of EIA).

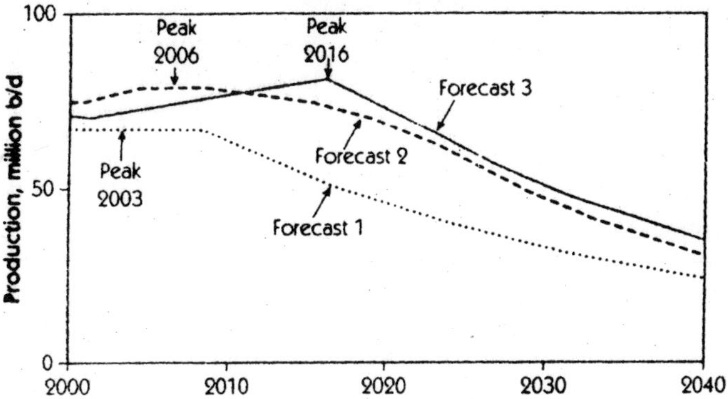

Fig. 7. Future world oil production (Courtesy of Oil & Gas Journal).

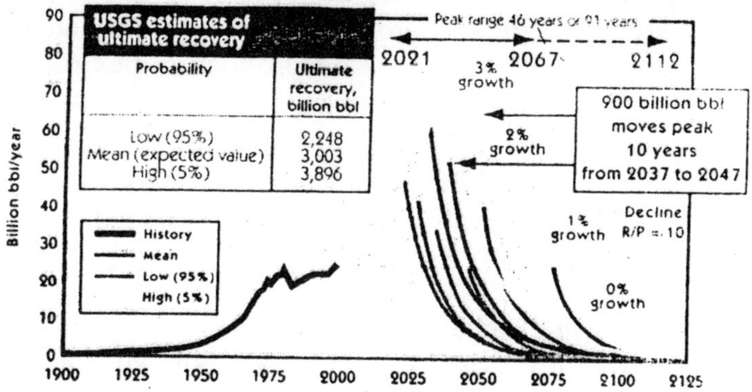

Fig. 8. Conventional oil production forecasts (Courtesy of Oil & Gas Journal)

the Persian Gulf. As other big oil producers like Russia and the United States peter out in the future, the Middle East's share of global production becomes proportionately large. See Table 1. Several trends have raised spirits that Western might depend less on OPEC oil in the future. Supplies from Russia have swelled, hindered only by its capacity to export the oil. Central Asian countries like Kazakhstan have found enormous new oil fields. And offshore West Africa and Brazil have seen some huge oil strikes. Even these new supplies will pale in comparison to Middle Eastern oil resources. National Iranian Oil projects an irreversible decline in production

Table 1. Middle East Share of production (Country of Oil and Gas Journal)

	2000	*2005*	*2010*	*2020*
		Million b/d		
World	63.24	59.48	59.61	46.04
Middle East	20.83	18.84	23.17	22.03
Ratio ME/world, %	32.9	31.7	38.9	47.8

*The 64 major oil-production nations.

Source : Colin Compbell, Association for the Study of Peak Oil database for conventional oil endowment, February 2002

beginning in 2006-07, due mainly to falling output from countries outside the Persian Gulf. See Fig. 9. Japan has virtually no oil resources. Europe's large North Sea fields are mostly mature, and U.S. crude oil production has recently hovered at 50-year lows. America's dependence on imports will grow from 53 percent of its consumption in 2002 to a projected 70 percent in 2025. See Fig. 10. Global gas reserves are growing, and trade in the form of liquefied natural gas (LNG) is thriving. The world's output of conventional gas might peak as early as 2020. Japan has almost no gas. Europe's large fields are mature, and the United States will rely more on gas imports in the future with increases in consumption being led by the power generation sector. See Fig. 11. Saudi Arabia is the only country with substantial extra oil

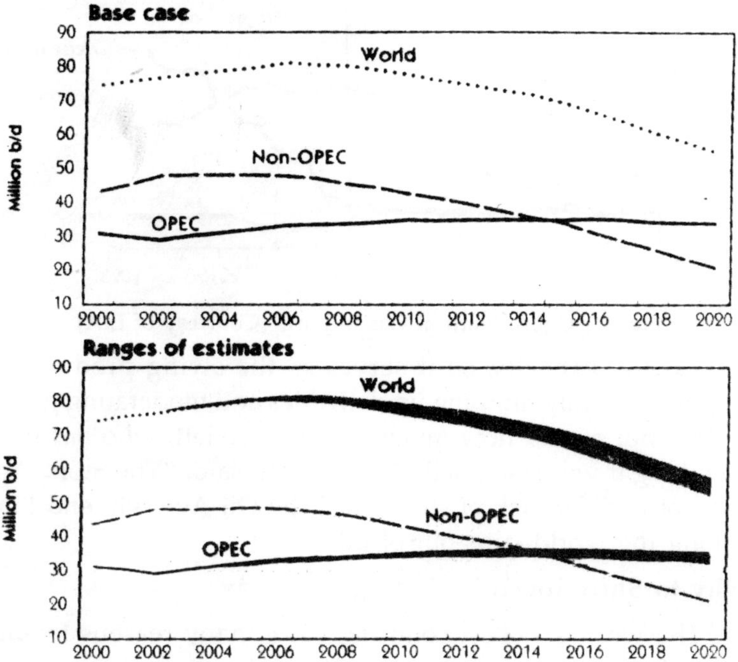

Fig. 9. Oil Production outlook (Courtesy of Oil and Gas Journal).

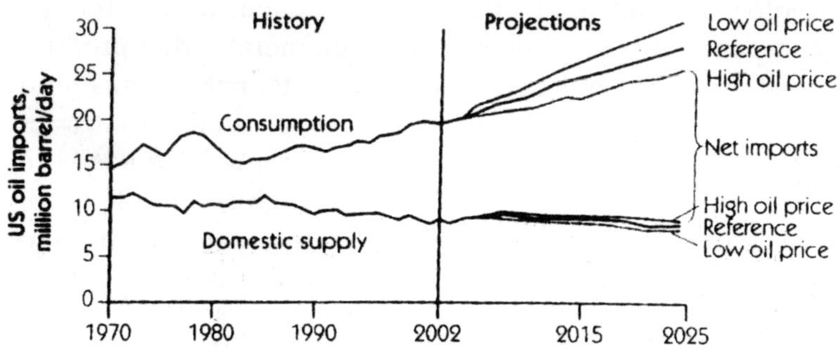

Fig. 10. U.S.A. oil imports (Courtesy of EIA).

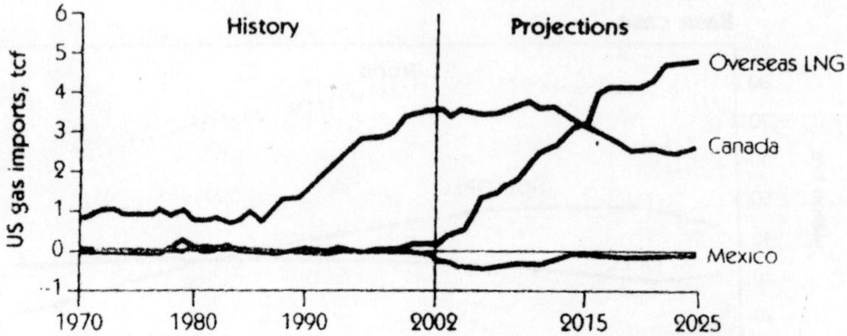

Fig. 11. U.S.A. Natural Gas imports (Courtesy of EIA).

production capacity, so it serves as the swing producer in charge of rapidly ramping up deliveries and moderating prices. It does not matter how much oil we have left, who has it, or how long it will last. Sheik Zaki Yamani said, "The Stone Age did not end for lack of stone, and the Oil Age will end long belong the world runs out of oil."

Why to Shift Towards Hydrogen Energy

The world's richest countries have many reasons to shift towards hydrogen energy systems, i.e., to slow down global warming and control air pollution, to improve efficiency and conserve energy, to reduce oil consumption and mitigate dependence on imports, and to take advantage of technological innovations that meet consumer needs. Today's oil companies are actually energy conglomerates that produce not just crude oil but petroleum products, natural gas, and other fuels and chemicals. But hydrogen does offer routes for the oil industry to profit. Energy companies are eager to supply and fuel that their customers night want. The oil/ energy industry pioneers in promoting hydrogen are BP and Shell, both based in Europe, and America's Chevron Texaco. They have joined with several of the world's major auto—makers in demonstrating hydrogen fuel cell vehicles and fueling stations. Government funding would be essential during the early stages of building a hydrogen infrastructure. Hydrogen fuel cells are one of the nost promising type of micropower, by virtue of their efficiency and cleanliness.

Internal-combustion engines can he modified to accept hydrogen or hydrogen-methane fuels, and eventually microturbines and large turbines also could operate on hydrogen. Future micropower systems like hydrogen fuel cells could deliver electricity 99.9999 per cent of the time, with only 32 seconds of downtime per year aot counting scheduled maintenance. Hydrogen fuel cell micropower can augment the grid supply, especially during peak hours.

Micropower promises to help relieve some of the problems facing electricity utilities, i.e., peak electricity consumption, completion, and growing demand and more reliable, higher quality power. Micropower can help the ytility meet its peak demand by serving major customers or 1 supplementing the utility's local distribution feeder lines in areas where the grid is highly congested. This is one of the clearest benefits of micropower to the electric fustry, i.e., it can improve grid reliability by relieving congestion and reducing peak load. Additional benefits to utilities and power providers include the Dtential to sell or trade emission credits and to exploit new business opportunities. Many of the world's biggest manufacturers see a profitable market in fuel cells, hydrogen production units, storage tanks, and other equipment needed for hydrogen use. Many scientists believe that government support is essential to accelerate a global transition to a future hydrogen energy economy, or could be required for it to happen at all. The European Union (EU) announced in 2002 a bold plan for Europe to become "the first hydrogen economy superpower of the 21st century". The European Union's research is aimed at reducing the cost of hydrogen production, solving storage problems, and integrating renewable sources into hydrogen fuel production over the longer term. One of Europe's most visible programs is called Clean Urban Transport for Europe (CUTE), which is demonstrating 30 hydrogen fuel cell-powered public buses, three in each of ten cities. As early as 1974, Japan started Project Sunshine, which included a hydrogen budget reportedly in excess of $3 billion through 2000. In the early

1990s, Japan's hydrogen research morphed into a 30-year plan with funding of another $2 billion. All along, Japan's industry has been a global leader in developing fuel cell technology. Japanese utilities are mainly receptive to micropower, and Japan has also led implementation of hydrogen fuel cells in vehicles and development of fueling infrastructure. American's energy policy is a subject of global debate, since the United States consumes such a large share of the world's resources. DOE planned to invest a total of $1.7 billion in hydrogen-related R&D through 2010. America's fuel cell research projects also address critical cost and durability issues. Three Centres of Excellence will focus on hydrogen storage research, led by the National Renewable Energy Laboratory, Los Alamos National Laboratory, and Sandia National Laboratories. In addition to hydrogen vehicle programmes, the United States has formulated a nationwide standard for connecting stationary fuel cells and other micropower plants to the utility grid, which should make them easier to site and build.

Of the 50 U.S. states, 23 offer financial incentives for fuel cell technologies. In addition, 23 states are considering adoption of the IEEE's national grid interconnection standards, which should promote the installation of micropower systems, and 15 states are instituting or considering net metering rules, which would allow micropower units to sell electricity back to grid. California leads the states in hydrogen fuel cell vehicle and infrastructure initiatives, primarily through the California Hydrogen Highway programme and the California Fuel Cell Partnership. A similar Hydrogen Highway project is starting up in Illinois. Hawaii has been researching hydrogen for almost 20 years and recently boosted its requirements for utilities to use renewable energy sources. Like California and Illinois, Canada is planning a Hydrogen Highway in British Columbia along 130 km. corridor from Vancouver to Whistler, with an extension to Victoria. According to the National Hydrogen Study, all of Australia's buses and 10 to 20 percent of other vehicles might run on hydrogen by 2030, and fuel cells could account for upto 5 percent commercial and residential micropower. China and other Asian countries are stepping up their hydrogen research programmes. Some fuel cell vehicles already are operating in China. China's research institutions focus generally on PEM (Polymer electrolyte membrane) fuel cell technology in transportation applications. Also, China has substantial installed capacity of micropower systems in industrial sizes. India is also working in hydrogen and fuel cells programmes. Some fuel cell vehicles already are operating in India. Nearly one million vehicles will the running on Indian roads by 2020 using hydrogen which will also be used to produce approximately 1000 MW of electricity, according to the roadmap prepared by a steering group set up by the government to promote the gas as future fuel. After finalising a hydrogen energy roadmap, the government is now preparing a strategy to harness solar energy as part of efforts to promote renewable energy sources in the country. The ministry of non-conventional energy sources is making a Solar Photovoltaic Technology Roadmap for the country upto 2022, in line with the 11th, 12th and 13th Five-Year plans. Iceland decided in 1999 to transform itself into the world's first hydrogen economy. Iceland's plan is to use its cheap, clean power to produce hydrogen by electrolysis and ultimately to eliminate petroleum products and use hydrogen fuel cells for transportation. All of the island's 180,000 vehicles and its fleet of more than 2000 boats will be switched from traditional fuel within 30 to 50 years. A joint venture called Iceland New Energy Ltd. was formed to develop hydrogen production technology and fuel cell applications. A smaller scale projĕct was taking place in Norway's smallest town, the island of Utsira, where energy comapny Norsk Hydro built the world's first combined hydrogen-wind power plant. The electrical output from one of two wind turbines is used to make hydrogen, which is stored in a tank and reconverted to electricity on demand by a fuel cell. The second wind turbine sends power into the grid, making the island a net exporter of electricity.

Barriers and Challenges

Cost is the biggest challenge, i.e., primarily the cost of delivering hydrogen and the complex logistics involved. Hydrogen can be transported fairly cheaply by pipeline, but building a new pipeline network for hydrogen is prohibitively expensive in the short term, through it might be a long-term solution in certain strategic areas. For the next few years, compressed or liquified hydrogen can be trucked to fueling stations. This is too expensive a method to use for very long. According to the National Research Council (NRC), the service life of today's fuel cells is much too short, and fuel cell costs are 10 to 20 times too high for market success. To satisfy consumers, fuel cells in vehicles would have to last about 5000 hours, which would translate to 150,000 to 200,000 miles. Also, vehicles will have to store enough hydrogen, without affecting cargo or passenger space, to travel more than 500 km., which is one of the U.S. DOE's key goals. Fuel cell vehicle range is still much too short. One of the greatest thing about hydrogen is that it can be produce from water or from just about any fuel on the planet. But how to do this cost-effectively is a scientific challenge. Generating the electricity, converting it to hydrogen, and converting it back to electricity obviously adds costs and energy losses, and these are particularly significant when hydrogen becomes a commodity transportation fuel, said NRC. Producing hydrogen from natural gas and other fossil fuels releases carbon dioxide, which would need to be captured and stored (sequestered). Sequestration could well act as a stepping-stone to a renewable-based hydrogen economy. The biggest obstacle to micropower has been connecting units with the utility grid. The key to the ultimate market success of small micropower system is the ability to safely, reliably, and economically connect to the utility grid. Another potential showstopper is the utility tariff and rate structure, which can discriminate against micropower. Local siting restrictions and permitting requirements, including air quality regulations, can impose burdensome approval process that inhibit micropower projects, especially in small sizes because the costs and siting and permitting do not scale down fully with project size. Safety is an especially important issue in the hydrogen vehicle market. Even NRC envisions that the path toward a hydrogen economy is neither simple nor straightforward, and it presents major hurdles. Hydrogen is a promissory note for humanity's future on earth.

Fundamentals and Background

Hydrogen is the source of the sun's heat and light, which is radiated to the earth in enormous amounts. Hydrogen—fueled reactions also supply most of the energy given off by other stars. Its atomic structure is the smallest, lightest, and simplest of all the elements. On earth hydrogen is not found free in nature. Hydrogen combines with all other elements except inert gases, so it creates more compounds than any other elements. Hydrogen can be produced by unlocking the chemical bonds in water, hydrocarbon fuels and other compounds. But these methods consume energy, because the chemical bonds in these substances are strong and stable. Hydrogen is usually considered an energy carrier, i.e., a way to transport and store energy that is produced elsewhere, from other sources. Hydrogen contains more energy per unit of weight of any known fuel, e.g., about three times the energy of gasoline weighing the same amount and almost seven times that of coal. Hydrogen's energy content is 52,000 Btu per pound (120.7 kilojoules per gram). When cooled to a liquid, hydrogen takes up just 1/700th as much space *as* it does in its gaseous form. Hydrogen can also be stored in compounds called metal hydrides, and possibly in the future in microscopic structure made of carbon. Hydrogen is highly flammable in the presence of air. Also, it has a wide range of flammability, meaning that it will burn in low concentrations as well as high ones (4 percent to 74 percent by volume in air). Hydrogen can not be detected by people's sense of smell, so a leak of pure hydrogen could be hazardous if it accumulates. Hydrogen produces no harmful emissions when its combined electrochemically with oxygen. The only product is pure water. Hydrogen also can form nitrogen oxides (NO_x) when it's burned with air, which contains about 80 percent nitrogen. Hydrogen produces zero soot emissions (particulates).

Hydrogen can be produced from water, hydrocarbon fuels, or other compounds. Electrolysis produces the two gases, hydrogen and oxygen, when an electric current is applied. In the reverse reaction, hydrogen combines with oxygen, producing water and giving off large amounts of heat (an exothermic reaction). Today hydrogen can be produced by electrolysis, but it's expensive because it uses a lot of electricity. Only about 4 percent of the world's hydrogen supply comes from electrolysis, mostly for use in processes requiring very pure hydrogen, such as electronics manufacturing. Although the electrical energy needed to split water exceeds the energy contained in the hydrogen product, eventually this electric power could come from wind turbines, solar energy, or other renewable resources. Nearly all of the hydrogen produced today (96 percent) comes from steam reforming of fossil fuels, mostly natural gas (48 percent). Some is also produced from reforming oil (30 percent) and coal (18 percent). Several advanced techniques are being developed to produce hydrogen in the future. These include gasification of coal and biomass, which produces a gas mixture from which hydrogen can be extracted. Two new methods being developed would use solar energy to split the water molecule : (1) photobiological techniques exploit algae and bacteria to produce hydrogen in the presence of sunlight, and (2) photoelectro-chemical processes split water into hydrogen and oxygen using sunlight and semiconductor electrodes. The water molecule can also be split into hydrogen and oxygen using heat and chemicals, at very high temperature.

Fuel Cell Technology

Fuel cells are similar to batteries, but instead of generating power from stored chemicals, fuel cells combine hydrogen with oxygen in an efficient electrochemical process that is clean and flameless. Electric power and pure, distilled water, along with heat then cane be recovered and used. Fuel cells need no charging. They will operate as long as hydrogen fuel is supplied. In a fuel cell, the hydrogen molecule's atoms are split into protons and electrons. The fuel cell's electrolyte lets the protons pass through, but it diverts the electrons through external wiring, allowing their energy to be captured as electricity. When the protons and electrons are reunited, the hydrogen molecules combine with oxygen to form water. To obtain the desired amount of electrical power, individual fuel cells can be connected into stacks. Increasing the stack's number of cells boosts its voltage, while increasing the cells' surface area boosts its current. Fuel cells release heat in varying amounts. When this heat is recovered and used in cogeneration applications, the overall system efficiency increases. Types of fuel cells are phosphoric acid, molten carbonate, solid oxide, alkaline cells, and PEM (polymer electrolyte membrane or proton exchange membrane).

PEM fuel cells deliver high power density and offer the advantages of low weight and volume, compared to other types. They operate around 80°C to 100°C. PEM fuel cells are good for vehicles and micropower applications. PEM technology uses a solid polymer membrane (thin plastic film) and porous carbon electrodes containing a platinum catalyst or other noble metals. See Fig. 12. Phosphoric acid fuel cells used liquid phosphoric acid as an electrolyte. This acid is contained in a Teflon-bonded silicon carbide matrix, and porous carbon electrodes contain a platinum catalyst. Phosphoric acid fuel cells are used mainly for stationary power generation, but some have been applied in large vehicles such as city buses. It is one of the most mature cell types and the first to be used commercially. They are upto 80 per cent in cogeneration electricity and heat, but only 37 percent to 55 percent efficient at producing electricity alone. Phosphoric acid fuel cells also deliver less power than other types, so they are usually large and heavy. Solid oxide fuel cells generate large amounts of useful high-temperature heat.

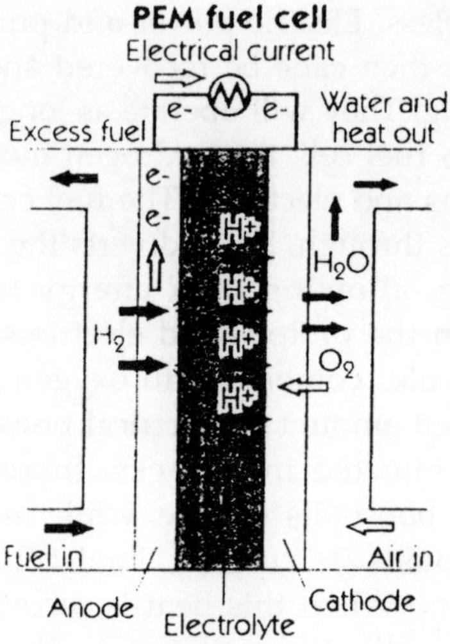

Fig. 12. Schematic of PEM fuel cell (Courtesy of DOE).

These cells are around 45 percent to 65 percent efficient at converting fuel to electricity. In cogeneration applications, fuel use efficiencies could reach 85 percent. These cells use a hard, non-porous ceramic compound as the electrolyte. They operate at very high temperature, around 1000°C. These cells reform fuels internally, so no costly reformer is needed, and a variety of fuels can be used. They can run on gases made from coal. Alkaline fuel cells use a solution of potassium hydroxide in water as the electrolyte and can use a variety of non-precious metal catalysts. These cells operate between 100°C and 250°C. These cells reach efficiencies of 60 percent in space applications. Their operating lifetimes are relatively short. Molten carbonate fuel cells are suitable for utility power plants and industrial applications and do not need precious-metal catalysts. They use an electrolyte composed of a molten carbonate salt mixture suspended in. a porous, chemically inert ceramic lithium-aluminium oxide matrix. The efficiency of these fuel cells approach 60 percent and with cogeneration, they can reach 85 percent. Their electrolyte is corrosive and cell life is short. Table 2 gives summary of these fuel cell types.

Table 2. Fuel Cell Technologies

Fuel cell type	*Temp. range*	*Efficiency*	*Electrolyte*	*Capacities*	*Primary application*	*Notes*
Polymer eiectrolyte or proton exchange membrane	< 100° C (<212°F)	50-60%	Polymer membrane (thin plastic film)	100 W to 250 kW per cell	Transportation, stationary	Fast startup, high power density, rapid response to power demand. relatively rugged
Phosphoric acid	160°-220°C (320-430°F)	37–55%; up to 72-80% with heat recovery	Concentrated phosphoric acid	25-250 kW per cell	Stationary	Fuel of choice is Fuel of choice is natural gas
Solid oxide	800°-1,000°C (1,500-1,800°F)	45-65%; up to 70-85% with heat recovery	Solid nonporous cermic materials	200 W per cell; 300 kW to 3 MW per module	Stationary, utility	Typically applied in stack of hundreds; a plant might produce up to 10 MW
Alkine	23°-250°C (70-482°F)	50-60%	Potassium hydroxide solution (35-50% KOH)	2.2 kW	Spacecraft	Being developed for other applications
Molten Carbonate	650°-660°C (1,200°F)	45-60% 70-85 with heat recovery	Melted carbonate salt mixture	250 kW to > 1 MW	Stationary, utility	Corrosive electrolyte limits durability

*Without recovery of cogenerated heat, unless otherwise noted.

Fuel cells produce divert current (dc) electricity. An inverter is needed to change the fuel cell's power from dc to ac. Stationary fuel cells use natural gas as their fuel instead of hydrogen, so an onsite reformer is part of the package. The reformer extracts hydrogen from natural gas or other hydrocarbon fuels. When used in a car or other vehicle, the fuel cell supplies power to an electric motor. Fuel cells generate electricity from hydrogen fuel, and the vehicles are refueled.

Uses of Hydrogen

Two applications use the greatest amounts of hydrogen : (1) manufacturing ammonia, and (2) refining crude oil. Ammonia is an important fertilizer and industrial chemical, and hydrogen is a critical ingredient in refinery processes such as hydrocracking and hydrogeneration, which produce gasoline, heating oil, and other petroleum products. In the food industry, edible fats and oils are solidified using hydrogen. Manufacturing a numerous other commercial products require hydrogen, e.g., dyes, drugs, plastics, vitamins, cosmetics, soaps, lubricants, and cleaners. Significant quantities of hydrogen are used in manufacturing methanol and electronic components. Hydrogen is also used to recover pure metals from their compounds and to generate very high temperatures for arc welding and glass cutting. In the electric power industry, hydrogen reduces friction in rotating equipment and is used to cool large generators, motors, and frequency changers. The exploration of outer space needs substantial amounts of liquid hydrogen as a rocket fuel. Recent history of hydrogen and fuel cell research and development is given in Table-3. An excellent, detailed history of hydrogen appears in Tomorrow's Energy by Peter Hoffman (2001).

Applications and Markets

A few oil/energy conglomerates have become pioneers in promoting hydrogen, e.g., BP and shell, both based in Europe, and America's Chevron Texaco. British Petroleum (BP) already produces about 5000 metric tons of hydrogen

Table 3. Recent history of hydrogen and fuel cell R & D

1987	Government study urges Canada to make hydrogen energy technology a national mission
	1st fuel cell bus project in United States begins with hybrid design
1988	Maiden flight of Soviet Union passenger jet with one engine concerted to liquid hydrogen
	First flight of airplane fueled only on liquid hydrogen, a four-set Grumman flow by William Conrad in Florida
	Soviet Union's high level of hydrogen research activities is revealed at World
	Hydrogen Energy Conference in Moscow
	Canada launches solid polymer electrolyte fuel cell research program
	Germany begins sea trials of hydrogen fuel cell submarine
	Study begins shipping electrolytically generated hydrogen from Quebec to Europe
1989	National Hydrogen Association is launched in Washington, DC
	Effort begins to establish international technical standards for hydrogen energy
	BMW builds 1st test sand for hydrogen-powered internal-combustion (*i-c*) engines
1990	German iab word's 1st solar-powered hydrogen production plant
	Soviet Union and West German plan to develop propulsion technology of liquid hydrogen jetliner prototype
	Environmental costs of fossil fuel burning are estimated at $ 2.3 trillion, or $ 460 per capita world wide; cost is equivalent to $ 1/gal gasoline in the US
	Hydrogen exhibits debut at ACHEMA, world's premier triannual chemical equipment industry show in Frankfurt
	GM begins work on 10-kW methanol PEM fuel cell
1991	Tests begin Germany on liquid hydrogen refueling device for cars and buses
	Fuel cell-battery hybrid, a converted Ford Fiesta mail-deliver car, tested in Pannsylvania
	Mazda unveils HR-X concept car using hydrogen-fueled rotary engine

1992 Grid-independent solar house in Germany uses hydrogen for long-term energy storage

US Vice President AL Gore book, Earth in the Balance : Ecology and the Human Spirit

1993 Ballard rolls out world's 1st PEM fuel in Canada

Japan plans 30-year $2 billion program to promote hydrogen energy international via We-Net

Ballard and Diamler-Benz collaborate on fuel cells for cars an buses

California funds study of fuel cell locomotives

1994 Funding is won fuel three pickup trucks in North America on hydrogen produced from solar energy and water

Daimler-Benz displays 1st NECAR fuel vehicle in Germany

Saudi-German Hysolar demonstration plant begins operation near Riyadh

Ballard PEM shuttle buses operating in Canada

Quebec-EU effort unveils 1st of four hydrogen-powered buses

Europe's 1st fuel bus debuts in Brussels, he 87-kW Eureka alkaline cell hybrid

BMW displays four generations of LH2 fueled I-c engine cars

1995 Chicago tests three hydrogen buses using Ballard PEM fuel cells

Daimler-Benz plans to convert am commuter airplane engine to liquid hydrogen

1996 Molten carbonate fuel plant senates electricity in California using natural gas

Daimler-Benz NECAR 2 minivan is unveiled in Germany, 1st consumer-friendly, pollution-free fuel cell passenger vehicle

Toyota debuts experimental SUV using PEM cell

Liquid hydrogen bus operating in Germany, I-c engine converted from natural gas

1st hydrogen golf delivered in California, using PEM fuel cell

1997 Chrysler show mockup PEM fuel cell passenger car that would use hydrogen extracted onboard gasoline

Hydrogen's blame for Hindenburg disaster is challenged

Daimler-Benz and Ballard to spend $ 300 million on developing fuel cells for transportation; Ford joins team

NECAR 3 is unveiled, to run on 50-kW Ballard PEM fuel cell using methanol

Daimler-Benz unveils prototype NEMUS using 250-kW PEM fuel cell

Japan's Musashi institute of Technology displays LH_2 fueled Nissan station wagon

Mazda unveils Demion hybrid station wagon using 20-kW PEM cell

U. S. presidential adverse urge expansion DOE's hydrogen program

1998 GM and Opel launch global PEM fuel cell project for European cars Opel shows experimental Zafira minivan using fuel cell

1st U.S. residential fuel is installed, in a ranch home in New York state

Norwegian conglomerate Norsk Hydro plans electric generation from hydrogen-fueled stem turbines

Iceland lays groundwork for its hydrogen economy

Shell sets up renewables division and hydrogen team

Zevco debuts its alkaline fuel cell Millennium in London with Shell support

U.S. DOE publishes 5-years strategic plan for hydrogen program 1999

Shell creates hydrogen division

Europe's 1st Hydrogen stations open in Hamburg and Munich

Daimler Chrysler introduces NECAR 4, shows fuel cell jeep concept vehicle

Ford unveils 75-kW fuel p 20000 research vehicle and mockup of fuel cell SUV, opens hydrogen fueling station at its Michigan research lab.

The Icelandic Hydrogen and Fuel Cell Co. is created by team of Icelandic companies/institutions and three multinationals

California languages Fuel Partnership with automakers, oil companies, and Ballard

BMW unveils 5th-generation LH_2 car using liquid hydrogen in I-c- engine and opens refueling station in Munich with a fully automated fuel pump

2000 Words 1st production-ready PEM fuel cell for automotive use is unveiled by Ballard, a 70-kW unit for 1st-generation fuel cell cars

GM shows fuel cell version of Precept concept car, 105-kW PWM cell

Ford shows Think FC5 75-kW fuel cell prototype designed for methanol

Zembus is launched in Belgium, a diesel city bus converted to hydrogen

Bayembus debuts Munich, two PEM fuel cell buses rolled out

American researchers describe experimental renewable hydrogen production based on great algae

BMW plans world's 1st commercial hydrogen-fueled car, would use internal-combustion engine

per day for industrial uses and is involved in fuel cell vehicle demonstrations in Europe, Asia, Australia, and North America. Shell planned to spend upto $1 billion during 2001-2006 on hydrogen energy R&D. Shell's hydrogen division is demonstrating hydrogen fueling applications in the three major hydrogen markets, i.e., Japan, Europe and North America. Chevron Texaco America company will design and build uptc six hydrogen fueling stations, including one based on onsite steam reforming of natural gas that will dispense upto 150 kg/day of hydrogen and use any excess to generate electricity from a stationary fuel cell. This hydrogen station will initially support three fuel cell transit buses in California. Also, a Chevron Texaco unit was developing its Halias technology, which makes hydrogen from natural gas or propane. ONGC Energy Centre Trust, India, dedicated to holistic research in non-conventional energy source in the premises of Rajiv Gandhi Urja Bhavan coming up in New Delhi, has taken up 3 projects : (1) Thermal-Chemical Reactor for hydrogen, (2) geo-bio reactors, and (3) fuel cell.

Hydrogen fuel cell vehicles are coming up in the world market and generating the most excitement in public. Most of the fueling stations being installed for these vehicles demonstrations use small, onsite reformers or electrolytic generators to provide hydrogen, so fuel cell vehicles no longer need to carry their own fuel processor onboard to reform gasoline, methanol, or natural gas. Auto-makers have shifted toward onboard hydrogen storage instead. This has led the industry to wind down its efforts to develop onboard processors for fuel cell vehicles. In 2004 General Motors set a world distance record for fuel cell vehicles, travelling 9751 kilometres and cross 14 countries, from northern Norway to the Portuges capital of Lisbon, the continent's most western point. GM' s goal is to make fuel cell vehicle technology commercially viable by 2010. The record was set by GM' s HydroGen 3 fuel cell prototype. See Fig. 13. Ford Motor Co. began production of a fleet cell-powdered Focus sedans in late 2004, which will be deployed in several cities worldwide. Two

Fig. 13. GM HydroGen 3 fuel cell prototype, travelled more than 9700 km, setting a world distance record (Courtesy of GM).

Honda FCX hydrogen fuel cell-powered *cars* were delivered in 2004 to the City of San Francisco, which planned to build refueling infrastructure to support their daily operation. During 2004 United Parcel Service (UPS) was operating a Daimler Chrysler F-Cell car on a daily express-delivery route around Ann Arbor, MI. A strategic alliance between Ballard Power Systems and automakers Daimler Chrysler and Ford has resulted in PEM fuel cells being used in Citaro buses, Mercedes and Focus cars, and other fuel cell vehicles being demonstrated. Toyato has developed a hydrgeon fuel cell-battery hybrid vehicle based on its Highlander mid-sized sport utility vehicle. A hybrid fuel cell vehicle based on Nissan Motor Co's X-Trail SUV was leased by Japan's Cosmo Oil Co., which also operates Toyota and Honda fuel cell vehicles. BMW plans to offer a hybrid gasoline-hydrogen car based on an internal-combustion engine rather than a fuel cell. One of Europe's most prominent hydrogen programmes, CUTE, is demonstrating 30 fuel cell-powered public buses, three in of ten cities, i.e., Amsterdam, Barcelona, Hamburg, London, Luxembourg, Madrid, Porto (Portugal), Reykjavik (Iceland), Stockholm, and Stuttgart (Germany). The Japan Hydrogen Fuel Cell (JHFC) demonstration project is Japan's first extensive research that involves actual operation of fuel cell vehicles for demonstration purposes. A joint venture called Iceland New Energy Ltd. is developing hydrogen production technologies and fuel cell applications for Iceland, which plans to be the world's first hydrogen-powdered economy before 2050. California leads the U.S.A. in hydrogen fuel cell vehicle and infrastructure initiatives. See Fig. 14. Demonstration and development of hydrogen vehicles and fueling stations are given in Tables 4 and 5.

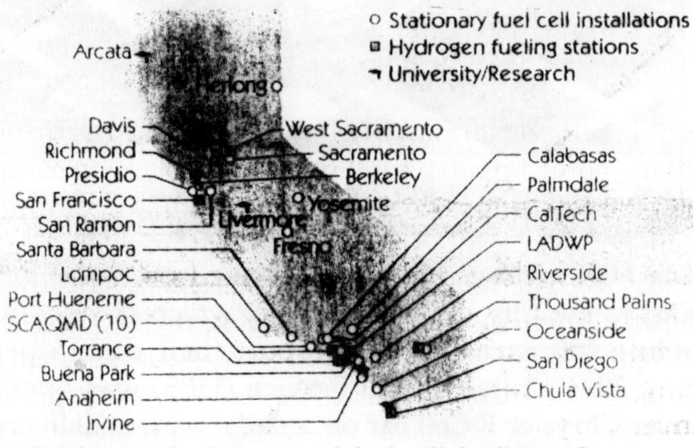

Fig. 14. California's hydrogen and fuel cell facilities (Courtesy of The State of California).

Table 4. Demonstration and Development of Hydrogen Vehicles

Automaker	*Vehicles*	*Partners*	*Locations*	*Fueling Stations*	*Dates*	*Notes*
BMW	7-Series car					Internal-combustions engine runs on liquid hydrogen
Daimler Chrysler	Thirty 280-kW Citaro urban transit buses	European Union GUJTE project	Amsterdam Barcelona; Hamburg; London; Luxembourg; Madrid; Porto, Portugal; Reykjavik, Iceland; Srockolm, Strugart, Germany	BP, Shell	2001-2006	
	Mercedes-Benz A-Class fuel cell delivery car	United Parcel Service	Ann Arbor, MI	U.S. EPA facility		
	Three Dodge Sprinter fuel cell delivery trucks	United Parcel Service	Los Angeles, Sacramento, Ann Arbor, MI	Existing	2004-2005	1st U.S. medium-duty package delivery trucks using hydrogen fuel cells
	Mercedes-Benz fuel cell A. Class	German fleet customers	Berlin	Public station available	2004	
	Three 205-kW Citro buses	China's Ministry of Science and Technology	Bejing	BP	2005 2007	
	Six cars	Singapore's Economic Development Board	Singapore	BP		

Automaker	Vehicles	Partners	Locations	Fueling Stations	Dates	Notes
Ford	Up to 30 67-kW Focus passengers cars	BP, U.S. DOE/ Freedom CAR	Sacramento, CA (10); Orlando, FL and Detroit, ML	To be built by BP; one existing at UC. Davis	2005	Sacramento vehicles operated by state/city government and Local utility
	Fuel cell delivery truk	U.S. Postal Service	Various U.S.			Real-world, limited use
GM	Six Hydro Gen 3 fuel cell minivans	Shall, U.S. Postal service	Washinton, D.C.		2004	U.S.A. 1st hydrogen pump at retail station
	Hydro Gen 3 fuel cell minivas	Linde AG	Europe marathon road test (Norway to Portugal)	Mobial station accompanied vehicle	2004	Set world distance record of 6,059 miles
	Three Hydro Gen 3 fuel cell cars	FedEx, METI/ JHFC project	Tokyo area		2003-04	1st commercial test of fuel cell while in Japan
Honda	Two 78-kW FVX fuel cell passenger cars		San Francisco		2004	One-year lease with 2nd-year option
	Two FUX fuel cell passengar	South cars	Coast Air Quality Management District	Southern Californis		
	Two FIX fuel cell passengar cars		New York state Japan		2005	On-road tests of cold-weather fuel cell stack
Nisan	X-Trail 85-kW SUV		Cosmo Oil	Japan	2004	Lithium-ion battery
Peugeot Citroen	Fuel cell cars	Millennium Cell; Gaz de France	Europe		2004	Hydrogen on Demand fuel system
Toyota	Prius fuel cell hybrid	Texaco Ovonic venture				Demonstrates onbord metal hydride storage
	Highlander SUV hybid	University of California-Irvine	Southern California	Stuart Energy Station	2004	
Volkswagen	Santana fuel cell sedans	Shanghi Auto Industry	China's Tongiu University		2005	Shanghi Auto makes almost in China

Table 5. Demonstration and Development of Hydrogen fueling Stations

Oil Company	*Vehicles*	*Partners*	*Locations*	*Dates*	*Notes*
BP	Fifteen Chrysler Citaro urban transit buses	CUTE	Barcelona; Hamaburg London, Porto Portugal, Stuttgart. Germany	2001-2006	
	Three Daimler Chrysler Citaro urban transit buses		Path, Austrilia		Hydrogen supplied by BP's Kwinana refinery
	Hydrogen powered passenger cars		Singapore		
	Hydrogen powered passengers cars		Los Angelers		
	Airport vehicles	Linde, HEW, BMW	Munich		1st public station hydrogen
	Public refueling station for range of alternative fuels		Berlin		
	Up to 30 67-kW Focus passenger cars	Ford U.S. DOE/ Freedom CAR	Sacramento, CA (10), Orlando, FL and Detroit, MI	2005	
	Three Daimler Chrysler Citaro urban transit buses		China's Manistry of Science and Technology	Beijing	205
	Daimler Chrysler Citaro urban transit buses	China'Ministry of Since and Technology	Shanghi	2005	
Shell	Three fuel cell buses	Ector/CUTE, Norsk Hydro	Reykjavik, Iceland	opend April 2003	Shall partner in legend New Energy Ltd
	Three fuel cell buses	CUTE, Amsterdam transport company (GVB)	Amsterdam	2003	Test in dense city traffic conditions on normal bus routes

Oil Company	*Vehicles*	*Partners*	*Locations*	*Dates*	*Notes*
	Three fuel cell buses	CUTE	Luxembourg		Test hilly terrain
		JMFC/METI	Takyo area		Shell to blud and operate one of five stations
	Six Hydro Gen 3 minivans	GM, U. S. Postal Service	Washington, D.C.	2004	U.S.'s 1st hydtogen pump at retail station
		Future residential fuel cell vehicles, Home Fueler	Stuart Energy Systems		

Automakers and energy companies are working with manufacturers of hydrogen fueling equipment to develop small, multipurpose systems for homes and businesses. With partner Honda R&D, Plug Power is developing the Home Energy Station, i.e., a fuel cell system that uses natural gas to provide electricity and heat in the form of hot water, plus hydrogen for fuel cell vehicle. See Fig. 15. With partner Shell,

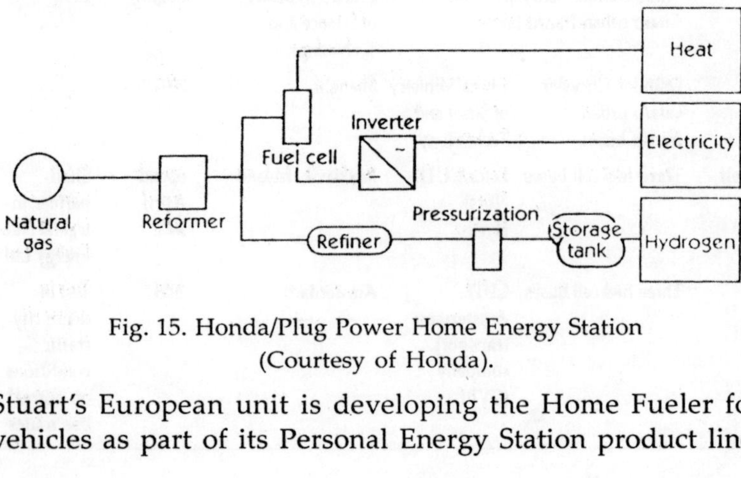

Fig. 15. Honda/Plug Power Home Energy Station (Courtesy of Honda).

Stuart's European unit is developing the Home Fueler for vehicles as part of its Personal Energy Station product line.

Stuart is also demonstrating a small fueling station that operates directly on solar photovoltaic power. The U.S. DOE funded development of the world's first hydrogen station that provides both vehicle fuel and electricity. Many electric utilities worldwide offer products or services related to micropower. In the U.S. DTE Energy has built a Hydrogen Technology Park near Detroit where water will be used in produce hydrogen for fuel cell power plants and vehicles (Busby, Rebecca L., 2005). DTE is also building a microgrid that will be powered by hydrogen, natural gas, and sunlight, which will serve the energy needs of Next Energy Corp' s new headquarters building and other facilities at Tech Town, a research and business technology park in Detroit. A micropower network was under construction in Ontario at the University of Toronto's Missisauga Campus as part of the Hydrogen Village Partnership project. Hawii hopes to demonstrate hydrogen generation from renewable energy sources at a Hydrogen Power Park proposed for the state's Big Island. Many businesses could profit from a burgeoning hydrogen economy using fuel cells in vehicles and power plants. Most of the stationary fuel cell systems already on the market get their hydrogen fuel from natural gas via a reforming process. Fuel cell micropower systems on the market are mostly sized for large buildings and are not commercially available for homeuse, except for a 1-kW fuel cell unit introduced in Japan in 2004. UTC began fuel cell research in 1958 and has supplied fuel cells to all of America's 100-plus manned space flights, including the Space Shuttle. More than 250 Pure Cell units, which are based on phosphoric acid technology, have been installed in 19 countries on five continents. Solid oxide fuel cells are the speciality of Siemens/ Westing-house. See Fig. 16. Fuel Cell Energy, Inc.'s high-temperature Direct Fuel Cell products use natural gas or other hydrocarbon fuels directly without extracting the hydrogen separately in an external reformer. Instead, the hydrogen is produced inside the cell and consumed immediately. Following installation of the first fuel cell in 2004, GM and Dow

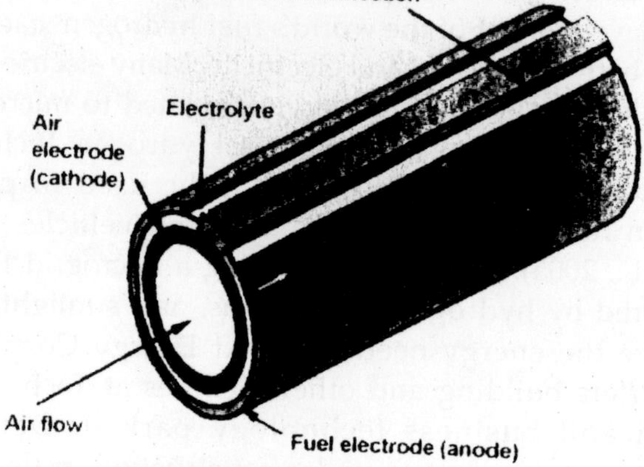

Fig. 16. Siemens/Westinghouse solid oxide fuel cell (Courtesy of Siemens/Westinghouse).

launched the second phase, a 1-MW integrated pilot plant. Plug Power and Ballard both are advancing PEM fuel cell technology for stationary power, including some models on wheels that could be called portable. Plug Power supplies hydrogen PEM micropower plants called GenSyn in sizes of 2.5 to 5 kW which are designed to run in parallel with the grid but can switch to standby power mode during outages. Microturbines are very small turbines based on automotive turbocharger technology with outputs of 25 to 300 kW. In hybrid applications such as Siemens/Westing—house' s microturbines can be powered by the fuel cell's by-product heat. Fuel cell technology is being used to run boats, trains, and planes. Fuel cells can be used to power a variety of portable devices, from handheld electronics such as cellphones and boom-boxes to large equipment such as portable generators. In portable applications, fuel cells could last much longer than batteries before refueling is required, and they should soon complete on cost as well. A 50-Watt solid oxide fuel cell was introduced in 2004 that runs on propane but can be adapted to natural gas or other hydrocarbon fuels. The future of a hydrogen economy based on fuel cells might depend on consumer demand for new products and services that we can not imagine today.

Production and Supply

Huge amount of hydrogen are produced and consumed at oil refineries, chemicals manufacturing plants, and other industrial operations around the world. The two primary conventional methods of producing hydrogen today are reforming of hydrocarbon fossil fuels and electrolysis of water. The least expensive, most common process in the United States is catalytic steam reforming of natural gas (mostly methane), while some European nations use nuclear power for electrolysis. Several advanced technologies are being develop to produce hydrogen in the future. These include gasification of biomass and coal, photoelectrochemical water-splitting using sunlight, biological methods that produce hydrogen from algae and bacteria, and high-temperature water-splitting using chemical and solar or nuclear heat. Although most industrial hydrogen is measured by volume, i.e., standard cubic feet (scf) or normal cubic metres (nm^3). Hydrogen for vehicle fueling can also be measured by weight (kilograms) or gge. A kilogram of hydrogen is the energy equivalent of about a gallon of gasoline. A full-size fueling station serving more than 500 vehicles would need to produce about 1000 kg/d, or more than 300,000 kg/yr. Carbon emissions are measured in kilograms of carbon produced per kilogram of hydrogen produced. The cost of storing carbon is estimated at \$37 per metric tonne, which translates to about \$10 per metric tonne of CO_2. The cost of carbon sequestration is fairly small.

In the first step of reforming natural gas, methane (CH_4) reacts with steam at temperatures of about 800° to 900°C, accelerated by a nickel catalyst. This reforming step produces a synthesis gas, or syn—gas, composed of hydrogen (75 percent) , carbon monoxide (15 percent), and CO_2 (10 percent). Then a reaction with additional steam converts the carbon monoxide to CO_2, and produces more hydrogen, which can be separated from the syngas and purified. CO_2 is removed by adsorption process. Syngas can also be used to many purposes including power generation and oil refining. The methane steam reforming process can be represented by the following equation :

$$CH_4 + 2H_20 \rightarrow 4H_2 + CO_2$$

Steam reforming process is shown in Fig. 17. Two variations of catalytic steam reforming are in use: (1) partial oxidation, and (2) autothermal reforming (Busby, 2005). Once captured, carbon dioxide can be stored in underground reservoirs, absorbed in oceans or infected deep underwater, or converted to rock-like materials. In geological sequestration CO_2 would be stored in underground formations such as depleted oil and gas reservoirs, unmineable coal deposits, and salt caverns. Norway's Statoil has been injecting and sequestering CO_2 underground since 1996. BP is planning on of the world's largest CO_2 storage project at the In Salah gas field in Algeria, where about 1.1 million typ will be sequestered. Another sequestration project is under way in Canada, where CO_2 from a coal gasification plant in the United States is piped over the border and injected in the Weyburn oil fields for enhanced oil recovery and CO_2 storage. In the US oil industry, a total of about 25 million typ of CO_2 is injected for enhanced recovery. Researchers are looking at ways to protect certain ecosystems and enhance their ability to absorb CO_2, e.g, forests, agricultural land, biomass crops, deserts, other waste lands, and wetlands.

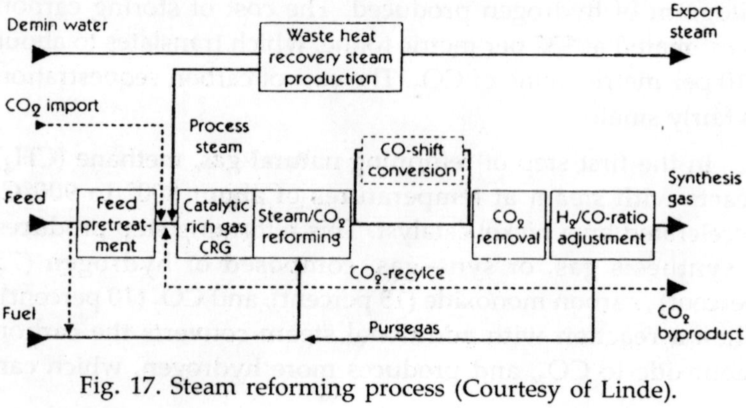

Fig. 17. Steam reforming process (Courtesy of Linde).

The primary route for producing hydrogen from coal is via gasification. Gasification breaks coal down into its basic chemical constituents. The coal is exposed to steam, along with carefully controlled amounts of air or oxygen, resulting in partial oxidation at high temperatures and pressures. Other solid fuels such as biomass can also be gasified. Gasification will increasingly be integrated with turbines for lower emissions and greater efficiency. See Fig. 18. Even with advanced technologies hydrogen production from coal gasification would release about twice as much carbon as natural gas reforming does. Solid biomass can be gasified to make biogas, which can be processed into hydrogen. Many forms of biomass such as animal waste are suitable for a biological digestion process called anaerobic formation. Once

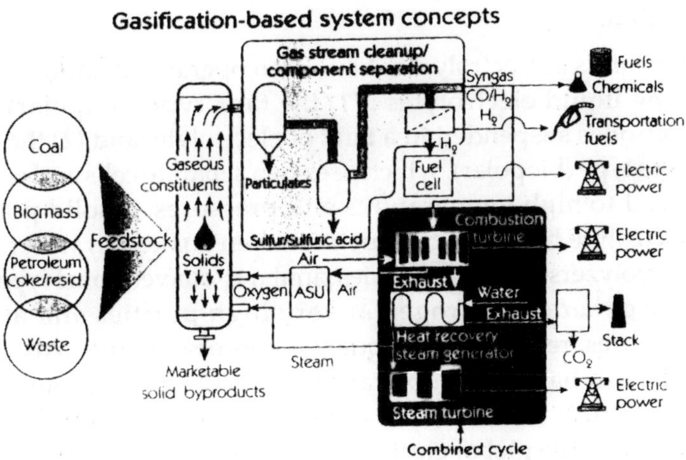

Fig. 18. Gasification of coal and other hydrogen feedstocks (Courtesy of U.S. DOE).

the biogas has been generated, subsequent steps to produce hydrogen are similar to those used in natural gas reforming and coal gasification. Gasification of biomass to produce electricity and heat is a well-proven process, with commercial plants in operation worldwide. In some cases, instead of gasifying the biomass, the material is pyrolysed, i.e. a decomposition process that produces usable liquids (bio-oils). These liquids can yield not only hydrogen but also valuable fuels, such as biodiesel and ethanol, and chemicals such as phenolic resins, which are used to make adhesives and other products. Ethanol can be converted to hydrogen in large refineries. From an environmental standpoint, biomass's attraction is that the fuel is carbon-neutral. Producing hydrogen from biomass is thermodynamically inefficient and expensive. Biomass gasification in a mid-size plant using today's technologies produces hydrogen costing more than $7 per kg. Hydrogen cost for central steam methane reforming with carbon capture and storage is $1.33 per kg. Hydrogen cost for central coal gasification plant with carbon capture storage is $1.23 per kg. During electrolysis, an electric current passes through water and splits it into hydrogen and oxygen.

Two kinds of electrolyzers have been operated in industry, both using liquid electrolytes : (1) the tank type (unipolar), with electrodes suspended in a tank of electrolyte, and (2) the filter-press type (biopolar), which uses two separate cells and is better suited to high temperatures and pressures. A solid polymer electrolyte becomes conductive when soaked in water. PEM electrolyzers reach efficiencies similar to conventional types, but they generate hydrogen at very high purities and at high pressures, reducing subsequent compression costs. Also, PEM units can handle abrupt variations in electrical input, which can disrupt conventional electrolyzers. Five manufacturers dominate the global electrolyzer market and produce systems with varying hydrogen production capacities suitable for particular fueling station size. See Table 6. At today's electrolyzer efficiencies, electricity prices would have to be below 4 cent to 5.5 cent per kWh to produce hydrogen costing less than $3 per kg. Nuclear electricity is the only existing large-scale option for carbon-free electrolysis of water into hydrogen. A Shell study suggested the hydrogen production from nuclear energy is not an efficient process, either by electrolysis or by direct thermochemical water-splitting (using

Table 6. Available Electrolyzers for Hydrogen fueling Station Applications.

Company	*Hydrogen production rate*		*Cars*	*Station size*
	Kg/d	*kg/yr*	*served*	
Norsk Hydro	22-1,046	7,875-381, 864	39-1, 909	Small neighborhood (5-50 cars) up to commercial fueling station (> 500 cars)
Sturat Energy	6-194	2, 364-70,863	12-354	Small neighborthood to commercial fueling station
Teledyne	6-91	2,205-33,069	11-165	Small neighborhood to small fuelling station (1500-500 cars)
Portion Energy	1-22	396-7,875	2-39	Home (1-5 cars (to small neighbothood
Avalence	0.9-11	315-3,939	1.6-20	Home to small neighborhood

heat and chemicals). Shell favours fossil fuel feedstocks and carbon sequestration. Gas-cooled reactors are being designed that could make hydrogen more efficiently by operating at higher temperatures (700° to 1000°C). These plants might electrlyze steam or therochemically split water. Solar energy collected by PV (photo-voltaic) panels and canopies can be used to power electrolyzers and supply pollution-free hydrogen to fueling stations and other applications. Todays' solar PV modules cost about \$3 to \$6 per watt. To complete with conventional power generation alone, not including hydrogen production, PV modules would have to cost less than \$1 per watt. At \$1 per watt, PV systems could generate electricity costing 9.8 cent per kWh and produce hydrogen via electrolysis at a total cost of \$6.18 per kg. This assumes sunlight availability of 20 percent and capital costs of \$1.54 per kg for electrolysis, hydrogen storage, and fuel dispensing. High-temperature thermochemical water-splitting can be powered by solar energy rather than a nuclear reactor. The idea is to concentrate the sun's heat intensely, using an array of mirrors on the ground aimed at a tower. Heated to thousands of degrees, steam dissociates into hydrogen and oxygen.

Photolytic processes for producing hydrogen include photoelectrochemical and photobiological techniques. In photoelectrochemistry, semiconductors immersed in liquid electrolyte receive sunlight, resulting in a photocurrent within the cell that splits the water molecule. In addition to absorbing the solar energy, the semiconductor functions as an electrode. Under specific conditions, the pigments in certain types of algae absorb solar energy. An enzyme in the algae cell acts as a catalyst to split the water molecule and release hydrogen. A good wind sites, electricity can be generated at costs of 4 cent to 7 cent per kWh, when the turbine are running 30 percent of full power on average. The Norwegian island of Utsira began producing hydrogen from wind power in 2004, making the island self-sufficient in energy use. The system incorporates two wind turbines and a Norsk Hydro electrolyzer, along with hydrogen storage equipment and a fuel cell for generating power on demand. With existing technology small-scale wind power can produce hydrogen costing $6.64 per kg., according to NRC. With anticipated technology improvements, wind-powered hydrogen production costs could be reduced to $2.86 per kg. without grid backup. See Table 7. Hydropower generates roughly 20 percent of the world's electricity. Countries with abundant hydropower, such as Canada and Brazil, could become leaders in implementing large-scale hydrogen production based on renewable electrolysis. Geothermal energy plants have operated for decades in Italy, New Zealand, and California, demonstrating the sustainable character of the resource. From 1940 to 1975, Iceland shifted all its space heating equipment from oil to geothermal heat. Plants are to switch all of its cars, trucks, buses and ships to hydrogen power by 2050. Our oceans are the world's largest solar energy collector and energy storage system. Ocean thermal energy conversion (OTEC) technology exploits the temperature difference

Table 7. Wind-powered hydrogen costs

	Current technology		*Future technology*	
	With grip backup	*Without grid backup*	*With grid backup*	*Without grid backup*
Average electricity cost, cent/kWh	6	6	4	4
Wind turbine capacity factor, %	30	30	40	40
Hydrogen cost, $/kg	6.64	10.69	3.38	2.86
Carbon emissions, kg C/kg H_2	3.35	0	2.48	0

Source: NRC.

between the warm surface of the sea and its colder depths. Hawaii and Japan have built OTEC plants producing less than 100 kilowatts. Tidal energy recovers power from the ebbing and flowing of the ocean's tides. Canada, Norway, Scotland, and the Azores have operated tidal energy plants, which incorporate dams at the entrance to tidal basins. The UK's Department of Trade and Industry is funding $90 million (£ 50 million) in tidal energy research. Some scientists are also seeking ways to generate power from the oceans' waves, which is estimated in the millions of megawatts. A 750 kW were energy converter called Pelamis began providing power to the UK grid in 2004. The International Partnership for a Hydrogen Economy comprise 15 nations, i.e., Australia, Brazil, Canada, China, France, Germany, Iceland, India, Italy, Japan, Korea, Norway, Russia, the United Kingdom, and the United States, plus the European Commission, which are advancing the transition to a global hydrogen economy. Currently about a million tonnes of hydrogen are produced annually in the United States. Table 8 gives the hydrogen production from U.S. domestic resources.

Storage and Safety

Hydrogen energy systems of the future will depend on safe, reliable ways to store hydrogen. Our state-of-the-art hydrogen storage technologies are compression and

Table 8. Hydrogen Production from U.S. Domestic Resources

Technology/ Resource	*Needed for Hydrogen*	*Current Availability*	*Current Consumption*	*Consumption Factor Increase*	*Construction/Footprint Required*
Reforming and/or Partial Oxidation					
Natural gas	95 million tpy	28 billion tons recoverable	475 million tpy	1.2	400 dedicated plants (100 million scf/d)
Biomass	400-800 million tpy	800 million tpy residue/ waste + 300 million tpy dedicated crops	200 million tpy (3 quads for hear, power and electricity)	2-4	400-600 dedecated plants
Coal	310 million tpy	126 billion tons recoverable (bituminous)	1100 million tpy (all grades)	1.3	280 dedicated plants
Water Electrolysis					
Wind	555 Gw_e	3,250 GW_e	4 GW_e	140	Available capacity North Dakota (≥ Class 3)
Solar	740 Gw_e	2,300 kWh/ m^2-yr (SW U.S.)	<1Gw_e	>740	3,750 sq miles (approx area of white Sands Missile Range, NM)
Nucler	216 Gw_e	N/A	98 Gw_e	3.2	200 dedicated plants (1-1.2 GW_e)
Thermo chemical water-splitting					
Nuclear	300 GW_{th}	N/A	0	N/A	125 Dedicated Plants (2.4 Gb_e)

Source: U.S. DOE Hydrogen Posture Plan.

liquefaction. Because hydrogen takes up so much space, it has to be compressed or liquefied to store useful quantities. Hydrogen holds more energy by weight than any known fuel, it contains less energy per unit of volume than competing fuels. Most compressed hydrogen tanks operate at ambient temperature and store the gas at pressures of 5,000 to 10,000 psi (350 to 700 bar). Compressed hydrogen tanks are in use onboard fuel cell vehicles, in portable and onsite power generators, and in uninterruptible power supply systems, where fuel cells replace batteries. Hydrogen liquefies at supercold (cryogenic) temperatures (–253°C, or –423°F). In rts liquid state, hydrogen takes up just 1/700th as much volume at the gaseous form. Compression and liquefaction are physical methods of storing molecular hydrogen. Hydrogen atoms bound into hydrides and other compounds cannot spill, vent, or burn, making them safer than conventional physical storage. Three mechanisms bind hydrogen into storage materials : (1) absorption, (2) adsorption, and (3) chemical reaction. Metal hydrides are heavy, and tradeoff is involved in selecting materials. Aluminium compounds called alanates are considered to *be* most promising of the complex metal hydrides. The most advanced chemical storage material is sodium borohydride. The mical creates a nontoxic, nonflammable solution with water and produces hydrogen when exposed to a catalyst. When the catalyst and solution are separated, the system stops generating hydrogen. The spent solution is recyclable. Carbon materials can hold hydrogen in minuscule structures called nanotubes. These forms of carbon could store and release huge quantities of hydrogen. In nanotubes, carbon atoms are linked together in hexagons like chicken wire and rolled into single-layer tubes. The most obvious general obstacles to overcome in storing hydrogen are the weight and size of the container and its contents, especially in automotive applications. Table 9 gives the hydrogen storage grand challenge. Hydrogen can be as safe as other fuels that we use today, or even safer, with proper handling and controls. Hydrogen is so much lighter

Table 9. Hydrogen storage Grand Challenge (Centres of Excellence)

Chemical Hydrogen Center LANL / PPNL	*Metal Hydride Center SNL*	*Carbon Center NIREL*
Los Alamos National Laboratory (Los Alamos, Nm)	Sandia National Laboratories (Livemore, CA)	National Renewable Energy Laboratory (Golden, CO)
Pacific Northwest National Laboratory (Richland, WA)	Stanford University (Stanford, CA)	California Institute of Technology (Pasadena, CA)
University of Pennsylvania (Philadelphia, PA)	General Electric (Niskayuna, NY)	Duke University (Durham, NC)
UCLA (Los Angeles, CA)	University of Hawaii (Honolulu, HI)	Penn State University (University Park, PA)
University of California-Davis (CA)	California Institute Technology (Pasadena, CA)	Rice University (Houston, TX)
Penn State University (University Park, PA)	Jet Propulsion Laboratory (Pasadena, CA)	University of Michigan (Ann Arbor, MI)
University of Washington (Seattle, WA)	HRL Laboratories (Malibu, CA)	University of North Carolina (Chapel Hill, NC)
University of Alabama (Tuscaloosa, AL)	University of Illinois (Champaign, IL)	University of Pennsylvania (Philadelphia, PA)
Rohm and Haas (Philadelphia, PA)	Univ of Pittsburgh/ Carnegie Mellon Univ (Pittsburgh, PA)	Oak Ridge National Laboratory (Oak Ridge, TN)
Millennium Cell (Eatontown, NJ)	NIST (Gaithersburg, MD)	Lawrence Livemore National Laboratory (Livemore, CA)
Intermatix (Moraga, CA)	University of Nevada-Reno (Reno, NV)	NISR (Gaithersburu, MD)
US Borax (Boron, CA)	Oak Ridge National Laboratory (Oak Ridge, TN)	Air Product (Allentown, PA)
	University of Utah (Salt Lake City, UT)	
	Intermatix Corporation (Moraga, CA)	
	Brookhaven National Laboratory (Brookhaven, NY)	

Prime	*Individual Projects Partners*	*Research Areas*
TIAX LLC (Cambridge, MA)	Gas Technology Institute (IL) Yale University (CT) University of Oklakoma (OK)	Lifecycle and cost analysis
University of Missouri (ST. Louis, MO)	Pacific Northwest National Laboratory (WA)	New materials
University of Connecticut (Storrs, CT)	Pacific Northwest National Laboratory (WA)	New materials
Michigan Technological University (Houghton, MI)	None	Chemical hydrides
Gas Technological Institute (two projects) (Chicago, IL)	Super Graphite Co. (IL) NEXGEN Fueling (MN)	Carbon Off-board storage
Alfred University (Alfred, Ny)	Savannah River Technology Center (SC) Mo-Sci Corporation (MO) CERALINK (NY)	New processes
Carnegie institute of Washington (Washington, DC)	None	New materials
Research Triangle Institute (Research Triangle Park, NC)	State Scientific Research Institute (Moscow, Russia) ATK/Thiokol Propulsion (UT)	Chemical hydrides
State University of New York (Syracuse, NY)	PorsGen, LLC (MA)	Carbon
TOFTEC, Inc (Gainesville, FL)	University of Florida Gainesville (FL)	New processes
University of Michigan (ANN Arbor, MI)	Northwestern University (IL) Los Almos National Laboratory (NM)	New materials
University of Pennsylvania (Philadelphia, PA)	Drexel University (PA) NIST (MD)	Carbon
University of California-Berkeley (CA)	Lawrence Berkeley National Laboratory (CA)	New materials
University of California-Santa Barbara (CA)	Los Alamos National Laboratory (NM)	New materials

than air, it rises rapidly when released, creating turbulent diffusion and reducing its concentration below the lower flammability limit. Hydrogen can ignite more easily than gasoline or natural gas, and it has a wide range of flammable concentrations in air. Table 10 gives the properties of

Table 10. Properties of Hydrogen and other Fuels

	Hydrogen	*Natural gas*	*Propane*	*Gasoline Vapour*
Density relative to air	0.07	0.55	1.52	4.0
Molecular weight	2	16	44	107
Density, kg/m^3	0.084	0.651	1.87	4.4
Diffusion coefficient, cm^2/s	0.61	0.16	0.12	0.05
Explosive energy, MJ/m^3	9	32	93	407
Flammability range, vol%	4 to15	5 to 15	2 to 10	1 to 8
Detonation range, vol%	18 to 59	6 to 14	3 to 7	1 to 3
Minimum ignition energy, mJ	0.02	0.29	0.26	0.24
Autoignition temp. in air, °C	565-581	539	454-509	257
Flame speed, cm/s	346	43	47	42

Source: U.S. DOE; NRC

hydrogen and other fuels. Hydrogen flame produces very little radiant energy and so no sooty particles, smokes, or poisonous emissions. Safety research is focusing on development of sensors for detecting hydrogen leaks. Chemical additives are being developed that would give hydrogen a smell that is detectable by humans. Precautions around hydrogen would be no smoking, no refueling with the engine running, and no use of cellphones around the fuel. The possibility of static electricity igniting hydrogen would have to be prevented by built-in grounding systems.

Transportation and Distribution

Transportation and distribution of hydrogen is not easy, and a lot of new equipment will have to be installed before hydrogen becomes convenient to use. This infrastructure will consists of vehicle fueling stations in the near term, when onsite production units will supply most of our hydrogen. Later on, as vehicles and micropower plants proliferate and demand for hydrogen grows, we might need to build regional hydrogen distribution hubs and possibly special pipelines if our supplies come from central hydrogen production plants. Unlike liquid fuels, the cost of delivering hydrogen to dispersed customers is extremely high, roughly five times more expensive than producing the hydrogen. Transportation and distribution strategies would evolve tailored to regional and local resources, population, and geographic factors, as well as hydrogen demand patterns and production capabilities. Compressed hydrogen at 5,000 psi contains 3 megajoules of energy per litre as a cryogenic liquid, 8 megajoules. Both compare unfavourably to gasoline's energy content to 32 megajoules per liter. Most hydrogen today is consumed onsite where it is produced near refineries and chemicals manufacturing plants, so the transportation and distribution network in industrial countries is negligible. Industrial gas companies who sell merchant hydrogen do move some volumes around, mainly on trucks and through dedicated pipelines. In road transport, trucks can carry compressed gas in loads of cylinders or in a single large tube trailer. Compressed gas trucks and trailers typically travel only 100 to 200 miles from the production facility. For longer distances, upto 1000 miles, cryogenic tankers carry liquid hydrogen. Some liquid hydrogen is also shipped by rail or barge. The liquid fuel is vapourized at the customer site. Hydrogen pipelines could cost 75 percent more, or even double the amount in the smallest diameter. See table 11. Four major components are needed for a compressed gas hydrogen fueling station : (1) hydrogen production, (2) compression, (3) storage, and (4) fuel dispensing. Hydrogen can be produced at a central plant today at a cost ranging from \$ 0.96 to \$1.22 per kg, depending on the feedstock (natural gas or coal) and whether or not carbon is sequestered. Pipeline shipment and dispensing of hydrogen adds an estimated cost of \$0.96 per kg. Over-the-road shipment of liquid hydrogen and dispensing at a vehicle fueling station is estimated to cost from \$1.40 to \$2.42 per kg.

Table 11. Pipeline Construction costs

Pipe diameter, Inch	*Capital cost, \$/mile*	
	Natural gas	*Hydrogen*
3	200,000	400,000
9	500,000	900,000
12	600,000	1,000,000
14	800,000	1,400,000

Source : Argonne National Laboratory[6].

References

1. Blankinship, Steve 2003; "When will the hydrogen arrie?" Power Engineering, January.
2. Bossel, Ulf, 2003; "The physics of the hydrogen economy"; Europe Fuel Cell News, Vol. 10, No. 2, July.
3. Bushy, Rebecca L; 2005; "Hydrogen and fuel cells'. A Comprehensive Guide"; PennWell Corporation, 1421 South Sheridan Road, Tulsa, Oklahoma 74112, USA.
4. Duncan, Richard C., 2003; "Three world oil forecast predict peak production"; Oils & Gas Journal, May 26, 18-21.
5. Eliasson, Baldur and Bossel, Ulf, 2000; "The future of the hydrogen economy : Bright or bleak?" Paper presented at Fuel Cell World, Lucerne, July 5.
6. Geiger, Stefan, 2004; "Fuel cell market survey Automotive hydrogen infrastructure"; Fuel Cell Today, May 5.
7. Hoffmann, Peter, 2001; "Tomorrow's energy: Hydrogen, fuel cells, and the prospects for a cleaner planet"; The MIT press, Cambridge, MA.
8. Maugeri, Leonardo, 2003; "Time to debunk mythical links between oil and politics;" Oil & Gas Journal, December 15, pp. 18-28.
9. Moritis, Guntis, 2003; "$C0_2$ sequestration adds new dimension to oil, gas production"; Oil & Gas Journal, March 3, pp. 39-44.
10. Rafkin, Jeremy, 2002; "The hydrogen economy : The creation of the worldwide energy web and the

redistribution of power on earth;" Penguin Group (USA) Inc., New York.

11. Samsen Bakhtiari, A.M., "Middle East oil production to peak within next decade"; Oil & Gas Journal, July 7, pp. 20-28.
12. Zink, John C; 2003; "Trends favours nuclear - hydrogen economy"; Power Engineering, April.

Annexure–1

HYDROGEN COST CALCULATIONS

Table 1. Caste and carbon dioxide emissions: central station natural gas Steam reforming plants.

	Current technology		*Future technology*	
	without sequestration	*with sequestration*	*without sequestration*	*with sequestration*
Capital investment, 10^6 $				
H_2 production	453.39	623.75	326.85	425.54
Distribution	724.75	724.75	532.98	532.98
Dispensing	714.51	714.51	507.42	507.42
Total capital investment	1,892.66	2,063.01	1,367.25	1,465.95
Production costs, $/kg H_2				
Variable costs				
Feed	0.75	0.79	0.71	0.73
Electricity	0.03	0.08	0.03	0.06
Non-fuel O & M[a]	0.01	0.02	0.01	0.01
Subtotal variable costs	0.79	0.89	0.74	0.80
Fixed costs[b]	0.06	0.08	0.04	0.05
Capital charges[c]	0.18	0.25	0.13	0.17
Total production costs	1.03	1.22	0.92	1.02
Distribution costs, $/kg H_2				
Variable costs				
Electricity	0.01	0.01	0.01	0.01
Non-fuel O & M[a]	0.02	0.02	0.01	0.01
Subtotal variable costs	0.03	0.03	0.02	0.02
Fixed costs[b]	0.09	0.09	0.07	0.07
Capital charge[c]	0.29	0.29	0.21	0.21
Total distribution	0.42	0.42	0.31	0.31

Continued ....

Dispensing costs, \$/kg H_2				
Variable costs				
Electricity	0.14	0.14	0.11	0.11
Non-fuel O & M[a]	0.09	0.09	0.06	0.06
Subtotal variable costs	0.23	0.23	0.17	0.17
Fixed costs$_b$	0.05	0.05	0.04	0.04
Capital charges$_c$	0.25	0.25	0.18	0.18
Total dispensing costs	0.54	0.54	0.39	0.39
Hydrogen costs, \$/kg				
Production	1.03	1.22	0.92	1.02
Distribution	0.42	0.42	0.31	0.31
Dispensing	0.54	0.54	0.39	0.39
CO_2 disposal	—	0.09	—	0.08
Carbon tax	0.13	0.02	0.12	0.02
Total H_2 costs	2.11	2.28	1.73	1.82
Carbon dioxide vented				
Kg C/kg H_2	2.51	0.42	2.39	0.35
Direct use	2.45	0.26	2.34	0.24
Indirect use	0.06	0.16	0.05	0.12
Kg CO_2/kg H_2	9.22	1.53	8.75	1.30
Direct use	8.99	0.95	8.56	0.88
Indirect use	0.23	0.58	0.18	0.42
Carbon charge				
\$/kg	0.13	0.02	0.12	0.02
Carbon sequestered				
Kg CO_2/kg H_2	—	8.56	—	7.91
Carbon	—	2.34	—	2.1.6

[a]Non-fuel O & M = 1% yr of capital
[b]Fixed costs = 5% yr of capital
[c]Capital charges = 18% yr of capital
Source: National Research Council, *The Hydrogen Economy: Opportunities, costs, Barriers, and* R & D *Needs.*

Table 2. Costs and carbon dioxide emission: central station coal gasification plants.

	Current technology		Future technology	
	without sequestration	*with sequestration*	*without sequestration*	*with sequestration*
Capital investment, 10^6 $				
H_2 production	1,151.92	1,1777.33	868.18	889.97
Distribution	724.75	724.75	532.98	532.98
Dispensing	714.51	714.51	507.42	507.42
Total capital investment	2,591.18	2,616.59	1,908.58	1,930.38
Production costs, \$/kg H_2				
Variable costs				
Feed	0.21	0.21	0.19	0.19
Electricity	0.11	0.17	0.04	0.08
Non-fuel O&M[a]	0.03	0.03	0.02	0.02
Sub variable costs	0.35	0.41	0.25	0.30
Fixed costs[b]	0.15	0.15	0.11	0.11
Capital charges[c]	0.46	0.47	0.35	0.36
Total production costs	0.96	1.03	0.71	0.77
Distribution costs, \$/kg H_2				
Variable costs				
Electricity	0.01	0.01	0.01	0.01
Non-fuel O&M[a]	0.02	0.02	0.01	0.01
Subtotal variable costs	0.03	0.03	0.02	0.02
Fixed costs[b]	0.09	0.09	0.07	0.07
Capital charge[c]	0.29	0.29	0.21	0.21
Total distribution	0.42	0.42	0.31	0.31
Dispensing costs, \$/kg H_2				
Variable costs				
Electricity	0.14	0.14	0.11	0.11
Non-fuel O&M[a]	0.09	0.09	0.06	0.06
Subtotal variable costs	0.23	0.23	0.17	0.17
Fixed costs[b]	0.05	0.05	0.04	0.04
Capital charges[c]	0.25	0.25	0.18	0.18
Total dispensing costs	0.54	0.54	0.39	0.39

Continued ....

Hydrogen costs, $/kg				
Production	0.96	1.03	0.71	0.77
Distribution	0.42	0.42	0.31	0.31
Dispending	0.54	0.54	0.39	0.39
CO_2 disposal	—	0.16	—	0.15
Carbon tax	0.26	0.04	0.23	0.03
Total H_2 costs	2.17	2.19	1.63	1.64
Carbon dioxide vented				
Kg C/kg H_2	5.12	0.82	4.56	0.60
Direct use	4.90	0.49	4.50	0.45
Indirect use	0.21	0.33	0.07	0.15
kg CO_2/kg H_2	18.76	3.00	16.73	2.21
Direct use	17.98	1.80	16.49	1.65
Indirect use	0.77	1.20	0.25	0.56
Carbon charge				
$/kg	0.26	0.04	0.23	0.03
Carbon sequestered				
kg CO_2/kg H_2	—	16.19	—	14.84
Carbon	—	4.41	—	4.05

Table 3. Cost of future central station nuclear thermal waste-splitting plants.

	Future technology
Capital investment, 10^6 $	
H2 production	2,468.19
Distributing	532.98
Dispending	507.42
Total capital investment	3,508.59
Production costs, $/kg H_2	
Variable costs	0.20
Feed	0.20
Decommission fund	0.06
Non-fuel O&Ma	0.06
Subtotal variable costs	0.32
Fixed costsb	0.31
Capital chargec	1000
Total production costs	1.63
Distributing costs, $/kg H_2	
Variable costs	
Electricity	0.01
Non-fuel O&M[a]	0.01
Subtotal variable costs	0.02
Fixed costs[b]	0.07
Capital charge[c]	0.21
Total dispending costs	0.31
Dispensing costs, $/kg H_2	
Variable costs	
Electricity	0.11
Non-fuel O&M[a]	0.06
Subtotal variable costs	0.17
Fixed costs[b]	0.04

Continued ....

Capital charge[c]	0.18
Total dispending costs	0.39
H_2 costs $/kg	
Production	1.63
Distribution	0.31
Dispending	0.39
Total H_2 costs	2.33

[a]Non-fuel O&M = 1 %/yr of capital
[b]Fixed costs = 5%/yr of capital
[c]Capital charges = 18%/yr of capital
Source: National Research Council, *The Hydrogen Economy: Opportunities, costs, Barriers, and* R&D *Needs,*

Table 4. Costs of mid-Aize natural gas steam reforming plants.

	Current technology		*Future technology*	
	without sequestration	*with sequestration*	*without sequestration*	*with sequestration*
Capital investment, 10^6 $				
H_2 production	21.52	29.26	17.12	23.06
Distribution	34.73	34.73	18.54	18.54
Dispending	20.70	20.70	9.01	9.01
Total capital investment	76.95	84.69	44.67	50.61
Production costs, \$/kg H_2				
Variable costs				
Feed	0.79	0.82	0.74	0.79
Electricity	0.04	0.10	0.03	0.08
Non-fuel O&M[a]	0.03	0.03	0.02	0.03
Subtotal variable costs	0.86	0.96	0.79	0.90
Fixed costs[b]	0.13	0.17	0.10	0.13
Capital charge[c]	0.40	0.54	0.32	0.43
Total dispending costs	1.38	1.67	1.21	1.46
Distribution costs, \$/kg H_2				
Variable costs				
Labor	0.09	0.09	0.09	0.09
Fuel	0.01	0.01	0.01	0.01
Electricity	0.50	0.50	0.36	0.36
Non-fuel O&M[a]	0.06	0.06	0.03	0.03
Subtotal variable costs	0.65	0.65	0.49	0.49
Fixed costs[b]	0.28	0.28	0.15	0.15
Capital charge[c]	0.88	0.88	0.47	0.47
Total dispending costs	1.80	1.80	1.10	1.10
Dispensing costs, \$/kg H_2				
Variable costs				
Electricity	0.06	0.06	0.06	0.06
Non-fuel O&M[a]	0.13	0.13	0.06	0.06

Continued ....

Subtotal variable costs	0.18	0.18	0.11	0.11
Fixed costs[b]	0.08	0.08	0.03	0.03
Capital charge[c]	0.36	0.36	0.16	0.16
Total dispending costs	0.62	0.62	0.30	0.30
Hydrogen costs, $/kg				
Production	1.38	1.67	1.21	1.46
Distribution	1.80	1.80	1.10	1.10
Dispending	0.62	0.62	0.30	0.30
CO_2 disposal	—	0.09	—	0.09
Carbon tax	0.13	0.02	0.12	0.02
Total H_2 costs	3.94	4.20	2.74	2.97

[a]Non-fuel O&M = 1 %/yr of capital
[b]Fixed costs = 5%/yr of capital
[c]Capital charges = 18%/yr of capital
Source: National Research Council, *The Hydrogen Economy: Opportunities, costs, Barriers, and* R&D *Needs,*

Table 5. Caste of mid-size biomass gasification plants.

	Current technology		*Future technology*	
	without sequestration	*with sequestration*	*without sequestration*	*with sequestration*
Capital investment, 10^6 \$				
H_2 production	121.04	123.91	59.04	60.53
Distribution	34.73	34.73	18.54	18.54
Dispensing	20.70	20.70	9.01	9.01
Total capital investment	176.46	179.33	86.59	88.08
Production costs, \$/kg H_2				
Variable costs				
Feed	0.98	0.98	0.42	0.42
Electricity	0.29	0.41	0.14	0.21
Non-fuel O&M[a]	0.15	0.16	0.07	0.08
Subtotal variable costs	1.42	1.54	0.64	0.71
Fixed costs[b]	0.77	0.79	0.37	0.38
Capital charge	2.44	2.50	1.19	1.22
Total dispending costs	4.63	4.82	2.21	2.32
Distribution costs, \$/kg H_2				
Variable costs				
Labor	0.09	0.09	0.09	0.09
Fuel	0.01	0.01	0.01	0.01
Electricity	0.50	0.50	0.36	0.36
Non-fuel O&M[a]	0.06	0.06	0.03	0.03
Subtotal variable costs	0.65	0.65	0.49	0.49
Fixed costs[b]	0.28	0.28	0.15	0.15
Capital charge[c]	0.88	0.88	0.47	0.47
Total dispending costs	1.80	1.80	1.10	1.10
Dispensing costs, \$/kg H_2				
Variable costs				
Electricity	0.06	0.06	0.06	0.06
Non-fuel O&M[a]	0.13	0.13	0.06	0.06

Continued ....

Subtotal variable costs	0.18	0.18	0.11	0.11
Fixed costs[b]	0.08	0.08	0.03	0.03
Capital charge[c]	0.36	0.36	0.16	0.16
Total dispending costs	0.62	0.62	0.30	0.30
Hydrogen costs, $/kg				
Production	4.63	4.82	2.21	2.32
Distribution	1.80	1.80	1.10	1.10
Dispensing	0.62	0.62	0.30	0.30
CO_2 disposal	—	0.26	—	0.17
Carbon tax	0.03	–0.31	0.01	–0.21
Total H_2 costs	7.07	7.19	3.63	3.68

[a]Non-fuel O&M = 1 %/yr of capital
[b]Fixed costs = 5%/yr of capital
[c]Capital charges = 18%/yr of capital
Source: National Research Council, *The Hydrogen Economy: Opportunities, costs, Barriers, and* R&D *Needs,*

Table 6. Cost of mod-size grid-based electrolysis plants

	Current technology	*Future technology*
Capital investment, 10^6 $		
H_2 production	84.78	9.71
Distribution	34.73	18.54
Dispensing	20.70	9.01
Total capital investment	140.20	37.26
Production costs, $/kg H_2		
Variable costs		
Feed	–0.08	–0.08
Electricity	2.43	2.11
Non-fuel O&M[a]	0.11	0.01
Subtotal variable costs	2.46	2.04
Fixed costs[b]	0.54	0.06
Capital charges[c]	1.71	0.20
Total dispending costs	4.70	2.30
Distribution costs, $/kg H_2		
Variable costs		
Labor	0.09	0.09
Fuel	0.01	0.01
Electricity	0.50	0.36
Non-fuel O&M[a]	0.06	0.03
Subtotal variable costs	0.65	0.49
Fixed costs[b]	0.28	0.15
Capital charges[c]	0.88	0.47
Total dispending costs	1.80	1.10
Dispensing costs, $/kg H_2		
Variable costs		
Electricity	0.06	0.06
Non-fuel O&M[a]	0.13	0.06
Subtotal variable costs	0.18	0.11
Fixed costs[b]	0.08	0.03

Continued ....

Capital charges[c]	0.36	0.16
Total dispending costs	0.62	0.30
Hydrogen Costs, $/kg		
Production	4.70	2.30
Distribution	1.80	1.10
Dispensing	0.62	0.30
Total H_2 costs	7.36	3.91

[a]Non-fuel O&M = 1 %/yr of capital
[b]Fixed costs = 5%/yr of capital
[c]Capital charges = 18%/yr of capital
Source: National Research Council, *The Hydrogen Economy: Opportunities, costs, Barriers, and* R&D *Needs,*

Table 7. Onsite natural gas system reforming units.

	Current technology	*Future technology*
Capital investment		
10^6 $	1.85	0.96
H_2 costs, $/kg		
Variable production costs		
Feed	1.37	1.17
Electricity	0.15	0.12
Non-fuel O&M	0.12	0.06
Subtotal variable costs	1.64	1.35
Fixed production costs[b]	0.23	0.12
Capital charges[c]	1.64	0.85
Total dispending costs	3.51	2.33
Carbon tax	0.17	0.14
Total H_2 costs	3.68	2.47
Carbon dioxide vented		
kg C/kg H_2	3.31	2.82
Direct use	3.11	2.67
Indirect use	0.19	0.15
kg CO_2/kg H_2	12.13	10.34
Direct use	11.42	9.79
Indirect use	0.71	0.55

[a]Non-fuel O&M = 1 %/yr of capital
[b]Fixed costs = 5%/yr of capital
[c]Capital charges = 18%/yr of capital
Source: National Research Council, *The Hydrogen Economy: Opportunities, costs, Barriers, and* R&D *Needs.*

Table 8. Caste and carbon emissions: onsite electrolysis units using grid power.

	Current technology	*Future technology*
Capital investment		
10^6 $	2.54	0.57
H_2 costs, $/kg		
Variable production costs		
Electricity	3.84	3.31
Non-fuel O&M[a]	0.16	0.04
Subtotal variable costs	4.00	3.35
Fixed production costs[b]	0.32	0.07
Capital charges[c]	2.26	0.51
Total dispending costs	6.58	3.93
Carbon tax	0.24	0.21
Total H_2 costs	6.82	4.13
Carbon dioxide vented		
kg C/kg H_2	4.97	4.13
Indirect use	4.97	4.13
kg CO_2/kg H_2	15.13	15.13
Indirect use	15.13	15.13

[a]Non-fuel O&M = 1 %/yr of capital
[b]Fixed costs = 5%/yr of capital
[c]Capital charges = 18%/yr of capital
Source: National Research Council, *The Hydrogen Economy: Opportunities, costs, Barriers, and* R&D *Needs.*

Table 9. Costs of onsite electrolysis units based on wind turbine power

	Current technology	*Future technology*
Capital investment		
10^6 $	6.86	0.89
H_2 costs, $/kg		
Variable production costs		
Electricity	3.29	1.90
Non-fuel O&M[a]	0.44	0.06
Subtotal variable costs	3.73	1.95
Fixed production costs[b]	0.87	0.11
Capital charges[c]	6.09	0.79
Total production costs	10.69	2.86.
Total H_2 costs	10.69	2.86

[a]Non-fuel O&M = 1 %/yr of capital
[b]Fixed costs = 5%/yr of capital
[c]Capital charges = 18%/yr of capital
Source: National Research Council, *The Hydrogen Economy: Opportunities, costs, Barriers, and* R&D *Needs,*

Table 10. Costs and carbon: emissions : onsite electrolysis unite based on hybrid-wind turbine/grid power.

	Current technology	*Future technology*
Capital investment		
10^6 $	2.75	0.59
H_2 costs, $/kg		
Variable production costs		
Electricity	3.67	2.75
Non-fuel O&M[a]	0.17	0.04
Subtotal variable costs	3.85	2.78
Fixed production costs[b]	0.35	0.07
Capital charges[c]	2.44	0.52
Total production costs	6.64	3.38
Carbon tax	0.17	0.12
Total H_2 costs	6.81	3.50
Carbon dioxide vented		
kg C/kg H_2	3.85	2.48
Indirect use	3.35	2.48
kg CO_2/kg H_2	12.28	9.08
Indirect use	12.28	9.08

[a]Non-fuel O&M = 1 %/yr of capital
[b]Fixed costs = 5%/yr of capital
[c]Capital charges = 18%/yr of capital
Source: National Research Council, *The Hydrogen Economy: Opportunities, costs, Barriers, and* R&D *Needs.*

Table 11. Costs of onsite electrolysis units based on solar PV power.

	Current technology	*Future technology*
Capital investment		
10^6 $	9.94	1.43
H_2 costs, $/kg		
Variable production costs		
Electricity	17.48	4.64
Non-fuel O&M[a]	0.63	0.09
Subtotal variable costs	18.11	4.73
Fixed production costs[b]	1.16	0.18
Capital charges[c]	8.82	1.27
Total production costs	28.19	6.18
Total H_2 costs	28.19	6.18

[a]Non-fuel O&M = 1 %/yr of capital
[b]Fixed costs = 5%/yr of capital
[c]Capital charges = 18%/yr of capital
Source: National Research Council, *The Hydrogen Economy: Opportunities, costs, Barriers, and* R&D *Needs.*

Table 12. Costs and carbon emissions: onsite electrolysis units based on hybrid solar-PV/grid power.

	Current technology	*Future technology*
Capital investment		
10^6 \$	2.74	0.59
H_2 costs, \$/kg		
Variable production costs		
Electricity	6.57	3.58
Non-fuel O&M[a]	0.17	0.04
Subtotal variable costs	6.74	3.61
Fixed production costs[b]	0.35	0.07
Capital charges[c]	2.43	0.52
Total dispending costs	9.52	4.21
Carbon tax	0.19	0.17
Total H_2 costs	9.71	4.37
Carbon dioxide vented		
kg C/kg H_2	3.83	3.30
Indirect use	3.83	3.30
kg CO_2/kg H_2	14.04	11.11
Indirect use	14.04	12.11

[a]Non-fuel O&M = 1 %/yr of capital
[b]Fixed costs = 5%/yr of capital
[c]Capital charges = 18%/yr of capital
Source: National Research Council, *The Hydrogen Economy: Opportunities, costs, Barriers, and* R&D *Needs.*

Table 13. Fueling station costs using current technology.

Design Basis

2,740 kg/dH_2

4,875 fuel cell vehicles supported

114 kg/h daily average

5 dispensers

22-hour operation

*Gaseous hydrogen**		*Liquid hydrogen***	
	Capital costs, 10^6 $		
Compressors	0.62	Liquid pump/vaporizer	0.506
Buffer storage	0.38	Liquid storage	0.529
Dispensers	0.07	Buffer storage	0.403
Subtotal equipment	1.07	Dispensers	0.075
		Subtotal equipment	1.513
Facilities/permitting	0.27	Facilities/permitting	0.378
Engineering/startup	0.11	Engineering/startup	0.151
Contingencies	0.11	Contigencies	0.151
Working capital/misc.	0.08	Working capital/misc.	0.106
Total capital costs	1.63	Total capital costs	2.300
	Hydrogen costs, $/kg H2		
Variable costs		Variable costs	
Non-fuel O&M	0.09	Non-fuel O&M	0.13
Electricity	0.14	Electricity	0.06
Subtotal variable costs	0.23	Subtotal variable costs	0.18
Fixed operating costs	0.05	Fixed operating costs	0.08
Capital charge	0.25	Capital charge	0.36
Total	0.54	total	0.62

*Hydrogen delivered pipeline from station, one of 438 stations supplied. Pipeline capital costs estimated at $725 million and operating costs at $0.42/kg H2 using current technology.

*Hydrogen delivered by tanker trunk from mid-size plant, one of 9 station supplied. Trucking capital costs estimated at $34.7 million (including trunk) and operating costs at $1.80/kg H_2 using current technology.

Source: National Research council, *The Hydrogen Economy: Opportunities, Costs, Barriers,* R&D *and Needs.*

Table 14. Fuel station costs using future technology.

Design Basis

2,740 kg/dH_2

4,875 fuel cell vehicles supported

114 kg/h daily average

5 dispensers

22-hour operation

*Gaseous hydrogen**		*Liquid hydrogen***	
Capital costs, 10^6 $			
Compressors	0.31	Liquid pump/vaporizer	0.304
Buffer storage	0.38	Liquid storage	0.113
Dispensers	0.07	Buffer storage	0.202
Subtotal equipment	0.76	Dispensers	0.040
		Subtotal equipment	0.659
Facilities/permitting	0.19	Facilities/permitting	0.165
Engineering/startup	0.8	Engineering/startup	0.066
Contingencies	0.08	Contigencies	0.066
Working capital/misc.	0.5	Working capital/misc.	0.046
Total capital costs	1.16	Total capital costs	1.001
Hydrogen costs, $/kg H2			
Variable costs		Variable costs	
Non-fuel O&M	0.06	Non-fuel O&M	0.06
Electricity	0.11	Electricity	0.06
Subtotal variable costs	0.17	Subtotal variable costs	0.11
Fixed operating costs	0.04	Fixed operating costs	0.03
Capital charge	0.18	Capital charge	0.16
Total	0.39	total	0.30

*Hydrogen delivered pipeline from station, one of 438 stations supplied. Pipeline capital costs estimated at $533 million and operating costs at $0.31/kg H_2 using future technology.

**Hydrogen delivered by tanker trunk from mid-size plant, one of 9 station supplied. Trucking capital costs estimated at $18.5 million (including trunk) and operating costs at $1.10/kg H_2 using future technology.

Source: National Research council, *The Hydrogen Economy: Opportunities, Costs, Barriers,* R&D *and Needs.*

Annexure–2

USEFUL ABBREVIATIONS AND GLOSSARY

absorption	A process in which a gas or liquid is drawn into another substance to form a compound. An example is the absorption of gaseous hydrogen by a metal, forming a hydride.
a-c	Alternating-current. Electrical current in which the electrons flow in both directions, from positive to negative and from negative to positive, in the same conductor.
acidic	A solution with a pH level below 7.0. Acids are the opposite of basic or alkaline solutions'.
adsorption	The adhesion of molecules to the surface area of solids or liquids. For example, gaseous hydrogen is adsorbed onto porous ceramic materials.
AFC	Alkaline fuel cell. A fuel cell technology that uses potassium hydroxide (KOH) or other alkaline solution as an electrolyte.
alkaline	A solution with a pH higher than 7.0. Alkaline solutions, also called basic solutions, are the opposite of acids.
alternative fuel	A popular term for unconventional fuels. Typically, alternative fuels are derived from natural gas, biomass, or other non-polluting or less-polluting sources such as hydroelectric, wind, or solar power.

alternator	A device that produces alternating-current electricity. Also called a synchronous generator or a-c generator
anion	A negatively charged ion.
ANL	Argonne National Laboratory (U.S.)
anode	One of two electrodes in an electrochemical cell. In a fuel cell, the anode is electrically negative. In an electrolysis system, the anode is electrically positive.
ANSI	American National Standards Institute
ARB	Air Resources Board (California)
ASME	American Society of Mechanical Engineers
avoided cost	The price utilities pay for electricity produced by cogenerating micropower plants. The utility's avoided cost equals whatever it would have cost the utility to generate the power.
bar	Metric unit of pressure, or force per unit of area, equal to 100,000 Pascals.
baseload	The primary source of round-the-clock electrical power supply; the minimum required at a steady rate over a specified period of time.
basic	A solution with a pH higher than 7.0. Basic solutions, also called alkaline solutions, are the opposite of acids.
bcm	Billion cubic meters. Metric unit that measures volume.
biomass	Biomass is organic material of various types including inedible plants, undesirable species that create a nuisance, crops grown specifically as biomass crops, leftovers from agricultural crops, organic industrial waste such as wood chips from sawmills, animal waste from farming operations, solid waste collected in

	urban areas, and biogases generated from landfills and sewage treatment plants.
black hydrogen	Hydrogen produced from coal or nuclear power rather than from clean, renewable power sources.
borate	A class of boron-oxygen compounds.
Borax	A type of borate and a common ingredient in laundry detergents.
boron	A relatively light element (atomic weight of 10.8) represented by the symbol "B" on the periodic table.
Btu	British thermal unit. Unit that measures heat, equal to the amount required to raise the temperature of one pound of water by one degree Fahrenheit.
byback rate	The price at which utilities purchase electricity from third parties such as operators of micropower plants.
by-product	A substance produced from a process that is not the main product. For example, when a fuel cell uses hydrogen and oxygen to produce electricity, the by-product is water.
C_3H_8	Propane. A component of natural gas and the main component of liquefied petroleum gas. Propane is usually extracted from natural gas and sold separately.
CaFPC	California Fuel Cell Partnership]
CARB	California Air Resources Board
carbon	A relatively light element (atomic weight of 12) represented by the symbol "C" on the periodic table. Carbon is a constituent in all hydrocarbons and other organic compounds.
carbon-	A process that could result in no net emissions

neutral	of carbon, such as biomass conversion.
catalyst	A chemical that increases the rate of a reaction without being consumed. The catalyst lowers the activation energy required, allowing the reaction to proceed more quickly or at a lower temperature. In a fuel cell, catalysts facilitate the reaction of oxygen and hydrogen.
catalyst poisoning	A process in which impurities bind to a catalyst, reducing its ability to facilitate the desired chemical reaction.
cathode	One of two electrodes in an electrochemical cell. In a fuel cell, the cathode is electrically positive. In an electrolysis system, the cathode is electrically negative.
cation	A positively charged ion.
CBO	Congressional Budget Office (U.S.)
cell	An individual electrochemical unit consisting of two electrodes and an electrolyte. Examples include fuel cells and electrolytic cells.
CFCs	Chlorofluorocarbons. Chemical compounds containing carbon, chlorine, and fluorine which were found to deplete the earth's protective ozone layer.
CH_2IP	Compressed Hydrogen Infrastructure Program (Canada)
CH_3CH_2OH	Ethanol, or ethyl alcohol. A clear, colorless liquid that is the same alcohol found in beer, wine, and liquor. Ethanol is produced by fermenting a sugar solution with yeast.
CH_3OH	Methanol, or methyl alcohol. Methanol, the simplest of all alcohols, is a flammable, poisonous liquid used as a fuel, fuel additive, chemical feedstock, and potential energy carrier.

CH_4 — Methane. A colorless, odorless, flammable gas that is the main constituent of natural gas.

CHP — Combined heat and power. A system that generates electricity and recovers heat for useful purposes. Also called cogeneration. Fuel cells can be applied in CHP systems.

climate change — The warming of the earth's climate over millions of years, which is thought to be caused by carbon dioxide and other greenhouse gases in the atmosphere. Also called global warming.

CO — Carbon monoxide. A colorless, odorless gas that is also poisonous. Carbon monoxide results from incomplete combustion of carbon with oxygen.

CO_2 — Carbon dioxide. A colorless, odorless gas produced by combustion of hydrocarbon fuels, the respiration of living organisms, and other processes. Carbon dioxide is a greenhouse gas and a major contributor to global warming.

cogeneration — A system that generates electricity and recovers heat for useful purposes. Also called combined heat and power, or CHP. Fuel cells can be applied in cogeneration systems.

combustion — The process of burning, also called oxidation Combustion occurs when a fuel or other substance combines with oxygen or air in the proper proportions and in the presence of a spark or other heat source.

composite — A substance created by combining different materials to obtain certain properties or characteristics. Each constituent retains its physical identity.

cryogenic	Very low temperatures, often those at which gases change into liquid form.
CSIRO	Commonwealth Scientific and Industrial Research Organization (Australia)
CSLF	Carbon Sequestration Leadership Forum CTFCA Canadian Transportation Fuel Cell Alliance
CUTE	Clean Urban Transport for Europe. A demonstration project that operates 30 fuel cell buses, three in each of 10 cities.
d-c	Direct-current. Electrical current in which the electrons flow in only one directions, from positive to negative or from negative to positive.
demand charge	Charges for the use of electricity based on the maximum power consumed during a specified period of time.
density	Mass per unit of volume. Density varies with temperature and pressure.
DG	Distributed generation. Power that is generated at or near the customer's site, usually in relatively small amounts. Also called micropower.
DOE	Department of Energy (U.S.)
DOT	Department of Transportation (U.S.)
$/kg-d	Cost in dollars per kilogram of hydrogen produced per day.
EC	European Commission
EEA	Ecological City Transport System (Iceland)
EE	Eastern Europe
EEA	European Environment Agency
EERE	Energy Efficiency and Renewable Energy (office within the U.S. Department of Energy)

EIA	Energy Information Administration (U.S.)
electrode	One of two electronically conducting parts of an electrochemical cell, such as a fuel cell or electrolyzer. An electrode can be a rod, a sheet, or a more complex structure.
electrolysis	An electrochemical process in which an electrical current passes through an electrolyte, causing a chemical reaction. For example, electrolysis splits the water molecule into hydrogen and oxygen.
electrolyte	A substance that conducts charged ions from one electrode to the other inside a fuel cell or electrolyzer.
electrolyzer	An electrochemical device that produces hydrogen and oxygen from water.
electron	An atomic particle that has a negative electrical charge. Electricity is the flow of electrons.
endothermic	A process that requires heat to take place.
energy carrier	A liquid or gas in which energy can be stored in a chemical form and transported. Also a non-material carrier such as electricity or solar radiation.
energy density	Amount of energy in a given volume.
EPA	Environmental Protection Agency (U.S.)
EPRI	Electric Power Research Institute (U.S.)
ethanol	See CH_3CH_2OH.
EU	European Union
EUR	Estimated ultimate recovery
exothermic	A process that gives off heat when it takes place.
FCV	fuel cell vehicle
flammability	The range of flammability in which a gas and

limits	air are in the right proportions to burn when ignited. Below the lower limit, there is not enough fuel to burn. Above the higher limit, there is not enough oxygen to support combustion.
PSU	Former Soviet Union
fuel cell stack	Individual fuel cells connected in series. Increasing the stack's number of cells boosts its voltage.
fuel cell	An electrochemical cell that converts the chemical energy contained in a fuel (such as hydrogen) directly into electricity through a reaction with oxygen. The electrochemical reaction is flameless.
fuel processor	Device used to extract hydrogen from hydrocarbon fuels, usually by reforming natural gas. Some fuel processors can accept other fuels such as propane, ethanol, methanol, or gasoline.
gge	Gallon of gasoline equivalent. The quantity of fuel such as hydrogen which contains the same amount of energy as a gallon of gasoline.
GHG	Greenhouse gas. These gases, which include carbon dioxide and methane, are thought to cause global warming.
global warming	A gradual process in which greenhouse gases in the earth's atmosphere allow the sun's rays in, but prevent heat from being radiated back into space.
grid	The network of equipment that transmits and distributes electricity.
GW	Gigawatt. Metric unit that measures power, equal to one billion Watts or 1,000 megawatts.
GW_e	Gigawatt-electrical
GW_{th}	Gigawatt-thermal

H_2	Hydrogen. The lightest element (atomic weight of 1). Hydrogen is a colorless, odorless, flammable gas that liquefies at cryogenic temperatures (–253°C, or –423°F). Hydrogen forms water when burned or when combined with oxygen in a fuel cell.
h2EA	h2 Early Adopters. A Canadian government-industry program to demonstrate hydrogen technologies that further the transition toward a hydrogen economy in Canada.
heat exchanger	A mechanical device such as a radiator that is designed to move heat from one part of a system to another or from one mass to another mass.
heating value	The amount of energy produced by combustion of a fuel. See HHV and LHV.
HHV	Higher heating value. The amount of energy produced by combustion of a fuel, including the heat given off when water vapor in the combustion products condenses.
HOD	Hydrogen on Demand™, a type of hydrogen generation system.
hp	Horsepower. Unit that measures the rate of doing work, equal to 746 Watts.
hydrocarbon	An organic fuel containing hydrogen and carbon alone or in combination with other elements. Hydrocarbon fuels include coal, oil, gasoline, methane, and propane.
hydro-cracking	A method of breaking down complex hydrocarbons into their various components, using hydrogen and a catalyst.
hydrogen economy	An economic system that uses hydrogen as the primary or secondary energy carrier.

hydro-genation	The process of chemically combining with hydrogen. For example, edible oils are hydrogenated to prolong their shelf life.
IEEE	Institute of Electrical & Electronics Engineers
IGCC	Integrated gasification combined cycle. A system that integrates coal gasification with two turbines operating in a combined cycle. The synthesis gas produced from coal is burned as fuel in a combustion turbine-generator. The turbine's exhaust heat is used in a boiler to create steam that powers a second turbine-generator.
inorganic	A compound that does not contain carbon.
ion	Atom or molecule that carries a positive or negative charge because of the loss or gain of electrons.
IPCC	Intergovernmental Panel on Climate Change (United Nations)
IPHE	International Partnership for the Hydrogen Economy ISO International Organization for Standardization
ISO	International Organization for Standardization
J	Joule. Metric unit that measures the amount of work done or energy expended by a force of 1 Newton acting through a distance of 1 meter.
JHFC	Japan Hydrogen and Fuel Cell demonstration program
kg	Kilogram. Metric unit that measures mass or weight, equal to about 2.2 pounds.
kg/d	Kilograms per day
kg/yr	Kilograms per year
kPa	Kilopascal. Metric unit that measures pressure, equal to 1,000 Pascals.

kW	Kilowatt. Metric unit that measures power, equal to 1,000 Watts or about 1.34 horsepower.
kWh	Kilowatt-hour. Metric unit that measures electrical energy.
LANL	Los Alamos National Laboratory (U.S.)
LH_2	Liquid or liquefied hydrogen
LHV	Lower heating value. The amount of energy produced by combustion of a fuel, not including the heat given off when water vapor in the combustion products condenses.
LLNL	Lawrence Livermore National Laboratory (U.S.)
LNG	liquefied natural gas
LPG	Liquefied petroleum gas. A mixture of hydrocarbon gases such as propane and butane that have been liquefied for storage and use.
m^3	Cubic meters. Metric unit that measures volume.
MCFC	Molten carbonate fuel cell. A type of high-temperature fuel cell that uses molten carbonate salt mixture as an electrolyte, suspended in a porous, chemically inert ceramic lithium-aluminum oxide matrix.
membrane	A layer of thin film that acts as an electrolyte in fuel cells and electrolyzers.
metal hydride	A compound created when a metal or alloy absorbs gaseous hydrogen. In metal hydride storage technology, hydrogen fills the spaces in the metal's crystalline lattice structure, but occupies no additional space. When the metal hydride is heated, hydrogen is released.
methane	See CH_4.

methanol	See CH_3OH.
METI	Ministry of Economy, Trade and Industry (Japan)
microgrid	A group of homes or larger buildings that are interconnected and serviced by multiple micropower units.
micropower	Any small electricity generation unit (less than 20 megawatts), usually located at or near the power customer's site. Hydrogen fuel cells and other small power generators can be used in micropower plants. Also called distributed generation.
microturbine	A very small turbine based on automotive turbocharger technology with output ranging from 25 to 300 kilowatts.
mJ	Megajoule. Metric unit that measures energy, equal to one million Joules.
MPa	Megapascal. Metric unit that measures pressure, equal to one million Pascals.
mpg	miles per gallon
MW	Megawatt. Metric unit that measures power, equal to one million Watts.
MW_e	Megawatt-electric. Metric unit that measures electrical power.
MW_{th}	Megawatt-thermal. Metric unit that measures thermal power.
NAE	National Academy of Engineers (U.S.)
NAS	National Academy of Science (U.S.)
NASA	National Aeronautics and Space Administration (U.S.)
natural gas	A naturally occurring mixture of hydrocarbon gases, primarily methane (CH_4).
neutron	An atomic particle that has no electrical charge.

Newton	Metric unit that measures the amount of force that produces an acceleration of 1 meter per second when exerted on a mass of 1 kilogram.
NGLs	Natural gas liquids. Hydrocarbons heavier than methane that are found in some natural gas, including condensate, butane, propane, and ethane.
nm^3	Normal cubic meters. Metric unit that measures volume.
NO_x	Nitrogen oxides. Chemical compounds of nitrogen and oxygen that are created at high temperatures during the combustion of fuels. Nitrogen oxides contribute to urban smog and can cause acid rain.
NRC	National Research Council (U.S.)
NREL	National Renewable Energy Laboratory (U.S.)
OPEC	Organization of Petroleum Exporting Countries
organic	A compound containing carbon
OTEC	Ocean thermal energy conversion. A technology that exploits the temperature difference between the warm surface of the sea and its colder depths.
oxidation	The process of combining with oxygen, accompanied by the loss of one or more electrons from the atom or molecule being oxidized. Combustion, or burning, is a type of oxidation, but oxidation can also take place electrochemically without a flame as in a fuel cell. The rusting of metals is a slow oxidation process.
Pa	Pascal. Metric unit that measures pressure, or force per unit area. One Pascal is the pressure generated by a force of 1 Newton acting on

an area of 1 square meter. It is a small unit and is more often used as a kilopascal (kPa) or megapascal (MPa).

PAFC — Phosphoric acid fuel cell. A type of fuel cell that uses concentrated liquid phosphoric acid (H_3PO_4) as an electrolyte—the acid is contained in a Teflon-bonded silicon carbide matrix—and porous carbon electrodes containing a platinum catalyst.

partial oxidation — A type of reforming reaction in which some of the feedstock is burned as fuel to generate the heat required for subsequent reactions, but combustion is quenched before it is complete.

particulates — Sooty particles produced from burning coal, diesel fuel, and other heavy hydrocarbons.

peak demand period — Daily and seasonal times of maximum electricity demand.

peak power — Electricity supplied during peak demand periods.

peakshaving — Reducing consumption of electricity during peak demand periods.

PEM — Polymer electrolyte membrane or proton exchange membrane. A thin plastic film that serves as the electrolyte in a fuel cell or electrolyzer.

PEM electrolyzer — A type of electrolyzer that uses a solid polymer (thin plastic film) as an electrolyte.

PEMFC — PEM fuel cell. A type of low-temperature fuel cell that uses a solid polymer (thin plastic film) as an electrolyte and porous carbon electrodes containing a platinum catalyst or other noble metal.

PNNL — Pacific Northwest National Laboratory (U.S.)

primary energy	Sources of energy found in nature such as coal, oil, and natural gas.
propane	See C_3H_8
proton	An atomic particle that has a positive electrical charge.
PSA	Pressure swing adsorption. A process for removing carbon dioxide from a gaseous stream.
psi	Pounds per square inch. Unit that measures pressure, or force per unit area.
psig	Pounds per square inch gauge.
PV	Photovoltaic. Systems of solar cells that convert the sun's light energy directly into an electric current. In photovoltaic cells, sunlight is absorbed by semiconducting materials such as crystalline silicon, allowing electrons from their atoms to flow through an external circuit and generate electricity.
real-time pricing	Electricity rate structure that charges premium prices for power during peak demand periods. Also called time-of-day rates.
reformer	A device in which hydrocarbon fuels or feedstocks are reacted with steam in the presence of a catalyst to produce a hydrogen-carbon monoxide synthesis gas from which hydrogen is separated and purified.
reforming	A chemical process that uses steam and a catalyst to convert hydrocarbon fuels or feedstocks into a hydrogen-carbon monoxide synthesis gas from which hydrogen is separated and purified.
renewable energy	Energy derived from resources that are virtually unlimited because they are renewed by nature within a short time. Examples

	include solar energy, wind power, and hydroelectric power.
scf	Standard cubic feet. Unit that measures volume.
shift reaction	One of the steps in reforming natural gas or other hydrocarbons. The shift reaction changes the carbon monoxide to carbon dioxide and produces more hydrogen.
SMR	steam methane reforming.
SNL	Sandia National Laboratories.
sodium borohydride	An advanced chemical storage material that combines hydrogen with sodium borate (essentially, the familiar laundry detergent Borax) The chemical creates a nontoxic, nonflammable solution with water and produces hydrogen when exposed to a catalyst. When the catalyst and solution are separated, the system stops generating hydrogen.
SOFC	Solid oxide fuel cell A type of fuel cell that uses a hard, non-porous ceramic compound as the electrolyte. They operate at very high temperatures—around 1,000°C (1,800°F), which means they do not require an expensive precious-metal catalyst. High-temperature operation also allows solid oxide cells to reform fuels internally
SO_x	Sulfur oxides. Compounds containing sulfur and oxygen. Sulfur oxides, created by combustion of coal and other sulfurous fuels, can cause acid rain.
syngas	A synthesis gas containing hydrogen and carbon monoxide that is produced during the reforming of natural gas or other hydrocarbons.

tcf	Trillion cubic feet. Unit that measures volume.
time-of-day rates	Electricity pricing structure that charges premium rates for power during peak demand periods. Also called real-time pricing.
ton	U.S. unit of weight equal to 2,000 pounds.
tonne	Metric unit that measures weight, equal to 1,000 kilograms or about 2,200 pounds.
tpy	Tons or tonnes per year
turbocharger	A compressor used to increase the pressure and density of gases entering an engine. The compressor is driven by a turbine that extracts energy from the engine's exhaust gas.
U.N.	United Nations
UPS	Uninterruptible power supply
UV-IR	Ultraviolet-infrared detector
VOCs	Volatile organic compounds. Compounds that have a high vapor pressure and low water solubility and which contribute to urban smog. Many VOCs are artificial chemicals used and produced in .the manufacture of paints, pharmaceuticals, and refrigerants. VOCs typically are industrial solvents such as trichloroethylene and fuel additives such as methyl tertiary butyl ether (MTBE).
W	Watt. Metric unit that measures power, or the rate of doing work. One Watt equals I Joule per second.
We-Net	World Energy Network (Japan)
wheeling	Third-party transportation of power on utility transmission lines.
ZEV	Zero-emission vehicle. A vehicle that has no tailpipe emissions, no evaporative emissions, no emissions from gasoline refining or sales, and no onboard emission-control systems that can deteriorate over time.

Conversion Factors :

Distance		
1 mile	=	1.609347 km
1 km	=	0.62137 mile
Volume		
1 scf	=	0.028317 nm^3
1 nm^3	=	35.3145 scf
1 gallon	=	3,785 liters
1 liter	=	0.264 gallon
1 m^3	=	1,000 liters
Vehicle fuel use		
1 mpg	=	0.4251 km/liter
1 km/liter	=	2.352 mpg
Mass		
1 kg	=	2.2046 lb
1 lb	=	0.4536 kg
1 ton	=	0.978 tonne
1 metric ton	=	1.023 tons
	=	2,204.6 lb
	=	1,000 kg
Pressure		
1 psi	=	0.06895 bar
	=	6.895 kPa
1 bar	=	14.5 psi
	=	100k Pa
	=	0.1 MPa
1 MPa	=	145 psi
Temperature		
delta °F	=	1.8°C

Continued ....

delta °C	=	0.555°F
°F	=	1.8°C + 32
°C	=	(°F – 32)0.555
Energy/Work		
hp	=	746 W
	=	0.746 kW
kW	=	1.34 hp
	=	1,000 W
MW	=	1,000, 000 W
Btu	=	1,055 J
Btu	=	1.055 kJ
kJ	=	0.948 Btu
kWh	=	3,600,000 J
	=	3,600 kJ
	=	3.6 MJ
Energy content		
1 gallon gasoline	=	1 kg H_2
	=	380 scf H_2
	=	10 nm^3 H_2
1 kg H_2	=	1 gallon gasoline
100 scf H_2	=	9.30 kWh HHV
	=	7.87 kWh LHV
	=	31,740 Btu HHV
	=	26,840 Btu LHV

Appendix–A

RISING OIL PRICES : HUGE BURDEN FOR SOCIETY

Introduction

The surging price of oil appears to be at the root of all our economic woes. On 27 June, 2008 oil price has touched $ 142 per barrel in international market. It was only spring last year (2007) that price of crude oil was around the $50 a barrel mark. Goldman Sachs recently said, "$200 a barrel could be a reality in the not-too-distant future in the case of a major disruption". The reality of $200 a barrel by the end of the year (2008) is seen by some experts as unlikely, in part because OPEC (Organisation of Exporting Petroleum Countries) has been steadily increasing in production since December 2007. Also demand is slowing and the USA petrol consumption in January 2008 was 4 percent down on January 2007, reports the US Department of Energy (USDOE). In China, growth in oil imports is easing, reports the International Energy Agency (IEA), from 10 percent a year to 6 percent. In addition, world surplus oil production capacity has risen from 1.5 million barrels a day a few years ago, to over three million barrels today. Rex Tillerson, Chairman of Exxon Mobil says the record run in oil prices is related more to speculation and a weakening dollar than supply and demand. In dollars, the price of oil has jumped dramatically. This is partly due to the 30 percent drop in its value against major currencies since 2002. Measured against the Euro the price of oil appears less dramatic. A very important influence is the geo-political situation, such as the tension between the USA and Iran, the security situation in Iraq, and talk of imposing sanctions on the Sudan. The UK consumes 1.7 million barrels of oil a day.

Almost three-quarters of Britain's imports of crude oil are from Norway.

Contributing Factors

There have been problems including strikes, insufficient refining capacity and the weather conditions that have contributed to recent price increases as well as the seasonal needs of the Northern Hemisphere to build up its inventories to prepare for the upcoming winter season when demand will peak. Production is lessening in some oil producing states such as Iran and Venezuela, as a result of management failures to undertake the necessary investment over the long-term, to maintain production, observes Robert Mabro of Oxform Institute of Energy Studies (OIES). In terms of financial markets, oil has been experiencing a series of record highs since last October 2007 as investors have fled stock markets and taken refuge in dollar denominated assets. Increasingly, speculators hedge funds and investors are using the futures market as *a* hedge or bet against inflation and a declining dollar. It is clear investment flows into the oil market that do not have anything to do with the demand and supply of oil. The oil market is stating to resemble the gold market which has also been soaring. Much of the speculation is dependent on data which is often inaccurate. Such increasing speculation in the futures markets adds pressure for the price of oil to increase in dollar terms, in both the short-term and long-term. Market prices for electricity, gas and coal have begun to climb. Electricity companies have been able to turn away from oil to alternative and competitively priced forms of fuel such as coal and natural gas. This has resulted in an increase in demand for such energy sources and caused pressure on prices. It is difficult to directly compare nuclear energy with fossil fuels, though it is said to be price competitive with other fuels in the generation of electricity by its promoters. Compared with other fuels it has relatively higher capital costs, waste disposal and environmental costs that make it harder to make a direct price comparison.

The Future Price of Oil

For G8 countries like Britain, the impact on dramatic oil price is likely to be less severe than the first oil price shock in 1972-73, when the price of petroleum quadrupled. The jump in oil prices has magnified existing economic troubles rather than were the primary cause of economic problems. The UK is benefiting from high fuel taxes, because nearly 70 percent of the price of a liter of petrol is made up of fuel duty and VAT. Taxes act as a cushion against major oil price fluctuations. The proportional increase will be less than in low fuel tax countries like America where the tax is around *20* percent of the price at the petrol pumps. Dr. Adnan Shihab-Eldin, OPEC's President, has pointed out that "predicting the price of oil is extremely difficult. Not only must one take into account the fundamental factors like supply and demand, but one must also anticipate the non-fundamentals, like geopolitical tensions and possible supply disruptions". According to the United States Department of Energy, in the short-term the price of oil is likely to fall due to a slowdown in the American economy, reduced consumption of oil caused by high oil prices, and increased OPEC production since December 2007 that has led to increased world oil inventories. The threat to supplies from a war between the USA and Iran has decreased, while supplies from Iraq continue to improve.

In the longer-term, most analysts agree that the price of oil is likely to continue its upward trend, but how fast it will climb will depend on how fast world demand may increase, plus the usual security, technological, economic and political factors, plus the decisions of the futures market. A further unknown variable is the extent to which new fields will be opened up. Already, some OPEC countries are nearing the end of their ability to export surplus oil, due to internal political and management problems. However, others are investing in new technology and engineers to boost and extend the life span of existing fields. New methods of exploration including increased use of 3-D seismic data have reduced drilling risk and led to the discovery of fields in the Arctic Ocean. Also, directional and horizontal drilling has improved production in many oil fields, and new recovery methods have enhanced existing oil wells. Elsewhere in the world, exploration and development of new oil fields, is likely to gather pace, especially if current high prices are maintained. The very same high price levels are likely to further encourage governments to develop alternative energy sources. The Arctic seems to be offering the prospect of new opportunities to explore and develop that are free from the political instability of the Middle East. Big gas discoveries have already been made off the South Kara/Yamal and East Barents Sea and across most of Arctic Canada. The best oil potential may be in the Pechora Sea, Baffin Bay and on the North Slope, although several other basins could become attractive. It is estimated that 400 billion barrels of oil equivalent gas and oil reserves still remain. While the Arctic icecaps continue to shrink due to global warming, this is making it much easier and economic for the world's oil companies to explore and develop new oil fields, in regions which until now had been at the frontiers of technology and costly to exploit. Developments off Norway's North Cape, Russia's Stockman fields and Alaska's North Slope are just the beginning and it is likely, in the near future, with the melting of the ice cap such developments in the high Arctic will be common place.

Present Scenario

The price of oil is determined by supply and demand. When price go up, consumers reduce demand, and eventually this leads to a fall in prices. The demand for oil in rich countries is slowing today with rising prices. We see this up-and-down price cycle less in oil. Because many governments subsidise oil consumption, and so keep demand artificially high. This then keeps world oil prices artificially high. Each developing country believes it is virtuously subsidizing its own consumers. But when many developing countries do so, notably high populated ones like China and India, they push up global demand for oil, and so push up global prices high too. They become victims of their own subsidies. Back in the 1970s, rich countries cut domestic taxes and imposed price controls to protect consumers after OPEC quadrupled prices. This kept oil demand and prices high. Only when the USA abolished price controls progressively after 1979 did imports crash, and later would prices crashed too. It was a signal lesson on the folly of trying to shield consumers from the reality of high oil prices.

Rich countries have learned from history, but developing countries have not. The demand for oil in rich countries is slowing today with rising prices. Petrol consumption has fallen in the USA as the price has risen to $4 per gallon. US demand for gas-guzzling large cars has collapsed, and General Motors wants to sell its Hummer brand, the largest car of all. All these positive outcomes flow from passing on the burden of OPEC to the consumer. But China, India and many developing countries have tried to keep oil prices artificially low. Thus, they have kept demand artificially high. And that is why OPEC is able to sell oil at $139 per barrel, despite a global slowdown. Indians government has reluctantly increased the price of petrol by Rs. 5 per Itr., diesel by Rs. 3 per Itr. and cooking gas by Rs. 50 per cylinder on 5th June 2008. These timid increases will plug barely one-tenth the implicit gap. Even this has been cushioned by cuts in excise and customs duty by the center, and the VAT by State governments (Many Indian states have already takes action in these matters and have reduced oil, diesel and gas pries nominally).

Any proposal to ration oil in view of rising global crude prices could turn out to be *a* disaster. Imposing a formal allocation system to streamline supply and demand of petrol and diesel would, instead of resolving the problem, encourage hoarding and black-marketeering. Then there are logistical problems. On what basis would the rationing system work? Since petrol and diesel are used largely for transportation, any rationing project will face difficulty in apportioning available fuel resources in an equitable manner. Ascertaining need and working out logistic could be a nightmare. Relying solely on oil for fuel is no longer a sustainable option. Alternative sources of energy need to be made available commercially. We simply have to step up research in solar, wind and biofuel energy from sources like the jatropha plant, biomass and waste, and perhaps sugarcane. USA has already started converting 10 percent of her maize crops into biofuel energy. Other countries should follow the example of USA, but it should not create food-shortage in the world market. Reducing energy wastage could offset initial high costs. Besides, the steep rise in the price of oil has made alternative fuels attractive. India, like Brazil already has, should immediately start its shift away form oil dependency. Sweden has declared its intention to kick its dependence on oil by the year 2020 by focusing on biofuels and wind energy. Oil-fired heating systems are being replaced with boilers using bio-pellets, leading to an 85 percent fall in heating oil sales. Denmark is harvesting wind energy on a large scale.

Sources

1. Nicholas Newman, 2008; The high price of oil; E&T Jornal, Vol. 3, No. 8, 10 May-23 May, pp. 46-49.
2. The Times of India, Newspaper.

Appendix–B

SEISMIC INSTRUMENTS WITHOUT LAND CABLES

Introduction

Al the recent SEG Convention in San Antonio, Texas, there were half a dozen different land seismic instruments which claimed as one of their main benefits the ability to work without digital spread cables. There is nothing novel in the notion of a wireless seismic recorder but there is something special about these latest cable-free products, and some of them have already made an impact. They will certainly benefit the Indians exploration industry.

Most of these latest systems claim to be designed for a new-era of land acquisition in which there is a major trend to far lower costs, HSE exposure is much reduced and channel counts can easily sore to five or even six figures. At least one manufacturer seems to believe that by 2010, half of all land channels sold could be cable-free. However, neither exaggeration nor wishful thinking are new to seismic equipment marketing so, before there is a rush to discard all existing cabled hardware, we should take a closer look at what actually is happening.

Cable Land Seismic Systems

Digital cable telemetry systems first hit the market 'in 1979. We are now almost thirty years on so no one can deny the long run of success enjoyed by this technology; in many ways it is what made 3D acquisition viable on land. But most technologies do not survive three decades without giving way to new ways of doing things, at least at some level, and cabled systems look like being no exception. Cable-free hardware is already being used in anger so, even if cable telemetry dominates another five years, no one can claim that cable did not get a good run for its money. It should receive our eternal gratitude for how far it brought onshore exploration before we pass the batten of land geophysics on to something more up-to-date.

So what has made this most conservative of industries reconsider its acquisition options? In my view, responsibility (blame or credit, depending on your position) for the move to "newera cable-free" rests mostly with the oil companies themselves. In the past, I feel that system producers rather than the data end-users have mostly been responsible for development decisions in acquisition hardware, with some manufacturers apparently paying little more than lip service to what oil companies wanted. In some respects this is quite reasonable because no hardware company that I know of operates as a charity. Therefore, design choices are, more often than not, made of course with profits in mind rather than what may necessarily allow progress in acquisition geophysics - an industry where it has long been safer to create a minor variation on an established theme than to write a whole new symphony. For some while there has only been very little variety on Central Europe. Side-by-side use of new-era cable-free system and land cable system, offer as to the way we acquire land data there seems to have been much greater choice in margarine than options in land instrumentation. It was not a situation which could persevere for ever.

In the mid-late nineties, data end-users at workshops and conventions, started to exercise their collective muscle and suggested that recording hardware needed to experience a quantum leap. In-the-know oil company geophysicists, slowly at first, then more vocally, demanded to know why the technology we regularly take for granted in digital cameras and mobile phones should not be used to help us record land seismic data at much lower cost, with very many more channels and less harm to the environment^ There was a feeling that land instrumentation should be more Wallmart than Wall Street, the sort of thing you might even find one day on eBay.

Cable systems were never going to be able to take such a giant leap for seismic-kind because some considered them already almost as perfected as they are going to get after thirty years. As Hamlet put it, they were "hoist by their own petar"; the very ubiquity of cables demonstrated its shortcomings better than alternative technologies had been successful in pointing out its weaknesses when cable systems are sometimes stretched inappropriately into the modern acquisition era. One major cable technology short-coming Deploying new-era cable-free equipment in rain forest, is the problem as channel counts rise to many thousands.

Historically, it was of course digital cable telemetry which started to make possible the transport of very much more data down one twisted pair than analog transmission permitted. Products such as Texas Instruments' DFS5 used a couple of conductors to pass data from only one geophone trace, a data rate in modern terms we may think of in round figures as 10 kbits/second. The latest cable systems send one thousand times this much data down one twisted pair but that's the problem. The laws of physics in general, and transmission theory in particular, both elicit a price for this. This price is in terms of cables, forced to transfer very high frequency data, can become increasingly susceptible to small physical damage making problems for the flow of high rate digital information which, if the frequency had remained lower, would make no difference at all.

Total system weight is another issue regularly highlighted by oil companies as something which increases the cost per channel of operations. The telemetry cable itself makes up perhaps three quarters of system-specific weight and this is very difficult to reduce since that would mean making the cable weaker or taking away some conductor pairs. Both of these are the opposite of what we need when thinking of improved HSE or large channel count acquisition. An extra nail in cable's coffin is that they have to be joined by digital connectors, all of which must work well for the spread to operate and, as channel counts try inexorably to increase, the issue of serial dependency then looms large too.

This is not to say that cable systems do not claim to be able to operate within range of some of the channel counts now being discussed. Specifications of some cable products claim that they will work with tens of thousand of channels -and well they may though no one has tried it. However, since some recent geophysical papers speak about the need for anything from fifty thousand to three million channels per crew, then almost by their own admission, cable systems will not solve these problems.

So given that there are now tried and tested alternatives, it is now reasonable to ask the question whether cable is any longer either the most appropriate or only way to grow in an industry otherwise much changed from the late seventies. When there was no technological alternative to cable, then one could understand the reticence to start the move away but with all the new cable-free products, then we may consider that cable may at least be reaching the autumn of its years for some applications. Not everyone will want tens or hundreds of thousands of channels on each crew, but if new technology can achieve this for an acceptable economic and environmental price, then think how much benefit it will also bring to smaller operations.

Cable-free Variety

Modern cable-free hardware comes in two broad categories and, out of the six systems mentioned above, three fall into each camp. The first includes those which store all data in local memory for later harvesting - sending nothing at all back by radio, not even a status byte. This is a "shoot blind" approach but this characteristic endows such products with the massive advantage of being by far the lowest cost to buy and to operate. Secondly, there is hardware which sends something back over some period of time over some distance. Currently none in this latter category seem capable of high data-rate sustained throughput in all seismic environments from more than a rather limited number of channels, and then at relatively high cost. You will not yet find this in the text books on seismic instrumentation but given the recent arrival of this new-era philosophy to the industry, I would like to suggest a relationship which covers the current engineering and commercial issues in operating with any the cable-free technology.

When a value is assigned between 1 and 10 to each of the following five characteristics and then the product taken, you arrive at a figure between 1 and 100,000 which in some way represents the difficulty of gelling any cable-free system to work in a particular acquisition environment. Stricth speaking, this derived value would have somewhat strange units but we may as well think of it in terms of cost, and the higher this value, the greater the cost.

The five characteristics are: (*i*) how much data, i.e how many channels and whether the full record or just status, (*ii*) how quickly, i.e data rate, (*iii*) from how far away, i.e the farthest channels, (*iv*) the weight per channel for any particular operation and (*v*) the serial reliability of any part of the transmission process. They are multiplicative because they can each affect the other. The lower the product, the more channels it is likely to be able to afford to buy and to use.

Shoot-blind systems are easiest to deal with because their factor for characteristic (*i*) is zero, and thus the product zero too. Cable systems can also be partially considered in this equation and do well as long as the amount of data is not overstretched. In other words channel count, weight and serial reliability must be kept reasonable - as they are for crews with just a few thousand channels. For non-shootblind cable-free systems, even a small data packet or short range transmission poses problems because it means the introduction of some form of transmitter and associated circuitry inside each box. This in turn means greater complexity, power consumption and weight, which translates into higher cost to buy and to operate, and thus a high derived value - the exact opposite of what this industry wants cable-free to achieve. Nevertheless, even cable-free systems which do send something back (depending on technology) may well offer advantages over a cable system. In either case, nothing approaches the cost-to-use which shoot-blind cable-free offers.

One advantage which cable systems are still seen as having over cable-free is that they offer realtime data from the entire connected spread for purposes of data quality control. If this is just to provide a means of supporting instant quality control checking of channels and sensors, then how important is this when such hardware nowadays tends to show incredible reliability? Another function provided by realtime checking is that it allows the observer to know quickly if sensors or ground units are not where and how they were deployed. But is laying 100 km of fragile and expensive cable still the best use of manpower to achieve this end? The real question to ask is: if the technology which lets us perform these QC feats automatically reduces the number of affordable channels -and thus increases HSE exposure and reduces the data quality of a final section - then are we now looking at a choice between data quality or data quality control? It cable-free shoot-blind channels really are now as low cost (to buy and to use) compared to all other technologies as the above equation indicates, then this is a discussion which the industry must undertake with some urgency.

However, no matter how one considers the necessity of realtime QC of each trace, where cable systems do still come out on top is their ability to monitor spread noise in real time, alerting the observer of when it may be necessary to stop acquisition. So does this mean that we have to stick with expensive systems after all, just to keep a noise monitoring function?

This is to make the situation too black and white because the reality is that we would like not to have to limit ourselves to a stark choice between high tec costly cabled hardware or simple low-cost cable-free. We ought to be able to choose functionality from both ends of the cost and technology spectra to suit any acquisition application. This would require shoot-blind cable-free systems to be able to work side-by-side cabled systems. And this is exactly what at least one of these new-era systems has been designed to do, permitting seamless integration of the two technologies enabling a sort of hybrid exploration to take place. So how did this new era start?

The Birth of New-era cable-free Acquisition Technology

The world's first new-era cable-free system was brought to life by the mid-size US oil company Aspect Energy in 2001. Unhappy with the cost and risk of cable-based acquisition, Aspect put their money where their mouth was, and through the subsidiary Ascend Geo, started work on a new type of seismic system. From the beginning, Aspect had various needs in mind but they can be summed up with thoughts of: many more affordable channels, much lower operating costs, greater flexibility and less environmental exposure. They came to the conclusion that shoot-blind cable-free hardware, appropriately deployed, would be the only one able to fit the bill.

After a few versions of systems which only saw life in the workshop, the third generation "Ultra" system was sent to Central America in 2004 to replace a cable instrument. Operators found that this cable-free hardware could be deployed at twice the spatial density of the cable system for around the same crew effort. Since the system had not been in the field before and considering the rainy season of this area, this was definitely being thrown in at the deep end. Nevertheless, the use of this revolutionary technology resulted in the first oil discovery in that country after 50 dry holes suffered by some of the majors.

This was also first ever exploration success for a new-era, shoot-blind, cable-free system. Since then, further generations of the same cable-free system in stand-alone mode have been deployed in various countries including Belize, resulting in six more discovery wells and an expanded programme reaching into Guatemala is planned. It has also been used side-by-side cabled systems in North America and Europe, for 2D, 3D and 3C/9C. As the system enjoys wider spread use, it evolves further with the introduction of new features specific to this type of acquisition.

Seamless Integration

If the undisputed raison d'etre of cabled systems is now just their ability to look at noise in real time while shoot-blind cable-free systems offer the lowest cost to buy and to operate, then these are the natural technologies to integrate together. Cable-free can be used on parts of the survey where would be difficult or impossible to use cabled systems. We can also combine these different types of hardware across the entire spread at some ratio of channels which enables enough noise monitoring to take place, while simultaneously acquiring better spatial sampled data than could ever be afforded with cable systems alone. In some places, such as the Middle East, this ratio of cable-free to cabled may be 20:1 whereas in others it may just be 2:1.

This integration philosophy also gives rise to the idea that we should not only look at the cost of a specific crew but also the incremental cost of adding cable-free channels to it. Perhaps mathematically we could say that a cabled system of x channels may cost $\$y$ to operate. With $2x$ cable channels is may be $\$z$ $(z > y)$, but with x cabled channels and x cablefree channels the cost would be less than $z, and possibly by a large figure.

Cable-free is also breathing new life in to analog geophones, saving significant costs to crew operations at the same time as providing higher quality data. Deployed as smaller arrays connected to many more cable-free channels than was affordable in the past, crews are deploying a higher number of actual seismic traces but using no more geophones since strings can be half the length and with half the elements used previously. This gives the benefit of better spatial sampling along with the advantages of a hardwired array, perhaps at no increase in operational cost.

Finally, by doing away with the problems of laying easily damaged cable, cable-free systems also have found applications in passive acquisition. Going against policies which have been in place for twenty or more years, some oil companies are now so keen to reap the benefits of this new way of acquiring data that they are currently considering buying their own cable-free hardware to permit much lower cost 4D and other forms of on-shore permanent monitoring.

Source : Health, Roger Bog, 2007. What's new in the rapidly changing face of land seismic instrumentation; Geohorizons 12, No. 2, pp. 33-39.

Appendix–C

3C ACCELEROMETERS FOR SEISMIC ACQUISITION

Introduction

Coil based gcophones are a proven technology that has been used for a long time by the industry Recent advances in Micro Electro Mechanical System (MEMS) now provide sensors with adequate sensitivity, low noise, and dynamic range to be applicable to seismic acquisition. MEMS accelerometers have the potential to provide broader bandwidth, more accurate amplitude, and less sensitivity to planting tilt. Together with the renewed interest for 3C recording, triggered by the success of OBC surveys' these trends have incited manufacturers to develop and market new digital sensors.

Several recent papers (J. Tessman et al., EAGE, 2002; R.R. Kendal et al., EAGE, 2002) have presented the advantages of three-component acquisition with single digital sensors based on MEMS, and the advent of these sensors has been promoted as the next big advance in land seismic acquisition, much like the shift to 24-bits ten years ago. Has this technology really advanced to the point that it can, or should, be used for general-purpose land seismic acquisition? This paper will address the advantages and disadvantages for the general application of single 3C digital sensors.

Why Accelerometers for Digital Sensors?

Ground motion can be measured as displacement, velocity or acceleration. The mass/spring assembly is the model used for all these measurements. With a soft spring, the mass (the coil in the geophone) does not move and represents the reference for displacement or velocity measurements. In case of a stiff spring, the mass does move with the case, but with a small residual displacement related to the acceleration. This acceleration can be measured either by the strain on the spring (e.g. low cost, low power, high distortion air bags) or by a feedback force applied to the mass to cancel the displacement (e.g. high performance digital sensors requiring power supply).

In this last implementation the sensor based on MEMS is analog, while the control loop and the output provided by an Application Specific Integrated Chip (ASIC) are digital. Such "digital" sensor is small. A MEMS accelerometer is a tiny silicon chip which size (~1 cm) and weight (< 1 g) are much less than that of a coil based sensor (3 cm long & 76 g cartridge). Within the chip, the residual displacement between the inertia! mass and the frame is in the order of a few nanometers. Manufacturing such a "digital" sensor is expensive due to the cost of MEMS + ASIC. Therefore only one sensor per active channel will be used to record the output of every ASIC (i.e. a single sensor configuration is always used).

These MEMS accelerometers improve the seismic receiver performances compared to the coiled geophones. They also provide the benefit of a full digital data transmission from the sensor to the Central Unit.

How it Compares with Coiled Geophone?

From the specification point of view the essential benefit of MEMS accelerometers is their broadband linear phase & amplitude response that may extend from 0 (DC) to 800 Hz within 1 dB. With MEMS, low frequency recording (< 10 Hz) are not prevented by the resonant frequency (Figure 1) that is far above the seismic band pass (1 kHz). This makes it possible to record the Direct Current (DC) related to the gravity acceleration that is a useful reference for sensitivity calibration and tilt measurement. Since acceleration increases with frequency (at constant velocity), accelerometers also fit well with high frequency measurements. In this domain

(> 50 Hz) the floor/electric noise of the MEMS becomes less than the one of the equivalent geophone/station electronics.

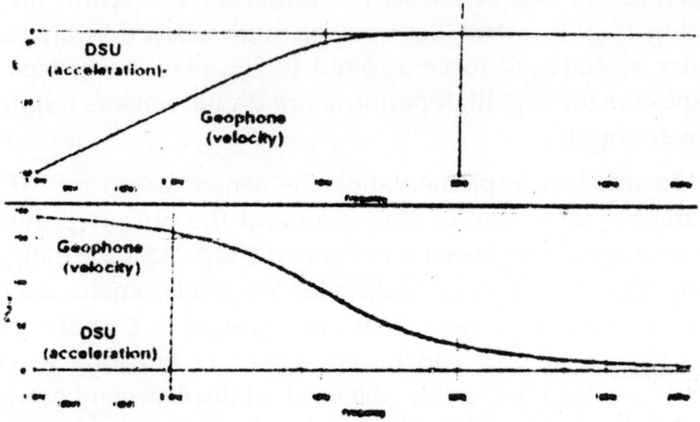

Fig. 1. Linear phase and amplitude responses of a Digital Sensor Unit (DSU) with MEMS compared with a 10 Hz geophone. The responses are in the velocity domain for the geophone, and in the acceleration domain for the DSU.

These broadband capabilities offer potential for a dramatic improvement in the vertical resolution of seismic data, which depends on the ratio between the maximum and minimum frequencies of the signal (Fmax/Fmin = 2^n, *n* being the number of octave). MEMS accelerometer is particularly suited for recording low frequency signals (< 5 Hz) like reflections at the main boundaries between lithological formations, or even an earthquake. At this frequency range the problem is more on the source side because such LF signal cannot be emitted with a sufficient S/N ratio. Recording of high frequencies is limited by their strong attenuation during propagation. However MEMS sensors should be able, if close enough, to listen to micro-seismic events (~ 500 Hz) as fluids move in the reservoir during oil & gas production.

The total dynamic range of a 24 bits recording system using MEMS (120 dB, the upper scale corresponding to -90 dB distortion) seems to be less than the one of the same system using single geophones (135 dB, the upper scale corresponding to –65 dB distortion). This apparent limitation of MEMS sensors is related to the different levels of distortion taken into consideration, and also to the floor noise of the digital accelerometer that is higher than the one of the equivalent geophone/station electronics (at least below 50 Hz). In practical situations (including the distortion) a MEMS sensor is more suited to record a weak signal in presence of strong noise (near offsets) while a geophone (and even more a string of geophones) is more effective in recording a weak / deep reflection in presence of low noise (far offsets).

Amplitude calibration of a MEMS sensor and its stability over aging & temperature variations are better than the geophone ones. Overall, performances of a digital sensor, where MEMS's are integrated with the station electronics in a single housing, are improved compared to a conventional station electronics that is connected during the same survey to different strings of geophones of variable characteristics.

The Full Digital Transmission

In the early 1970's, the A/D converter of the first digital recording system was implemented in the Central Unit. One analog pair for each of the channels was used for transmission between strings of geophones and the recording truck (Figure 2). Noise pick-up coming from electromagnetic (EM) interferences, signal cross-talk and sensitivity to leakage were common. 30 years later, the electronics distributed in the seismic network makes it possible to digitize close to the geophone groups. Only two pairs are necessary for telemetric transmission of 10,000+ channels in real-time. Sensitivity to leakage is less, digital data being controlled by each node of the seismic network, and retransmitted if necessary. However noise pick-up may still contaminate the strings of geophones. Today, the ultimate step is completed by integrating the sensor with the station electronics. It would have been possible to put in the same case a coiled geophone with the station electronics. Actually, integration of the MEMS accelerometer with the corresponding ASIC and station electronics is more effective, particularly for 3C sensors.

Advantages of the full digital transmission has been demonstrated. During field tests, records by bunched geophones were compared to MEMS sensors at the same location (Figure 3). 50 Hz is picked up below a high voltage line is obvious on the shot point recorded by bunched phones. On the corresponding FK diagram the EM noise interferes strongly with signal (K = 0). This noise does not occur on any of the 3 components of the MEMS sensors thanks to the full digital transmission.

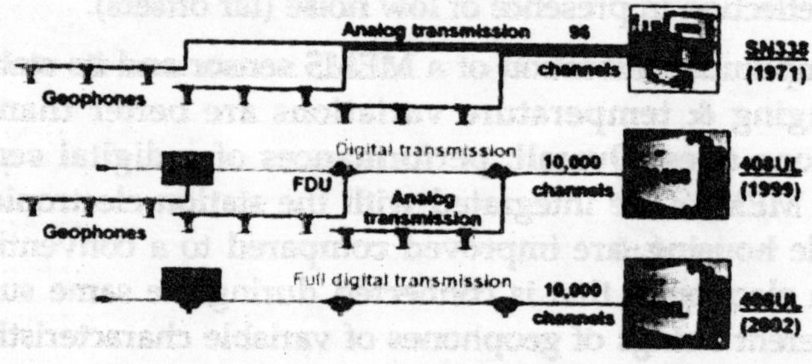

Fig. 2. With the first digital recording system all transmissions between geophone groups and Central Unit, including the A/D converter, were still analog. 30 years later, only the transmission between geophone groups and the Field Digitizing Unit (FDU) was analog. Today, the Digital Sensor Unit (DSU) makes it possible the full digital transmission.

Fig. 3. Shot point comparison between the vertical component of a Digital Sensor Unit (DSU3) and bunched phones planted at the same location (photo). Strong pick up of a high voltage line is due to analog transmission up to the station electronics. FK diagram shows this 50 Hz noise interfere with signal. DSU data are not contaminated at all. (Data courtesy of BatchNeftGeofisika)

Digital Sensors to Replace Arrays of Geophones?

Arrays of geophones may tremendously improve the dynamic range of a receiver point by reducing the ambient & organized noises. Whatever the mounting in series or in parallel of N geophones, the dynamic range of this array is improved by 10 × logN dB, as the signal-to-ambient noise is reduced by the square root of N. For organized noise attenuation, geophones are laid out to provide array filtering. The size of the array and the number of wired geophones should be large enough to sample properly the maximum wavelength of the ground roll.

Despite these advantages of the arrays field geophysicists would like to get rid of these large and heavy geophones arrays that slow crew productivity, require expensive logistic, deteriorate first breaks and lower signal band pass. At a first glance, the use of single digital sensors would have many operational and geophysical advantages over geophone arrays. Layout & positioning are easier compared to geophone strings, and this is even more relevant for 3C receiver points. Recording is isotropic (no azimuth dependant array filtering), and the high frequency content of the signal is not attenuated by intra-array static's. However these benefits are only true in an ideal world where reflected signal is not contaminated by noise i.e. in a situation where a single coiled geophone would have been sufficient.

Practically, the spacing of single sensors should decrease with respect to length of a geophone array. This shorter spacing will not attenuate noise while recording. It will provide enough multiplicity (fold coverage) to decrease the ambient noise while stacking data. Denser spatial sampling will also prevent the organized noise from aliasing for efficient application of FK filtering. Therefore we cannot expect to get better looking shot point displays while recording single digital sensor. The benefits (larger frequency content, accurate amplitude) will only show up with the final sections, after data processing.

New Requirements for Acquisition Geometry

How many of these MEMS sensors would be necessary to replace a string of N geophones? It is unlikely that anyone will record as many single digital sensors as hard wired geophones, and it is probably not necessary, even though that would provide excellent noise attenuation.

If we consider the Ground Roll (GR), often the strongest noise, the digital sensor spacing D should be such that the GR wavelength L = Va/Fa (Va, apparent velocity; Fa, apparent frequency) will be sampled at least two times, i.e. D = Va/2Fa. This provides often values in the range of 3 to 30 m. Figures 4 & 5 are comparison of FK diagrams on two SP's recorded at the same location with different spatial sampling. At 10 m spacing, the very low velocity ground roll (330 m/s, i.e. as low as the air blast) is aliased and interferes with signal. At 3.33 m spacing, GR is still aliased but it vanishes at high frequencies (70 Hz) before to intersect signal. Considering this maximum frequency limitation of the noise it is possible to use a spacing (adequate sampling, D) a little more than half of the GR wavelet (Nyquist sampling, D) as suggested by G.J. M. Baeten et al. (SEG, 2000).

Up to now, we have considered that all propagations were 2D. In case of 3D acquisition or complex near surface generating backscattered noise, it would be necessary to sample the noise properly both in the inline and cross line directions. Such areal sampling would require a corridor of single digital sensors equivalent to the patches of hard wired geophones. Since digital sensors are directly connected to a telemetry cable. Deployment of such receiver line would need to lay out several parallel cables (Figure 6) instead of only one telemetry cable for all geophones. A quick calculation of the channel requirement for a 3D swath of 4 × 4 Km^2 with 100 m between receiver lines, each one made of 5 individual cables with single digital sensors at 10 m spacing, provides a figure of 80,000 active channels. This amount is still above the real-time capability of all recording systems at 2 ms sampling. Today, this type of single sensor arrangement is only compatible with a 2D acquisition.

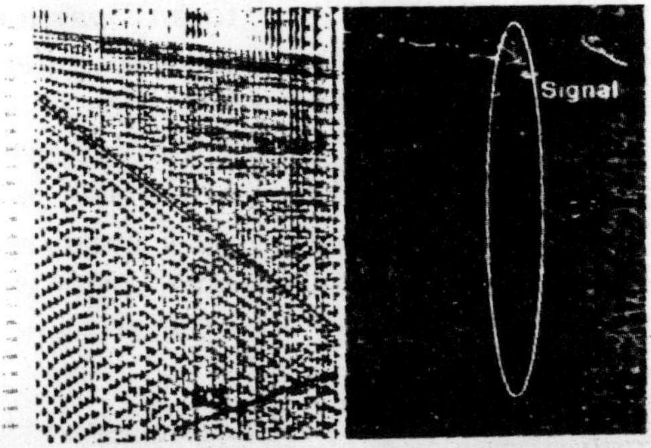

Fig. 4. Shot point (GR, ground roll, BS, back scattering) with 10 m spacing between single digital sensors. On FK diagram, GR is aliased and interferes with signal. (Data courtesy of CGG).

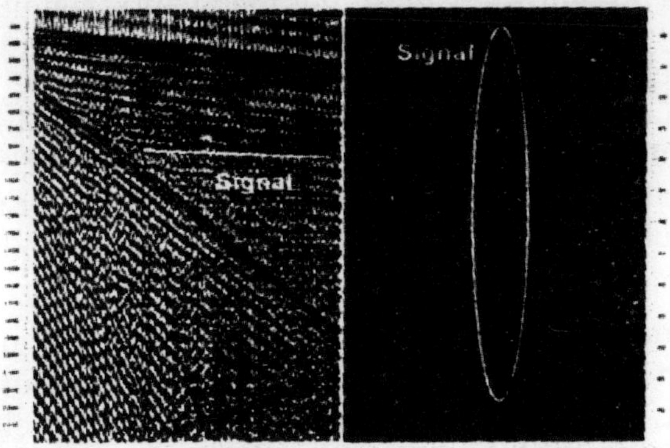

Fig. 5. Shot point with 3.3 m spacing between single digital sensors. On FK diagram, GR is still aliased but does not interfere with signal. (Data courtesy of CGG).

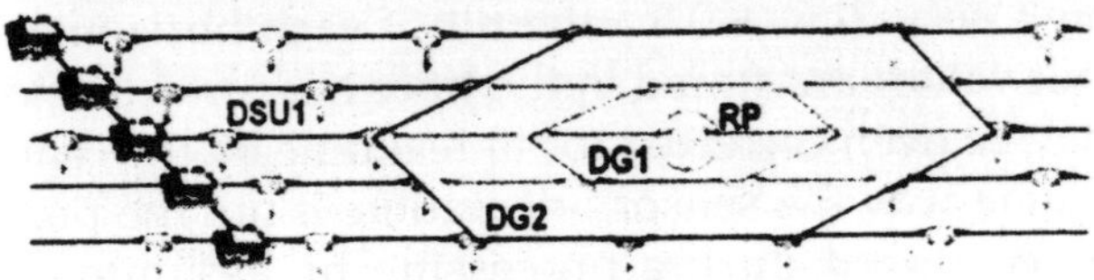

Fig. 6. Uncommitted 2D acquisition design made of a corridor of 1C single digital sensor units (DSU1) connected along parallel telernetric cables. At a given point receiver (PR) different types of digital group (DG1, DG2) may be considered to reduce ambient noise and filter the ground roll.

Due to the continuous spatial sampling, this corridor of single sensors provides some sort of universal acquisition design since it is not committed to any particular type of noise. Different single sensor combinations, often referred as digital group forming, may be used to attenuated noise after the recording of all single digital sensors. Since groups are overlapping from point-to-point, each single sensor may be used into different digital groups. At a given receiver point this group forming may even involve larger digital arrays along with increasing travel time and decreasing S/N ratio.

A New Era for 3C Recording

Connecting strings of triphones to a telemetry cable is an extra task involving heavy equipment, lots of wire and many connectors. Also planting, levelling and orienting properly all these triphones is painful but mandatory: the final output being the electric sum of all triphones connected to the same station electronics, any correction is impossible at a later stage. Having sensors and station electronics integrated in the same housing, as it is for the 408UL 3C Digital Sensor Unit (DSU3), will reduce overall weight and wiring errors, and should make multi-component surveys faster, better and cheaper.

Of course, planting a 3C digital sensor would need some attention in order to get the proper coupling, but insuring its exact verticality is not mandatory. This is related to a unique feature of the MEMS based 3C digital sensor: their ability to measure the continuous effect of the gravity vector. This vector is used as a reference to automatically compute with high accuracy (± 0.5°) the tilt of each horizontal sensor. These tilt values are stored in the trace header extensions, and data may be even corrected for in real time by the central unit. In the same way the sensor orientation, if not the proper one, may be corrected during processing by assuming a radial propagation between the source and the single sensor (3D surveys only).

Tilt measurement is only one aspect of the advantages provided, in term of vector fidelity, by the MEMS based 3C digital sensors. In addition to their broadband capabilities (0-800 Hz linear response) is the very precise orthogonality of the sensors (± 0.25° accuracy) and their accurate and stable amplitude calibration (± 0.25% accuracy).

This 3C digital sensor technology is already field proven as many surveys have already been completed. Data from Figures 7 & 8 are from a 2D acquisition with explosive recorded with 408UL in North America. These data evidence

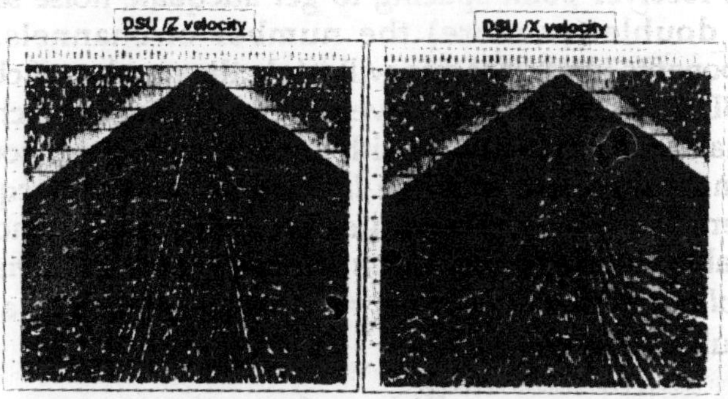

Fig. 7. Real time display of DSU3 shot points (Z & X components) in the doghouse after velocity conversion and low cut filtering (10 Hz). (Data courtesy of Veritas DGC & Devon).

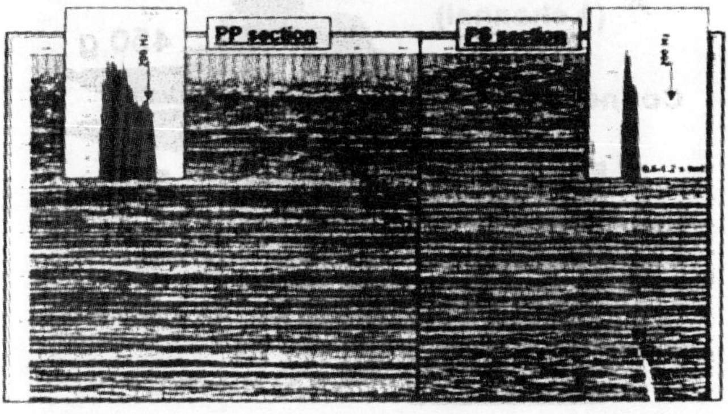

Fig. 8. Comparison of PP & PS final sections corresponding to the previous SP's. PS section is squeezed to PP time assuming a constant Vp/Vs = 3. The frequency content of the PP section is above 200 Hz, while in the PS section most of the HF above 70 Hz has been attenuated. The reflectivity of the two sections recorded in sand shale formations is quite different. (Data courtesy of Veritas DGC & Devon).

the broadband capabilities of the MEMS 3C digital sensor (DSU3). High frequency preservation while stacking has required careful static definition and efficient deconvolution after noise attenuation. On the final PP section, the frequency spectrum of the signal in a 0.4-1.0s window is above 200 Hz, and sinnal bevond 300 Hz is evidenced down to 0.2 s twt.

Crew Productivity with Single 3C Digital Sensors

Seismic data acquisition with high-density single digital sensors will require recording large number of channels. Short receiver point spacing to get adequate noise sampling may double (or more) the number of channels. Three components instead of one will triple the number of channels. For 3D's this may mean several tens of thousand channels. To maintain productivity with such high channel count, the ground equipment must be *lightweight,* and the acquisition system *low power*. Transmission redundancy should be available thanks to *multi-path telemetry,* and *real-time quality control* of the spread & of the seismic data should be available for quick diagnostic.

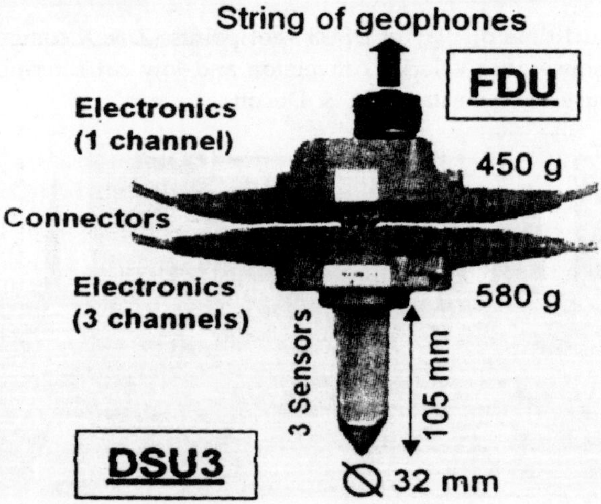

Fig. 9. Back-to-back comparison of a 408UL station electronics (FDD) that should be connected to a string of geophones with a 408UL 3C digital sensor (DSU3) that includes 3 sensors with the corresponding electronics.Connectors are the same to be able to switch easily from analog to digital sensors.

As implemented in the 408U.L recording system (Figure 9), the 580 g of a 3C Digital Sensor Unit (DSU3 including the base assembly with the telemetry cable, all station electronics for the three channels and the three MEMS sensors) compare favourably with the 450 g of the 1C Field Digitizing Unit (FDU including the same base assembly and the electronics for only one channel to be connected to a string of geophones). This comparison illustrates the high level of sensor/electronics integration that makes it possible to use MEMS accelerometers

Considering cost associated with manpower and USE issues related to the use of vehicles a seismic crew should use the smallest number of batteries, each one with a maximum duration (i.e. the recording system must be low power). Even the fact that MEMS would require some power while geophone does not is not a disadvantage for digital sensor recording. At least with the 408UL recording system, the overall consumption of a DSU3 (400 mW) is less the equivalent consumption of three FDD's connected to triphones (420 mW).

Distributed electronics with computing and buffering capabilities as implemented in the most advanced telemetry cable systems makes secure data transmission possible. In case of a cable failure the use of multiple transverses between the receiver lines and the central units will permit the seismic network to reroute data through a different path.

As the number of channels increases up 10,000+, manual or visual checking of all the system and data quality becomes impossible. This explains the importance of automated real-time quality control as already implemented for single digital sensor. As example in the 408UL system the tilt measured from the residual DC on the horizontal components can be checked continuously. The result is not only stored numerically but also visualized graphically with a warning colour telling if tilt is above a predefined threshold. In addition each of the MEMS includes a built-in reference accclerometer that provides a continuous control of the instruments including distortion, gain, phase & cross-talk. At the end of the recording seismic data may be visualized component by component, and several attributes (signal, noise, frequency content, faulty trace ...) are available on a trace-by-trace or shot-by-shot basis to continuously monitor the acquisition process.

Since MEMS sensors record acceleration and not velocity, as for conventional geophones, real time integration from one domain to the other has been made available. To makes it possible a one-to-one comparison between analog & digital sensors, MEMS broadband seismic data may be in addition filtered as a geophone does (10 Hz low cut filtering & damping, Figure 10).

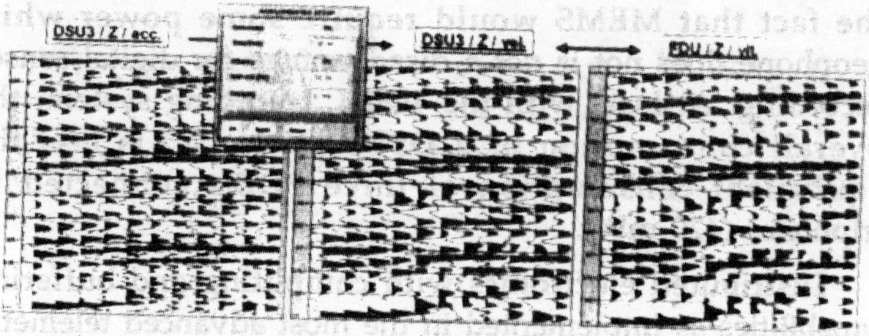

Fig. 10. Real time QC of shot points (Z component) coming from Digital Sensor Units (DSU3) and conventional geophone strings (FDU) laid out at the same location and recorded by the same 408UL Central Unit. For visual comparison it is possible in real time to integrate acceleration data into the velocity domain, and to apply low cut filtering to mimic geophone data.

Conclusion: Is it Time to Use Digital Sensors?

MEMS based single digital sensors offer new capabilities compared with conventional arrays of geophones. The sensor itself (MEMS + ASIC) should provide better vector fidelity thanks to its accurate and stable calibration (amplitude & orthogonality), and to its broadband linear response (from DC to 800 Hz). Tight integration of the sensor with the station electronics makes possible not only size/weight reduction, but also lower power consumption. For the first time it provides a full digital transmission, from the sensor to the Central Unit, less sensitive to electromagnetic pick-up, cross-talk & leakage. Overall MEMS technology offers the potential to reduce operation costs while improving data quality. However there are two types of limitations to the use of MEMS sensors: one is geophysical and related to the fact that digital sensors are recorded as single sensors; the other is economic and is due to the cost of manufacturing digital sensors.

If single sensor recording provides obvious advantages for deployment and signal preservation, these benefits are strongly balanced by the inability of single sensors to attenuate any ambient/organized noise. Records by single digital sensors will be dominajed by noise, and this domination will be even worse if we consider point receiver should be used in conjunction with point source (i.e. without any source array filtering). In noisy areas with strong, dispersive and backscattered ground roll and with high ambient noise this may prevent from recording any usable signal.

To be able to recover signal, all this noise should be attenuated while processing. For ambient noise reduction the fold coverage should increase. This is possible by decreasing the spacing and increasing the number of single digital sensors vs. conventional geophone arrays. For organized noise attenuation, the point receiver spacing should also decrease, perhaps not down to the geophone spacing, but at least down to the Nyquist distance necessary to keep the corresponding ground-roll unaliased. For both ambient & organized noises this implies to increase the number of point receivers and channel capabilities (i.e. normally to increase the cost of acquiring data). Thus a question arises: does it make sense to invest and operate single digital sensors instead of conventional geophone array?

To answer this question, let us consider a receiver configuration that should be valid for low noise areas' (a six geophone string deployed over 30 m) and assume one single digital sensor (1C or 3C) may replace two geophones or triphones (i.e. the 5 m spacing between geophones is replaced by the 10m spacing between DSU's). We will compare three different configurations equivalent to this 30 m receiver Analog 1C array (Figure 11): the same array where geophones are replaced by triphones (Analog 3C); a line of DSU3 with 10 m spacing (Digital 3C); the same line with DSU1 (Digital 1C).

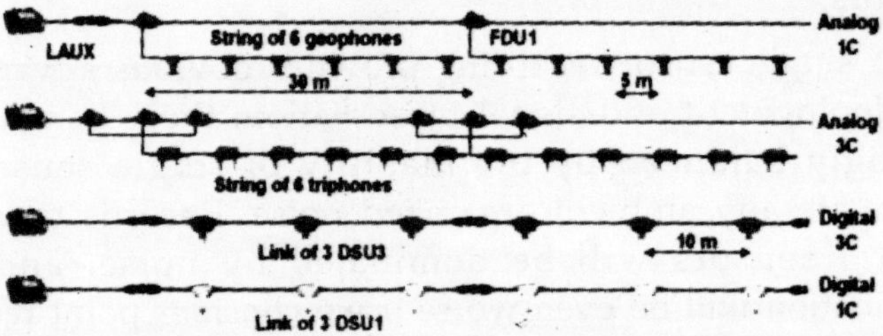

Fig. 11. A conventional 1C/30 m/6 geophone string receiver point (Analog 1 C) is compared with the corresponding Analog 3C receiver point. Assuming one digital sensor (every 10 m) may replace two geophones (every 5 m), the corresponding Digital 3C and Digital 1C receiver points are displayed.

As an indicator of capital expenditure (CAPEX) we consider the cost of a 30 m receiver line equivalent to the Analog 1C array (reference of 1). As indicator of operational

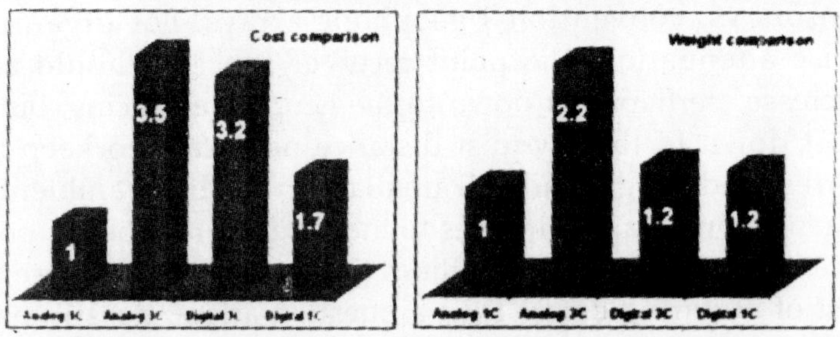

Fig. 12. Cost (for CAPEX) and weight (for OPEX) comparison of the four configurations presented in Figure 11. Numbers are relative to the conventional analog 1C configuration (reference = 1).

expenditure (OPEX) we choose the weight of the same 30 m receiver lines compared to the weight of the three other configurations. Cost/weight of the central unit, the crossing units, the line units and the associated batteries are not taken into consideration.

From the cost/weight comparison in the histograms (Figure 12), two obvious conclusions come up:

- in case of 3C acquisition it is already cheaper for both CAPEX & OPEX to use a Digital 3C array;
- it is still more expansive to invest in a dense digital array (1C or 3 C) than in an conventional analog 1C array, but the operational costs are close.

However if the overall cost of an acquisition project is used as a reference (it is much larger than the CAPEX amortization) the added cost of using a Digital 3C line instead of an Analog 1C may be as small as 5 to 10% (J. Gibson et al., TLE, 2003). PP data may be better. Thanks to the improved spatial sampling and broad band capabilities of the MEMS sensors. PS data may not be used immediately, but will be available to solve specific reservoir characterisation problems if needed at a later stage of the field development. Therefore we feel it is worth weighting the potential long term benefit of using a Digital 3C line compared to the small incremental cost of this technology for some general 2D or 3D acquisition using short linear geophone arrays.

Source : MOUGENOT Denis, 2003; "MEMS Based 3C accdenometers for land seismic acquioition.Isit time?; Geohorizons, Vol. 8, No. 2, July, pp. 20-25.

Appendix–D

STREAMER POSITIONING FOR ADVANCED 3D AND HD APPLICATIONS

Introduction

Correlated positioning errors can have a detrimental impact on the resolution of 3D surveys. The potential impact on 4D is even more serious. These problems can be addressed by the use of more rigorous DigiRANGE II fully cross braced acoustic positioning networks, and through the use of advanced on-board systems, such as ORCA. In this paper, we will review the

- history of marine streamer positioning
- accuracy of current marine positioning systems
- impact of correlated positioning cross on 3D and 4D seismic data

We will then discuss cost effective strategies to mprove positioning accuracy, with minimum impact on operational effeicinecy and streamer noise.

History

In the mid-1980's, the standard technology for streamer positioning was based on tangent measurements (provided by magnetic compasses) at discrete points along each cable. This allowed for an estimate of the cable shape (and hence an estimate of the receiver locations) at the time of each shot. At that time, most acquisition contracts were written to contain specifications that the distance between compasses along each cable would be 300 meters to allow for adequate streamer shape estimation. In the 1990's, the ability to place limited acoustic networks near the front, middle and tail end of the streamers led to a significant improvement in positioning accuracy. Further incremental improvements in positioning accuracy have occurred as the result of continuous improvement in measurement techniques (better compass calibrations and more reliable acoustics). New algorithms for detecting and eliminating random and systematic errors in the measurement data (multipathing/ reflections, velocity variations and residual compass biases) have lead to further improvements. The next step in this evolution in streamer positioning techniques is the arrival of third generation acoustic systems, capable of providing full acoustic cross bracing along the entire length of the cable. The evolution of streamer positioning is schematically shown in Figure 2.

Fig. 1. Integrated magnetic heading sensor and cable leveling device ("bird") mounted on towed streamer.

Accuracy of Current Systems

For in-water positioning networks typically used today, some rules of thumb can be applied :

- Receiver errors are smallest at the ends of the cable, where acoustic networks tie receiver locations directly to surface GPS observations. Due to the complexities of acoustic propagation around the propellers and the energy source, the errors are usually the least at the far end of the cable.
- Errors tend to increase as the distance from the GPS points increases.
- If a mid cable acoustic network is present, errors are reduced in the area of the mid cable network.

The magnitude of the errors depends on a number of factors, including :

- Performance of measurement devices.
- Density and geometry of measurements (streamer length).
- Environmental conditions (acoustic and compass degradations can degrade in poor weather).
- Survey location (probability of reflected acoustic signals increases in difficult water bottom conditions, and with significant thermal gradients.)
- Data processing techniques

The standard deviations (calculated using Concept Systems GeoMatrix software) shown in Figure 3 are based on some fairly conservative estimates of measurement noise based on North Sea data, and the offsets shown are longer than typically used in North Sea work. Positioning errors are commonly of the same order of magnitude as 50% of the crossline bin size.

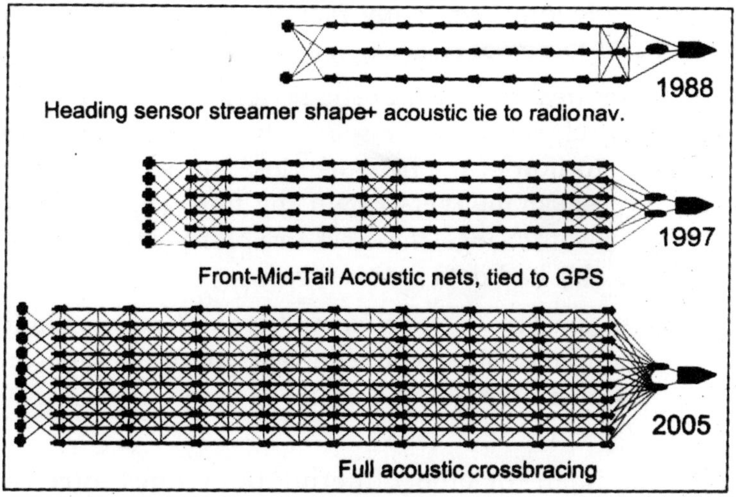

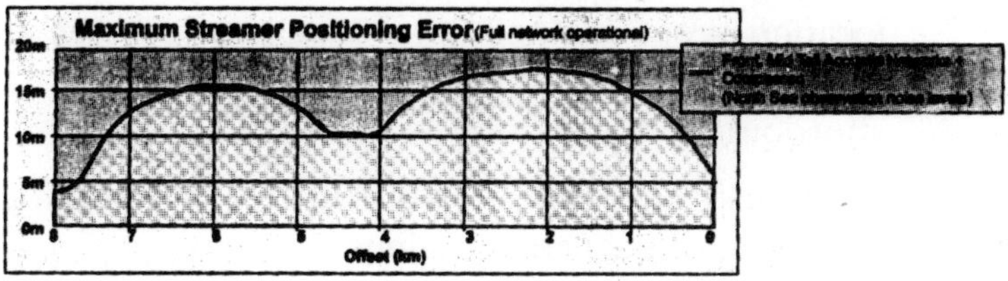

Fig. 3. Typical 3D streamer positioning errors as a function of source-receiver offset.

What is the Impact of Positioning Errors on the 3D and 4D Seismic Image ?

The precise impact of positioning errors will depend upon the geology, and seismic data processing techniques. Regardless of the processing technique, in the presence of dip, Gaussian distributions of error will lead to some loss of high frequency data. Provided that the bin size is small enough to adequately sample the structure, then the loss of high frequency associated with these errors is typically small enough to be acceptable for most 3D imaging applications.

Unfortunately, positioning errors are NOT purely

Gaussian. In practice, many factors conspire to introduce spatial and temporal correlations.

- An area of poor acoustic performance caused by the vessel wake and the source arrays commonly creates distortion of the network close to the vessel. As the vessel maneuvers down the line, and winds and currents change, the exact area of the network affected by this bad data area can vary.
- As the vessel maneuvers, "ripples" are transmitted along the cable, with a wavelength of the same order of magnitude as the vessel motion - typically 500 - 2,000m.
- Kalman (or other) filtering techniques force some temporal consistency in the errors. If a receiver position is calculated 5m to the north of its true location at one shotpoint, it will still be approximately 5m to the north of its true location at the next shotpoint.
- Network adjustment algorithms will tend to distribute errors across regions of a network, creating transient, but systematic spatial distortions. If a receiver position is calculated 5m to the north of it's true location, the adjacent receivers (both in-line and crossline) will probably be approximately 5m to the north of their true location as well.

Given these circumstances, it is more reasonable to think of positioning errors as "clusters" of errors that drift around a zero mean, but are not necessarily zero mean at any shot, receiver or CMP location. In the presence of geological dip, the result of these errors is not simply a high cut filter, but also a subtle spatially variant time shift.

Provided that the survey is properly designed, the errors should be less than a single sample period, and within normal tolerances for a traditional 3D structural survey.

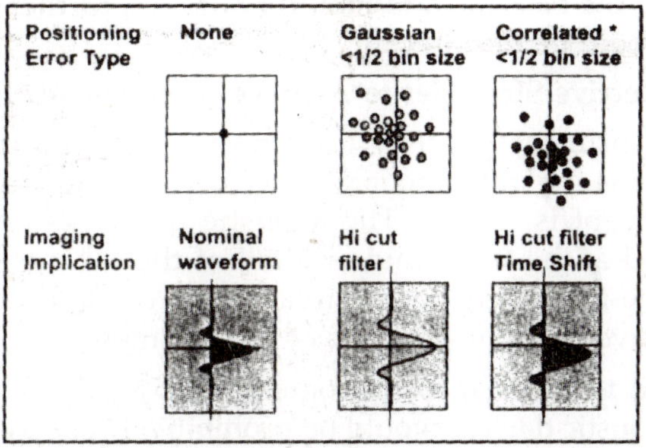

Fig. 4. Illustration of impact of positioning errors on seismic wavelet.

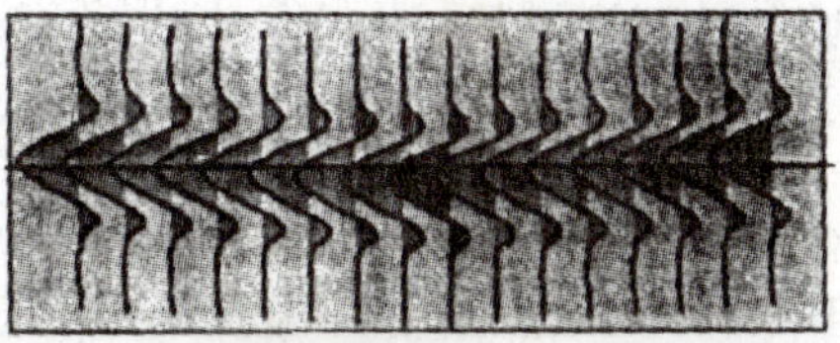

Fig. 5 (*a*) Effect of spatially correlated positioning errors on 3D seismic image Baseline Monitor Difference.

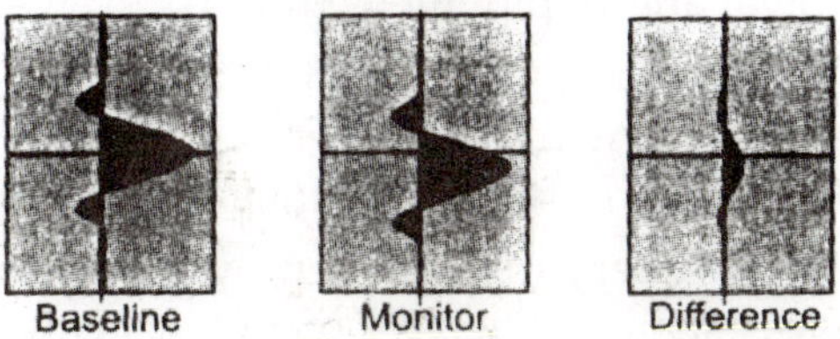

Fig. 5 (*b*) Impact on 4D difference signal caused by changes in positioning correlation between baseline and monitor.

Whilst these correlated errors may be acceptable for most 3D applications, they can become a limiting factor for 3D surveys seeking enhanced resolution, and for many 4D applications.

For 4D surveys, there is another factor that can create correlated errors between surveys. Traditional navigation processing techniques require a skilled operator, making many subjective decisions about what data to include or exclude, or what filtering algorithms to apply. If different operators work on the baseline and monitor surveys, further systematic biases could be introduced:

Cost Effective Strategies to Achieve Adequate 4D Positioning

The primary strategy to improve streamer positioning accuracy is the implementation of full acoustic cross bracing. The concept is simple. The acoustic networks traditionally deployed at the front, mid and tail of the cable are extended along the full length of the streamer network. This can result in improvements in accuracy of 60% or more.

With traditional technologies, the cost of adding all the extra acoustic devices would be prohibitively expensive. Input/Output's solution is to upgrade 50% of the compass birds deployed on the cable, and replace them with DigiRANGE II acoustic birds. This means that for every heading sensor observation removed from the network, 6-8 direct range observations are added.

Benefits of this approach include : -

- 60% improvement in positioning accuracy.
- No additional external devices mounted on the streamer. (No increase in noise, no increase in retrieval and deployment time.)
- The additional redundancy and continuity in the acoustic network allows estimation of spatial and temporal variations in propagation velocity.
- If the streamers are to be deployed with lateral steering devices such as DigiFIN of I/O systems, the streamer shape may have cusps (kinks) at the locations of the lateral steering devices. In this case, heading sensors cannot be used as the primary method of streamer shape estimation. Full acoustic cross bracing is a necessary pre-requisite to applying lateral streamer steering technology as shown, for example in Figure 7 for DigiRANGE II of I/O systems.

Many oil company specifications currently require a "magnetic heading sensor to be placed every 300 meters along the streamer". It should be noted that the upgrade strategy advocated here requires revisions to these specifications

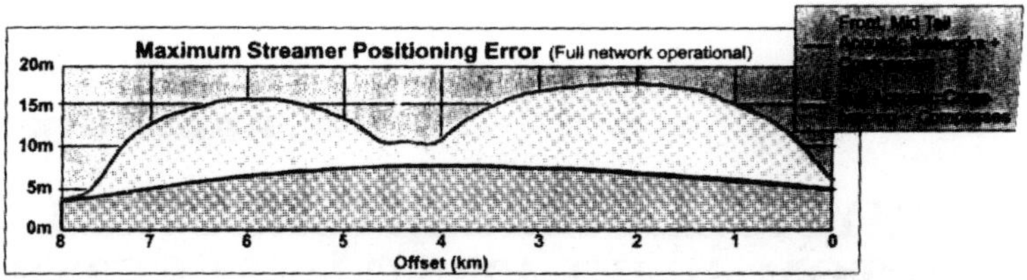

Fig. 6. Full acoustic cross bracing provides 60% improvement in maximum error.

Although DigiRANGE II can be used with any integrated navigation system, the next generation of integrated navigation and instrument room data management systems, including ORCA from Concept Systems, support a number of features that have particular application to advanced 3D and 4D surveys. ORCA contains features to allow automated computation of final co-ordinates within a few minutes of the completion of data acquisition. This feature eliminates many of the delays in traditional processing, but it , also eliminates the subjectivity associated with individual data processors. Other key ORCA advances to improve 3D and 4D image quality while increasing operational efficiency include advanced planning and data acquisition techniques such as intelligent line selection and steering strategies to optimize 3D coverage and/or 4D repeatability.

Fig. 7. DigiRANGE II Acoustic Bird.

Source : Musser James A., Ridyard Dave, and Dr. Hupkens Erik, 2006; Stremer positioning for aduanced 3D and 4D applications; Vol. 11, No. 2, pp. 4-7.

Appendix–E

PHYSICAL PARAMETERS FROM BOTTOM SIMULATING REFLECTOR AND GAS-HYDRATES

Summary

To determine various physical parameters like porosity, density, thermal conductivity, electrical resistivity, geothermal gradient or heat flow using associated probes at depth below the seafloor are not always feasible. The base of gas-hydrates stability field is marked by an anomalous reflector, known as BSR or bottom simulating reflector. The temperature at BSR can be determined from the pressure-temperature relation of the gas-hydrates phase curve. Using the seafloor temperature and the temperature at the BSR, we can calculate the geothermal gradient of an area. We present a case study to determine various physical parameters using the BSR identified on a seismic data set in the Arabian Sea. The depth of the BSR is found to be 495 m beneath the seafloor (1715 m). Taking the seafloor temperature from the oceanographic data, we determine the geothermal gradient as 34.34 °C/km. The seafloor porosity, average density, resistivity of background sediments at BSR, resistivity of hydrated sediments at BSR, average thermal conductivity, heat flow and the maximum saturation of gas-hydrates are calculated as 54%, 1.98g/cc, 2.4 Ωm, 3.0 Ωm, 1.267 W/m/K, 43.55 mW/m^2 and 13% respectively. From this study we show that presence of gas-hydrates increases the electrical resistivity and decreases the thermal conductivity of the sedimentary formations.

Introduction

Gas-hydrates have attracted the whole scientific community due to their widespread occurrences in nature, potential as future energy resources, possible role in climate change and geo-hazards (Kvenvolden, 1998). To understand these aspects, physical parameters like porosity, density, hydrate-saturation, thermal conductivity, temperature, resistivity, geothermal gradient and heat flow associated with the hydrates reservoirs provide important data. However, measurement of these parameters using probes at depth below the seafloor is not only difficult but also quite expensive. The most prominent marker for the investigation of gas-hydrates is the BSR, which very often represents the base of gas-hydrates stability field. Gas-hydrates are crystalline form of water and low molecular weight hydrocarbons (mainly methane). These are formed at high pressure (8-30 MPa) and cooled temperature (10 to 2°C) in submarine sediments where methane concentration is sufficiently high (Sloan, 1998; Kvenvolden, 1998). Guided by the thermo-barometric stability conditions, gas-hydrates are found within few hundred meters below the seafloor (Minshulletal., 1994; Lee et al, 1996; Yuan et al., 1996). The BSR is identified based on its characteristic features of (*i*) mimicking the shape of seafloor, (*ii*) cutting across the dipping strata, (*iii*) opposite polarity with respect to the seafloor event etc. Here we present a case study of how to quantify the amount of gas-hydrates and derive various other physical parameters from the BSR, identified on a seismic section in the Makran accretionary prism (Sain et al., 2000).

Since pure gas-hydrates have much higher seismic velocity than that of normal oceanic sediments, presence of gas-hydrates increases the seismic velocity that again depends on the concentration of hydrates, whereas free-gas underlying the gas-hydrates reduces the velocity appreciably up to few %. From the seismic data, we can determine the velocity-depth function across a BSR. The background or reference functions are defined as the variation of physical properties with depth in absence of gas-hydrates and free-gas.

Figure 1 displays the phase diagram of gas-hydrates in which the solid line represents the pure methane-hydrate phase curve with the pressure converted into depth assuming hydrostatic conditions in both water and sediments. The dashed line represents the hydro-thermal curve and the dotted-solid line represents the geothermal curve. The figure shows the zone from the seafloor down to a depth up to few hundred meters where gas-hydrates are stable. The base of the gas-hydrates stability field is associated with a seismic reflector, known as BSR, which represents a physical interface between the gas-hydrates bearing sediments above and the gas-charged or water bearing sediments below.

Estimation of Physical Parameters

Figure 2 shows a seismic section in the Makran accretionary prism, where a BSR at 495 m below the seafloor

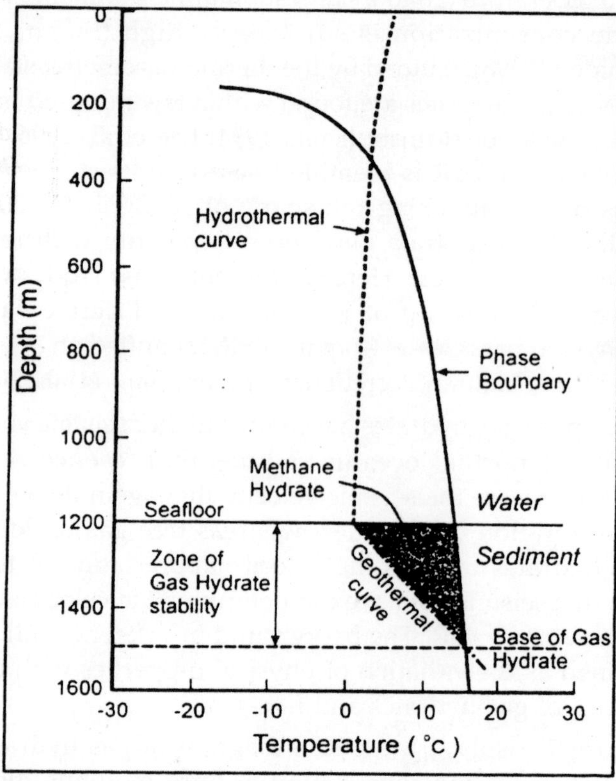

Fig. 1. A schematic phase diagram of submarine gas-hydrates and the stability zone (modified after Sloan, 1998)

(1715 m) has been identified based in its characteristic features. Using the waveform inversion to the pre-stack seismic data, Sain etal (2000) determined the fine scale velocity structure across the BSR. Here we consider the velocity-depth function at CDP 4400 for calculating the hydrates saturation and other physical properties. The seafloor velocity is 1.78 km/s. The velocity at 285 m below the seafloor starts increasing and reaches to a maximum value of 2.2 km/s at BSR followed by a sudden decrease to a value of ~1.4 km/s. Since the velocity of free-gas bearing sediments below the BSR remains almost unaffected at more that 5% saturation, it is hard to quantify the amount of free-gas. So we restrict our calculation of hydrates saturation and physical parameters 'up to the BSR depth only.

Porosity and Density

To determine the porosity at the seafloor, first we prepare a nomogram of P-wave velocity (V_p) versus seafloor porosity (ϕ). For a given porosity (ϕ), V_p can be calculated using the two-phase weighted equation of Nobes et al. (1986) as

$$\frac{1}{V_P} = \frac{W\phi}{V_1} + \frac{(1-W\phi)}{V_2} \qquad ...(1)$$

where W is the weighting factor and is taken as 1.2. Due to unconsolidated nature of marine sediment V_1 and V_2 used in equation (1) are calculated as

$$\frac{1}{\rho_b V_1^2} = \frac{1-\phi}{\rho_m V_m^2} + \frac{\phi}{\rho_w V_w^2} \qquad ...(2)$$

and

$$\frac{1}{V_2} = \frac{1-\phi}{V_m} + \frac{\phi}{V_w} \qquad ...(3)$$

where V_m and V_w are the P-wave velocities of sediment matrix and water respectively. ρ_b, ρ_m and ρ_w are the densities of the sediment as a whole, matrix and water respectively. We use V_m = 4.50 km/s, V_w =1.5 km/s, ρ_m = 2.76 g/cc. ρ_m = 1.05g/cc for sandy sediments (Minshull and White, 1989) in the study area. The velocities for assumed seafloor porosities at steps of 1 % are determined using equations (1), (2) and (3), and the nomogram is shown in Figure 3(*a*). Associated with the seafloor velocity of 1.78 km/s, we find the seafloor porosity as 54%. Error in velocity will produce error in all other parameters. Assuming ±5% error in the seafloor velocity, i.e. velocity varying between 1.69 and 1.87 km/s produces seafloor porosity from 49.5% to 59%. Background porosity, $\phi(z)$ at any depth, z below the seafloor for un-consolidated marine sediments can be calculated using the Athy'slaw (1930) as

$$\phi(z) = \phi_0 e^{-(z/\lambda)} \quad ...(4)$$

where ϕ_0 is the porosity at the seafloor, which is already calculated. Using the compaction factor (λ) equal to 1.44/' km (Minshull and White, 1989), we calculate the background porosity-depth function along with the error bounds (Figure 3(*b*)). The porosity at BSR is determined as 38.3% that can vary from 35% to 41.8% due to ±5% error in velocity.

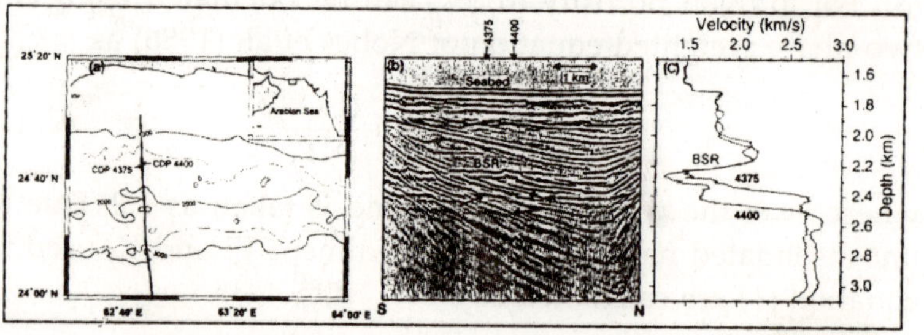

Fig. 2. (*a*) Location of the study area (represented by rectangle) in the Makran accretionary prism in the Arabian Sea. (*b*) Seismic section along thick solid line covering CDPs 4375 and 4400. displaying clear BSR at 495 m below seafloor and cutting across dipping strata (*c*) Velocity depth function derived using full waveform inversion at CDPs 4375 and 4400 (after Sain *et al.*, 2000).

Using equation (2), we calculate the bulk density at the seafloor as 1.82 g/cc corresponding to velocity (1.78 km/ s) and porosity (54%) at the seafloor. The background density as a function of depth and the error bounds (Figure 3(c)) are calculated using the porosity-bulk density (ρ_b) relation as per Nobes et al. (1986).

$$\rho_h = \rho_w\phi + \rho_m(1 - \phi) \quad ...(5)$$

The average density for the Makran region is determined asl .98g/cc, which can vary from 1.9 g/cc to 2.04 g/cc due to assumed error in velocity.

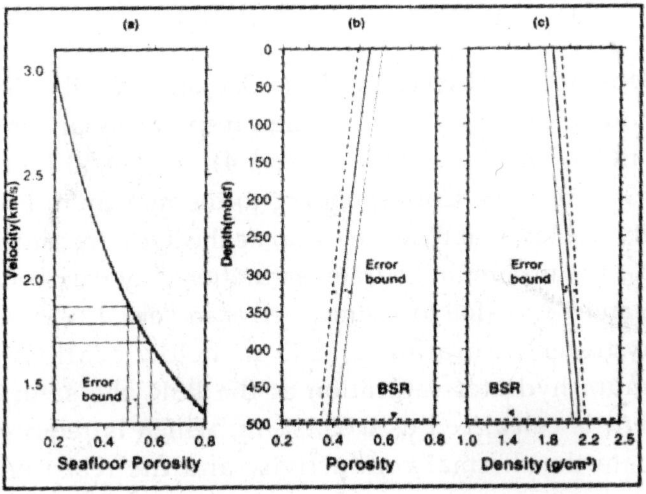

Fig. 3. (*a*) The nomogram of velocity versus seafloor porosity along with the lower- and upper-bounds, (*b*) Background porosity-depth function along with the lower- and upper-bounds, (c) Background density-depth function along with the lower- and upper-bounds.

Hydrates Saturation

Under the assumption of gas-hydrates saturation, *S* increasing with depth and becoming maximum at BSR, we calculate the hydrates saturation at BSR as follows. A nomogram (Figure 4) of V_P versus gas-hydrates saturation is prepared by varying the hydrates saturation from 0 to 80% at interval of 1% using the three-phase weighted equation of Leeetal. (1996) as

$$\frac{1}{V_P} = \frac{W\phi(1-S)}{V_1} + \frac{1-W\phi(1-S)}{V_2} \quad ...(6)$$

V_1 and V_2 used in equation (6) are calculated as

$$\frac{1}{\rho_b V_1^2} = \frac{1-\phi}{\rho_m V_m^{\ 2}} + \frac{S\phi}{\rho_h V_h^{\ 2}} + \frac{(1-S)\phi}{\rho_w V_w^{\ 2}} \qquad ...(7)$$

and

$$\frac{1}{V^2} = \frac{1-\phi}{V_m} + \frac{S\phi}{V_h} + \frac{(1-S)\phi}{V_w} \qquad ...(8)$$

Here, ρ_h (= 0.92 g/cc) and V_h (= 3.3 km/s) are the density and P-wave velocity of pure hydrates respectively, and ρ_b (=2.1 g/cc) is the density at BSR (Figure 4). V_m = 4.50 km/sand ϕ =38.3% are used. Corresponding to the maximum P-wave velocity (2.2 km/s) at BSR, we calculate the hydrates saturation as 13%. The maximum hydrates saturation may vary between 12.5% and 13.5% due to assumed error in velocity. Assuming 0% hydrates saturation at 285 m below seafloor and maximum hydrates saturation at the BSR, the saturation gradient is calculated as 0.057 %/m, which is required to calculate the thermal conductivity and the resistivity of hydrated sediments.

Geothermal Gradient

Using the water depth versus seafloor temperature curve (Figure 5) obtained from the real data, we find the sea-floor temperature as 4°C corresponding to the water depth of 1715m. The water and the sediments upto the BSR is converted to an equivalent pressure of 27.23 Mpa that corresponds to the BSR temperature of 21°C (Figure 6). The difference in temperatures at the BSR and seafloor divided by the depth of BSR below the seafloor yields the geothermal gradient of 34.34 °C/km. The ±5% error in assumed velocity changes the pressure at BSR from 27 to 27.5 Mpa that hardly affect the geothermal gradient estimated for the region.

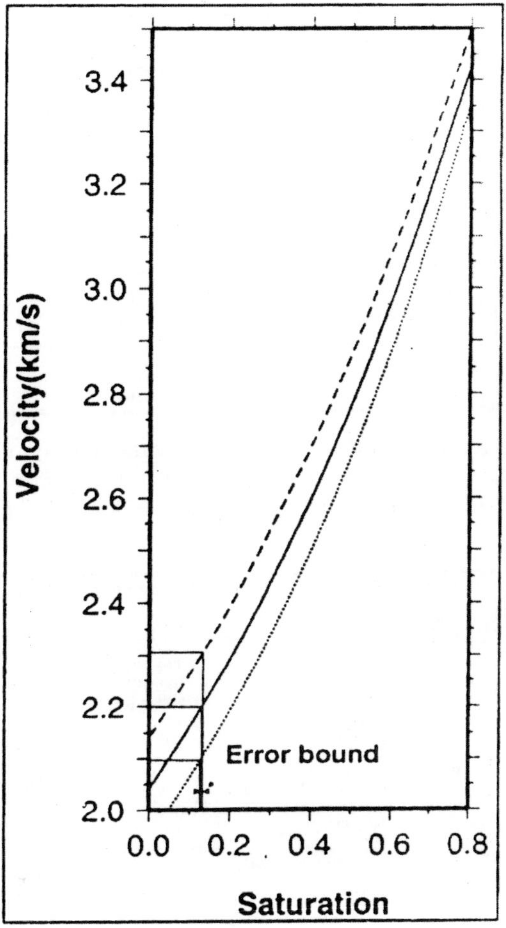

Fig. 4. The nomogram of velocity versus gas-hydrates saturation calculated using the porosity at the BSR along with the lower and upper-bounds.

Thermal Conductivity

The thermal conductivity of an n-component system is generally expressed as (Grevemeyer and Villinger, 2001)

$$K = \prod_{i=1}^{n} K_i^{v_i} \qquad ...(9)$$

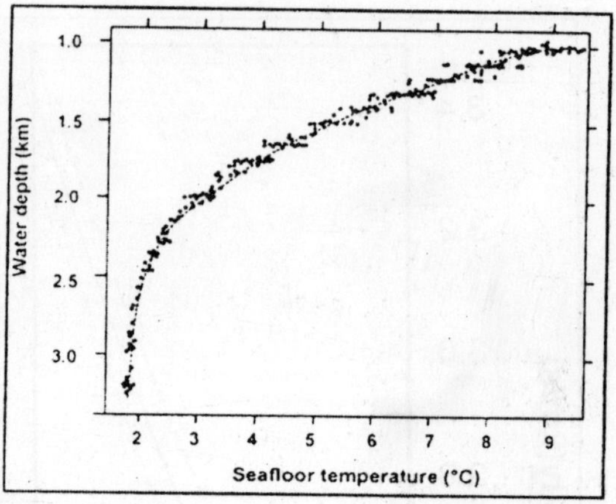

Fig. 5. Seafloor temperature at various water depths in the Gulf of Oman. Data provided by the Marine Information and Advisory Services of the Institute of Oceanographic Sciences (Minshull and White. 1989).

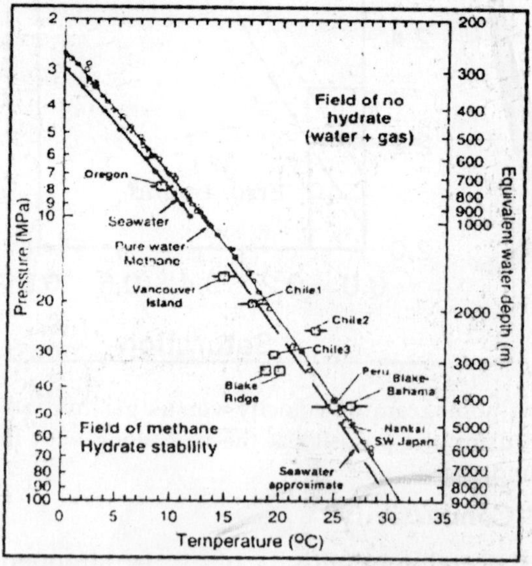

Fig. 6. The pressure-temperature phase diagram for the methane gas-hydrates stability field. The solid line is the seawater curve from the equation-of-state computation for artificial seawater (Dickens and Quinby-Hunt, 1994; Englezos and Bishnoi, 1988). BSR temperatures in DSDP-ODP drill holes are also indicated (Ganguly et al., 2000).

where, K_i and v_i are the conductivity and volume percent of the ith component. Using equation (9) we can derive the background thermal conductivity-depth function from the porosity-depth function using the relation between porosity and thermal conductivity K_s as

$$K_s = K_m^{(1-\phi)} K_w^{\phi} \quad ...(10)$$

where, ϕ and $(1 - \phi)$ are volume fraction of water and the matrix in the sediment respectively K_m and K_w are 2.5 and 0.6 W/m/K, representing the thermal conductivities of the matrix and water respectively. The value of K_m was obtained by taking the best-fitting geometric mean of matrix conductivities of unconsolidated sediments from several continental margins of the world (Grevemeyer and Villinger, 2001).

The thermal conductivity of the hydrated sediment. K_{hs} in the depth interval between 285 to 495 m below seafloor can be similarly determined as

$$K_{hs} = K_m^{(1-\phi)} K_h^{s\phi} K_w^{(1-S)\phi} \quad ...(11)$$

where K_h (=0.4 W/m/K) represents the thermal conductivity of pure hydrates.

Using equations (10), we calculate the background thermal conductivity and the associated error bounds (Figure 7) as a function of depth below the seafloor. The thermal conductivity of the hydrated sediment calculated using equation (11) is also shown by dotted-dashed lines in Figure 7. We see that the thermal conductivity of hydrated sediments decreases with respect to the background trend. The average thermal conductivity of the sedimentary formation and hence the heat flow are calculated as 1.267 W/m/K and 43.55mW/m^2 respectively. The estimated values match quite accurately with the published results of 1.27 W/m/K and 43 mW/m^2 for thermal conductivity and heat flow respectively near the study area (Grevemeyer and Villinger, 2001; Kaul et al., 2000). The lower and upper bounds in thermal conductivity and heat flow are calculated as 1.2 W/m/K and 41 mW/m^2, and 1.34 W/m/K and 46 mW/m^2 respectively.

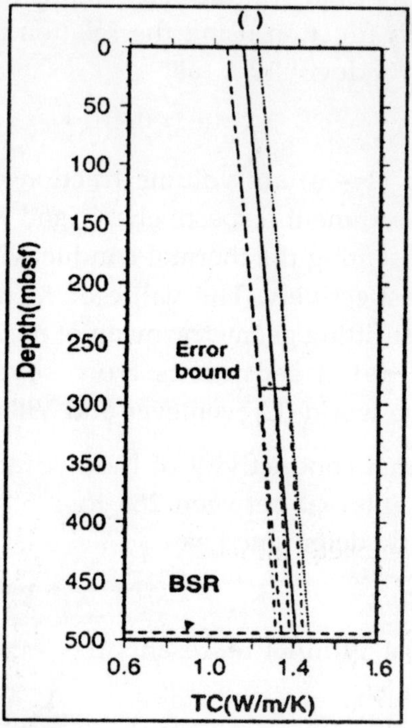

Fig. 7. Background thermal conductivity versus depth along with the lower- and upper-bounds. The thermal conductivity variation of hydrated sediment is also shown.

Resistivity

The resistivity of the hydrated sediments, R_t can be calculated using the Archie's law (Nobes et al., 1986) as

$$S_w^n = \frac{R_0}{R_t} \qquad ...(12)$$

where S_w, n and R_0 are respectively the water saturation, saturation exponent and the background resistivity i.e. the resistivity of the formation when sediment pores are filled only with water. The background resistivity, R_0 is calculated as

$$R_0 = \frac{a\,R_w}{\phi^m} \qquad \text{...(13)}$$

where ϕ, R_w, m and a are the porosity, water resistivity, cementation factor and a constant respectively. The Archie's parameters are taken as a =0.9, m =2.7 and n = 1.9 (Collet, 2000). The R_w is calculated using the relation of Nobes et al (1986) as

$$R_w = 1/\left(3+\frac{T}{10}\right) \qquad \text{...(14)}$$

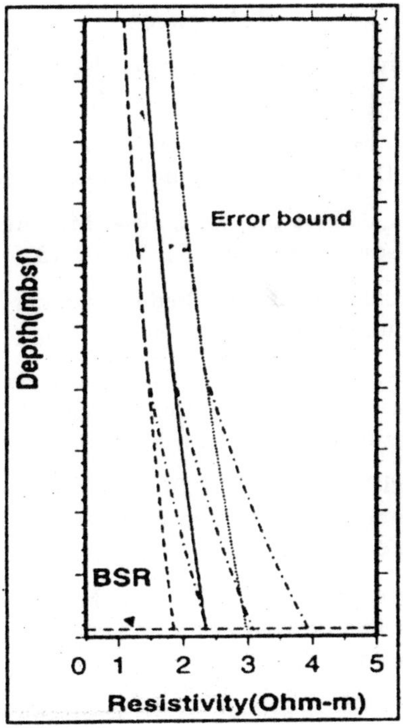

Fig. 8. Background resistivity versus depth function along with the lower- and upper-bounds. The resistivity variation of hydrated sediment is also shown.

where T is the formation temperature that can be calculate]d at different depths using the derived geothermal gradient and the seafloor temperature. The variation of background resistivity with depth and the associated error bounds are shown in Figure 8. The resistivity of the hydrated sediment is also shown in Figure 8. The study shows that the background resistivity at BSR varies from 1.90 to 3.0 Ω-m. Whereas presence of gas-hydrates increases the formation resistivity and the value at BSR varies between 2.4 and 4.0 Ω-m. This indicates that the seafloor electrical resistivity profiling can be used for the identification and quantification of gas-hydrates, particularly at regions where BSR is not detected on seismic section but gas-hydrates are found while drilling.

References

Athy, L. F., Density, porosity and compaction of sedimentary rocks. Am. Assoc. Pet. Geol. Bull, 1930, 14, 1-24.

Collet, T. S., Quantitative well-log analysis of in-situ natural gas hydrates [Ph. D. dissert.], Colorado School of Mines, 2000.

Dickens, GR. and Quinby-Hunt, M.S., 1994. Methane hydrate stability in sea water, *Geophys. Res. Lett.*, 21, 2115-2118.

Englezos, P. and Bishnoi, P.R., 1988. Prediction of gas-hydrate formation in aqueous solutions. *Am. Inst. Chem. Eng., 34,* 1718-1721.

Ganguly, N. Spence, G D., Chapman, N.R. and Hyndman, R. D., 2000. Heat flow variations from bottom simulating reflectors on the Cascadia, margin, *Mar. Geol.*, 164, 53-68.

Grevemeyer, I. and Villinger, H., 2001. Gas hydrate stability and the assessment of heat flow through continental margins, *Geophys. J. Int.*, 145, 647-660.

Kaul, N., Rosenberger, A. and Villinger, H., 2000. Comparison of measured and BSR-derived heatflow values, Makran accretionary prism, Pakistan. *Mar. Geol.*, 164, 37-51.

Kvenvolden, K.A., 1998. A primer on the geological occurrence of gas hydrate. In Henriet, J. P. and Mienert, J. (editors), Gas hydrates: Relevance to the World Margin Stability and Climate Change, *Geological Society, London, Special Publications,* 137, 9-30.

Lee, M. W., Hutchinson, D. R., Collett, T. S. and Dillon, W. P., 1996. Seismic velocities for hydrate-bearing sediments using weighted equation, *J. Geophys. Res.*, 101, 20347- 20358.

Minshull, T.A., Singh, S.C. and Westbrook, G.K., 1994. Seismic velocity structure at a gas hydrate reflector, offshore western Colombia, full waveform inversion, *J. Geophys. Res.* 99, 4715-4734.

Minshull, T. A. and White, R., 1989. Sediment compaction and fluid migration in the Makran accretionary prism, *J. Geophys. Res.*, 94, 7387-7402.

Nobes, D. C., Villinger, H., Davis, E. E. and Law, L. K., Estimation of marine sediment bulk physical properties at depth from seafloor geophysical measurements. *J. Geophys. Res*, 1986, 91, 14033-14043.

Sain, K., Minshull, T. A., Singh, S. C. and Hobbs, R. W., 2000. Evidence for a thick free gas layer beneath the bottom simulating reflector in the Makran accretionary prism. *Mar. Geol.*, 164, 37-51.

Sloan, E.D., *Clathrate hydrates of natural gases, 2" edn.. Marcel Dekkerlnc. Publishers, New York, 1998.*

Yuan. T., Hyndman, R. D., Spence, G D. and Desmons, B., 1996. Seismic velocity increase and deep-sea gas hydrate concentration above a bottom simulating reflector on the northern Cascadia continental slope. *J. Geophys. Res*, 101. 13,655-13,671.

Source: SAIN KALACHAND, 2006, Estimation of various physical perameters from BSR and quantification of gas-hydrates-a case study; Geohorizens, Vol. 11, No. 2, July, pp. 18-23.

Appendix–F

FAMOUS WORLD'S QUATIONS

Tol 29-10-2006

1. Obstacles are those frightful things you see when you take your eyes off your goal. —*Henry Ford*
2. Friendship marks a life even more deeply than love. Love risks degenerating into obsession, friendship is never anything but sharing. —*Elie Wiesel*
3. Education is when you read the fine print. Experience is what you get if you don't. —*Pete Seeger*
4. Fashion is a form of ugliness so intolerable that we have to alter it every six months. —*Oscar Wilde*
5. Everyone believes very easily whatever they fear or desire. —*Jean de La Fontaine*
6. I have sometimes thought of marrying, and then I have thought again. —*Noel Coward*
7. History will be kind to me for I intend to write it.

   —*Winston Churchill*
8. A friend is a gift you give yourself.

   –*Robert Louis Stevenson*
9. A book is a uersion of the world. If you do not like it, ignore it; or offer your own version in return

   —*Salman Rushdie*

Tol 23-9-2003

10. Knowledge speaks, but wisdom listens. —*Jimi Hendrix*

Tol 18-8-2006

11. What looms over us is no dark fate but our own past.

    —*S Radhakrishnan*

Tol 12-11-2006

12. Always do right. This will gratify some people and astonish the rest. —*Mark Twain*
13. The man who has confidence in himself gains the confidence of others. —*Anonymous*
14. Experence is not what happens to a man; it is what a man does with what happens to him. —*Aldous Huxley*
15. When the character of a man is not clear to you, look at his friends. —*Japanese Proverb*
16. Just because you are blind, and unable to see my beauty doesn't mean it does not exist. —*Margaret Cho*
17. It takes a great deal of courage to stand up to your enemies, but even more to stand up to your friends.

    —*J K Rowling*
18. It is mistake to try to look too far ahead. The chain of destiny can only be grasped one link at a time.

    —*Sir Winston Churchill*
19. I never think of the future, it comes soon enough.

    —*Albert Einstein*

Tol 1-2-2007

20. Great things are not done by impulse, but by a series of small things brought together. —*Vincent Van Goch*

Tol 17-7-2006

Bennett, Coleman & Co., Ltd.

21. The foolish man seeks happiness in the distance, the wise man grows it under his feet. —*James Oppenhein*

Tol 10-12-2006

22. When you do the common things in life in an uncommon way, you will command the attention of the world. —*George Washington Carver*
23. No person is you friend who demands your silence, or denies your right to grow. —*Alice Walker*

24. Whenever I climb I am followed by a dog called 'Ego'.

—Friedrich Nietzsche

25. How on earth are you ever going to explain in terms of chemistry and physics so important a biological phenomenon as first love? *—Albert Einstein*

26. Never let your sense of morals get in the way of doing what's right. *—Isaac Asimov*

27. Small opportunities are often the beginning of great enterprises. *—Demosthenes*

28. Love at first sight is easy to understand; it is when two people have been looking at each other for a lifetime that it becomes a miracle. *—Amy Bloom*

29. Work for something because it is good, not just because it stands a chance to succeed. *—Vaclav Havel*

Tol 16-2-2008

A THOUGHT FOR TODAY

30. If your actions inspire others to dream more, learn more, do more and become more, you are a leader.

—John Quincy Adams, former American president

Tol 1-12-2006

A THOUGH FOR TODAY

31. The policy of beings too cautious is the greatest risk of all. *—Jawaharlal Nehru*

Tol 17-12-2006

32. Who bravely dares must sometimes risk a fall.

—Tobias George Smollett

33. It seems that ambition makes most people wish to be loved rather than to love others. *—Aristotle*

34. Three can keep a secret if two of them are dead.

—Benjamin Franklin

35. I believe that ignorance is the root of all evil. And that no one knows the truth. —*Molly Ivins*

36. While we read history we make history. —*George William Curtis*

37. Education is what survives when what has been learned has been forgotten. —*B F Skinner*

38. Reading all the good books is like a conversation with the finest men of past centuries. —*Rene Descartes*

39. Never assume the obvious is true. —*William Safire*

40. The secret of being a bore is to tell everything. —*Voltaire*

41. Live as if you were to die tomorrow. Learn as if you were to live forever. —Mahatma Gandhi

Tol 9-5-2006

42. *Let us learn from the past to profit by the present, and from the present to live better in the future.* —*William Wordsworth*

Tol 3-12-2006

43. *The true measure of a man is how he treats someone who can do him absolutely no good.* —*Samuel Johnson*

44. Only two things are infinite, the universe and human stupidity, and I am not sure about the former. —*Albert Einstein*

45. Happiness is good health and a bad memory. —*Ingrid Bergman*

46. You got to be careful if you don't know where you're going, because you might not get there. —*Yogi Berra*

47. The nice thing about egotists is that they don't talk about other people. —*Ucille S Harper*

48. In any contest between power and patience, bet on patience. —*W B Prescott*

49. The nice thing about being a celebrity is that if you bore people they think it's their fault. —*Henry Kissinger*

50. I shall not waste my days in trying to prolong them.

—Ian L Fleming

Tol 27-7-2007

51. Service which is rendered without joy helps neither the servant nor the served. But all other pleasures and possessions pale into nothingess before service which is rendered in a spirit of joy. *—M K Gandhi*

Tol 18-1-2006

52. The view of the earth from the moon fascinated me-a small disc, 240,000 miles away. Raging nationalistic interests, famines, wars, pestilence don't show from that distance..... *—Frank Borman, Commander, Apollo 8*

Tol 30-3-2005

53. The earth is nobler than the world we have put upon it. *—J B Priestley*

Tol 19-11-2006

54. Laughter is the shortest distance between two people.

—Victor Borge

55. To live a creative life, we must lose our fear of being wrong. *—Joseph Chilton Pearce*

56. The heart of a fool is in his mouth, but the mouth of a wise man is in his heart. *—Benjamin Franklin,*

57. We are rarely proud when we are alone. *—Voltaire*

58. An injury is much sooner forgotten than an insult.

—Lord Chesterfield

59. Yes and no are very powerful words. Mean them when you say them. Respect them when you hear them.

—Michael Josephson

60. A friend is one who knows you and loves you just the same. *—Elbert Hubbard*

61. to accomplish a great things, we must not only act, but also dream; not only plan, but also believe.

—Anatole France

Tol 14-10-2006

62. I know that my unity with all people cannot be destroyed by national boundaries and government order. *—Leo Tolstoy*

Information is the oxygen of the modern age. It seeps through the walls topped with barbed wires, it wafts across the electrified borders. *—Ronald Reagan*

You live in the age of interdependence. Borders can't count for much or stop much, good or bad anymore.

—Bill Clinton

Tol 24-12-2006

63. *Those who say it can't be done are usually interrupted by others doing it.* *—James A Baldwin*

64. One of the keys to happiness is bad memory.

—Rita Mae Brown

65. Slow down and enjoy life. It's not only the scenery you miss by going too fast-you also miss the sense of where you are going and why. *—Eddie Cantor*

66. To live a creative life, we must lose our fear of being wrong. —Edward gibbon

67. Never deprive someone of hope; it might be all they have. *—Jackson Brown*

68. Life is a foreign language; all men mispronounce it.

—Tryon Edwards

69. Never pretend to a love which you do not actually feel, for love is not ours to command. —Alan Watts

70. All human actions have one or more of these seven causes: chance, nature, compulsion, habit, reason, passion, and desire. *—Aristotle*

71. The secret of being a bore is to tell everything.*—Voltaire*

Tol 11-10-2006

72. You must not lose faith in humanity. Humanity is an ocean; if a few drops of the ocean are dirty, the ocean does not become dirty. *—Mahatma Gandhi*

Tol 3-8-2006

73. Whatever is begun in anger ends in shame.
—Benjamin Franklin

Tol 8-10-2006

74. A goal is a dream with a deadline. *—Napoleon Hill*
75. If you surrender completely to the moments as they pass, you live more richly those moments.
—Anne Morrow Lindbergh
76. The miracle is not to fly in the air, or to walk on the water; but to walk on the earth. *—Chinese Proverb*
77. Love is the only force capable of transforming an enemy into friend. *—Martin Luther King*
78. If you are successful, you may win false friends and true enemies. Succeed anyway. *—Mother Teresa*
79. There are two kinds of failures: those who thought and never did, and those who did and never thought.
—Laurence J Peter
80. The difference between the impossible and the possible lies in determination. *—Tommy Lasorda*
81. In matters of style, swim with the current; in matters of principle, stand like a rock. *—Thomas Jefferson*

Tol 23-10-2005

82. Luck is what you have left over after you give 100 percent. *—Langston Coleman*

Tol 20-10-2005

83. All the powers in the universe are already ours. It is we who have put our eyes and cry that it is dark.
—Swami Vivekananda

Tol 21-5-2006

84. I not only use all the brains that I have, but alı that I can borrow. —*Woodrow Wilson*

Tol 25.3.2007

85. You can never plan the future by the past. —*Edmund Burke*

86. He who does not get fun and enjoyment out of every day....needs to reorganize his life. —*George M Adams*

87. The roots of true achievement lie in the will to become the best that you can become. —*Harold Taylor*

88. When something can be read without effort, great effort has gone into its writing. —*Enrique Jardiel Poncela*

89. One secret of success in life is for a man to be ready for his opportunity when it comes. —*Bengjamin Disraell*

90. The brain is a wonderful organ. It starts working the moment you get up in the morning and does not stop until you get into the office. —*Robert Frost*

91. I don't need a friend who changes when I change and who nods when I change and who nods when I nod; my shadow does that much better. —*Plutarch*

92. You, yourself, as much as anybody in the entire universe, deserve your love and affection. —*Buddha*

Tol 29-8-2000

93. There is no one without faults, not even men of God. They are men of God not because they are faultless, but because they know their faults, they strive against them, they do not hide them, and are ever ready to correct themselves. I look only to the good qualities of men. Not being faultless myself, I won't presume to probe into the faults of others. —*Mahatma Gandhi*

Tol 1-4-2007

94. Worrying is like a rocking chair: it gives you something to do, but gets you nowhere. —*Van Wilder*

95. The man who doesn't read good books has no advantage over the man who can't read them.

—Mark Twain

96. If it were not for hopes, the heart would break.

—Thomas Twain

97. It is always better to have no ideas than false ones; to believe nothing, than to believe what is wrong.

—Thomas Jefferson

98. Where there is the greatest love, there are always miracles. *—Willa Cather*

99. Friendship is not for merriment but for stern reproach when friends go astray. *—Thiruvalavar*

100. Education is a weapon whose effects depend on who holds it in his hands and at whom it is aimed.

—Joseph Stain

101. When we love, we always strive to become better than we are. *—Paulo Coelho*

Tol 8-1-2006

102. There is no greatness where there is no simplicity.

—Leo Tolstoy

Tol 18-7-2007

103. A fine is a tax for doing wrong. A tax is a fine for doing well.

Tol 8-6-2008

104. Who looks outside-dreams. Who looks inside-awakes.

—Carl Gustav Jung

Tol 21-5-2006

105. The best way to cheer yourself up is to try to cheer somebody else up. *—Mark Twain*

Tol 23-9-2005

105. Human Judges can show mercy. But against the laws of nature, there is no appeal. *—Arthur C Clarke*

Appendix–G

NEWS IN FOCUS

Tol 9-9-2008

BEAMS OF LIFE IN SWISS TUNNEL?

Rays From Particle Collider May Lead to Better Cancer Treatments —**Jonathan Leake**

The giant new particle collider at Europe's search, which is due to start work on Wednesday, is being linked to spectacular spin-offs including improved cancer treatments, systems for destroying nuclear waste and insights into climate change.

"Everyone is looking at the start up of the Large Hadron Collider [LHC] but Cern has many other research programmes with important practical uses," said Paul Collier, who runs the control room at the European Organisation for Nuclear Research (Cern).

The first beams of particles have been successfully fired around nearly half of the 17-mile tunnel in Switzerland, where Cern is based. Linked research has already spurred useful by-products.

In a typical year, the huge machine, which will smash particles into each other at enormous speed, should generate enough data to fill 56 m CDs. That means physicists have had to create a sophisticated system for organizing information extremely quickly. The Grid, as they call it, is likely to become the model for many other systems designed to handle large volumes of data.

Another project has suggested a potentially radical new way of dealing with nuclear waste. Cern's physicists found that firing a beam of protons (a type of sub-atomic particle) into blocks of lead could generate a shower of neutrons (another sub-atomic particle)-and that these could then be used to break down radioactive waste into harmless stable elements. A Cern spokesman said the technique was being studied by industry.

Cern has also contributed to medical research, treating cancers with beams of charged particles such as protons, carbon ions and even antimatter.

Antimatter does not exist naturally, but Cern can make it using a smaller accelerator called the proton synchrotron. This machine is also involved in generating the protons that will orbit around the LHC. The interest in such beams arises because existing forms of radiation therapy may kill cancers but also cause extensive damage to surrounding tissue.

Particle beams could minimize such damage as they can be tuned to pass through healthy tissue and deposit energy only in the tumour.

Cern's latest research project may prove the most controversial. It is building a laboratory to investigate the theory that the rate of cloud formation in the atmosphere is linked to the level of cosmic rays. Cloud formation is a a vital component of climate and weather, and the project could place Cern at the heart of the debate on whether other factors besides greenhouse gases are involved in climate change.

Tol 10-9-2008

TODAY, EXPERTS TO RECREATE BIG BANG

Fingers Crossed As Skeptics Fear Tests Could Produce 'Black Holes' Endangering Planet

Geneva: It has been called an Alice in Wonderland investigation into the makeup of the universe or dangerous tampering with nature that could spell doomsday.

Whatever the case, the most powerful atom-smasher ever built comes online on Wednesday, eagerly anticipated by scientists worldwide who have awaited this moment for two decades.

The multibillion-dollar Large Hadron Collider will explore the tiniest particles and come ever closer to re-enacting the big bang, the theory that a colossal explosion created the universe.

The machine at Cern, the European Organization for Nuclear Research, promises scientists a closer look at the makeup of matter, filling in gaps in knowledge or possibly reshaping theories.

The first breams of protons will be fired around the 17-mile tunnel to test the controlling strength of the world's largest superconducting magnets. It will still be about a month before beams traveling in opposite directions are brought together in collisions that some skeptics fear could create micro "black holes" and endanger the planet.

The project has attracted researchers of 80 nationalities, some 1,200 of them from the US, which contributed $4 million of the project's price tag of nearly $4 billion.

The Cern collider is designed to push the proton beam close to the speed of light, whizzing 11,000 times a second around the tunnel 150 to 500 feet under the French Swiss border.

Once the beam is successfully fired counterclockwise, a clockwise test will follow. Then the scientists will aim the beams at each other so that protons collide, shattering into fragments and releasing energy under the gaze of detectors filling cathedral-sized caverns at points along the tunnel.

Cern dismisses the risk of micro black holes, subatomic version of collapsed stars which can suck in planets and other stars.

Tol 13-9-2008

ACROSS THE UNIVERSE

The Collider could Unravel Many of Nature's Mysteries

—Brian Greene

New York : Three hundred feet below the outskirts of Geneva lies part of a 17-mile-long tubular track, circling its way across the French border and back again, whose interior is so pristine and whose nearly 10,000 surrounding magnets so frigid, that it's one of the emptiest and coldest regions of space in the solar system. The track is part of the Large Hadron Collider, a technological marvel built by physicists and engineers, and described alternatively as heralding the next revolution in our understanding of the universe or, less felicitously, as a doomsday machine that may destroy the doomsday machine that may destroy the planet.

After more than a decade of development and construction, involving thousands of scientists from dozens of countries at a cost of some $8 billion, the "on" switch for the collider was thrown this week. So what we can expect? The collider's workings are straightforward: at full power; trillions of protons will be injected into the otherwise empty track and set racing in opposite directions at speeds exceeding 99.999999 per cent of the speed of light-fast enough so that every second the protons will cycle the entire track more than 11,000 times and engage in more than half a billion head-on collisions.

The raison d'etre for creating this microscopic maelstrom derives from Einstein's famous formula, $E=mc^2$, which declares that much like euros and dollars, energy ("E") and matter or mass ("m") are convertible currencies (with "c"-the speed of light-specifying the fixed conversion rate). By accelerating the protons to fantastically high speeds, their collisions provide a momentary reservoir of tremendous energy, which can then quickly convert to a broad spectrum of other particles. It is through such energy matter conversion that physicists hope to create particles that would have been commonplace just after the big band, but which for the most part have long since disintegrated.

Here's a brief round-up the sort of long-lost particles the collisions might produce and the mysteries they may help unravel. One the mysteries that continues to stump physicists is the origin of mass. We can measure with fantastic accuracy the mass of an electron, a quark and most every other particle, but where does mass itself come from? More than 40 years ago, a number of researchers, including peter Higgs, an English physicist, suggested an answer: perhaps space is pervaded by a field, much like the electromagnetic fields generated by cellphones and radio broadcasts, that acts like invisible molasses.

The one component of the standard model that remains stubbornly unconfirmed is the very notion of the Higgs' "molasses" field. However, collisions at the Large Hadron Collider should be able to chip off little chunks of the ubiquitous Higgs field (if it exists), creating what are known as Higgs bosons or Higgs particles. If these particles are found, the standard model, more than a quarter-century after its articulation, will finally be complete.

A tantalizing idea considered since the early part of the last century is that the universe might have more than the three spatial dimensions of common experience. For many years Einstein was a strong proponent of this idea. He had already shown that gravity was nothing but warps and curves in the familiar dimensions of space (and time); the new idea posited that nature's other forces (for example, the electromagnetic force) amounted to warps and curves in additional, as yet unknown, spatial dimensions. Difficulties in applying the idea mathematically resulted in Einstein ultimately losing interest. But decades later, string theory revived it: the mathematics of string theory not only requires extra dimensions but has shown how to resolve the issues that flummoxed Einstein. And now, remarkably, there's a chance-albeit a smali one-that the collider may find evidence for the extra dimensions.

Now for the possibility that's generated the fuss. Recent work in string theory has suggested that the collider might produce black holes, providing physicists with a spectacular opportunity to study them in a laboratory. The common conception is that black holes are fantastically massive astrophysical bodies with enormous gravitational fields. But in reality, a black hole can have any mass. Take an orange and squeeze it to a sufficiently small size (about a billionth of a billionth of a billionth of a metre across) and you'd have a black hole-with the mass of an orange.

Physicists have realized that the collider's proton-proton collision might momentarily pack so much energy into such a small volume that exceedingly tiny black holes may form-black holes even lighter than the one theoretically created by the orange, but black holes nevertheless. Why might one worry that this would be a problem? Because black holes have a reputation for rapacity. If a black hole is produce under Geneva, might it swallow Switzerland and continue on a ravenous rampage until the earth is devoured?

It's reasonable question with a definite answer: no. work that made Stephen Hawking famous established that tiny black holes would disintegrate in a minuscule fraction of a second, long enough for physicists to reap the benefits of having produced them, but short enough to avoid their wreaking any havoc.

Should any of the particles described above be produced at the Large Hadron Collider, from Higgs particles to black holes, corks will rightly pop in physics department worldwide. But the most exciting prospect of all is that the experiments will reveal something completely unanticipated, something that forces us to rethink our most cherished explanations. Confirming an idea is always gratifying. But finding what you don't expect opens new vistas on the nature of reality. And that's what humans live for.-*NYTNS*

The writer is a professor of maths and physics at Columbia University.

Tol 12-8-2008

SEALS REVEAL ANTARCTIC'S DEEPEST SECRETS

—Jonathan Leake

Scientists are uncovering the deepest secrets of the freezing Antarctic waters by enlisting elephant seals to carry probes to places never before reached by humans.

The seals can reach depths of 6,500ft, so revealing information about the ocean's greatest mysteries. Scientists from the British Antarctic Survey and St Andrews University tracked about 80 seals with sensors. In recent years, some regions, such as the Antarctic Peninsula, have shown sign of warming, and many ice shelved have been breaking up. The data collected by elephant seals could show if warmer currents are disrupting the polar circulation. The research has also provided intriguing insight to one of Elephant seals only come ashore for short periods. The other nine months are spent entirely at sea-mostly underwater.

Tol 3-7-2008

INDIA SETS UP RESEARCH BASE AT NORTH POLE

India on Tuesday commissioned its permanent research base at the North Pole which will enable scientists to carry out studies on a range of subjects including climate change in one of the cleanest environments on earth. The research station-Himadri-was inaugurated by Earth sciences minister Kapil Sibal at Ny-Alesund, on the west coast of Spitsbergen. Situated 1,200 km from the North Pole, Ny-Alesund is the northern most international research village, managed by Kings Bay, the Norwegian government held company that runs the logistics at the research station.

The station was set up following two expeditions by Indian scientists to Ny-Alesund in the last 11 months. The maiden expedition to the Arctic was launched in August last year under the leadership of Rasik Ravindra, director National Centre for Antarctic and Ocean Research, Goa which was followed up by an other team of seven scientists led by Prof A K Gwal of Barkatullah University, Bhopal, who spent 4 weeks in Ny-Alesund.

Tol 9-9-2008

INDIA WILL AVOID 5MN TONES OF CO_2 EMISSIONS BY 2012

—Nitin Sethi IINN

New Delhi: For those who believes India is not doing enough to check the growth of its greenhouse gas emissions, here is some news that should serve as an eye-opener: Through carbon trading projects under the Clean Development Mechanism, more than 5 million tones of carbon dioxide will be avoided by 2012-cutting back 10% of the country's greenhouse gas emissions every year.

Official figures show the government has cleared more than 1,000 projects for carbon trading, the highest in the world, followed by China, attracting investments worth Rs 119,662 crore in these green ventures.

The Clean Development Mechanism is a market-driven device under the UN Framework on Climate Change that allows industries in developing countries to get funds to make their plants and production facilities a bit greener.

Under the convention, rich countries are expected to reduce the greenhouse gas emissions by a fixed percentage by 2012. But realizing that transition would be costlizing that transition would be costlier in developed countries, the treaty allows rich countries to instead fund green transitions in developing countries and claim credit of the reduced emissions against their targets.

So companies or other entities in India undertake a change in their existing processes that rduces emission against which they are provided carbon credit certificates (each worth a tonne of carbon dioxide not emitted), which they can sell to the rich countries. A single project such as this can generate anything from 100 to a million carbon credits, depending on the amount of emission it cuts back on. But the price that an Indian entrepreneur gets in an open market for his certificate depends entirely on how much rich countries really need to meet their targets. If their demand is higher, the certificate, quite naturally, attracts a better price.

At the moment, countries are negotiating what targets rich nations should accept in 2012-when their first phase of commitments ends. Naturally, India has demanded rich countries take on more ambitious targets and this would benefit India by way of funds to go green while also helping developed nations meet their "clean" commitments.

The rich countries, despite a lot of rhetoric, have so far been trying to keep their targets as low as possible and demanding that India should also undertake fixed targets of its own, even though the UN convention on climate change has no such provision.

This would require India to divert money from its development and poverty alleviation programmes to instead fund the "green drive" that is required to a crisis created by rich countries, climate negotiators have pointed out. Big the carbon pie will become in days come, therefore, is linked critically what direction the international ations on climate change, which are conclude by 2009, take.

ToI 11-8-2008

N POLE MAY HAVE NO ICE LEFT BY 2013

The meltdown in the Arctic is speeding up and as a result the north pole could be ice-free by 2013 instead of in 60 years as predicted earlier, scientists have warned.

Their apprehension are based on computer studies of satellite images that reveal that ice at north pole melted at an unprecedented rate last week-the disappearance is said to have exceeded the record loss of more than a million square kilometers in 2007 as global warming tightened its grip.

"It does not really matter whether 2007 or 2008 is the worst year on record for Arctic sea ice," the Observer quoted Wieslaw Maslowski of the Naval Postgraduate School in Monterey as saying. "The crucial point is that ice is clearly not building up enough over winter to restore cover and that when you combine current estimates of be thickness with the extent of the ice cap, you get a very clear indication that the Arctic is going to be ice-free in summer in five years."

Using the US navy super-computers, his team produced a forecast which indicated that by 2013 there will be no ice in the Arctic-other than a few outcrops on islands near Greenland and Canada between mid-July and mid-September.

Added another scientist, Peter Wadhams of Cambridge University: "When we did the first climate change computer models, we thought the Arctic's summer ice cover would last until around 2070...It is now clear we did not understand how thin the ice cap had already become-for Arctic ice cover has since been disappearing at ever increasing rates. Every few years we have to revise our estimates downwards."

Tol 27-5-2008

TO STOP YOUR CO_2 EMISSION, BURY IT

Millions of Tonnes Buried by Norwegian Platform

Sleipner Platform: With planet Earth engaged in a heated race against global warming, "carbon capture and storage" (CCS) has brought a ray of hope, and a Norwegian gas platform is leading the way.

The Sleipner platform in the North Sea, a mammoth steel and cement structure, has successfully buried millions of tones of CO_2 under the seabed for the past 12 years in a pioneering project.

Using a simple metallic tube measuring 50 centimetres (20 inches) in diameter, the platform operator, Norwegian oil and gas group StatoilHydro, has injected some 10 million tones of CO_2 into a deep saline aquifer one kilometer under the sea.

"We bury every year the same amount of CO_2 as emited by 300,000 to 400,000 cars," said Helge Smaamo, the manager of the Sleipner rig, a structure so large that the 240 employees ride three-wheeled scooters to get around.

The project is far from a philanthropic initiative to save the climate: StatoilHydro decided to test the carbon capture and storage (CCS) idea 250km off the Norwegian coast for purely financial reason.

The natural gas extracted by Sleipner has a carbon dioxide content of 9%, almost four times the commercial quality target of 2.5%, requiring the company to reduce the level by filtering it with amines on a platform adjacent to the main structure.

Since it was already being filtered, the question was then whether to release the CO_2 into the atmosphere or to capture it.

A carbon tax imposed as of 1991 on Norway's offshore sector led the group to opt for the second solution, despite an initial cost of $100 million to drill a well and install a compressor, and annual operating costs of $5 million. "We save money by injecting (CO_2) gas rather than releasing it," said Olav Kaarstad, special advisor at StatoilHydro. With the carbon tax at its current level of $66 per tonne, StatoilHydro would have to pay $66 million a year to release one million tones of CO_2into the atmosphere.

But all this does not make diesel powered generator that provides electricity and compresses the gas, and the flare that burns off the impurities, together release a total of 900,000 tonnes of CO_2 per year-as much as the volume of gas buried under the seabed each year. The idea of CCS is however a hotly debated idea.

Greenpeace, which published a report in early May entitled "False hope. Why carbon capture and storage won't save the climate," is spearheading the opposition.

Tol 28-7-2008

WARMING'S UPSIDE IN GREENLAND

Island's Independence Movement is set to Benefit from Climate Change **—Stephan Faris**

Greanland's ice sheet represents one of global warming's most disturbing threats. The vast expanses of glaciers-massed, on average, 1.6 miles deep-contain enough water to raise sea levels worldwide by 23 feet. Should they melt or otherwise slip into the ocean, they would flood coastal capitals, submerge tropical islands and generally redraw the world's atlases. The infusion of fresh water could slow or shut down the ocean's currents, plunging Europe into bitter winter.

Yet for the residents of the frozen island, the residents of the frozen island, the early stages of climate change promise more good, in at least one important sense, than bad. A *Retreating glaciers have uncovered pockets of lead and zinc. The island's minerals are becoming more accessible* Danish protectorate since 1721, Greenland has long sought to cut its ties with its colonizer.

But while proponent of complete independence face little opposition at home or in Copenhagen, they havne't been able to overcome one crucial calculation: the country depends on Danish assistance for more than 40% of its gross domestic product.

Climate change has the power to unsettle boundaries and shake up geopolitics, usually for the worse. But while most of the world sees only peril in the island's meltwater, Greenland's independence movement has explicitly tied its fortunes to the warming of the globe.

The island's ice cover has already begun to disappear. Greenland's fishermen are applauding return of warm-water cod. Shops in island's capital have suddenly begun to offer locally produced potatoes and broccoli-crops unimaginable few years earlier.

But the real promise lies in what may be found under the ice. Near the town of Uummannaq, about halfway up Greenland's coast, retreating glaciers have uncovered pockets of lead and zinc. Gold and diamond prospectors have flooded the island's south. Alcoa is preparing to build a large aluminum smelter. The island's minerals are becoming more accessible even as global commodity prices are soaring. And with more than 80% of the land currently iced over, the island has begun to reveal its riches.

Offshore, where the Arctic Ocean is rapidly thawing, expectations are even higher. Greenland's northeastern waters could contain 31 billion barrels of undiscovered oil and gas.

In November, Greenlanders will vote on a referendum that would leverage global warming into a path to independence. The proposed pland for self-rule, drafted in partnership with Copenhagen, is expected to pass overwhelmingly.

Tol 13-9-2008

Waste is a terrible thing to mind-Recycle

IT'S A GAS

An Entire City could Get Powered by Methane from Bio-sewage

San Antonio in the United States could become the first city to draw all its energy requirements from methane gas generated from the city's water treatment system through recycling 14.000 tonnes of biosolids in sewage annually. The methane source includes human waste that if left untreated and unutilized, would only pollute soil and water. Treating bio-waste, however, could generate an average of 1.5 million cubic feet of gas a day-enough to fill 1,250 tanker trucks daily-according to the system's chief operating officer. A by-product of human and organic waste, methane is the chief component of natural gas that can fuel generators, power plants and furnaces.

Closer home, gobar gas-natural gas obtained from methane released by cattle waste-as a green alternative to diesel and other fossil fuels have been taken up seriously, particularly in rural households. However, a lack of adequate hygiene is a constraint because the gas formation-in the large containers filled with gobar-makes the drum's lid rise, and there is spillage all around the plant. So, in India gobar gas plants are fertile breeding grounds for mosquitoes and other pests. But this is not an insurmountable problem. Gobar gas plants could be expanded and diversified to include energy extraction from all kinds of biomass and the gas so produced could fuel power stations-as San Antonio proposes to do-and with improved sanitation, the experiment could yield good results for several Indian cities.

As a renewable resource, biomass-either from plants, agriculture and forestry residues, animal or human waste-is biodegradable and so is far more eco-friendly than petroleum derived fuels. And they are relatively easier to source and process, unlike the sophisticated instruments and know-how required to extract oil of refine coal. Ethanol derived from biofuels has a very high octane rating. It might deliver less energy than gasoline, but by blending about 10 per cent ethanol land petrol or diesel together, a feasible balance is achieved with no perceptible effct on fuel economy.

America's space agency NASA is sponsoring a joint project to turn human waste into a power source for spaceships using a process that could also produce other chemicals that can be used on board. Instead of turning up our noses at the idea of recycling human waste and other biosolids in sewage, it would be worthwhile to exploit the immense potential hidden in what we routinely regard as being useless.

Tol 16-7-2008

A GREEN GAS

Methane Extracted from Coalfields to be Used as Clean Fuel for Vehicles

A proposal to supply coalbed methane to Kolkata to replace the city's diesel-dependence is being welcomed in all quarters, since it would reduce pollution levels in the area. Methane will be extracted from coalfields in Jharia, Jharkhand, by using converters imported from France. The gas will be transported by road to Kolkata in steel containers until such time as new pipelines are laid and distribution networks worked out. Initially, methane will be used to power autos, taxis and buses that currently run on diesel, often adulterated Eventually, the plan is to extend gas supply for household cooking purposes as well. The Oil and Natural

Gas Corporation has signed an agreement with a private company for distribution to commence in January 2009.

Coalbed methane as a source of clean natural gas has immense potential for India, especially since there are rich sources in the Jharkhand and West Bengal regions. Methane gas is found trapped in fissures in coal and extraction reduces explosion hazards in mines, thereby reducing safety risks for miners. When burnt as fuel, methane has zero emission, whereas when released into the atmosphere its global warming potential is 21 times that of carbon dioxide over a span of 100 years.

There are, however, several factors that have hampered the realization of this clean fuel potential in India. Though the country is rich in reserves of bituminous coal containing methane, the reserves are depths of up to 1,200 metres and need appropriate drilling equipment apart from know-how for extraction.

In the process of coalbed methane extraction, water from the coalbed is first pumped out and since the the water is usually rich in sodium, its salinity makes it unfit for irrigation or drinking purposes. So, waste-water disposal from coalbed methane deposits is something that needs looking into in order not to adversely affect the local water table or stunt plant growth. Unless it is diluted sufficiently with normal water, saline content will be far too high. This, and the fact that converters to extract methane from coalbeds are not available locally, makes it imperative for India to have ties with other countries for technology and know-how transfer. China is on the job, showering tax breaks and subsidies on coalbed methane extraction companies and having an agreement with the US for technology inputs. India should speed up its coalbed methane projects in order to generate clean fuel in areas easily accessible from coal-bearing zones.

Tol 8-8-2008

Top 10 Varsities with International Students

University	*No. of foreign students (05-06)*
Indira Gandhi National Open University	3,000
University of Pune	2,455
Manipal University	1.417
University of Delhi	1,055
Birla Institute of Technology & Science, Pilani	912
Bharati Vidyapeeth, Pune	441
University of Mysore	389
Osmania University, Hyderabad	314
Aligarh Muslim University	250
Banaras Hidu University, Varanasi	214
Total	10,447

Tol 29-6-2008

Earth's twin hiding in Milky Way?

After recently discovering three super-Earths, astronomers say its' just a matter of time before they find a planet identical to ours, which might be hiding in the Milky Way galaxy. According to a report in Space.com, the three super-Earths are worlds more massive than ours. "Being able to find three Earth-mass planets around a single star really makes the point that not only may many stars have one Earth, but they may very well have a couple of Earths," said Alan Boss, a planet theorist at Carnegle institution of Washington.

International Students in Indian Universities (continent-wise)

Continents	*2004-05*	*2005-06*
Asia	9,849	10,493
Africa	2,005	2,403
America	593	654

Europe	178	206
Australasia (Oceania)	55	71
Miscellaneous	587	629
Total	13,267	14,456

Varsities with over 100 International Students

Jamia Hamdard, Delhi	240
Jamia Millia Islamia, Delhi	108
Periyar University, Salem	117
Swami Vivekanand Yoga Anusandhan Sansthan, Bangalore	153

Tol 26-5-2008

HUGE CRACKS APPEAR IN ARCTIC ICE CAP

London: Research during an expedition by the Canadian military has found dramatic evidence of the break-up of the arctic ice cap, in the form of vast cracks.

According to a report by BBC News, scientists traveling with the troops found major new fractures during an assessment of the state of giant ice shelves in Canada's far north.

The team found a network of cracks that stretched for more than 16 km onward Hunt, the area's largest shelf.

"I was astonished to see these new cracks," said Derek Muelle, one of the expedition's scientists. "It means the ice shelf is disintegrating, the pieces are pinned together like a jigsaw but could float away," he added.

According to another scientist on the expedition, Dr Luke Copland of the University of Ottawa, the new cracks fit into a pattern of change in the Arctic.

"We're seeing very dramatic changes; from the retreat of the glaciers, to the melting of the sea ice," said Copland. "We had 23% less (sea ice) last year than we've over had, and what's happening to the ice shelves is part of that picture," he added. When ice shelves break apart, they drift offshore into the ocean as "ice islands", transforming the very geography of the coastline.

Ayles Ice Island, an iceberg the size of Manhattan, has split into two in the past year, each vast chunk of ice now 640km south of its original position. The rapid changes in the Arctic have reignited disputes over territory. The Canadian military's expedition was billed as a "sovereignty patrol", the lines of snowmobiles flying Canadian flags in a display of control.

After the record Arctic melting last year, all eyes are now on what happens to the sea ice this summer: Although its maximum extent last winter was slightly greater than the year before, it was still below the long-term average.

ToI 30-7-2008

There's Gold in Trash

Ethanol Produced from Waste Promises to Reduce Vehicle Emission by 90 per cent

First-generation bioethanol fuels are neither cost-competitive nor do they significantly reduce greenhouse gas emissions. They also require the use of food crops such as sugarcane, corn or soybean, which means they cannot be produced in sufficient quantities without threatening food supplies. Second-generation biofuels, on the other hadn, could be the real alternative for the future because they can solve such problems and supply a larger proportion of our fuel supply sustainably, affordably and with greater environmental benefits, Moreover, since they use non-food biomass like grain stalks, shavings, switchgrass or husk, they neatly sidestep the contentious "food or fuel" debate. The problem is, extracting ethanol from such difficult feedstock.

But now it seems a chemical company in England has circumvented that issue, too, by developing a method to produce ethanol in large quantities from municipal solid waste, organic commercial waste and agricultural residues amongst other things. The waste is first superheated to produce gases and then fed to naturally occurring bacteria that efficiently produce ethanol which is purified to make the fuel ready to be blended for use in cars. One tonne of dried waste can yield around 400 literes of bioethanol. It's claimed this type of ethanol produces 90 per cent less net greenhouse gas emissions than petrol. The first commercial plant is expected to be set up in two years.

According to the United Kingdom's National Non-Food Crops Cantre, this is a breakthrough in two areas: technologically because producers can use municipal solid waste which, at least partially, solves the problem of waste disposal and landfill area reduction; and commercially because we could now have the potential to produce large volumes of bioethanol viably across the world.

Although some car manufacturers have already developed engines that can run efficiently on both bioethanol and conventional fuel, most automobiles still need to use a 10 to 20 per cent blend with conventional fossil fuels. Still, for motorists who are constantly facing rising prices at petrol stations around the world it should come as a welcome relief-especially if economies of scale can bring down a part of the cost of the fuel they consume. It's also about time that manufacturers seriously start building more cars that run using only biofuels and substantially bring down a part of the cost of the fuel they consume. It's also about time that manufacturers seriously start building more cars that run using only biofuels and substantially bring down vehicle emission. Their oil lobbies are running out of excuses now.

ToI 15-7-2008

FIRM TURNS CO_2 EMISSIONS INTO 'GREEN CARBON'

Washington : A small company in the US is developing an alternative for carbon sequestration that takes carbon dioxide (CO_2) and tailings from mining operations and turns the mix into materials of a "higher order" for use in a variety of industrial, agricultural, and environmental applications, which has been dubbed as 'green carbon'.

According to a report in ENN (environmental News Network), Carbon Sciences, founded by CEO Derek McLeish, has developed a relatively simple technology that puts the brew under pressure and temperature to create PCC (precipitated calcium carbonate). Traditionally, calcium carbonate is produced through an energy intensive process using expensive materials such as limestone. The 'green carbon' technology takes this normally exhaustive process and simplifies it, thus producing a useful, benign material while transforming carbon emissions instead of simply sequestering it.

Carbon neutral operations don't release any additional CO_2 into the atmosphere, nor do they reduce CO_2 levels either. When applying the technology to a carbon neutral process, say an ethanol plant, that process actually reduces the amount of CO_2 thus making it carbon negative.

30-7-2008

THERE'S GOLD IN TRASH

Ethanol Produced from Waste Promises to Reduce Vehicle Emissions by 90 per cent

First-generation bioethanol fuels are neither cost-competitive nor do they significantly reduce greenhouse gas emissions. They also require the use of food crops such as sugarcane, corn or soybean, which means they cannot be produced in sufficient quantities without threatening food supplies. Second-generation biofuels, on the other hand, could be the real alternative for the future because they can solve such problems and supply a larger proportion of our fuel supply sustainably, affordably and with greater environmental benefits. Moreover, since they use non-food biomass like grain stalks, shavings, switchgrass or husk, they neatly sidestep the contentious "food or fuel" debate. The problem is, extracting ethanol from such difficult feedstock.

But now it seems a chemical company in England has circumvented that issue, too, by developing a method to produce ethanol in large quantities from municipal solid waste, organic commercial waste and agricultural residues amongst other things. The waste is first superheated to produce gases and then fed to naturally occurring bacteria that efficiently produce ethanol which is purified to make the fuel ready to be blended for use in cars. One tonne of dried waste can yield around 400 litres of bioethanol. It's claimed this type of ethanol produces 90 per cent less net greenhouse gas emissions than petrol. the first commercial plant is expected to be set up in two years.

According to the United Kingdom's National Non-Food Crops Centre, this is a breakthrough in two areas: technologically because producers can use municipal solid waste which, at least partially, solves the problem of waste disposal and landfill area reduction; and commercially because we could now have the potential to produce large volumes of bioethanol viably across the world.

Although some car manufacturers have already developed engines that can run efficiently on both bioethanol and conventional fuel, most automobiles still need to use a 10 to 20 per cent blend with conventional fossil fuels. Still, for motorists who are constantly facing rising prices at petrol stations around the world it should come as a welcome relief—especially if economies of scale can bring down a part of the cost of the fuel they consume. It's also about time that manufacturers seriously start building more cars that run using only biofuels and substantially bring down vehicle emissions. Their oil lobbies are running out of excuses now.

3-5-2008

GLOBAL TEMPS WILL CLIMB AFTER 2020: EXPERTS

—Nitin Sethi ITNN

New Delhi : Research carried out scientists from Leibniz Institute of Marine Sciences and Max Plank Institute of Meteorology, both based in Germany, has said that Earth's temperatures will be in check for the next 10 years. However, temperatures would finally reach the predicted higher levels by the end of 2020. All predictions of global temperature changes are based on complex mathematical models that create future scenarios according to parameters and data that scientists feed in. due to numerous physical phenomena involved, these predictions work better when the average temperature increase for a longer period-several decades-is calculated. The break through has come with scientists being able to predict changes that could occur over 10 year intervals-what climatologists consider a much shorter time period.

The scientists studies temperatures measured on the surface of oceans-a crucial factor in determining variations of global average temperatures. They were able to predict workings of a critical phenomenon called meriodional overturning circulation (MOC). It brings warm water into the north Althantic, releasing heat into the atmosphere. This then returns to cooler waters in the southern portions f the ocean. But MOC is known to change intensity over decades.

Researchers were able to predict that MOC would weaken over the next decade and as a result would cool north Altantic waters, consequently keeping global temperatures under control. MOC, in a sense, would work just the way EI Nino and La Nina do to affect global temperatures in the Pacific Ocean. These are more familiar in India as they can impact monsoons. While the research might have brought down the immediate threat levels globally and can allow government and decision-makers-especially in US, Europe and north Africa-to plan for lower levels of crisis management, there could be other spinoffs.

This kind of predictive studies also help simulate once models get better, precipitation in regions at more accurate levels.

Tol 12-7-2008

TINY FRACTURES MAY HELP PREDICT QUAKES

Washington : Scientists working at California's San Andreas Fault have detected subtle geological changes occurring hours before an earthquake that could enable them to develop an early-warning system aimed at saving lives.

Their instruments detected geological changes most likely caused by tiny fractures forming in the rock ahead of an impending earthquake due to stress in the earth's crust, according to seismologist Paul Silver of the Carnegie Institution in Washington, one of the researchers. "It's the opening up of cracks before an earthquake," Silver said. The research, published in the journal Nature, was conducted using wells dug 0.6 miles deep into the quakeprone fault at Parkfield, California.

Their equipment generated and recorded seismic waves before, during and after two small quakes, allowing them to observe these small, predictive geological changes. In the first case, the geological signals occurred 10 hours before a magnitude 3 quake in December 2005. The same sort of signals also occurred two hours before a magnitude 1 quake that happened five days later; the researchers said.

"We are very encouraged by these observations, and we are planning for more experiments to confirm whether these changes are part of the general physical processes before an earthquake," seismologist Fenglin Niu of Rice University in Houston said.

Scientists have made strides in under-standing earthquakes, but finding changes in the earth's crust that could allow for an advance prediction has remained difficult. Current earthquake warning systems provide at best a few seconds notice before an earthquake strikes. The findings were published just two months after a powerful earthquake in China. The May 12 quake in Sichuan province killed about 80,000 people, with many killed when buildings such as schools collapsed.

Tol 12-5-2008

GEOPHYSICISTS SAY NEW METHOD COULD FORECAST EARTHQUAKES

New York : Geophysicsts from Britain and China have developed a new methodology to seismic monitoring that could help forecast the time, size and sometimes even the location of earthquakes.

The new method exploits a phenomenon called shear-wave splitting, in which seismic 'shear' waves traveling through rocks are split into ttwo components, which vibrate parallel and perpendicular relative to microscopic cracks, according to a report published in Nature.

These two shear wave components travel through the ground at different speeds, and so reach detectors at different times. The alignment of these microscopic cracks reflects the amount of stress in the Earth's crust. The more stress, the more the cracks are aligned, and the bigger the gap between the two waves' arrival.

So far efforts to predict the tremors have proved futile.

In the past, Nature says researchers have gauged the build-up of strain in earthquake zones indirectly, by looking at satellite maps of surface ground movement. But this gives only a rough idea of the stress changes deeper down, where earthquakes originate. Stresses have also been monitored directly at fault lines, but such localized data doesn't show when and where slippage will occur.

The researchers' evidence, the report says, suggests that they could perhaps issue an hour's warning be fore a small quake and months be fore a big one.

Tol 9-5-2008

AUSTRALIAN PLATYPUS GENOME A LINK TO EVOLUTION

Sydney : Australia's duckbilled platypus-an egg-laying, furry animal with web feet is part bird, part reptile and part mammal according to its gene map.

A team of international scientists released the platypus genome on Thursday, saying its complex sequence would aid the study of human evolution-particularly the development of the immune, nervous and reproductive systems.

"Its probably the most eagerly awaited genome since the chimp genome because platypuses are so weird," said Jenny Graves, head of Comparative Genomics Group at Australian National University.

The Nature paper analyzed the genome of a female platypus named Glennie. Its genome contained roughly 18,500 genes, similar to other vertebrates. The researchers found genes that support lactation and egg laying, and genes responsible for venom production, which evolved from reptile genomes.

"You see genes that look reptile-like, genes that look reptile-like, genes that look bird-like and genes that look mammal-like. It's a pretty amazing picture," Rick Wilson, director of the Genome Center at Washington University in St Louis, said.

Tol 27-5-2008

NATURE'S CLUES TO PREDICTING AN EARTHQUAKE

Tangshan (China) : Well before this city was destroyed by an earthquake 32 years ago, the coming disaster was loudly preceded by strange animal behavior and other bizarre signals that survivors wish they heeded.

"The animals were trying to tell us something. If only we knew that, not so many people would have died," said Fu Wenran, a retired farmer whose wife was among the estimated 240,000 who perished in Tangshan's quake on July 28,1976. Several survivors of the disaster in this northern city-still the deadliest earthquake of modern times-said the toll in this month's quake in southwestern China could have been minimized if such clues had been validated.

Dogs erupted in wild howing and barking hours before the quake struck. Mice and snakes skittered around crazily in the open. Horses and cows kicked at their stable walls. Water levels in local wells plunged in the weeks before, only to rise sharply in the hours preceding the quake

Chinese media reports buzzed with reports of mass migrations of thousands of frogs and toads near the quake region in Sichuan province just before the May 12 disaster. Whether linked to the quake or not, there is little dispute among scientists that animals can predict earthquakes, possibly through sensitivity to pressure waves.

"Physical and chemical stimuli emanate from the earth prior to an earthquake and animals probably sense that," said George Pararas-Carayannis, a chemist and oceanographer. The 1976 Tangshan quake was a tour de force of clues, survivors say.

Fu, then a farmer on the city's outskirts, said dogs erupted in wild howling and barking hours before the quake struck at 3.42am. Mice and snakes skittered around crazily in the open. Horses and cows kicked at their stable walls.

Water levels in local wells plunged in the weeks before, only to rise sharply in the hours preceding the quake, with many overflowing, he said. Even Tangshan's people behaved strangely, he said.

"People were irritable and confused. There were many fights that night," said Fu. At the time, the bad tempers were blamed on a sudden heat wave, strangely unforeseen by weather forecasts, said Chang Qing, 71, then a local photographer.

Mysterious brilliant lights have also been seen in skies before large earthquakes since ancient times.

"It looked like explosions. Bright sudden flashes. But there was no sound," said Jiang Mo, 59, who recalls seeing them while lying awake in the pre-dawn heat. Dubbed "earthquake lights", some scientists believe they many be the products of a traumatized mind, while geologists suggest a link to electromagnetic forces from deep underground.

Yet animal behaviour is widely believed to hold the most promise in forecasting.

Tol 1-5-2008

EXPLORE ALL OPTIONS

Biofuels Require the Right Kind of Feedstock to be Viable in Future

With oil hitting a record high of $120 a barrel, the time to anticipate and develop a future alternative energy source was, perhaps, yesterday. But even a recent and radically different approach to producing sustainable energy in the form of biofuels derived from plants is now also suddenly looking down the barrel of the environmentalists' gun, even though these fuels can reduce greenhouse gas emissions. In particular, they question whether biofuel crops such as corn and soybeans in the United States, sugarcane in Brazil or palm oil in south East Asia, for instance, will ultimately compete for land with food crops, thus driving up staple price.

In certain places like the US they will, since the government inappropriately subsidises corn cultivation while levying high tariffs on much more energy-efficient Brazilian sugar ethanol. But in Brazlil itself, for example, it won't because the country has enough grasslands for plantation space without encroaching on its rainforest ecosystem. Besides, there are other reasons why food prices are skyrocketing. These include areas in Africa such as Sudan where there's suddenly been a slump in the ability to distribute food, places where production is declining to the point where export caps have to be put in place, increase and improvement in people's diets-in China and India, for instance-and economic factors like fertilizer prices and transportation costs.

Of course, risks still remain and plant fuel production has its own inherent problems that need to be addressed, but it's also a fact these are still first generation biofuels and the technology is still in its infancy. It would be a clear case of throwing the baby out with the bathwater if the whole movement were to be jettisoned now for being part of the problem instead of the solution as some people are beginning to believe.

The better way to go about it is to invest in the right feedstock-the basis of second-generation plant fuels. In India, a more viable solution would be to speedily increase political and industrial support for biofuel implementation from non-food crops because these can also include waste biomass, grain stalks and shavings. One alternative could be to use sugarcane of which there is already excess production. If farmers can be incentivised to utilize a part of this yield in future for ethanol production, it would neither eat into sugar supplies nor affect food prices by diverting land meant for food crop cultivation.

Tol 11-2-2008

SUPER EYE MAY CRACK MYSTERIES BEHIND GALAXIES

Jonathan Leake

Europe is to launch the most powerful space telescope over built, with the ability to capture light from stars that were born and died up to 13 billion years ago.

The Herschel space telescope, named after an 18th-century British astronomer, could help solve the mystery of how galaxies and stars formed and how these processes eventually gave rise to life-bearing planets like Earth.

Last week, the assembly of Herschel moved into its final stage at the European Space Agency's research and technology centre in Noordwijk, Holland, with the arrival of the 3.5m mirror that will become the heart of the instrument after its launch this cummer. Herschel will be far more powerful than Nasa's Hubble space telescope, which has a mirror of just 2.4 m.

"We will be able to look at some of the oldest objects in the universe," said Bruce Swinyard, professor of astronomical instrumentation at Cardiff University, who has helped design the telescope. "It is going to tell us a great deal about how galaxies originally formed."

It will complement rather than supplant in the infra-red spectrum, detecting radiation invisible to the human eye. Hubble, by contrast, collects mainly visible light.

One of the mysteries that is the growth of galaxies. The universe is dominated by such galaxies, each typically containing several hundred billion stars and surrounded by huge areas of emptiness. The Milky Way, which included Earth, is one of them.

Astronomers cannot even tell if stars arose first and then drew together to form galaxies or if it was the other way round, with huge clouds of gas accumulating and then condensing into stars.

"The light from those times is now all deep within the infrared spectrum where we cannot yet see it." Said Swinyard. "The instruments on Hershel will be the first to pick it up and tell us something about what happened back then."

Herschel will carry three main scientific instruments, including the spectral and photometric imaging receiver built by Cardiff University.

The kind of secrets that might be unveiled by Herschel were hinted at by an earlier ESA probe, the infrared space observatory when it peered, for example, at the Andromeda galaxy, one of the closest to our own. ISO showed it was made of concentric rings.

Tol 3-7-2008

EARTH'S PIERCING CRIES RECORDED IN OUTER SPACE

Scientists have been able to record the ear-piercing series of chirps and whistles which the earth emits and which could be heard by any aliens who might be listening. The sound is awful, the recording from space reveals.

Researchers have known about the radiation since the 1970s. It is created high above the planet, where charged particles from the solar wind collide with Earth's magnetic filed. It is related to the phenomenon that generates the colorful aurora, or Northern Lights.

The radio waves are blocked by the ionosphere, a charged layer atop our atmosphere, so they do not reach Earth. That's good, because the out-of-this-world radio waves are 10,000 times stronger than even the strongest military signal, the researchers said, and they would overwhelm all radio stations on the planet.

Theorists had long figured the radio waves, which were not well studied, oozed into space in an ever-widening cone, like light from a torch.

But new data from the European Space Agency's Cluster mission, a groups of four high-flying satellites, reveals the bursts of radio waves head off to the cosmos in beam-like fashion, instead.

Tol 12-7-2008

NEW EVIDENCE OF WATER ON MOON

Conclusion Reached After Scan of Samples Brought 40 Years Ago

Washington : Tiny green and orange glass bails brought back from the moon nearly 40 years ago by astronauts show evidence that water existed there from the very beginning, scientists reported on Wednesday.

They used a new method of analyzing elements in the lunar sand samples to show strong evidence of water, dating back 3 billion years. Their study, published in the journal Nature, could support evidence that water persists in shadowed craters on the moon's surface-and that the water could be native to the moon and that the water could be native to the moon and not carried there by comets.

Most scientists believe the moon was formed when a Mars-size body collided with Earth 4.5 billion years ago. The giant impact would have melted both proto-planets and sent molten debris into orbit around the Earth.

Some of this would have eventually coalesced into the moon, but the heat of the impact would have vaporized light elements such as the hydrogen and oxygen needed to make water-theoretically, anyway.

Erik Hauri of the Carnegie Institution for Sccience in Washington had developed a technique called secondary ion mass spectrometry or SIMS, which could detect minute amounts of elements in samples. His team was using it to find evidence of water in the Earth's molten mantle.

"Then one day I said, 'Look, why don't we go and try it on the moon glass?" Alberto Sall of Brown University, who helped lead the study, said. Saal, Hauri and colleagues were able to get about 40 of the little glass beads and break them apart for analysis. What they found overturned the conventional wisdom that the moon is dry.

Saal's team did not find water directly, but they did measure hydrogen, and it resembled the measurements they have done to detect hydrogen, and eventually water, in samples from Earth's mantle.

Tol 15-5-2008

'BELIEF IN GOD, ALIENS IS OK'

Vatican Scientist Backs life elsewhere

Vatican City : The Vatican's chief astronomer says there is no conflict between believing in God and in the possibility of "extraterrestrial brothers" perhaps more evolved than humans.

"In my opinion this possibility (of life on other planets) exists," said Jose Gabriel Funes, a 45-year-old Jesuit priest who is head of the Vatican observatory and a scientific adviser to Pope Benedict.

"How can we exclude that life has developed elsewhere," he told the Vatican newspaper L'Osservatore Romano in an interview explaining that the large number of galaxies with their own planets made this possible.

Asked if he was referring to beings similar to humans or even more evolved than humans, he said: "Certainly, in a universe this big you can't exclude this hypothesis".

In the interview headlined "The extraterrestrial is my brother," he said he saw no conflict between belief in such beings and faith in God.

"Just as there is a multiplicity of creatures on earth, there can be other beings, even intelligent, created by God. This is not in contrast with our faith because we can't put limits on God's creative freedom," he said.

"Why can't we speak of a 'brother extraterrestrial'? It would still be part of creation," he said.

Funes, who runs the observatory which is based south of Rome and in Arizona, held out the possibility that the human race might actually be the "lost sheep" of the universe.

"There could be (other beings) who remained in full friendship with their creator," he said.

Green aliens, UFOs visited UK: secret files

Alines from outer space have been visiting Britain for years and UFO sightings doubled after the film close Encounters was released in 1977, according to secret files collating reports by members of the public, the alien craft come in all shapes and colors but their occupants are uniformly green, the ministry of defence files show. The archives are the first batch of a four-year release programme of all the ministry's UFO files from 1978 to the present day. The ministry dismisses 90% of the reports as having mundane explanations and leave 10% with a question mark and the assurance they are no defence threat.

Christians have sometimes been at odds with scientists over whether the Bible should be read literally and issues such as creationism versus evolution have been hotly debated for decades. The Inquisition condemned astronomer Galileo in the 17th century for insisting that the earth revolved around the sun.

Funes said dialogue between faith and science could be improved is scientists learned more about the Bible and the Church kept more up to date with scientific progress.

Tol 3-8-2008

NEW WAY TO STORE SOLAR ENERGY FOR A RAINY DAY

Cambridge : A US scientist has developed a new way of powering fuel cells that could make it practical for home owners to store solar energy and produce electricity to run lights and appliances at night.

A new catalyst produces the oxygen and hydrogen that fuel cells use to generate electricity, while using far less energy than current methods. With this catalyst, users could rely on electricity produced by photovoltaic solar cells to power the process that produces the fuel, said the Massachusetts Institute of Technology professor who developed the new material.

"If you can only have energy when the sun is shining, you're in deep trouble. And that's why, in my opinion, photovoltaics haven't penetrated the market," Daniel Nocera, an MIT professor of energy, said in an interview at his Cambridge, Massachusetts, office.

"If I could provide a storage mechanism, then I make energy 24/7 and then we can start talking about solar."

Solar has been growing as a power source in the US. But is is still a tiny power source, producing enough energy to meet the needs of about 600,000 typical homes, and only while the sun is shining. Nocera said his development would allow people to bank solar energy as hydrogen and oxygen, which a fuel cell could use to produce energy when the sun was not shining.

"I can turn sunlight into a chemical fuel, now I can use photovoltaics at night," said Nocera, who explained the discovery in a paper written with Matthew Kanan published on Thursday in the journal Science.

Tol 23-4-2008

HAWKING: LIFE LIKELY ON OTHER PLANETS

Washington : Famed astrophysicist Stephen Hawking has been thinking a lot about the cosmic question, "Are we alone?" The answer is probably not, he says.

It there is life elsewhere in the universe, Hawking asks why haven't we stumbled onto some alien broadcasts in space, maybe something like an "alien quiz shows?"

Hawking's comments were part of a lecture at George Washington University in honor of Nasa's 50th anniversary. He theorized that there are possible answers to whether there is extraterrestrial life.

One option is that there likely isn't life elsewhere. Or maybe there is intelligent life elsewhere, but when it gets smart enough to send signals into space, it also is smart enough to make destructive nuclear weapons.

Hawking said he prefers the third option: "Primitive life is very common and intelligent life is fairly rare," he then quickly added: "Some would say it has yet to occur on earth."

So should you worry about aliens? Alien abduction claims come from "weirdos" and are unlikely. However, because alien life might not have NDA like us, Hawking warned: "Watch out if you would meet an alien. You could be infected with a disease with which you have no resistance."

The 66-year-old British cosmologist believes "if the human race is to continue for another million years, we will have to boldly go where no one has gone before." Boldly go where no one has gone before."

Hawking compared people who don't want to spend money on human space exploration to those who opposed the journey of Christopher Columbus in 1492. "The discovery of the New World made a profound difference to the old. Just think we wouldn't have had a Big Max or KFC."

Tol 26-7-2007

A NEW EARTH, 20 LIGHT YEARS AWAY

It's Potentially Habitable, Say European Experts

Washington : For the first time astronomers have discovered a planet outside our solar system that is potentially habitable, with Earth like temperatures, a find researchers described Tuesday as a big step in the search for 'life in the universe'.

The planet is just the right size, might have water in liquid form, and in galactic terms is relatively nearby at 120 trillion miles away. But the star it closely orbits, known as a 'red dwarf', is much smaller, dimmer and cooler than our Sun.

There's still a lot that is unknown about the new planet, which could be deemed inhospitable to life once more is known about it. And it's worth noting that scientists' requirements for habitability count Mars in that category: a size relatively similar to Earth's with temperatures that would permit liquid water.

However, this is the first outside our solar system that meets those standards.

"It's a significant step on the way to finding possible life in the universe," said University of Geneva astronomer Michel Mayor, one of 11 European scientists on the team that found the planet. "It's a nice discovery. We still have a lot of questions."

The results of the discovery have not been published but have been submitted to the journal *Astronomy and Astrophysic.*

Alan Boss, who works at the Carnegie Institution of Washington where a US team of a tronomers competed in the hunt for an Earth-like planet, called it "a milestone in this business".

The planet was discovered by the European Southern Observatory's telescope in La Silla, Chile, which has a special instrument that splits light to find wobbles in different wave lengths. Those wobbles can reveal the existence of other worlds.

What they revealed is a planet circling the red dwarf star, Gliese 581: Red dwarfs are low-energy, tiny stars that give off dim red light and last longer than stars like our sun. until a few years ago, astronomers didn't consider these stars as possible hosts of planets that might sustain life.

The discovery of the new planet, named 581 c, is sure to fuel studies of planets circling similar dim stars. About 80% of the stars near Earth are red dwarfs.

The new planet is about five times heavier than Earth. Its discoverers aren't certain if it is rocky like Earth or if it's a frozen ice ball with liquid water on the surface.

If it is rocky like Earth, which is what the prevailing theory proposes, it has a diameter about 11/2 times bigger than our planet. If it is an iceball, as Mayor suggests, it would be even bigger.

Tol 4-9-2008

BEYOND CARBON: EXPERTS WORRY ABOUT NITROGEN

Toolik Field Station (Alaska): As Anne Giblin was lugging four-foot tubes of Arctic lakebed mud from her inflatable raft to her nearby lab this summer; she said, "Mud is a great storyteller".

Giblin, a senior scientist at the Marine Biological Laboratory in Woods Hole, Massachusetts, is part of the Long Term Ecological Research network at an Arctic science outpost here operated by the University of Alaska at Fairbanks.

Public discussion of complicated climate change is largely reduced to carbon: carbon emission, carbon footprints, carbon trading. But other chemicals have large roles in the planet's health, and the one Giblin is looking for in Arctic mud, one that a growing number of other researchers are also concentrating on, is nitrogen.

In addition to having a role in climate change, nitrogen has a huge, probably more important biological impact through its presence in fertillzer. Peter Vitousek, a Stanford ecologist whose 1994 essay put nitrogen on the environmental map, co-authored a study this summer in the journal Nature that put greater attention on the nitrogen cycle and warned against ignoring it in favor of carbon benefits.

Public discussion of complicated climate change is largely reduced to carbon: carbon emissions, carbon footprints, carbon trading. But other chemicals have large roles in the planet's health, and the one that a growing number of other researchers are concentrating on, is nitrogen

For example, Vitousek said, "There's a great danger in doing something like, oh, overfertilizing a cornfield to boost biofuel consumption, where the carbon benefits are far outweighed by the nitrogen damage."

Soon after Vitousek's report, the journal Geophysical Research Letters branded as a "missing greendhouse gas" nitrogen trifluoride, which is used in production of semiconductors and in liquid-crystal displays found in many electronics.

Nitrogen causes more global warming than coal-fired plants. Nitrogen trifluoride, which is not one of the six gases covered by the Kyoto Protocol, the celebrated international global warming accord, is about 17,000 times more potent than carbon dioxide. Its estimated worldwide release into the atmosphere this year is equivalent to the total global-warming emission form Austria.

"The nitrogen dilemma," nitrogen dilemma," Vitousek added, "is not just thinking that carbon is all that matters. But also thinking that global warming is the only environmental issue. The weakening of biodiversity, the pollution of rivers, these are local issues that need local, attention. Smog. Acid rain. Coasts. Forests. It's all nitrogen."

James Galloway, an environmental sciences professor at the University of Virginia is developing a universal calculator for individual nitrogen footprints. "Reactive nitrogen isn't a waste product. We need it desperately. Just not too much and not too little. It's just more complicated than carbon."

Nitrogen is part of all living matter. When plants and animals die, their nitrogen is passed into soil and the nitrogen in the soil, in turn, nourishes plants on land and seeps into bodies of water. Giblin is pursuing her research because as the Arctic warms, the tundra's permafrost will thaw, and the soil will release carbon and nitrogen into the atmosphere.

Tol 1-9-2008

GETTING RID OF 'WARMING' GASES

Toxic Gases Can be Broken Down Before They Reach Atmosphere

By identifying a new way to wrestle fluorine from carbon compounds, chemists may now be able to break down certain types of greenhouse gases before they reach the atmosphere.

Some of the most potent manmade greenhouse gases are also among the most difficult chemicals to destroy, and the most persistent once released into the environment. Scientists report in the Science magazine that they have managed to force these gases to chemically react, turning them into more benign compounds.

For now, the process offers only a proof of concept. But the work opens the door to new ways of disposing of these materials. "Our process allows us to take a hydrofluorocarbon and transform it so that it's no longer a greenhouse gas," says study co-author Oleg Ozerov of Brandeis University in Waltham, Massachusetts.

The researchers found that a powerful acid, 'Lewis acide's, when used in organic solvents such as benzene, forces HFCs to swap out their fluorine atoms with hydrogen atoms

"It's a very hard nut to crack, andthey finally got it to work," says Robert Crabtree of Yale University.

Fluorocarbons, compounds in which carbon and fluorine atoms are bonded together, are a wide class of chemicals, with applications ranging from anaesthetics to non-stick pans. Those in a class called hydro-fluorocarbons, or HFCs, have been used as refrigeration fluids to replace chlorofluorocarbons, which were implicated in the thinning of the ozone layer.

Ironically, though, HFCs have been found to have a different drawback: They trap heat extremely well. Once released in the atmosphere, HFCs contribute to the greenhouse effect and to global warming.

Getting rid of HFCs is difficult, because carbon-fluorine bonds are notoriously resistant to change, or, chemically speaking, inert. That means HFCs are hard to break up through reactions with other substances. Fluorocarbons do react with some potent acids, but those tend to be expensive or they only work at very high temperatures. But Ozerov and Christos Douvris, now at the University of Colorado at

Boulder, have found a way to use acids as reusable catalysts, which don't get consumed while they help HFCs react chemically. This reaction also has the advantage of working at room temperature.

Ozerov and Douvris found out that a powerful acid, 'Lewis acids', when used in organic solvents such as benzene, force HFCs to react chemically with silanes, silicon-hydrogen compounds, leading the HFCs to swap out their fluorine atoms with hydrogen atoms.

The resulting compounds are then easier for chemists to deal with, Ozerov said. Crabtree said the chemical industry may now be able to find economical ways to dispose of existing stockpiles of HFCs, in the expectation that these chemicals will be banned sooner or later.

TOI 5-9-2008

GLOBAL WARMING PACKING POWER INTO HURRICANES

Warm Seas Convert More Energy into Cyclone Winds

Paris : Global warming is likely to boost the power of the strongest tropical cyclones, a new study says.

An additional 1^0C in sea temperature in tropical regions where eyclones breed could lead to a nearly one-third rise in the number of the most powerful storms, it says. "As the seas warm, the ocean has more energy to convert to tropical cyclone wind," say authors of the paper, released by London weekly Nature.

Previous research, based on observation over the past 30 years, has already suggested that hurricanes have become more intense as a result of warmer seas. But the observational record for the Atlantic is more detailed and goes back farther than for storms in the Indian Ocean, known as cyclones, or those in the Pacific, which are called typhoons.

Seeking to fill in the blanks, a trio of US scientists crunched satellite data for the period of 1981-2006 in all of these storm basins. They totted up the number of storms and the maximum wind speeds attained during each event, and compared this with sea-surface temperatures.

Over the 25 years under scrutiny, they saw no increase in the overall number of storms. But there was a significant increase in wind speed among the most powerful storms, or those in roughly the top quarter for intensity. Measurements of the energy pumped into the air from the warm waters—essentially fuel for hurricanes—has increased dramatically since the mid-1990s, mostly in the strongest of hurricanes.

The Atlantic is seeing an increase in storms rated among the strongest. In the past four years, eight storms reached Category 4 with winds of at least 211 kmph.

STORM FRONT: A satellite image shows a full disk western hemisphere view of the earth. (Left to right) Hurricanes Gustav (over the US Gulf coast),Hanna (over Haiti and Cuba), and Ike and Josephine can be seen churning further in the eastern Atlantic Ocean.

TOI 9-8-2008

NEW GEOLOGY MAP WILL HELP SAVE EARTH

Lillestroem (Norway) : Scientists unveiled the first digital map of the earth's geology and said it could guide oil and gas exploration and mining or pinpoint sites for burying greenhouse gases.

The map shows the world stripped of vegetation, water, soil and human structures by joining up existing data from the geological centers of 83 member nations in a planetary jigsaw on the internet.

"We have simply unlocked what already exists," said Ian Jackson, chief of operations at the British Geological Survey who is coordinator of the map that he said could be of interest to the public as well as many companies.

The mapping project so far covers about 70% of the globe—gaps include India and parts of Africa. Britain and France have contributed a total of $930,100 to the project. All countries provided their data for free.

THE GROUND BENEATH YOUR FEET: A digital map of the earth's geology. Scientists unveiled the map on Wednesday and said it could guide oil and gas exploration, mining and help pinpoint sites for burying greenhouse gases.

TOI 2-8-2008

CONFIRMED: SATURN MOON HAS LIQUID ON ITS SURFACE

Besides Earth, Titan Only Body In Solar System With Fluid

Pasadena (California) : At least one of many large, lake-like features on Saturn's moon Titan studied by the international Cassini spacecraft contains liquid hydrocarbons, making it the only body in the solar system besides Earth known to have liquid on its surface, Nasa said.

Liquid ethane is a component of crude oil. Cassini has made more than 40 close flybys of Titan, a giant planet-sized satellite of the ringed world.

Scientists has theorized that Titan might have oceans of methane, ethane and other hydrocarbons, but Cassini found hundreds of dark, lake-like features instead, and it wasn't known at first whether they were liquid or dark, solid material, JPL's statement said.

"This is the first observation that really pins down that Titan has a surface lake filled with liquid," Bob Brown, team leader of Cassini's visual and mapping instrument, said.

The instrument was used during a December flyby to observe a feature dubbed Ontario Lacus, in the south polar region, that is about 7,800 square miles, slightly larger than North America's Lake Ontario.

Cassini reached Saturn in mid-2004 and at the end of that year launched a probe named Huygens that parachuted to the surface of Titan the following January. The mission is a project of Nasa, the European Space Agency and the Italian Space Agency. Titan shows over whelming evidence of evaporation, rain, and fluid-carved channels draining into a liquid hydrocarbon lake.

Earth has a hydrological cycle based on water and Titan has a cycle based on methane. Scientists ruled out presence of water ice, ammonia, ammonia hydrate and carbon dioxide in Ontario Lacus. The observation also suggest the lake is evaporating. It is ringed by a dark beach, where the black lake merges with the bright shoreline.

FUEL FOR FUTURE? An image released by Nasa shows what experts believe to be seasize bodies of liquid hydrocarbon (shown in blue) on Titan's surface

Tol 26-1-2008

GIANT LEAP TO 'MAN-MADE' LIFE

—Andrew Pollack

Taking a significant step toward the creation of man-made forms of life, researchers reported on Thursday that they had manufactured the entire genome of a bacterium by painstakingly stitching together its chemical components.

While scientists had previously synthesized the complete DNA of viruses, this is the first time it has been done for bacteria, which are much more complex.

The feat is a watershed for synthetic biology, which involves the design of organisms to performs particular tasks, such as making biofuels. Synthetic biologists envision being able one day to design an organism on a computer, press the print button to have the necessary DNA made, and then put that DNA into a cell to produce a custom-made creature.

"What we are doing with the synthetic chromosome is going to be the design process of the future," said J Craig Venter, the boundary-pushing gene scientist. He assembled the team that made the bacterial genome as part of his well publicized quest to create the first synthetic organism. The work was published online on Thursday by Science.

But there are concerns that synthetic organism. The work was published online on Thursday by Science.

But there are concerns that synthetic biology could be sued to make pathogens, or that errors by well-intended scientists could produce organisms that run amok. In any case, there are many hurdles to over come before Venter's team was not designed from scratch, but rather was a copy, with only a few changes, of the genetic sequence of a tiny natural bacterium called My team has so far failed to accomplish the next and biggest step. That would be to insert the synthetic chromosome into a living microbe and have it boot up and take control of the organisms functioning.

H.T. 26-5-2008

GET HELIUM FROM SPACE

Balloon Sellers, power plants, doctors, deep-sea divers, and astronauts depend on it. So crucial is the rare gas helium in a range of energy, science, and engineering applications. India is now one of the few countries with the expertise to extract helium from natural gas. The ONGC, Saha Institute of Nuclear Physics and the Variable Energy Cyclotron Centre, Kolkata, and the Department of Science and Technology have jointly set up a pilot plan for this in Tamil Nadu.

Discovered in 1868 by British scientists, helium is found in natural gas deposits, and in the atmosphere were it accumulated over billions of years by the decay of uranium and thorium. Helium is inert (not chemically reactive with other elements or compounds), odourless, tasteless, and the lightest gas after hydrogen. Unlike hydrogen, however, it is non-flammable. This makes it ideal for use in weather ballons and—in its liquid state—as a cryogenic refrigerant for medical and industrial research. It eases breathing difficulties in asthmatic patients and deep-sea divers coming out of water. It cools the superconducting magnets in MRI scanners, nuclear fusion power plants, and electric systems, and Nasa uses it to pressurize space shuttle fuel tanks.

Although helium is the second most abundant element in the universe, on Earth we are fast running out of it. A by-product of fossil fuel extraction, helium is lighter than air and bubbles irrecoverably into the atmosphere. So its best source is extraterrestrial. At 93 million miles away, the sun is a wonderful, if inaccessible, helium factory. When the solar wind—the stream of charged particles emitted by the sun—strikes the moon, however, helium 3 is deposited in its powdery soil. Over billions of years, meteorite bombardment dispersed more than a million tons of helium 3 throughout the lunar surface. This is enough to power the world for thousands of year. The logistics of heating lunar soil to nearly 1000 C to liberate the gas and transporting it to Earth are daunting. But the moon would be a stepping-stone to other helium 3-rich sources like the atmospheres of Saturn, Uranus and Neptune.

Tol 3-8-2008

MARS CRAFT 'TOUCHED AND TASTED' WATER

Conclusive Proof That Water Exists On Red Planet

Los Angeles : Nasa scientists said that they had definitive proof that water exists on Mars after further tests on ice found on the planet in June by the phoenix Mars Lander.

"We have water," said William Boynton, lead scientist for the Thermal and Evolved-Gas Analyzer instrument on Phoenix, on Thursday.

"We've seen evidence for this water ice before in observation by the Mars Odyssey orbiter and in disappearing chunks observed by Phoenix last month, but this is the first time Martian water has been touched and tasted," he said, referring to the craft's instruments.

Nasa on Thursday also extended the mission of the Phoenix Mars Lander by five weeks, saying its work was moving beyond the search for water to exploring whether the red planet was ever capable of sustaining life.

"We are extending the mission through September 30," Michael Meyer, chief scientist for Nasa's Mars exploration program, told a televised news conference. The extension will add about $2 million to the $420 million cost of landing Phoenix on May 25 for what was a scheduled three-month mission, Meyer said.

Phoenix is the latest Nasa bid to discover whether water—a crucial ingredient for life—ever flowed on Mars and whether life, even in the form of mere microbes, exists or ever existed there. Phoenix touched down in May on an ice sheet and samples of the ice were seen melting away in photographs taken by the lander's instruments in June.

Boynton said that water was positively identified after the lander's robotic arm delivered a soil sample on Wednesday to an instrument that identifies vapors produced by heating.

Mission scientists said the extension would give time for more analysis of Martian samples. They plan to dig two additional trenches—dubbed "cupboard" and "neverland" — using the robotic arm on the Phoenix craft. "We hope to be able to answer the question of whether this was a habitable zone on Mars. It will be for future missions to find if anyone is home on this environment," Phoenix principal investigator Peter Smith told the news conference.

Mission scientists said in June that Martian soil was more alkaline than expected and had traces of magnesium, sodium, potassium and other elements. Meyer said the scientific proof of the existence of water meant that Phoenix could "move from looking for water to seeing whether there were habitats for life".

NOW, HUNT FOR LIFE: A panoramic view of Phoenix Mars Lander.

Appendix–H

IMPORTANT FIGURES

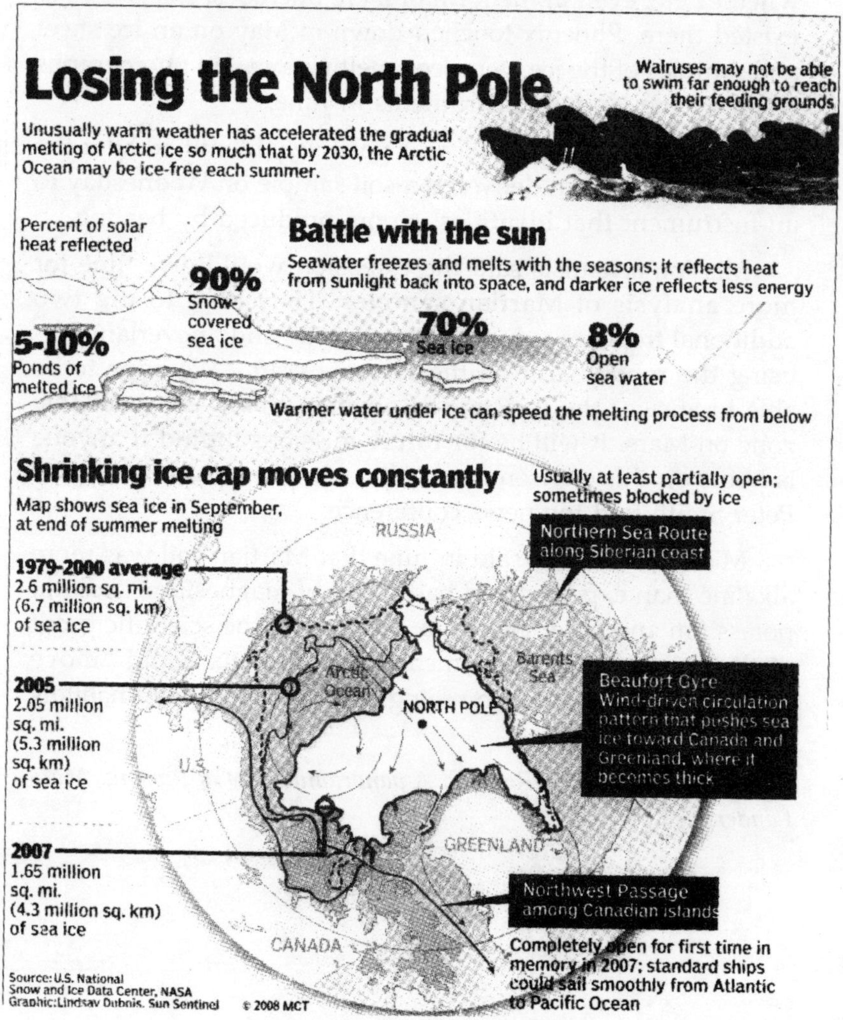

Worst natural disasters

Since 1900 with the highest estimated death tolls

[illegible]	[illegible]	[illegible]	[illegible]
1976 China 255,000	1931 China 3.7 million	1970 Pakistan 200,000	1998 Mitchi 14,500
2004 Indonesia 225,000	1970 Pakistan 200,000	1991 Bangladesh 131,000	1970 Fifi, Honduras 8,000
1920 China 200,000	1975 China 200,000	1965 Pakistan 47,000	1975 Flora, Caribb 7,200
1927 China 200,000	1971 Vietnam 100,000	1963 Pakistan 22,000	1971 Galveston, Tx 8,000
1923 Japan 140,000	1954 Iran 10,000	1971 India 10,000	2005 Katrina, US 1,800
2008 China 60,000		**2008 Myanmar 80,000**	

DELIVERY IN SPACE A WORLD RECORD

India's PSLV-C9 (polar satellite launch vehicle) successfully delivers 10 satellites into orbit from Sriharikota in AP, the first ISRO launch vehicle to do so

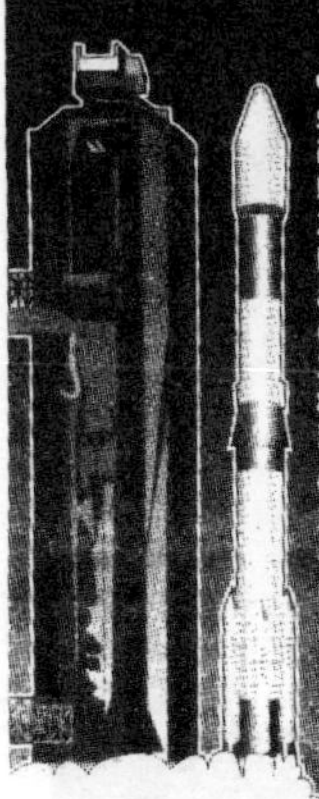

- Biggest satellite mission in the world. Russia holds 2nd record for hoisting 8 satellites a year ago. India on Monday put 2 Indian and 8 foreign satellites into orbit
- Rocket weighs 230 tonne, stands 44m tall. Tagged at $17.4 m, it carried a payload of 824kg

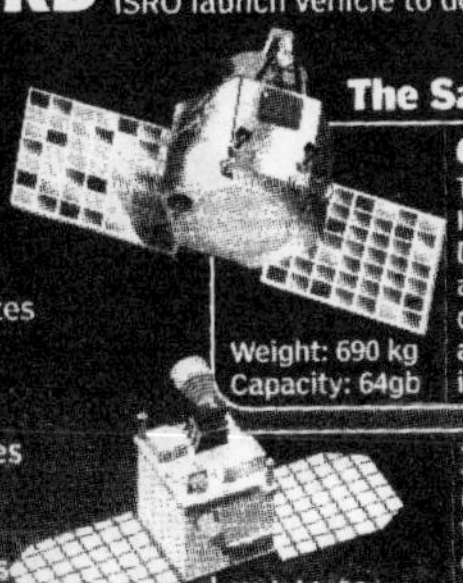

The Satellites

Cartosat-2A

The Rs 2b Cartosat-2A is the 13th Indian remote sensing satellite. Data from satellite will find applications in infrastructure development and management and also in land & geographical information systems

Weight: 690 kg
Capacity: 64gb

Indian Mini Satellite-1

IMS-1 has many new technologies for remote sensing. It employs 2 cameras (multispectral & hyper-spectral) and will serve other developing countries as well

Weight: 83 kg
Cameras: 2

Nanosatellites

Eight nanosatellites with a combined payload of 50kg were launched in this mission. They were from developed countries like Canada, Japan, Denmark, Germany and Netherlands

"It is a memorable moment for Team ISRO. The rocket stuck to its path without any deviation and delivered all the 10 satellites in their intended orbit

G MADHAVAN NAIR, Chairman, Isro

BRAVING THE COLD TERRAINS

PTI

TOUGH JOB: Soldiers guard a post at Nathu La on Monday

Giant wheels
Observation wheels, larger versions of the Ferris wheel, have become popular landmarks around the world; China will set a record in 2009.
Great Wheel of China
• To open in 2009 in Beijing
• 682 ft. (207 m) tall
• Weight 2,800 tons (2,840 metric tons)
48 capsules rotate as wheel turns; each holds 40 passengers
Automatic glass doors for loading; wheel turns once every 30 minutes
Ferris wheel milestones
Modern wheels evolved from 17th century Bulgarian "pleasure wheels"
Chicago 264 ft. (80 m)
Vienna 197 ft. (60 m)
Coney Island, N.Y. 135 ft. (41 m)
London 443 ft. (135 m)
Singapore 541 ft. (165 m)
Beijing
*Planned opening
1893
1897
1920
1999
2008*
2009*
Graphic: Renee Kwok, Sun-Sentinel

WHITE WONDER
PTI
TOI

Under the rubble

AFP

The *New Travel Weekly* with pictures of models in underwear amid rubble, in southwest Chongqing. The magazine has been shut down.

CHINA IN NUMBERS

The number of dead and missing climbed above **74,000**, while the confirmed number of people killed had risen to **51,151**. More than **247,000** hurt

To stop disease outbreaks among the **5** million people displaced, China's health ministry has sent more than **3,500** specialists in epidemic control to Sichuan

Doctors said **58** cases of gas gangrene have been detected and **30** amputations were done so far. **5.3** million leaflets on hygiene tips have been distributed among the affected people

900,000 tents will be sent to the disaster area over the next month, and up to one million makeshift structures by August

Saudi Arabia has sent more than **85,000** tents and **500,000** blankets, on top of a cash donation of **50** million dollars

China will spend more than **13** billion dollars on relief and reconstruction

1,600 wild pandas live in nature reserves in Sichuan, the badly affected province

80 percent of the bodies found in Sichuan province had been cremated or buried.

6,900 school rooms destroyed

Graphic: VINEY

The Oberoi Udaivilas is rated the best hotel in the world by Travel + Leisure

THE WORLD'S BEST HOTELS

(as ranked by Conde Nast Traveler)

Rank	Name	Company
2	Udaivilas	Oberoi Hotels
3	Vanyavilas	Oberoi Hotels
6	Amarvilas	Oberoi Hotels
18	Rajvilas	Oberoi Hotels
32	Hotel Monasterio	OEH
77	Hotel Bora Bora	OEH

(as ranked by Travel + Leisure)

Rank	Name	Company
1	Udaivilas	Oberoi Hotels
10	Amarvilas	Oberoi Hotels
11	Rajvilas	Oberoi Hotels
82	Taj Lake Palance	Taj Group
99	Mount Nelson	OEH

ASIA'S BEST HOTELS

(as ranked by Conde Nast Traveler)

Rank	Name	Company
1	Udaivilas	Oberoi Hotels
3	Amarvilas	Oberoi Hotels
4	Rajvilas	Oberoi Hotels
16	Taj Mahal Palace	Taj Group
34	Taj Lake Palace	Taj Group
51	Umaid Bhawan Palace	Taj Group
52	Taj Mahal Hotel	Taj Group
69	Leela Palace Kempinski	Leela Hotels

ASIA'S BEST RESORTS

(as ranked by Conde Nast Traveler)

Rank	Name	Company
1	Vanyavilas	Oberoi Hotels
2	Banyan Tree Phuket	Banyan Tree
3	Bali at Sayan	Four Seasons

PASSING THOUGHT / R K LAXMAN

Of course, I remember, father – I was just this high and all this around us was not there at the time of our tryst with destiny!